THE PERSONAL MBA

'A sterling effort . . . a book to be referred to at crucial moments'
Philip Delves Broughton, *Management Today*

'Cherrypicks the cleverest advice from the most effective business books
and condenses it into simple, memorable ideas and tools'
Smart.com

'Few people know how to get things done better
than Josh Kaufman'
David Allen, author of *Getting Things Done*

'A creative, breakthrough approach to business education. I have
an MBA from a top business school, and this book helped
me understand business in a whole new way'
Ali Safavi, Executive Director of International
Sales & Distribution, The Walt Disney Company

'Josh has synthesized the most important topics in business
into a book that truly lives up to its title. It's rare to find
complicated concepts explained with such clarity. Highly
recommended'
Ben Casnocha, author of *My Start-Up Life*

'Fundamentals are fundamentals. Whether you're an entrepreneur or
an executive at a Fortune 50 company, this book will help you succeed'
John Mang, Vice President, Procter & Gamble

'If you're thinking of starting a business, this book will radically
increase your confidence. If you're already running a business, this
book will help you identify weaknesses in your systems to get better
results. If you're thinking about plunging yourself into debt to get
an MBA, this book will challenge you to your core. Are you more
interested in becoming a better businessperson, or having a
document to hang on your wall to impress people?'
Daniel Joshua Rubin, Playwright and Portrait Artist

'I used the mental models in this book to create a profitable business in less than four weeks. Josh quickly dispels many mistaken beliefs about entrepreneurship, and his guidance has made me vastly more productive and successful, and my life more fulfilling'
Evan Deaubl, President and CEO, Tic Tac Code

'An absolutely amazing book! I'm highly recommending this to all creative types, for the best overview of the modern business mindset they need'
Derek Sivers, founder, CD Baby, sivers.org

'These concepts really work: I'm booked solid with clients, making eight times more money, feeling far less overwhelmed, and having a lot more fun. If you want to live up to your potential, you can't afford to miss this book'
Tim Grahl, Founder and CEO, Out:think Group

'After one hour with Josh, I immediately used his advice to bring in an extra $120,000 this year. These simple principles are astoundingly effective'
Dan Portnoy, Founder and CEO, Portnoy Media Group

ABOUT THE AUTHOR

Josh Kaufman is an independent business educator who helps people develop their business skills, start new ventures, and get ahead in their fields.

He founded PersonalMBA.com as an alternative to the business schools, and has introduced hundreds of thousands of readers to the most powerful business concepts of all time.

Before creating PersonalMBA.com, he worked for Procter & Gamble, where he launched major new products and developed P&G's global online marketing measurement strategy. He lives in Colorado.

www.personalmba.com

THE PERSONAL
MBA

*A World-class Business
Education in a Single Volume*

JOSH KAUFMAN

PORTFOLIO
PENGUIN

PORTFOLIO PENGUIN

Published by the Penguin Group
Penguin Books Ltd, 80 Strand, London WC2R ORL, England
Penguin Group (USA) Inc., 375 Hudson Street, New York, New York 10014, USA
Penguin Group (Canada), 90 Eglinton Avenue East, Suite 700, Toronto, Ontario, Canada M4P 2Y3
(a division of Pearson Penguin Canada Inc.)
Penguin Ireland, 25 St Stephen's Green, Dublin 2, Ireland (a division of Penguin Books Ltd)
Penguin Group (Australia), 707 Collins Street, Melbourne, Victoria 3008, Australia
(a division of Pearson Australia Group Pty Ltd)
Penguin Books India Pvt Ltd, 11 Community Centre, Panchsheel Park, New Delhi – 110 017, India
Penguin Group (NZ), 67 Apollo Drive, Rosedale, Auckland 0632, New Zealand
(a division of Pearson New Zealand Ltd)
Penguin Books (South Africa) (Pty) Ltd, Block D, Rosebank Office Park,
181 Jan Smuts Avenue, Parktown North, Gauteng 2193, South Africa

Penguin Books Ltd, Registered Offices: 80 Strand, London WC2R ORL, England

www.penguin.com

First published in the United States of America by Portfolio Penguin,
a member of Penguin Group (USA) Inc. 2010
First published in Great Britain by Portfolio Penguin 2011
This paperback edition with new material first published in the United States of America 2012
This edition published 2012

001

Printed in England by Clays Ltd, St Ives plc

ISBN: 978–0–670–91953–6

www.greenpenguin.co.uk

ALWAYS LEARNING   PEARSON

*To the millions of business professionals worldwide who work
to make people's lives better, in ways large and small.*

CONTENTS

2 Marketing 86

3 Sales 112

4   Value Delivery *143*

5   Finance *162*

6   The Human Mind *208*

7 Working with Yourself 252

8 Working with Others 307

9   Understanding Systems   346

10   Analyzing Systems   366

11   Improving Systems   388

KEY TERMS

A NOTE TO THE READER

Clear language engenders clear thought,
and clear thought is the most
important benefit of education.
—RICHARD MITCHELL, AUTHOR OF
THE GRAVES OF ACADEME

Many people assume that they need to attend business school to learn how to build a successful business or advance in their career. That's simply not true. The vast majority of modern business practice requires little more than common sense, simple arithmetic, and knowledge of a few very important ideas and principles.

The Personal MBA is an introductory business primer. Its purpose is to give you a clear, comprehensive overview of the most important business concepts in as little time as possible.

Each idea in this book is presented in plain language. Connections between these ideas are highlighted for easy reference. Once you know the essentials, you're free to focus on building your career, secure in the knowledge that you're considering the most important matters first.

Most "MBA alternative" books try to replicate the curricula of top-tier business school programs. That's not the focus of *The Personal MBA*. My aim is to help you build a solid understanding of general business practice from scratch, regardless of your current level of education or business experience.

Your time is valuable. I've made every effort to distill and condense a very large and diverse topic into an approachable volume you can read in a few hours. If additional research into specific topics is prudent in your situation, you'll know what to look for and where to begin.

Knowing where to start in common business situations is extremely valuable, whether you're a brand-new entrepreneur or a successful executive with decades of experience. Having a common language to label and think about what you notice opens the door to major improvements, whether you labor alone, with a small group of colleagues, or inside the largest corporation in the world.

This revised and updated edition of *The Personal MBA* features many new concepts that make the book's coverage of fundamental ideas even more comprehensive. In addition, small edits have been made to improve the clarity of the concepts included in the first edition, and new index features have been added to enhance the book's value as a long-term reference.

If you combine reading this book with real-world experience, you'll reap the rewards for the rest of your life. I hope this book helps you make more money, get more done, and have more fun in the process.

All my best,

Josh Kaufman
Fort Collins, Colorado
2012

Introduction

WHY READ THIS BOOK?

Just what the world needs . . . another business book!
—U.S. CUSTOMS AGENT AT JFK INTERNATIONAL AIRPORT,
AFTER ASKING ABOUT MY OCCUPATION

Life's tough. It's tougher if you're stupid.
—JOHN WAYNE, WESTERN FILM ICON

Since you're reading this book, chances are you want to make something important happen: start a business, get a promotion, or create something new in the world. It's also likely that a few things are holding you back from achieving your dream:

▶ *Business Angst.* The feeling that you "don't know much about business" and therefore could never start your own company or take more responsibility in your current position. Better to maintain the status quo than face the fear of the unknown.

▶ *Certification Intimidation.* The idea that "business is really complicated" and is a subject best left to highly trained "experts." If you don't have an MBA or similar expensive credentials, who are *you* to say you know what to do?

▶ *Impostor Syndrome.* The fear that you're already "in over your head" and it's only a matter of time before you're unmasked as a total fraud. No one likes a phony, right?

Here's the good news: everyone has these unfounded fears, and they can be eliminated quickly. All you need to do is learn a few simple concepts that will change the way you think about how business works. Once you've conquered your fears, you can accomplish anything.

If you're an entrepreneur, designer, student, programmer, or professional who wants to master the fundamentals of sound business practice, this book is for you. No matter who you are or what you're trying to do, you're about to discover a useful new way of looking at business that will help you spend less time fighting your fears and more time doing things that make a difference.

You Don't Need to Know It All

> As to methods, there may be a million and then some, but principles are few. The man who grasps principles can successfully select his own methods. The man who tries methods, ignoring principles, is sure to have trouble.
>
> —RALPH WALDO EMERSON, ESSAYIST AND POET

One of the beautiful things about learning any subject is the fact that *you don't need to know everything*—you only need to understand a few critically important concepts that provide most of the value. Once you have a solid scaffold of core principles to work from, building upon your knowledge and making progress becomes much easier.

The Personal MBA is a set of foundational business concepts you can use to get things done. Reading this book will give you a firm foundation of business knowledge you can use to make things happen. Once you master the fundamentals, you can accomplish even the most challenging business goals with surprising ease.

Over the past five years, I've read thousands of business books, interviewed hundreds of business professionals, worked for a *Fortune* 500 corporation, started my own businesses, and consulted with businesses ranging from solo operations to multinational corporations with hundreds of thousands of employees and billions of dollars in revenue. Along the way, I've collected, distilled, and refined my findings into the concepts presented in this book. Understanding these fundamental principles will give you the tools you can rely on to make good business decisions. If you invest the time and energy necessary to learn these concepts, you'll easily be in the top 1 percent of the human population when it comes to knowing:

▶ How businesses *actually* work.

▶ How to start a new business.

▶ How to improve an existing business.

▶ How to use business-related skills to accomplish your personal goals.

Think of this book as a filter. Instead of trying to absorb all of the business information that's out there—and there's a *lot* out there—use this book to help you learn what matters most, so you can focus on what's actually important: making things happen.

No Experience Necessary

People always overestimate how complex business is. This isn't rocket science—we've chosen one of the world's most simple professions.

—JACK WELCH, FORMER CEO OF GENERAL ELECTRIC

Don't worry if you're a complete beginner. Unlike many other business books, this book does not require any prior business knowledge or experience. I don't assume you're already the CEO of a large company who makes multimillion-dollar decisions on a daily basis. (But this book will still be very useful if you are!)

If you *do* have business experience, take it from many of my clients around the world who have MBAs from top schools—you'll find the information in this book more valuable and practical than anything you learned earning your degree.

Together, we'll explore 248 simple concepts that help you think about business in an entirely new way. After reading this book, you'll have a much more comprehensive and accurate understanding of what businesses *actually are* and what successful businesses *actually do*.

Questions, Not Answers

Education is not the answer to the question. Education is the means
to the answer to all questions.
—BILL ALLIN, SOCIOLOGIST AND EDUCATION ACTIVIST

Most business books attempt to teach you to have more *answers*: a technique for this, a method for that. This book is different. It won't give you answers—it will help you ask better *questions*. Knowing what's critically important in *every* business is the first step in making good business decisions. The more you know about the essential questions to ask in your current situation, the more quickly you'll be able to find the answers you need to move forward.

Mental Models, Not Methods

The limits of my language are the limits of my world.
—LUDWIG WITTGENSTEIN, PHILOSOPHER AND LOGICIAN

To improve your business skills, you don't need to learn everything there is to know—mastering the fundamentals can take you surprisingly far. I call these foundational business concepts *mental models*, and together, they create a solid framework you can rely on to make good decisions.

Mental models are concepts that represent your understanding of "how things work." Think of driving a car: what do you expect when you press down on the right-side pedal? If the car slows down, you'll be surprised—that pedal is supposed to be the accelerator. That's a mental model—an idea about how something works in the real world.

Your brain forms mental models automatically by noticing patterns in what you experience each day. Very often, however, the mental models you form on your own aren't completely accurate—you're only one person, so your knowledge and experiences are limited. Education is a way to make your mental models more accurate by internalizing the knowledge and experiences other people have collected throughout their lives. The best education helps you learn to see the world in a new, more productive way.

For example, many people believe things like "starting a business is risky," "to get started, you must create a massive business plan and borrow a lot of money," and "business is about who you know, not what you know." Each of these phrases is a mental model—a way of describing how the world works—but they're not quite accurate. Correcting your mental models can help you think about what you're doing more clearly, which will help you make better decisions:

INACCURATE MENTAL MODEL	ACCURATE MENTAL MODEL
Starting a business is risky.	Uncertainty is an ever-present but manageable part of business, and risks can be minimized.
In order to successfully create a business, you must create a flawless business plan before you start your business.	A written plan is secondary to understanding the critical functions of your business, and no matter how much you prepare, there will *always* be surprises along the way.
You must raise large amounts of capital before you start building your business.	Raising money is necessary only if it allows you to accomplish something that would otherwise be impossible (like building a factory).
It's not what you know, it's who you know.	Personal connections are important, but knowledge is key if you want to use those connections to your best advantage.

After learning the mental models in this book, many of my clients have realized that their picture of *what businesses are* and *how businesses work* was inaccurate—getting their venture off the ground would be far easier than they originally imagined. Instead of wasting valuable time and energy feeling intimidated and freaking out, learning these concepts gave them the freedom to stop worrying and start making progress.

This book will help you learn the fundamental principles of business quickly so you can focus your time and energy on actually *doing* useful things: creating something valuable, attracting attention, closing more sales, serving more customers, getting promoted, making more money, and changing the world.

Not only will you be able to create more value for others and improve your own financial situation, you'll also have more fun along the way.

My "Personal" MBA

Self-education is, I firmly believe, the only kind of education there is.
—ISAAC ASIMOV, FORMER PROFESSOR OF BIOCHEMISTRY AT BOSTON
UNIVERSITY AND AUTHOR OF OVER FIVE HUNDRED BOOKS

> This section describes the history of the Personal MBA as a project. You may find this context useful, but the primary value of this book is independent of my personal background. If you'd like to get to the material as quickly as possible, feel free to skip ahead to page 17.

People often ask me if I have an MBA. "No," I reply, "but I did go to business school."

As a student at the University of Cincinnati, I was fortunate enough to participate in the Carl H. Lindner Honors-PLUS program, which is essentially an MBA at the undergraduate level. The program was generously funded via scholarships, and as a result I had the remarkable opportunity to experience most of what business schools teach without the crippling burden of debt.

I've also been on the "fast track to corporate success." Through the University of Cincinnati's cooperative education program, I landed a management position at a *Fortune* 500 company—Procter & Gamble—during my second year of college. By the time I graduated in 2005, I had an offer to become an assistant brand manager in P&G's Home Care division, a role typically reserved for graduates of top MBA programs.

As I began my last semester of college, I started focusing less on my coursework and more on the future. My new job would require a solid understanding of business, and almost all of my peers and managers would have MBAs from top-tier schools. I briefly considered enrolling in an MBA program, but it made no sense to pursue an expensive credential to get the kind of job I already had, and my responsibilities would be demanding enough without adding a load of coursework by enrolling in a part-time program.

While considering my options, I remembered a bit of career advice that Andy Walter, the first associate director I reported to at P&G, had given me: "If you put the same amount of time and energy you'd spend completing an MBA into doing good work and improving your skills, you'll do just as well." (Andy doesn't have an MBA—he studied electrical engineering in college. He's now one of the company's top global IT managers, responsible for leading many of P&G's largest projects.)

In the end, I decided to skip business school, but not business education. Instead of enrolling in an MBA program, I skipped the classroom and hit the books, creating my own "Personal" MBA.

A Self-Directed Crash Course in Business

Many who are self-taught far excel the doctors, masters, and bachelors of the most renowned universities.

—LUDWIG VON MISES, AUSTRIAN ECONOMIST AND AUTHOR OF
HUMAN ACTION

I've always been an avid reader, but before I decided to learn everything I could about business, most of what I read was fiction. I grew up in New London, a small farm town in northern Ohio where the major industries are agriculture and light manufacturing. My mother is a children's librarian, and my father worked as a sixth grade science teacher, then as an elementary school principal. Books were a major part of my life, but business was not.

Before getting my first real job, I knew next to nothing about what businesses were or how they functioned, other than that they were places people went every day in order to draw a paycheck. I had no idea that companies like Procter & Gamble even existed until I applied for the job that swept me into the corporate world.

Working for P&G was an education in itself. The sheer size and scope of the business—and the complexity required to manage a business of that size—boggled my mind. During my first three years with the company, I participated in decisions across every part of the business process: creating new products, ramping up production, allocating millions of marketing dollars, and securing distribution with major retailers like Walmart, Target, Kroger, and Costco.

As an assistant brand manager, I was leading teams of thirty to forty

P&G employees, contractors, and agency staff—all of whom had competing projects, plans, and priorities. The stakes were huge and the pressure was intense. To this day, I can't help but marvel at the thousands of man-hours, the millions of dollars, and the enormously complex processes necessary to make a simple bottle of dish soap appear on the shelf of the local supermarket. Everything from the shape of the bottle to the scent of the product is optimized—including the text on the cardboard boxes used to ship inventory to the store.

My work at P&G, however, wasn't the only thing on my mind. My decision to skip business school in favor of educating myself developed from a side project into a minor obsession. Every day I would spend hour after hour reading and researching, searching for one more tidbit of knowledge that would help me to better understand how the business world worked.

Instead of using the summer after graduation to relax and go on vacation, I spent my days haunting the business stacks at the local bookstore, absorbing as much as I possibly could. By the time I officially started working full-time for P&G in September 2005, I had read hundreds of books across every discipline that business schools teach, as well as in disciplines that most business schools don't cover, such as psychology, physical science, and systems theory. When my first day at P&G finally arrived, I felt prepared to strategize with the best of them.

As it turned out, my self-education served me well—I was doing valuable work, making things happen, and getting good reviews. As time went on, however, I realized three very important things:

1. *Large companies move slowly.* Good ideas often died on the vine simply because they had to be approved by too many people.

2. *Climbing the corporate ladder is an obstacle to doing great work.* I wanted to focus on getting things done and making things better, not constantly positioning myself for promotion. Politics and turf wars are an inescapable part of the daily experience of working for a large company.

3. *Frustration leads to burnout.* I wanted to enjoy the daily experience of work, but instead I felt like I was running a gauntlet each day. It began to affect my health, happiness, and relationships. The longer

I stayed in the corporate world, the more I realized I wanted out. I desperately wanted to work on my own terms, as an entrepreneur.

The Wheat and the Chaff

It is important that students bring a certain ragamuffin, barefoot irreverence to their studies; they are not here to worship what is known, but to question it.

—JACOB BRONOWSKI, WRITER AND PRESENTER OF *THE ASCENT OF MAN*

If there's one thing I'm good at, it's taking in a huge amount of information and distilling it to the essentials. I'm a synthesist by nature, and my travels through the world of business literature quickly became an exercise in separating the diamonds from the rough.

The amount of business information being published every day is staggering. As of this writing, the Library of Congress has approximately 1.2 million business-related books in its general collection. Assuming you read at an average speed of 250 words per minute and an average book contains 60,000 words, it would take 528 years of around-the-clock reading to finish the entire collection, 822 years if you allowed yourself the luxury of food and sleep.

According to Bowker, the company responsible for assigning ISBN numbers for the publishing industry, over 11,000 new business books are published worldwide each year, adding to the millions of business books printed since the early 1900s. Amazon.com carries over 630,000 business-related titles, not counting audiobooks, e-books, or materials that are published without an ISBN.

Of course, books aren't the only source of business information available. Take magazines and newspapers, for example: 527 major business-related periodicals are currently tracked by the Wilson Business Periodicals Index. Every year, the WBPI adds over 96,000 records to its database of 1.6 million entries. That figure doesn't include blogs: according to Google Blog Search, there are currently over 110 million business-related blog posts on the Internet—a figure that is growing daily. There's certainly no shortage of business writers in the blog world: the blog search engine Technorati has indexed over 4 million bloggers who write about business-related topics.

Clearly, sifting through the massive amount of business information available would be an enormous challenge. My early business research was mostly haphazard—I simply went to a bookstore and picked up a book that looked interesting. For every great book I found, I had to wade through ten times as many hastily assembled texts by consultants who were more interested in creating a three-hundred-page business card than providing genuinely useful information.

I started to wonder: how much of what's out there—and there's a *lot* out there—I *really* needed to know. How could I separate the valuable information from the rubbish? I only had so much time and energy, so I started searching for a filter: something that would direct me to the useful knowledge and keep me away from the chaff. The more I searched, the more I realized it didn't exist—so I decided to create it myself.

I began tracking which resources were valuable and which ones weren't, then publishing my findings on my Web site, both as an archive and for the benefit of anyone interested. It was a personal project, nothing more: I was just a recent college graduate doing my best to learn something useful, and publishing my research for others seemed like a good use of time and energy.

One fateful morning, however, the Personal MBA went unexpectedly public, and my life changed permanently.

The Personal MBA Goes Global

Whoever best describes the problem is the one most likely to solve it.

—DAN ROAM, AUTHOR OF *THE BACK OF THE NAPKIN*

In addition to reading books, I was following several hundred business blogs. Some of the best business thinking was being published on the Internet months (or years) before it ever appeared in print, and I wanted to read it all as soon as it was available.

One of the bloggers I followed avidly was Seth Godin. A best-selling author (of books like *Permission Marketing, Purple Cow,* and *Linchpin*) and one of the earliest successful online marketers, Seth specializes in bold statements of big ideas designed to challenge you to do more, do better, question the status quo, and make a difference.

One particular morning, Seth was commenting on a recent news story: Harvard was rescinding the admission of 119 previously soon-to-be Harvard MBA students.[1] These prospective students had discovered an ethically dubious way to hack into the Harvard admissions Web site to view their application status before the official acceptance letters went out. The story quickly became a media frenzy, devolving into a debate about whether MBA students were naturally inclined to lie, cheat, and steal, or if business schools made them that way.

Instead of being outraged at the bad behavior of the applicants, Seth (unsurprisingly) had a different perspective: Harvard was giving these students a gift. By rescinding their applications, Harvard was giving these students a significant opportunity: the university was returning $150,000 and two years of their lives, which would otherwise have been spent chasing a mostly worthless piece of paper. "It's hard for me to understand," he wrote, "why [getting an MBA] is a better use of time and money than actual experience combined with a dedicated reading of 30 or 40 books."

"Holy cow," I thought. "That's exactly what I'm doing!"

Over the next two days, I created a list of the books and resources I had found most valuable in my studies,[2] then published it on my blog with a link to Seth's post, so anyone interested in figuring out how to do what Seth suggested would be able to find it. Then I typed a quick e-mail to Seth and sent him a link to my post.

Two minutes later, a post went up on Seth's blog directing people to my reading list, and a flood of readers from around the world started visiting my Web site.

Popular personal development and productivity blogs like Lifehacker .com picked up the story, which then spread to social media Web sites like Reddit, Digg, and Delicious. Within the first week of the Personal MBA's existence, thirty thousand people visited my little corner of the Internet to see what I was doing. Better yet, they started talking.

Some readers asked questions—where should they start? Others sug-

gested great books they'd read, helping me with my research. A few told me
the entire project was naive, and that I was wasting my time. Through it all,
I kept reading, researching, and developing the Personal MBA in my spare
time, and the business self-education movement began to snowball.

In a very short time, the Personal MBA grew from a one-man side project into a major global movement. The site, http://personalmba.com, has
been visited over 1.6 million times since it went live in early 2005, and the
project has been featured by *The New York Times, The Wall Street Journal,
Bloomberg BusinessWeek, Time, Fortune, Fast Company*, and hundreds of
other major news organizations and independent Web sites. In late 2008,
I left P&G to focus on building the Personal MBA full-time.

As much as I enjoyed the interest in my reading list project, I soon realized that providing a reading list wasn't enough. People read business books
to solve specific challenges or to improve themselves in some tangible way.
They're looking for solutions, and a list of books, while valuable, could only
do so much.

The books themselves aren't as important as the ideas and knowledge
they contain, but many of my readers were missing out because it took
hours of turning pages to get to the good stuff. Many Personal MBA readers started enthusiastically, then quit after reading a few books—it took too
long to reap the rewards, and the demands of work and family life inevitably intervened.

To help them, I had more work to do.

Munger's Mental Models

I think it's undeniably true that the human brain works in models. The
trick is to have your brain work better than the other person's brain
because it understands the most fundamental models—the ones
that do the most work.

—CHARLES T. MUNGER, BILLIONAIRE BUSINESS PARTNER OF
WARREN BUFFETT, CEO OF WESCO FINANCIAL, AND VICE-CHAIRMAN OF
BERKSHIRE HATHAWAY

My first glimpse into the future of the Personal MBA came when I discovered the work of Charles T. Munger.

Charlie was born in Omaha, Nebraska, shortly before the Great Depression. As a young man, Charlie skipped high school athletics in favor of reading to satisfy his intense curiosity about how the world worked. His early business experience consisted of working in a family-owned grocery store for $2 a day.

In 1941, Charlie graduated from high school. After two years of studying undergraduate mathematics and physics at the University of Michigan, he enlisted in the Army Air Corps, where he was trained as a meteorologist. In 1946, after leaving the army, he was accepted to Harvard Law School, even though he had never earned a bachelor's degree, which wasn't absolutely required at the time.

Charlie graduated from Harvard Law in 1948 and spent the next seventeen years practicing as an attorney. In 1965, he left the law firm he had created to start an investment partnership, which went on to outperform the market by 14 percent compounded annually over fourteen years—an astounding record given his complete lack of formal business education.

Charlie Munger isn't a household name, but Warren Buffett, Charlie's business partner, certainly qualifies. Buffett and Munger purchased Berkshire Hathaway, a floundering textile manufacturer, in 1975, turning it into a conglomerate investment holding company. Together, Buffett and Munger became billionaires.

According to Buffett, Charlie's mental-model-centric approach to business is a major contributing factor in the success of Berkshire Hathaway and Buffett's status as one of the world's wealthiest business owners: "Charlie can analyze and evaluate any kind of deal faster and more accurately than any man alive. He sees any valid weakness in sixty seconds. He's the perfect partner."[3]

The secret to Charlie's success is a systematic way of understanding how businesses actually work. Even though he never *formally* studied business, his relentless self-education in a wide variety of subjects allowed him to construct what he called a "latticework of mental models," which he then applied to making business decisions:

> *I've long believed that a certain system—which almost any intelligent*
> *person can learn—works way better than the systems most people use [to*
> *understand the world]. What you need is a latticework of mental models*

in your head. And, with that system, things gradually fit together in a way that enhances cognition.

Just as multiple factors shape every system, multiple mental models from a variety of disciplines are necessary to understand that system . . . You have to realize the truth of biologist Julian Huxley's idea that, "Life is just one damn relatedness after another." So you must have all the models, and you must see the relatedness and the effects from the relatedness . . . [4]

It's kind of fun to sit here and outthink people who are way smarter than you are because you've trained yourself to be more objective and more multidisciplinary. Furthermore, there is a lot of money in it, as I can testify from my own personal experience. [5]

By basing their investment decisions on their extensive knowledge of how businesses work, how people work, and how systems work, Buffett and Munger created a company worth over $195 billion—an astounding track record for a meteorologist-turned-lawyer from Omaha with no formal business education.

Discovering Munger's approach to business education was a huge validation. Here was a man who, decades before, had decided to do what I was doing—and it had worked extraordinarily well! Munger's method of identifying and applying fundamental principles made much more sense to me than most of the business books I'd previously read. I resolved to learn everything I could about the "mental models" Charlie used to make decisions.

Unfortunately, Charlie has never published a comprehensive collection of his mental models. He's given hints in his speeches and essays—even going so far as to publish a list of the psychological principles he finds most useful in *Poor Charlie's Almanack*, a recent biography—but there was no single text that contained "everything you need to know in order to succeed in business."

If I wanted to understand the fundamental principles of how every successful businessperson works, I'd have to discover them myself. To do that, I had to rebuild my understanding of business from the ground up.

Connecting the Dots

In all affairs, it's a healthy thing now and then to hang a question mark on the things you have long taken for granted.

—BERTRAND RUSSELL, RENOWNED PHILOSOPHER AND AUTHOR OF *THE PROBLEMS OF PHILOSOPHY* AND *THE PRINCIPLES OF MATHEMATICS*

Most business books (and business schools) assume that the student already knows what businesses are, what they do, and how they work—as if it were the most obvious thing in the world. It's not. Business is one of the most complex and multidisciplinary areas of human experience, and trying to understand how businesses work can be remarkably intimidating, even though they surround us every day.

Businesses are so much a part of daily life that it's easy to take the business world for granted. Day after day, businesses deliver what we want swiftly, efficiently, and with remarkably little fuss. Look around: almost every material good you're surrounded by right now was created and delivered to you by some sort of business.

Businesses invisibly create and deliver so many different things in so many different ways that it makes generalizations difficult: what do apple cider and airlines have in common? As it turns out, quite a bit—if you know where to look. Here's how I define a business:

Every successful business (1) creates or provides something of value that (2) other people want or need (3) at a price they're willing to pay, in a way that (4) satisfies the purchaser's needs and expectations and (5) provides the business sufficient revenue to make it worthwhile for the owners to continue operation.

Take away any of these things—value creation, customer demand, transactions, value delivery, or profit sufficiency—and you have something other than a business. Each factor is both essential and universal.

As I deconstructed each of those factors, I found additional universal requirements. Value can't be created without understanding what people want (market research). Attracting customers first requires getting their attention, then making them interested (marketing). In order to close a sale, people must first trust your ability to deliver on what's promised (value delivery and operations). Customer satisfaction depends on reliably exceeding the customer's expectations (customer service). Profit sufficiency requires bringing in more money than is spent (finance).

None of these functions is rocket science, but they're always necessary, no matter who you are or what business you're in. Do them well, and your business thrives. Do them poorly, and you won't be in business very long.

Every business fundamentally relies on two additional factors: people and systems. Every business is created by people and survives by benefiting other people in some way. To understand how businesses work, you must have a firm understanding of how people tend to think and behave—how humans make decisions, act on those decisions, and communicate with others. Recent advances in psychology and neuroscience are revealing why people do the things they do, as well as how to improve our own behavior and work more effectively with others.

Systems, on the other hand, are the invisible structures that hold every business together. At the core, every business is a collection of processes that can be *reliably repeated* to produce a particular result. By understanding the essentials of how complex systems work, it's possible to find ways to improve existing systems, whether you're dealing with a marketing campaign or an automotive assembly line.

Before writing this book, I spent several years testing the principles in this book with my clients and readers. Understanding and applying these "business mental models" has helped them launch new careers, land job offers from prestigious organizations in the corporate and academic worlds, get promoted, start new businesses, and in several cases go through the entire product development process (from idea to first sale) in less than four weeks.

These concepts are important because they work. Not only will you be able to create more value for others and improve your own financial situation, you'll find it noticeably easier to achieve what you set out to do—and you'll have more fun along the way.

For the Skeptics

You wasted $150,000 on an education you could have got for a buck fifty in late charges at the public library.

—MATT DAMON AS WILL HUNTING, *GOOD WILL HUNTING*

This section examines the benefits and detriments of traditional business school programs versus learning business outside of academia. If you've already enrolled in business school, completed an MBA program, or don't particularly care about the current state of business academia, this section won't be as valuable for you. Feel free to skip ahead to page 32.

This is a book about business concepts, not business schools. However, many people simply don't believe it's possible to reap the benefits of a comprehensive business education without forking over enormous sums of money for a name-brand diploma from an Ivy League school. This section, which will discuss the merits and downfalls of traditional MBA programs, is for the skeptics.

Should You Go to Business School?

There is a difference between (A) what an MBA does to help you prove your abilities to others and (B) what getting an MBA actually does to improve your abilities. They are two different things.

—SCOTT BERKUN, AUTHOR OF *MAKING THINGS HAPPEN* AND *THE MYTHS OF INNOVATION*

Every year, millions of individuals determined to make a name for themselves have the following thought: "I want to become a successful businessperson. Where should I get my MBA?" Since you're flipping through this book, you've probably wondered the same thing at some point in your life.

Here's the answer: five simple words that will save you years of effort and hundreds of thousands of dollars:

Skip business school. Educate yourself.

This book will show you how to succeed in business—without mortgaging your life.

Three Big Problems with Business Schools

> College: two hundred people reading the same book. An obvious mistake. Two hundred people can read two hundred books.
>
> —JOHN CAGE, SELF-TAUGHT WRITER AND COMPOSER

I have nothing against people who work in business schools: by and large, business school professors and administrators are lovely people who try their best and want to see their students succeed. Unfortunately, MBA programs around the world have three major systemic issues:

1. *MBA programs have become so expensive you must effectively mortgage your life to pay the price of admission.* "Return on Investment" is always directly related to how much you spend, and after decades of tuition increases, MBA programs are increasingly a burden to their students instead of a benefit. The primary question is not whether attending a university is a positive experience: it's whether or not the experience is worth the cost.[6]

2. *MBA programs teach many worthless, outdated, even outright damaging concepts and practices*—assuming your goal is to actually build a successful business and increase your net worth. Many of my MBA-holding readers and clients come to me after spending tens (sometimes hundreds) of thousands of dollars learning the ins and outs of complex financial formulas and statistical models, only to realize that their MBA program didn't teach them how to start or improve a real, operating business. That's a problem—graduating from business school does not guarantee having a useful working knowledge of business when you're done, which is what you actually need to be successful.

3. *MBA programs won't guarantee you a high-paying job, let alone make you a skilled manager or leader with a shot at the executive suite.* Developing skills such as decision making, management, and leadership takes real practice and experience, which business schools can't provide in the classroom, regardless of how prestigious the program is.

Instead of spending huge sums of money to learn marginally useful information, you can spend your time and resources learning things that actually matter. If you're ready and able to invest in improving your skills and abilities, you can learn everything you need to know about business on your own, without mortgaging your life for the privilege.

Delusions of Grandeur

> The very substance of the ambitious is merely the shadow of a dream.
>
> —WILLIAM SHAKESPEARE, *HAMLET*

It's easy to figure out why business school is attractive: it's sold as a one-way ticket to a permanently prosperous and comfortable life. It's a pleasant daydream: after two years of case studies and happy hour "networking," corporate recruiters will be shamelessly throwing themselves at you, each of them offering a prestigious and high-paying position at a top firm.

Your rise up the corporate ladder will be swift and sure. You'll be a CAPTAIN OF INDUSTRY, collecting huge bonuses and tabulating the value of your stock options while sitting behind an impressive-looking mahogany desk in the corner office on the top floor of a gigantic glass skyscraper. You'll be the big boss, telling other people what to do until it's time to go play golf or relax on your yacht. You'll be wined and dined all over the world, and the lowly masses will venerate you and your astounding achievements. Everyone will think you're rich, intelligent, and powerful—and they'll be damn right.

What price for the promise of riches, power, and glory? A few thousand dollars in application fees, an effortless scribble on a loan document, and you'll be on your way to the top! Not only that, you'll get a two-year vacation from actually working. What a fantastic deal!

Unfortunately, daydreams and reality are often quite different.

Your Money AND Your Life

There ain't no such thing as a free lunch.

—ROBERT HEINLEIN, AUTHOR OF *STRANGER IN A STRANGE LAND* AND *THE MOON IS A HARSH MISTRESS*

For the moment, let's assume you think business school is your ticket to everlasting success. You're in luck—getting into at least one business school is relatively easy. If you pay thousands of dollars in application fees, write enough personal statements that strike just the right balance of confidence and humility, and compliment the quality of the school's program in interviews, sooner or later some college or university will generously bestow upon you the chance to become the next Bill Gates.[7]

Here, though, is where the problems begin: business school is insanely expensive. Unless you're independently wealthy or land a massive scholarship, your only option is to effectively mortgage your life by taking out an enormous loan against your future earnings to pay the tuition.

Most prospective MBA students have already graduated from college with an undergraduate degree, so they're already carrying some level of student loan debt. According to FinAid.org, a college financial aid Web site, the average cumulative debt of a student who completed an undergraduate degree in the United States in 2009 is $22,500. For students who choose to pursue an MBA program after undergrad, total average cumulative debt is $41,687. That doesn't include providing for material needs like rent, groceries, and car payments, which are often funded via additional student loans.

Forty thousand dollars is a significant chunk of change, assuming you go to an *average* school—but who wants to be merely average? If you're shooting for offers from top-tier financial services companies like Goldman Sachs or major consulting companies like McKinsey and Bain (which are historically the highest-paying options for newly minted MBAs), you're going to have to attend a top-ten program, and that'll require a *lot* more than a measly forty grand.

Breaking Out the Benjamins

Who goeth a borrowing, goeth a sorrowing . . . A fool and his money
are soon parted.

—THOMAS TUSSER, SIXTEENTH-CENTURY ENGLISH FARMER AND POET

According to the 2011 *U.S. News & World Report* business school rankings,
the top fifteen MBA programs charge $40,983 to $53,208 *per year* for tuition.[8] That amount doesn't include fees, student loan interest, or living
expenses. In recent years, tuition has been increasing at a rate of 5 to 10
percent per year.[9]

According to data compiled by *Fortune* contributor John A. Byrne in
late 2011, eight business schools exceed $300,000 in costs once you account
for tuition, fees, living expenses, and the opportunity cost of lost wages:
Harvard, Stanford, Wharton, Columbia, Dartmouth, Chicago, MIT, and
Northwestern.[10] Harvard and Stanford top the list at a total cost of
$348,800 and $351,662, respectively. These costs are *before* student loan
charges: tack on 2 to 3 percent in origination fees and a 6 to 10 percent
compound annual interest rate on the loan balance, and you've accounted
for the true cost of enrolling in a top-tier business school.

Research conducted by *Bloomberg BusinessWeek* and PayScale indicates
that a typical graduate of a top-ranked MBA program collects $2.4 to $3.8
million in total career pay, depending on the program.[11] Based on these
numbers, you can expect to give up 8 to 10 percent of your expected lifetime earnings in exchange for two years of case studies and networking at
a top-ranked business school.

That's assuming you get in, of course. Top business schools are notoriously hard to get into—the programs can afford to be picky because of their
reputations. It's circular. The reputation of a business school is built on the
success of its graduates, so the top schools only admit those students intelligent and ambitious enough to make it through the rigorous selection
process—the ones who are already likely to succeed, MBA or no MBA.
Business schools don't *create* successful people. They simply *accept* them,
then take credit for their success.

If you get in, the school will do what it can to help you get a decent job,
but making things happen will always be *your* responsibility. If you're suc-

cessful in the years after graduation, the school will hold you up as a shining example of the quality of their program and will use the "halo effect" of your name to recruit more students. If you lose your job and go broke, you'll get neither publicity nor help, but the loan bills will keep rolling in. Sorry about your luck.

Here's what Christian Schraga, a 2002 graduate of the Wharton School of Business, had to say about his MBA experience in an essay on his Web site:[12]

> My been-there-done-that experience has taught me that a top MBA program provides some benefits, but at a steep price. If you are currently considering attending a full-time program, please stop to ask yourself whether or not you are willing to take the risk.
>
> Business school is a big risk. Should you choose to enroll, the only certainty is that you will shell out about $125,000. Such a figure correlates to a $1,500/month non-deductible loan repayment and a ten-year period of time in which you will not be able to save a red cent.
>
> If you think that this payment is worth it to earn the pedigree, the fraternity, the two years off, and a shot at the big bucks, then the MBA is right for you. If not, please do something else.

Wise words. If you don't absolutely need the sheepskin, don't enroll.

What an MBA Will Actually Get You

Hypocrisy can afford to be magnificent in its promises; for never intending to go beyond promises, it costs nothing.
—EDMUND BURKE, POLITICIAN AND POLITICAL THEORIST

In "The End of Business Schools? Less Success Than Meets the Eye," a study published in *Academy of Management Learning & Education*,[13] Jeffrey Pfeffer of Stanford University and Christina Fong of the University of Washington analyzed forty years of data in an effort to find evidence that business schools make their graduates more successful. Their hypothesis was remarkably straightforward:

If an MBA education is useful training for business, then the following should be true as a matter of logic: (1) having an MBA degree should, other things being equal, be related to various measures of career success and attainment, such as salary; and (2) if what someone learns in business school helps that person be better prepared for the business world and more competent in that domain—in other words, if business schools convey professionally useful knowledge—then a measure of how much one has learned or mastered the material, such as grades in course work, should be at least somewhat predictive of various outcomes that index success in business.

What Pfeffer and Fong found was astonishing and disturbing: business schools do almost nothing, aside from making money disappear from students' pockets:

Business schools are not very effective: Neither possessing an MBA degree nor grades earned in courses correlate with career success, results that question the effectiveness of schools in preparing their students. And, there is little evidence that business school research is influential on management practice, calling into question the professional relevance of management scholarship.

According to Pfeffer and Fong's study, it doesn't matter if you graduate at the top of your class with a perfect 4.0 or at the bottom with a barely passing grade—getting an MBA has zero correlation with long-term career success. None.

There is scant evidence that the MBA credential, particularly from non-elite schools, or the grades earned in business courses—a measure of the mastery of the material—are related to either salary or the attainment of higher level positions in organizations. These data, at a minimum, suggest that the training or education component of business education is only loosely coupled to the world of managing organizations.

That's tough to hear if you've forked over a few hundred thousand dollars to buy a degree whose sole purpose is to make you a more successful businessperson.

It gets worse: getting an MBA doesn't even have an impact on your total lifetime earnings. It takes decades of work simply to dig yourself out of the debt you took on to get the degree. Christian Schraga, the Wharton MBA, estimated that the ten-year "net present value" (a financial analysis technique used to estimate whether or not an investment is worthwhile) of a top MBA program is approximately negative $53,000 (that's bad). This assumes a pre-MBA base salary of $85,000, a post-MBA salary of $115,000 (a 35 percent increase), marginal tax rate increases (which you'll pay if your job requires moving to a major city), and a discount rate of 7 percent to account for opportunity cost (the opportunities you give up by spending money on business school instead of investing it in something else). In plain English: Schraga used a technique business schools teach to prove that getting an MBA from a top-tier school is a bad financial decision.

Assuming Schraga's assumptions are accurate, it takes twelve years of solid effort *just to break even*—and that's assuming everything goes according to plan. If you graduate into a bad job market, you're screwed.

Where Business Schools Came From

It is, in fact, nothing short of a miracle that modern methods of instruction have not entirely strangled the curiosity of inquiry.

—ALBERT EINSTEIN, NOBEL PRIZE–WINNING PHYSICIST

MBA programs don't make students more successful because they teach very few things that are actually useful in the working world. As Pfeffer and Fong state in their paper:

> *A large body of evidence suggests that the curriculum taught in business schools has only a small relationship to what is important for succeeding in business . . . If there is, in fact, only a slight connection between the skills needed in business and what is taught in graduate business programs, then the absence of an effect of the MBA or mastery of the subject matter on the careers of graduates is understandable.*

If you look at the curriculum of any business school, you'll notice a few assumptions about what you'll do after you graduate: you'll either be a C-level executive at a large industrial manufacturing or retail operation, become a consultant, become a corporate accountant, or work as a financier at an investment bank. Accordingly, the coursework is implicitly structured around keeping your massive operation running and/or doing sophisticated quantitative analysis—not doing any of the other critically important things that 99 percent of working businesspeople do in any given day.

The disconnect between the classroom and the working world makes sense when you realize that the concepts, principles, and techniques most business schools teach were designed for a very different world. Graduate schools of business started popping up at the end of the nineteenth century during the Industrial Revolution. The intent of early MBA programs was to train managers to be more scientific in an effort to make large operations more efficient.

Frederick Winslow Taylor, the pioneer of "scientific management" techniques that now form the foundation of modern management training, used a stopwatch to shave a few seconds off the average time a workman took to load iron ingots into a train car. That should give you a good idea of the underlying mind-set of most business school management programs.

Management was thought of mostly as an exercise in getting people to work faster and do exactly what they're told. The philosopher kings behind what passed for management psychology were Ivan Pavlov and, later on, B. F. Skinner, who believed that if you discovered and applied just the right stimulus, people would behave however you wanted. This mentality led to the widespread use of financial incentives to influence behavior: salary, bonuses, stock options, and so on, in an effort to encourage business professionals and managers to act in the best interest of corporate shareholders.

There's an enormous (and growing) body of evidence that direct incentives often undermine performance, motivation, and job satisfaction in the real world.[14] Despite more useful competing theories of human action,[15] the search for the magic stimulus continues in business school classrooms to this day.

In Search of Distribution

> Any technique, however worthy and desirable, becomes a disease
> when the mind is obsessed with it.
>
> —BRUCE LEE, WORLD-RENOWNED MARTIAL ARTIST

Marketing, on the other hand, was originally a way to get additional store distribution for physical products and keep expensive factory production lines busy. With the widespread adoption of the radio and television in the early twentieth century, it became possible to advertise to a large national audience, paving the way for national brands and national retailers. More advertising typically resulted in more distribution, which in turn resulted in more sales and even more money to spend on advertising, continuing the cycle. As decades passed, this self-reinforcing feedback loop resulted in a few dominant behemoths in each industry. Business schools became obsessed with how to capture market share and create gigantic companies quickly via ever-larger mergers, raising the financial stakes with each acquisition.

For entrepreneurs, venture capital became a must-have aspect of the business process—how else could you afford to build a factory or a national brand in a few short years? "Economies of scale" in production meant large companies could outcompete smaller rivals by offering similar products at lower prices. Investors wanted to see huge returns on their money quickly, prudence be damned, rewarding speculators who wrote business plans promising a huge exit in a short amount of time. Viable businesses were acquired and gutted in the name of conglomeration and "synergy," all with the blessing of business academia. The sheer enormity of integrating these gigantic, complex business systems was ignored or overlooked, leading most of the companies that attempted huge mergers to ruin.

Playing with Fire

Beware of geeks bearing formulas.

—WARREN BUFFETT, CHAIRMAN AND CEO OF BERKSHIRE HATHAWAY AND
ONE OF THE WEALTHIEST INDIVIDUALS IN THE WORLD

Finance, in the meantime, was steadily increasing in complexity. Before the twentieth century, accounting and finance were a matter of common sense and relatively simple arithmetic. The widespread adoption of double-entry bookkeeping (a thirteenth-century innovation) brought many benefits, like increased accuracy and ease of detecting anomalies like theft, at the cost of simplicity.

The introduction of statistics to financial practice simultaneously enhanced analytical capability at the cost of abstraction, increasing opportunities to fudge the numbers without anyone noticing. Over time, managers and executives began using statistics and analysis to forecast the future, relying on databases and spreadsheets in much the same way ancient seers relied on tea leaves and goat entrails. The world itself is no less unpredictable or uncertain: as in the olden days, the signs only "prove" the biases and desires of the soothsayer.

The complexity of financial transactions and the statistical models those transactions relied upon continued to grow until few practitioners fully understood how they worked or respected their limits. As *Wired* revealed in a February 2009 article, "Recipe for Disaster: The Formula That Killed Wall Street," the inherent limitations of deified financial formulas such as the Black-Scholes option pricing model, the Gaussian copula function, and the capital asset pricing model (CAPM) played a major role in the tech bubble of 2000 and the housing market and derivatives shenanigans behind the 2008 recession.

Learning how to use complicated financial formulas isn't the same as learning how to run a business. Understanding *what businesses actually do to create and deliver value* is essential knowledge, but many business programs have de-emphasized value creation and operations in favor of finance and quantitative analysis. In "Upper Mismanagement," journalist Noam Scheiber explores the reason behind the downfall of American industry:

> *Since 1965, the percentage of graduates of highly ranked business schools who go into consulting and financial services has doubled, from about one-third to about two-thirds. And while some of these consultants and financiers end up in the manufacturing sector, in some respects that's the problem . . . Most of GM's top executives in recent decades hailed from a finance rather than an operations background. (Outgoing GM CEO Fritz Henderson and his failed predecessor, Rick Wagoner, both worked their way up from the company's vaunted Treasurer's office.) But these executives were frequently numb to the sorts of innovations that enable high-quality production at low cost.*[16]

Process improvements are easy to skip if you want the business's short-term profit numbers to look good, even though they're essential to long-term viability. By ignoring the things that make a business operate more effectively, MBA-trained executives have unwittingly gutted previously viable companies in the name of quarterly earnings per share.

Meanwhile, the widespread practice of using large amounts of debt as leverage[17] created enormous companies with even more enormous obligations, amplifying returns in good years but making the firms catastrophically unstable during the slightest downturn. The "leveraged buyout" strategy taught in many business school classrooms—buying a company, financing massive expansion via debt, then selling the business to another company at a premium[18]—turned formerly self-sustaining companies into debt-bloated monstrosities, and the constant flipping of businesses from one temporary owner to the next turned financial markets into a game of musical chairs.

When financial wizardry and short-term returns trump prudence and long-term value creation, customers and employees suffer. The only people who benefit are the MBA-trained executive-level financiers and fund managers, who extract hundreds of millions of dollars in transaction fees and salaries while destroying previously viable companies, hundreds of thousands of jobs, and billions of dollars of value.

Business is about creating and delivering value to paying customers, not orchestrating legal fraud. Unfortunately for us all, business schools have de-emphasized the former in favor of teaching the latter.

No Reason to Change

Schools teach the need to be taught.
—IVAN ILLICH, PRIEST, THEOLOGIAN, AND EDUCATION CRITIC

The world is constantly changing, but business schools aren't changing with it. With the advent of the Internet and the widespread availability of new technologies, successful modern businesses tend to be smaller, require less capital to build, have less overhead, and require fewer employees. According to the U.S. Small Business Administration, small businesses represent 99.7 percent of all employer firms in the United States, employ half of all private-sector workers, have generated 64 percent of net new jobs over the past fifteen years, and create more than 50 percent of U.S. nonfarm gross domestic product (GDP).[19] You wouldn't know that from looking at b-school curricula: based on current standards, it seems that most MBA programs believe huge businesses are the only ventures worth managing.

Mass-market advertising is no longer able to reliably convert pennies to dollars. Inventories (if they exist at all) tend to be smaller, businesses depend on others for critical functions, and markets change and adapt extremely quickly. Speed, flexibility, and ingenuity are the qualities that successful businesses rely on today—qualities that the corporate giants of the past few decades struggle to acquire and retain, and business school classrooms struggle to teach.

The demands of the public market push executives to chase short-term earnings at the expense of long-term stability, creating waves of layoffs and severe budget cuts when times get tight or unexpected events occur. At the same time, more and more employees are looking for a greater sense of autonomy, flexibility, and security from their work—and they're finding these things outside of the confines of the traditional corporate job. How do you manage someone who doesn't really want to work for you in the first place?

MBA programs are trying to cope, but they're still teaching theories that are outdated, misguided, and even outright wrong. Even so, don't expect them to start doing things differently. Why bother, when MBA programs are profitable status symbols for the colleges and in such high demand? As long as students are still signing up, don't expect the hallowed halls of business schools to change their tune.

The Single Benefit of Business Schools

Institutions will try to preserve the problem to which they are the solution.

—CLAY SHIRKY, PROFESSOR AT NYU AND AUTHOR OF
HERE COMES EVERYBODY AND *COGNITIVE SURPLUS*

The one significant benefit that business schools *do* provide is better access to *Fortune* 500 recruiters, consulting firms, large accounting firms, and investment banks via on-campus recruiting and alumni networks. Upon graduating from a top-tier business school, you'll find it much easier to get an interview with a corporate recruiter who works for a *Fortune* 500, investment bank, or consulting firm. The effect is strongest immediately after graduation, then largely wears out within three to five years. After that, you're on your own: hiring managers no longer care so much about where you went to school—they care more about what you've accomplished since then.

Hiring managers typically use MBA programs as a filter when deciding whom to bring in for an interview. HR managers are busy, and since each student in the program has been prescreened, there's less of a chance the manager will be wasting precious time. Hiring directly from MBA programs also provides plausible deniability for the recruiter if the hire doesn't work out: "I'm not sure what the issue was—she graduated from Harvard Business School!"

The filtering aspect of MBA programs is very real, and difficult to overcome on your own. If you have your heart set on becoming a management consultant, international financier, or *Fortune* 500 fast-track management candidate, you may have to buy yourself a $150,000 interview. If you go this route, be aware of what you're getting yourself into *before* you apply—once you sign your life away, the debt will make it very difficult to change your mind.

If you're more interested in working for yourself or holding down an enjoyable job while having a life, getting an MBA is a waste of time and money. As Dr. Pfeffer says, "If you are good enough to get in, you obviously have enough talent to do well, regardless."

I Owe, I Owe—It's Off to Work I Go

Are you where you want to be if it doesn't work?
—LOUIS L'AMOUR, AUTHOR AND HISTORIAN

Let's say you go ahead and get your MBA. If you're "lucky," you may be hired by a big financial services or consulting firm, where you'll have the privilege of working twelve hours a day for around $100,000 a year. The money is certainly good, but you'll have a hard time maintaining any sort of life outside of work, and the pressure will be intense and relentless. Even if you don't like your job, you'd better keep pushing if you want to pay your tuition bills and make your investment "worth it."

Congratulations: you've used your intelligence and drive to condemn yourself to the life of an indentured servant.

If you do a good job, you'll become an executive, get a raise, and have the privilege of working one hundred–plus hours a week. You'd better not mind enjoying the fruits of your labor alone: top executives consistently have the highest rates of divorce and family relationship issues. As the saying goes: you can have anything you want, as long as you're willing to pay the price.

If you're not so "fortunate," you'll find a job that pays little more than what you'd be able to command without your MBA. Worse yet, graduating into an iffy job market means that you may graduate with a thousand-dollar-a-month loan payment without a job to foot the bill.

An unforgiving job market won't make student loan payments go away—in the United States, student loan debt cannot be forgiven, even if you declare bankruptcy. Regardless of how your life works out, your student loans will always be there, and your phone will ring with the calls of debt collectors until they're repaid.

I can't emphasize this enough: *the quickest and easiest way to screw up your life is to take on too much debt.* The primary reason people spend decades working in jobs they despise is to pay off their creditors. Financial stress can destroy relationships, threaten your health, and jeopardize your sanity. Is a shot at a desk in a corner office really worth it?

With heavy debt loads and questionable returns, MBA programs simply aren't a good investment—they're a trap for the unwary.

A Better Way

To educate educators! But the first ones must educate themselves! And for these I write.

—FRIEDRICH NIETZSCHE, PHILOSOPHER AND AUTHOR OF *THE WILL TO POWER* AND *THUS SPOKE ZARATHUSTRA*

Fortunately, you have a choice in how you go about educating yourself—a choice that can make you *more* successful than top MBA graduates while saving you hundreds of thousands of dollars. Studying the fundamentals of sound business practice and developing a network on your own can provide most of the benefits of business education at a fraction of the cost. Instead of wasting your time and hard-earned money learning outdated theories you'll probably never use, it's far better to spend your time and energy teaching yourself what you actually need to know to succeed.

If you're the type of person who's capable of getting into a top MBA program and doing what it takes to succeed after graduation, skipping business school and learning the fundamentals of business by reading this book may be the best decision you ever make.

What You'll Learn in This Book

When you first start to study a field, it seems like you have to memorize a zillion things. You don't. What you need is to identify the core principles—generally three to twelve of them—that govern the field. The million things you thought you had to memorize are simply various combinations of the core principles.

—JOHN T. REED, REAL ESTATE INVESTMENT EXPERT AND AUTHOR OF
SUCCEEDING

This book is designed to teach you the fundamentals of sound business practice as quickly and efficiently as possible. Here's a quick preview of what you'll learn:

How Businesses Work. A successful business, roughly defined, provides (1) something of value that (2) other people want or need at (3) a price they're willing to pay, in a way that (4) satisfies the customer's needs and expectations so that (5) the business brings in sufficient profit to make it worthwhile for the owners to continue operation. Together, the concepts in chapters 1 to 5 describe how every business operates and what you can do to improve your results.

How People Work. Every business is created by people and survives by benefiting other people. To understand how businesses work, you need a firm understanding of how people make decisions, act on those decisions, and communicate with others. Chapters 6 to 8 introduce you to a few major concepts in psychology that describe how the human mind processes the world, how you can work more effectively, and how you can create and strengthen professional relationships.

How Systems Work. Businesses are complex systems with many moving parts that exist within even more complex systems like industries, societies, cultures, and governments. Chapters 9 to 11 will help you understand how complex systems work, as well as help you analyze existing systems and find ways to improve them without provoking unanticipated consequences.

Here are a few things you *shouldn't* expect:

Management and Leadership Overload. Many business resources (and all business schools) conflate management and leadership skills with business skills; *they're not the same thing.* While management and leadership are important in the practice of business, they aren't the be-all and end-all of business education: without solid business knowledge, it's possible to organize and lead a group of people toward the accomplishment of the wrong objectives. Business is about the profitable creation and delivery of valuable offers to paying customers—management and leadership are simply a means to this end. We'll discuss the essentials of effective management and leadership in chapter 8, but in their proper context.

CFA/CPA-Level Finance and Accounting. Finance and accounting are very important topics, and we'll discuss the essential concepts and practices in chapter 5, including common mistakes and pitfalls. That said, we have many topics to explore, and finance is not the sole focus of this book. Deep examinations of financial analysis and accounting standards have filled thousands of books much longer than this one, and unless you plan on becoming a Chartered Financial Analyst (CFA) or a Certified Public Accountant (CPA), you should learn the basics of these topics, but leave the details to the specialists.

Fortunately, there's no need to reinvent the wheel: great books on finance and accounting already exist. If you're interested in exploring these topics in more detail after completing chapter 5, I recommend the following books:

- *Financial Intelligence for Entrepreneurs* by Karen Berman and Joe Knight
- *Simple Numbers, Straight Talk, Big Profits!* by Greg Crabtree
- *Accounting Made Simple* by Mike Piper
- *How to Read a Financial Report* by John A. Tracy

In addition, online courses like MBA Math (http://mbamath .com) and Bionic Turtle (http://bionicturtle.com) are available if you want to explore these topics in even greater depth. (Many business schools and corporate finance training programs recommend or require these courses prior to enrollment.)

Quantitative Analysis and Modeling. We'll discuss the fundamentals of measurement and analysis in chapter 10, but this book won't turn you into a Wall Street "quant" or a high-flying spreadsheet jockey. Statistics and quantitative analysis are very useful skills when used appropriately, but the actual techniques are very situational and beyond the scope of this book. If you're interested in learning more about statistical analysis after reading chapter 10, I recommend:

- *Thinking Statistically* by Uri Bram
- *How to Lie with Statistics* by Darrell Huff
- *Turning Numbers into Knowledge* by Jonathan G. Koomey, PhD

For an examination of more advanced methods of analysis, *Principles of Statistics* by M. G. Bulmer is a useful reference.

How to Use This Book

All truly wise thoughts have been thought already thousands of times; but to make them truly ours, we must think them over again honestly, until they take root in our personal experience.

—JOHANN WOLFGANG VON GOETHE, POET, DRAMATIST, AND POLYMATH

Here are a few tips that will help you get the most from this book:

Browse, skim, and scan. Believe it or not, you don't need to read a book cover to cover to benefit: browsing can give you better results with less effort. Periodically skim through this book until you find a section that grabs your attention, then commit to applying that concept to your work for a few days. You'll begin to notice significant differences in the quality of your work, as well as in your ability to "think like a businessperson."

Keep a notebook and pen handy. The purpose of this book is to give you ideas about how to make things better, so be prepared to capture your thoughts as you have them; it'll make it easier to review the major concepts later. Your notebook will also make it easy to shift from taking notes to creating detailed action plans as they occur to you.[20]

Review this book regularly. Keep it close to where you work so you can refer to it often, particularly before starting a new project. Repetition inevitably leads to mastery, and the better you internalize these concepts, the more you'll improve your results. I also recommend setting a reminder in your calendar to review this book or your notes every few months to reinforce your understanding and spark new ideas.

Discuss these ideas with your colleagues. Great things happen when everyone you work with knows these concepts and uses the same language to discuss how they apply to your business. After every idea, I've included a Web site link to a short reference summary of the concept, which you can include in an e-mail, proposal, blog post, or other communication. This helps ensure everyone is on the same page, particularly if the recipient isn't familiar with the concept you're referencing.

There's always more to explore. Each of these mental models has extremely broad applications, and it's impossible to explore every ramification of these concepts in a single book. There are many great resources in the world of business literature that can deepen your understanding if you'd like to learn more about a particular mental model. Join me at http://personalmba.com to explore these ideas in more detail and learn how to apply them to your daily life and work.

Let's begin.

1

VALUE CREATION

Make something people want . . . There's nothing more valuable than an unmet need that is just becoming fixable. If you find something broken that you can fix for a lot of people, you've found a gold mine.

—PAUL GRAHAM, FOUNDER OF Y COMBINATOR, VENTURE
CAPITALIST, AND ESSAYIST AT PAULGRAHAM.COM

Every successful business creates something of value. The world is full of opportunities to make other people's lives better in some way, and your job as a businessperson is to identify things that people don't have enough of, then find a way to provide them.

The value you create can take on one of several different forms, but the purpose is always the same: to make someone else's life a little bit better. Without value creation, a business can't exist—you can't transact with others unless you have something valuable to trade.

The best businesses in the world are the ones that create the most value for other people. Some businesses thrive by providing a little value to many, and others focus on providing a lot of value to only a few people. Regardless, the more real value you create for other people, the better your business will be and the more prosperous you'll become.

SHARE THIS CONCEPT: http://book.personalmba.com/value-creation/

The Five Parts of Every Business

A business is a repeatable process that makes money. Everything else is a hobby.

—PAUL FREET, SERIAL ENTREPRENEUR AND COMMERCIALIZATION EXPERT

Roughly defined, a business is a repeatable process that:

1. Creates and delivers something of value . . .

2. That other people want or need . . .

3. At a price they're willing to pay . . .

4. In a way that satisfies the customer's needs and expectations . . .

5. So that the business brings in enough profit to make it worthwhile for the owners to continue operation.

It doesn't matter if you're running a solo venture or a billion-dollar brand. Take any one of these five factors away, and you don't have a business—you have something else. A venture that doesn't create value for others is a hobby. A venture that doesn't attract attention is a flop. A venture that doesn't sell the value it creates is a nonprofit. A venture that doesn't deliver what it promises is a scam. A venture that doesn't bring in enough money to keep operating will inevitably close.

At the core, every business is fundamentally a collection of five **Interdependent** (discussed later) processes, each of which flows into the next:

1. *Value Creation*. Discovering what people need or want, then creating it.

2. *Marketing*. Attracting attention and building demand for what you've created.

3. *Sales*. Turning prospective customers into paying customers.

4. *Value Delivery*. Giving your customers what you've promised and ensuring that they're satisfied.

5. *Finance*. Bringing in enough money to keep going and make your effort worthwhile.

If these five things sound simple, it's because they are. Business is not (and has never been) rocket science—it's simply a process of identifying a problem and finding a way to solve it that benefits both parties. Anyone who tries to make business sound more complicated than this is either trying to impress you or trying to sell you something you don't need.

The **Five Parts of Every Business** are the basis of every good business idea and business plan. If you can clearly define each of these five processes for any business, you'll have a complete understanding of how it works. If you're thinking about starting a new business, defining what these processes might look like is the best place to start. If you can't describe or diagram your business idea in terms of these core processes, you don't understand it well enough to make it work.[1]

SHARE THIS CONCEPT: http://book.personalmba.com/5-parts-of-every-business/

Economically Valuable Skills

> Don't go around saying the world owes you a living. The world owes you nothing—it was here first.
>
> —MARK TWAIN, GREAT AMERICAN NOVELIST

If you want to improve your value as a businessperson, focus on improving skills directly related to the **Five Parts of Every Business**.

Not every skill or area of knowledge is **Economically Valuable**, and that's okay—there are many things worth pursuing for the sake of relaxation or enjoyment alone. You may enjoy whitewater rafting, but it's very unlikely anyone will pay you to shoot the rapids unless you apply your skills for the benefit of others. Make the leap from personal enjoyment to **Products and Services** (discussed later), however, and you'll find yourself getting paid—plenty of adventurous souls are willing to pay for rafting equipment and guides.

As Michael Masterson suggests in *Ready, Fire, Aim*, don't expect skills that aren't related to the Five Parts of Every Business to be economically rewarded. Find a way to use them to create Economic Value, and you'll inevitably find a way to get paid.

Any skill or knowledge that helps you create value, market, sell, deliver value, or manage finances is Economically Valuable—accordingly, these are the topics we'll discuss in this book.

SHARE THIS CONCEPT: http://book.personalmba.com/economically-valuable-skills/

The Iron Law of the Market

Market matters most; neither a stellar team nor fantastic product will redeem a bad market. Markets that don't exist don't care how smart you are.

—MARC ANDREESSEN, VENTURE CAPITALIST AND FOUNDER OF
NETSCAPE AND NING.COM

What if you throw a party and nobody shows up? In business, it happens all the time.

Dean Kamen, a renowned and prolific inventor whose creations include the Sterling engine, the world's first insulin pump, and water purification devices, poured over $100 million into the development of the Segway PT, a $5,000, two-wheeled, self-balancing scooter that he claimed would revolutionize personal transportation "in the same way that the car replaced the horse and buggy." When the Segway was made available to the public in 2002, the company announced that it expected to sell 50,000 units every year.

Five years into the business, the company had sold a total of 23,000 units—less than 10 percent of the initial goal. (The company's financial records are private, but it's safe to say they don't look good.)

The problem wasn't that the product was poorly designed—the technology that makes the Segway work is extremely sophisticated, and the benefits are significant: the Segway is a convenient, green urban car replacement. The problem was that very few people cared enough to spend $5,000 on a goofy-looking alternative to walking or riding a bike—the massive market that Kamen expected didn't exist.

The same thing happens to new businesses every day. Without enough revenue to sustain it, any business will fail. Your revenue is completely dependent on people actually *wanting* what you have to offer.

Every business is fundamentally limited by the size and quality of the market it attempts to serve. The *Iron Law of the Market* is cold, hard, and un-forgiving: if you don't have a large group of people who really want what you have to offer, your chances of building a viable business are very slim.

The best approach is to focus on making things people want to buy. Creating something no one wants is a waste. Market research is the business equivalent of "look before you leap." Books like *The New Business Road Test* by John Mullins can help you identify promising markets from the outset, increasing the probability that your new venture will be a success.

In the next few sections, we'll explore how to figure out what people want and need *before* investing your time and hard-earned money into creating something new.

SHARE THIS CONCEPT: **http://book.personalmba.com/iron-law-of-the-market/**

Core Human Drives

Understanding human needs is half the job of meeting them.

—ADLAI STEVENSON, POLITICIAN AND FORMER GOVERNOR OF ILLINOIS

If you're going to build a successful business, it's useful to have a basic understanding of what people want. The most well-known general theory of what people want is called "Maslow's hierarchy of needs," proposed by the psychologist Abraham Maslow in 1943. Maslow's theory was that people progress through five general stages in the pursuit of what they want: physiology, safety, belongingness/love, esteem, and self-actualization. Physiology represents the "lowest" level of human need, while self-actualization (the exploration of a person's innate potential) is the "highest."

In Maslow's hierarchy, each lower-level need must be met before a person can focus on higher-order needs. If you don't have enough food, or you're in physical danger, you're probably not paying too much attention to how much other people like you or how much personal growth you're experiencing.

In practice, I prefer Clayton Alderfer's version of Maslow's hierarchy, which he called "ERG theory": people seek existence, relatedness, and growth, in that order. When people have what they need to survive, they move on to making friends and finding mates. When they're satisfied with their relationships, they focus on doing things they enjoy and improving their skills in things that interest them. First existence, then relatedness, then growth.

ERG theory explains the general *priority* of human desires, but not the *methods* people use to satisfy them. For that, we must turn to other theories of human action. According to Harvard Business School professors Paul Lawrence and Nitin Nohria, the authors of *Driven: How Human Nature Shapes Our Choices*, all human beings have four **Core Human Drives** that have a profound influence on our decisions and actions:

1. *The Drive to Acquire.* The desire to obtain or collect physical objects, as well as immaterial qualities like status, power, and influence. Businesses built on the drive to acquire include retailers, investment brokerages, and political consulting companies. Companies that promise to make us wealthy, famous, influential, or powerful connect to this drive.

2. *The Drive to Bond.* The desire to feel valued and loved by forming relationships with others, either platonic or romantic. Businesses built on the drive to bond include restaurants, conferences, and dating services. Companies that promise to make us attractive, well liked, or highly regarded connect to this drive.

3. *The Drive to Learn.* The desire to satisfy our curiosity. Businesses built on the drive to learn include academic programs, book publishers, and training workshops. Companies that promise to make us more knowledgeable or competent connect to this drive.

4. *The Drive to Defend.* The desire to protect ourselves, our loved ones, and our property. Businesses built on the drive to defend include home alarm systems, insurance products, martial arts training, and legal services. Companies that promise to keep us safe, eliminate a problem, or prevent bad things from happening connect to this drive.

There's a fifth core drive that Lawrence and Nohria missed:

5. *The Drive to Feel.* The desire for new sensory stimulus, intense emotional experiences, pleasure, excitement, entertainment, and anticipation. Businesses built on the drive to feel include restaurants, movies, games, concerts, and sporting events. Offers that promise

to give us pleasure, thrill us, or give us something to look forward to connect with this drive.

Whenever a group of people have an unmet need in one or more of these areas, a market will form to satisfy that need. As a result, the more drives your offer connects with, the more attractive it will be to your potential market.

At the core, all successful businesses sell some combination of money, status, power, love, knowledge, protection, pleasure, and excitement. The more clearly you articulate how your product satisfies one or more of these drives, the more attractive your offer will become.

SHARE THIS CONCEPT: http://book.personalmba.com/core-human-drives/

Status Seeking

The society which scorns excellence in plumbing as a humble activity and tolerates shoddiness in philosophy because it is an exalted activity will have neither good plumbing nor good philosophy: neither its pipes nor its theories will hold water.

—JOHN W. GARDNER, FORMER PRESIDENT OF THE CARNEGIE CORPORATION

In addition to understanding *Core Human Drives*, it's important to understand that humans are social creatures. Like many other mammals, humans evolved to have a "pecking order," a relative ranking of *Power* (discussed later) or status in a group. Competing with other people for status and power brought many benefits, including access to food, mates, resources, and the protection of other group members.

Status considerations are no longer as critical to survival, but our brains developed to place a very high priority on social status. As a result, status considerations influence the vast majority of a person's decisions and actions.

Status Seeking is a universal phenomenon: neurotypical human beings care intensely about what other people think of them, and they spend a significant amount of energy tracking their relative status compared to other members of their group. When opportunities to increase status appear, most people will seize them. When given a choice between different

Alternatives (discussed later), people will typically choose the option with the highest perceived status.

In general, we like to be associated with people and organizations that we think are powerful, important, or exclusive or that exhibit other high-status qualities or behaviors. We also like to ensure other people are aware of our status: for proof, examine what people post on their Facebook profiles.

Status Seeking is a fact of human life: it's not necessarily bad or something to be avoided. On the contrary: Status Seeking can motivate people to accomplish amazing things. In the words of Alain de Botton, a philosopher and social critic, "If one *felt* successful, there'd be so little incentive to *be* successful."

Unchecked, this can lead people to make poor decisions: think of someone who purchases a large house, luxury car, and designer clothing, only to end up bankrupt or in severe debt. As an individual, paying attention to how much you value status is useful when making buying decisions, particularly when there are other options that can meet the same needs or desires at a lower cost.

As a business professional, it's important to understand that status considerations are present in every level of the Core Human Drives. When you make an offer to a new prospect, they will automatically and unconsciously examine how your offer will influence their social status. Consciously building *Social Signals* (discussed later) into your offer is almost always an effective way to increase its appeal to your target market.

SHARE THIS CONCEPT: http://book.personalmba.com/status-seeking/

Ten Ways to Evaluate a Market

> So often people are working hard at the wrong thing. Working on the right thing is probably more important than working hard.
>
> —CATERINA FAKE, FOUNDER OF FLICKR.COM AND HUNCH.COM

If you're thinking of starting a new business or expanding an existing business into a new market, it pays to do some research before you leap.

The *Ten Ways to Evaluate a Market* provide a back-of-the-napkin method you can use to identify the attractiveness of any potential market. Rate each of the ten factors below on a scale of 0 to 10, where 0 is extremely unattractive and 10 is extremely attractive. When in doubt, be conservative in your estimate:

1. *Urgency*—How badly do people want or need this right now? (Renting an old movie is typically low urgency; seeing the first showing of a new movie on opening night is high urgency, since it only happens once.)

2. *Market Size*—How many people are actively purchasing things like this? (The market for underwater basket weaving courses is very small; the market for cancer cures is massive.)

3. *Pricing Potential*—What is the highest price a typical purchaser would be willing to spend for a solution? (Lollipops sell for $0.05; aircraft carriers sell for billions.)

4. *Cost of Customer Acquisition*—How easy is it to acquire a new customer? On average, how much will it cost to generate a sale, in both money and effort? (Restaurants built on high-traffic interstate highways spend little to bring in new customers. Government contractors can spend millions landing major procurement deals.)

5. *Cost of Value Delivery*—How much would it cost to create and deliver the value offered, both in money and effort? (Delivering files via the Internet is almost free; inventing a product and building a factory costs millions.)

6. *Uniqueness of Offer*—How unique is your offer versus competing offerings in the market, and how easy is it for potential competitors to copy you? (There are many hair salons, but very few companies that offer private space travel.)

7. *Speed to Market*—How quickly can you create something to sell? (You can offer to mow a neighbor's lawn in minutes; opening a bank can take years.)

8. *Up-Front Investment*—How much will you have to invest before you're ready to sell? (To be a housekeeper, all you need is a set of inexpensive cleaning products. To mine for gold, you need millions to purchase land and excavating equipment.)

9. *Upsell Potential*—Are there related secondary offers that you could also present to purchasing customers? (Customers who purchase razors need shaving cream and extra blades as well; buy a Frisbee, and you won't need another unless you lose it.)

10. *Evergreen Potential*—Once the initial offer has been created, how much additional work will you have to put into it in order to continue selling? (Business consulting requires ongoing work to get paid; a book can be produced once, then sold over and over as is.)

When you're done with your assessment, add up the score. If the score is 50 or below, move on to another idea—there are better places to invest your energy and resources. If the score is 75 or above, you have a very promising idea—full speed ahead. Anything between 50 and 75 has the potential to pay the bills, but won't be a home run without a huge investment of energy and resources, so plan accordingly.

SHARE THIS CONCEPT: http://book.personalmba.com/ten-ways-to-evaluate-a-market/

The Hidden Benefits of Competition

> The competitor to be feared is one who never bothers about you at all, but goes on making his own business better all the time.
>
> —HENRY FORD, FOUNDER OF THE FORD MOTOR COMPANY AND ASSEMBLY-LINE PIONEER

One of the most common experiences of a first-time entrepreneur is discovering that your brilliant business idea isn't as original as you'd thought: other businesses are already offering similar products or services. This would shake anyone's confidence—after all, why bother when someone else is doing what you want to do?

Cheer up: there are *Hidden Benefits of Competition*. When any two markets are equally attractive in other respects, you're better off choosing to enter the one *with* competition. Here's why: it means you know from the start there's a market of paying customers for this idea, eliminating your biggest risk.

The existence of a market means you're already on the right side of the

Iron Law of the Market, so you can spend more time developing your offer instead of proving a market exists. If there are several successful businesses serving a market, you don't have to worry so much about investing in a dead end, since you already know that people are buying.

The best way to observe what your potential competitors are doing is to become a customer. Buy as much as you can of what they offer. Observing your competition from the inside can teach you an enormous amount about the market: what value the competitor provides, how they attract attention, what they charge, how they close sales, how they make customers happy, how they deal with issues, and what needs they aren't yet serving.

As a paying customer, you get to observe what works and what doesn't before you commit to a particular strategy. Learn everything you can from your competition, and then create something even more valuable.

SHARE THIS CONCEPT: **http://book.personalmba.com/hidden-benefit-of-competition/**

The Mercenary Rule

> Make money your god and it will plague you like the devil.
> —HENRY FIELDING, EIGHTEENTH-CENTURY NOVELIST AND SATIRIST

Becoming a **Mercenary** doesn't pay: don't start a business for the money alone. Here's why: starting and running a business *always* takes more effort than you first expect.

Even if you identify a business that will largely run itself, setting up the **Systems** (discussed later) necessary to run the business requires persistence and dedication. If the only thing that interests you about an opportunity is the money, you'll probably quit well before you find the pot of gold at the bottom of the landfill.

Pay very close attention to the things you find yourself coming back to over and over again. Building or finishing anything is mostly a matter of *starting* over and over again; don't ignore what pulls you. The trick is to find an attractive market that interests you enough to keep you improving your offering every single day. Finding that market is mostly a matter of patience and active exploration.

That said, don't ignore "boring" businesses until you investigate them; if you can find some aspect of the work that interests you and keeps you engaged, mundane markets can be quite attractive. "Dirty" businesses like plumbing and garbage collection certainly aren't sexy, but they can be quite lucrative because there's a significant ongoing need combined with relatively few people willing to step up and meet the demand.

If you find a way to make a necessary but dull market interesting enough to pursue, you may have discovered a hidden vein of gold waiting to be mined.

SHARE THIS CONCEPT: http://book.personalmba.com/mercenary-rule/

The Crusader Rule

> The zealous display the strength of their belief, while the judicious show the grounds of it.
>
> —WILLIAM SHENSTONE, EIGHTEENTH-CENTURY POET AND
> LANDSCAPE DESIGNER

Being a *Crusader* doesn't pay either. Every once in a while, you'll find an idea so fascinating it becomes hard to think about it objectively. The stars align, heavenly trumpets blare, and suddenly you have the unmistakable impression that you've found your calling.

In all the excitement, it's easy to forget that there's often a huge difference between an interesting idea and a solid business. In your optimism, forget ye not prudence: changing the world is difficult if you can't pay the bills.

Some ideas don't have enough of a market behind them to support a business, and that's perfectly okay. That doesn't mean you should ignore them: side projects can help you expand your knowledge, improve your skills, and experiment with new methods and techniques. I'm a huge advocate of pursuing side projects as long as you don't count on them to reliably produce income. Once you have your financial bases covered, crusade all you want.

Before attempting to launch a business, take the time to do a thorough evaluation using the *Ten Ways to Evaluate a Market*. If you're finding it difficult to be objective, find a trusted colleague or adviser to help you, then test it as quickly and as inexpensively as you can before you fully commit. A few hours spent in evaluation can prevent months (or years) of frustration and misplaced effort.

SHARE THIS CONCEPT: http://book.personalmba.com/crusader-rule/

Twelve Standard Forms of Value

> Value is not intrinsic; it is not in things. It is within us; it is the way in which man reacts to the conditions of his environment.
>
> —LUDWIG VON MISES, AUSTRIAN ECONOMIST

In order to successfully provide value to another person, it must take on a form they're willing to pay for. Fortunately, there's no need to reinvent the wheel—*Economic Value* usually takes on one of twelve standard forms:

1. *Product.* Create a single tangible item or entity, then sell and deliver it for more than what it cost to make.

2. *Service.* Provide help or assistance, then charge a fee for the benefits rendered.

3. *Shared Resource.* Create a durable asset that can be used by many people, then charge for access.

4. *Subscription.* Offer a benefit on an ongoing basis, and charge a recurring fee.

5. *Resale.* Acquire an asset from a wholesaler, then sell that asset to a retail buyer at a higher price.

6. *Lease.* Acquire an asset, then allow another person to use that asset for a predefined amount of time in exchange for a fee.

7. *Agency.* Market and sell an asset or service you don't own on behalf of a third party, then collect a percentage of the transaction price as a fee.

8. *Audience Aggregation.* Get the attention of a group of people with certain characteristics, then sell access in the form of advertising to another business looking to reach that audience.

9. *Loan.* Lend a certain amount of money, then collect payments over a predefined period of time equal to the original loan plus a predefined interest rate.

10. *Option.* Offer the ability to take a predefined action for a fixed period of time in exchange for a fee.

11. *Insurance.* Take on the risk of some specific bad thing happening to the policy holder in exchange for a predefined series of payments, then pay out claims only when the bad thing actually happens.

12. *Capital.* Purchase an ownership stake in a business, then collect a corresponding portion of the profit as a one-time payout or ongoing dividend.

Let's investigate these **Twelve Standard Forms of Value** in more detail.

SHARE THIS CONCEPT: http://book.personalmba.com/12-standard-forms-of-value/

Form of Value #1: Product

> Business is not financial science ... it's about creating a product or service so good that people will pay for it.
>
> —ANITA RODDICK, ENTREPRENEUR AND FOUNDER OF THE BODY SHOP

A **Product** is a tangible form of value. To run a Product-oriented business, you must:

1. Create some sort of tangible item that people want.

2. Produce that item as inexpensively as possible while maintaining an acceptable level of quality.

3. Sell as many units as possible for as high a price as the market will bear.

4. Keep enough inventory of finished product available to fulfill orders as they come in.

The book you're holding right now is a good example of a Product. It had to be written, edited, typeset, printed, bound, and shipped to bookstores in sufficient quantities before reaching your hands. Leave out any of these steps and you wouldn't be reading this right now. To make money, a book must be sold for more than it cost to create, print, and distribute.

Products can be durable, like cars, computers, and vacuum cleaners. They can also be consumable: goods like apples, donuts, and prescription medications are products as well. Products don't have to be physical—even though things like software, e-books, and MP3s don't have a distinct physical form, they are entities that can be sold.

Providing value in Product form is valuable because Products can be *Duplicated*. This book was only written once, but individual copies can be printed and delivered millions of times to readers all around the world. As a result, products tend to *Scale* better than other forms of value, since they can be Duplicated and/or *Multiplied* (all discussed later).

SHARE THIS CONCEPT: http://book.personalmba.com/product/

Form of Value #2: Service

> Everyone can be great because everyone can serve.
> — MARTIN LUTHER KING, JR., HUMAN RIGHTS ACTIVIST

A *Service* involves helping or assisting someone in exchange for a fee. To create value via Services, you must be able to provide some type of benefit to the user.

In order to create a successful Service, your business must:

1. Have employees capable of a skill or ability other people require but can't, won't, or don't want to use themselves.

2. Ensure that the Service is provided with consistently high quality.

3. Attract and retain paying customers.

A good example of a Service business is a barbershop. A haircut is not a *Product:* you can't purchase one from a shelf. The Service is the series of actions the stylist uses to transform your current hairstyle into the one you want. In this sense, doctors, freelance designers, massage therapists, lawn care providers, and consultants are all Service providers.

Services can be lucrative, particularly if the skills required to provide them are rare and difficult to develop, but the trade-off is that they're difficult to duplicate. Services typically depend on the Service provider's investment of time and energy, both of which are finite. A heart surgeon can only complete so many four-hour operations on any given day.

If you're developing a Service, be sure to charge enough to compensate for the time you'll be investing on a daily basis in providing the Service to your customers. Otherwise, you'll discover that you're working too hard for too little a reward.

SHARE THIS CONCEPT: http://book.personalmba.com/service/

Form of Value #3: Shared Resource

The joy that isn't shared dies young.

—ANNE SEXTON, PULITZER PRIZE–WINNING POET

A *Shared Resource* is a durable asset that can be used by many people. Shared Resources allow you to create the asset once, then charge your customers for its use.

In order to create a successful Shared Resource, you must:

1. Create an asset people want to have access to.

2. Serve as many users as you can without affecting the quality of each user's experience.

3. Charge enough to maintain and improve the Shared Resource over time.

Gyms and fitness clubs are a classic example of a Shared Resource. A fitness club may purchase forty treadmills, thirty exercise bikes, six sets of free weights, a set of kettlebells, and other useful but expensive equipment that lasts a long time. The club's members benefit by being able to access this equipment without having to purchase it themselves—instead, they pay an access fee, which is much easier for an individual to afford. (Most gyms combine access to their Shared Resource with *Services* and *Subscriptions*, a common example of *Bundling*—discussed later.)

Businesses like museums and amusement parks work in much the same way. Whether it means studying a Monet or riding a roller coaster, Shared Resources allow many people to take advantage of experiences that would otherwise be too expensive.

The tricky part about offering a Shared Resource is carefully monitoring usage levels. If you don't have enough users, you won't be able to spread out the cost of the asset enough to cover up-front costs and ongoing maintenance. If you have too many users, overcrowding will diminish the experience so much that they'll become frustrated, stop using the resource, and advise others not to patronize your business, diminishing your *Reputation* (discussed later). Finding the sweet spot between too few members and too many is the key to making a Shared Resource work.

SHARE THIS CONCEPT: http://book.personalmba.com/shared-resource/

Form of Value #4: Subscription

Please accept my resignation. I don't want to belong to any club that will accept me as a member.

—GROUCHO MARX, COMEDIAN

A *Subscription* program provides predefined benefits on an ongoing basis in exchange for a recurring fee. The actual benefits provided can be tangible or intangible—the key differences are (a) the expectation of additional value to be provided in the future and (b) that fees will be collected until the Subscription is canceled.

In order to create a successful Subscription, you must:

1. Provide significant value to each subscriber on a regular basis.

2. Build a subscriber base and continually attract new subscribers to compensate for attrition.

3. Bill customers on a recurring basis.

4. Retain each subscriber as long as possible.

Cable or satellite television service is a great example of a Subscription. After you sign up, the company will continue to provide television service as long as you make the payments. You don't have to call up the company every month to buy another thirty days' worth—the service continues as long as the invoice is paid.

Subscription is an attractive form of value because it provides more predictable revenue. Instead of having to resell to your existing customers every day, Subscriptions allow you to build a steady base of loyal customers over time. This model ensures a certain level of revenue coming in each billing period.

The key to Subscription offers is doing everything you can to keep customer attrition as low as possible. As long as you continue to make your customers happy, only a small percentage of your customer base will cancel each period, giving you the ability to plan your finances with more certainty. Any subscriber attrition you experience can be overcome by enrolling more customers.

SHARE THIS CONCEPT: http://book.personalmba.com/subscription/

Form of Value #5: Resale

Buy low, sell high.

—STOCK TRADER'S MAXIM

Resale is the acquisition of an asset from a wholesale seller, followed by the sale of that asset to a retail buyer at a higher price. Resale is how most of the retailers you're familiar with work: they purchase what they sell from other businesses, then resell each purchase for more than it cost.

In order to provide value as a reseller, you must:

1. Purchase a product as inexpensively as possible, usually in bulk.

2. Keep the product in good condition until sale—damaged goods can't be sold.

3. Find potential purchasers of the product as quickly as possible to keep inventory costs low.

4. Sell the product for as high a markup as possible, preferably a multiple of the purchase price.

Resellers are valuable because they help wholesalers sell products without having to find individual purchasers. To a farmer, selling apples to millions of individuals would be time-intensive and inefficient: it's far better to sell them all to a grocery chain and focus on growing more apples. The grocery then takes the apples into inventory and sells them to individual consumers at a higher price.

Major retailers like Walmart and Tesco, book retailers like Barnes & Noble, and catalog operations like Lands' End work in fundamentally the same way: purchase products at low prices directly from manufacturers, then sell them for a higher price as quickly as possible.

Sourcing good products at low prices and managing inventory levels are the keys to reselling. Without a steady supply of sellable product at a low enough price to turn a profit, a reseller will have a hard time bringing in enough revenue to keep going. Accordingly, most successful resellers establish close relationships with the businesses that supply their stock to ensure they continue to get a reliable supply of good assets at low prices.

SHARE THIS CONCEPT: http://book.personalmba.com/resale/

Form of Value #6: Lease

> The human species, according to the best theory I can form of it, is composed of two distinct races: the men who borrow and the men who lend.
>
> —CHARLES LAMB, ESSAYIST

A **Lease** involves acquiring an asset, followed by allowing another person to use that asset for a predefined amount of time in exchange for a fee. The asset can be pretty much anything: cars, boats, houses, DVDs. As long as an asset is durable enough to survive rental to another person and return ready for reuse, you can Lease it.

In order to provide value via a Lease, you must:

1. Acquire an asset people want to use.
2. Lease the asset to a paying customer on favorable terms.

3. Protect yourself from unexpected or adverse events, including the loss or damage of the leased asset.

Leasing benefits the customer by allowing the use of an asset for less than the outright purchase price. You may not be able to afford to spend tens of thousands of dollars to purchase a luxury car or a speedboat, but for a few hundred dollars a month, you can certainly lease or rent one. The same principle applies to housing: leasing makes it possible to live in an expensive building for much less than it would cost to purchase or build it yourself. After your lease is up, the asset can be leased by the owner to someone else.

To successfully provide value via Leases, you must ensure that the revenue from the Lease covers the purchase price of the asset before it wears out or is lost. Most assets have a limited useful life, so you must charge enough to bring in more revenue than the purchase price before the asset loses its value. In addition, be sure to plan for repair and replacement costs to ensure you're charging enough money to cover you in the event your asset is lost or damaged in use.

SHARE THIS CONCEPT: http://book.personalmba.com/lease/

Form of Value #7: Agency

> I wish to be cremated. One tenth of my ashes shall be given to my
> agent, as written in our contract.
>
> —GROUCHO MARX

Agency involves the marketing and sale of an asset you don't own. Instead of producing value by yourself, you team up with someone else who has value to offer, then work to find a purchaser. In exchange for establishing a new relationship between your source and a buyer, you earn a commission or fee.

In order to provide value via Agency, you must:

1. Find a seller who has a valuable asset.
2. Establish contact and trust with potential buyers of that asset.

3. Negotiate until an agreement is reached on the terms of sale.

4. Collect the agreed-upon fee or commission from the seller.

Sellers benefit from an Agency relationship because it generates sales that might not otherwise happen. Literary agents are a classic example: a potential author may have an idea for a book, but may not know anyone in publishing. By working with an agent who has preexisting connections in the publishing industry, it's far more likely the author will land a publishing contract. In exchange for finding a publisher and negotiating the deal, the agent gets a percentage of the book's advance and royalties.

Buyers also benefit from an Agency relationship—good agents can help them find great assets to purchase. Agents often act as a filter for buyers, who trust that the agent will bring their attention to assets worth purchasing and keep them away from bad deals. Residential real estate is a great example: working with an experienced buyer's agent who knows the area often makes purchasing a home in a new town much easier.

The key to Agency is to ensure that your fee or commission is high enough to make the effort worth it. Since most Agency relationships are dependent upon closing a sale, spend your time on activities that will result in a completed transaction, and ensure that the commission or fee from that transaction compensates you for the time and effort you put into closing the deal.

SHARE THIS CONCEPT: http://book.personalmba.com/agency/

Form of Value #8: Audience Aggregation

So long as there's a jingle in your head, television isn't free.
—JASON LOVE, MARKETING EXECUTIVE

Audience Aggregation revolves around collecting the attention of a group of people with similar characteristics, then selling access to that audience to a third party. Since attention is limited and valuable, gathering a group of people in a certain demographic is quite valuable to businesses or groups that are interested in getting the attention of those people.

In order to provide value via Audience Aggregation, you must:

1. Identify a group of people with common characteristics or interests.

2. Create and maintain some way of consistently attracting that group's attention.

3. Find third parties who are interested in buying the attention of that audience.

4. Sell access to that audience without alienating the audience itself.

Audience Aggregation benefits the audience because it provides something worthy of their attention. Magazines and advertising-supported Web sites are great examples: readers benefit from the information and entertainment these sources provide in exchange for being exposed to some level of advertising. If the advertising becomes obnoxious, they'll leave, but most people are willing to be exposed to a certain amount of advertising if the content is good.

Audience Aggregation benefits the advertiser because it gets attention, which leads to sales. Think of a conference or trade show: buying a booth in the center of a building full of people interested in what you have to offer can be a smart decision. Done well, advertising attracts attention, attention brings prospects, and prospects lead to sales. As long as the sales bring in more money than the cost of the advertising plus the business's **Overhead** (discussed later), the advertising can be a valuable tool to bring in new customers, which means the advertiser can continue to support the aggregator by purchasing more advertising.

SHARE THIS CONCEPT: http://book.personalmba.com/audience-aggregation/

Form of Value #9: Loan

Money talks—but credit has an echo.

—BOB THAVES, CARTOONIST AND CREATOR OF "FRANK AND ERNEST"

A **Loan** involves an agreement to let the borrower use a certain amount of resources for a certain period of time. In exchange, the borrower must pay the lender a series of payments over a predefined period of time, which is equal to the original loan plus a predefined interest rate.

In order to provide value via Loans, you must:

1. Have some amount of money to lend.

2. Find people who want to borrow that money.

3. Set an interest rate that compensates you adequately for the Loan.

4. Estimate and protect against the possibility that the Loan won't be repaid.

Used responsibly, Loans allow people to benefit from immediate access to products or services that would otherwise be too expensive to purchase outright. Mortgages allow people to live in houses without having hundreds of thousands of dollars in the bank. Auto Loans allow people to drive new vehicles in exchange for a monthly payment instead of a 100 percent down payment. Credit cards allow people to purchase goods and services immediately, then pay for them over the course of several months.

Loans are beneficial to the lender because they provide a way to benefit from excess capital. The addition of compound interest on top of the original loan (the "principal") means that the lender will collect much more than the original loan—in the case of long-term Loans like mortgages, often two to three times more.

After the Loan is made, little additional work is required on the part of the lender aside from collecting payments—unless the borrower stops making payments. Accordingly, the process of identifying how risky a particular Loan is—a process called "underwriting"—is critically important for lenders, who often require some sort of asset as collateral to protect against the risks of a Loan gone sour. If the Loan is not repaid, ownership of the collateral is transferred to the borrower, then sold to recoup any funds lost in the transaction.

SHARE THIS CONCEPT: http://book.personalmba.com/loan/

Form of Value #10: Option

You pays your money and you makes your choice.

—*PUNCH*, NINETEENTH-CENTURY BRITISH COMIC MAGAZINE, 1846

An **Option** is the ability to take a predefined action for a fixed period of time in exchange for a fee. Most people think of Options as financial securities, but they're all around us: movie or concert tickets, coupons, retainers, and licensing rights are all examples of Options. In exchange for a fee, the purchaser has the right to take some specific action—attend the show, purchase an asset, or buy a financial security at a particular price—before the deadline.

In order to provide value via Options, you must:

1. Identify some action people might want to take in the future.
2. Offer potential buyers the right to take that action before a specified deadline.
3. Convince potential buyers that the Option is worth the asking price.
4. Enforce the specified deadline on taking action.

Options are valuable because they allow the purchaser the *ability* to take a specific action without *requiring* them to take that action. For example, if you purchase a movie ticket, you have the ability to occupy a seat in the theater, but you don't *have to* if a better opportunity presents itself. When you purchase the ticket, all you're purchasing is the right to exercise the Option to see the movie at the time specified—nothing more.

Options are often used to keep specific courses of action open for a certain period of time before another transaction takes place. For example, in moving to Colorado from New York, my wife, Kelsey, and I put a deposit down on an apartment we hadn't seen in person. The deposit ensured that the landlord wouldn't rent the apartment to someone else before we moved. Once we signed the official rental agreement, the deposit became a standard rental security deposit. If we had decided not to move forward, the landlord would have kept the deposit in compensation for holding the apartment for us and would have been free to find another tenant. Thus, the Option was beneficial for both of us.

Options are often an overlooked form of value—flexibility is one of the **Three Universal Currencies** (discussed later). Find a way to give people more flexibility, and you may discover a viable business model.

SHARE THIS CONCEPT: http://book.personalmba.com/option/

Form of Value #11: Insurance

Take calculated risks. That is quite different from being rash.
—GENERAL GEORGE S. PATTON, COMMANDER OF THE U.S. THIRD ARMY IN
WORLD WAR II

Insurance involves the transfer of risk from the purchaser to the seller. In exchange for taking on the risk of some specific bad thing happening to the policy holder, the policy holder agrees to give the insurer a predefined series of payments. If the bad thing actually happens, the insurer is responsible for footing the bill. If it doesn't, the insurer gets to keep the money.

In order to provide value via Insurance, you must:

1. Create a binding legal agreement that transfers the risk of a specific bad thing (a "loss") happening from the policy holder to you.

2. Estimate the risk of that bad thing actually happening, using available data.

3. Collect the agreed-upon series of payments (called "premiums") over time.

4. Pay out legitimate claims upon the policy.

Insurance provides value to the purchaser by protecting them from downside risk. For example, a house can catch fire in any number of ways, and most homeowners don't have enough cash to purchase another if their home burns to the ground. Homeowners' Insurance transfers this risk to the insurer. If the home is destroyed by fire, the Insurance will compensate the homeowner and allow them to purchase a new home. If it isn't, the insurer gets to keep the premium payments.

Insurance works because it spreads risk over a large number of individuals. If an insurer writes policies for thousands or millions of homes, it's highly unlikely that every single one will burn to the ground at once—only a certain number of claims will have to be paid. As long as the insurer brings in more premium payments than it pays in claims, the insurer makes money. Car insurance, health insurance, and warranty coverage for consumer goods work the same way.

The more premiums an insurer collects and the fewer claims the insurer pays, the more money it makes. Insurers have a vested interest in avoiding "bad risks," maximizing premiums, and minimizing payments on claims. Accordingly, insurers must be constantly vigilant to avoid fraudulent activity, both by preventing fraudulent claims and by refraining from defrauding purchasers by collecting premium payments without paying legitimate claims. If an insurer fails to pay legitimate claims, they're likely to find themselves in court as policy holders use the legal system to uphold their Insurance contract.

SHARE THIS CONCEPT: http://book.personalmba.com/insurance/

Form of Value #12: Capital

Capital is that part of wealth which is devoted to obtaining further wealth.

—ALFRED MARSHALL, ECONOMIST AND AUTHOR OF
PRINCIPLES OF ECONOMICS

apital is the purchase of an ownership stake in a business. For parties that have resources to allocate, providing Capital is a way to help owners of new or existing businesses expand or enter new markets. Angel investing, venture capital, and purchasing stock in publicly traded companies are all examples of providing value via Capital, which we'll discuss in detail later in the *Hierarchy of Funding*.

In order to provide value via Capital, you must:

1. Have a pool of resources available to invest.

2. Find a promising business in which you'd be willing to invest.

3. Estimate how much that business is currently worth, how much it may be worth in the future, and the probability that the business will go under, which would result in the loss of your Capital.

4. Negotiate the amount of ownership you'd receive in exchange for the amount of Capital you're investing.

Businesses benefit from Capital investment because it enables them to gather the resources necessary to expand or enter new industries. Some industries, like manufacturing and financial services, require huge amounts of funding to start or expand. By taking on investors, business owners can secure enough funding to move forward quickly.

Investors benefit by acquiring a certain percentage of that company's ownership, which allows them to benefit from the business's activities without active involvement. Instead of leaving their money in a bank account, investors can allocate it to companies that are involved in promising ventures, which may provide a higher rate of return. If the business brings in a lot of cash, investors may benefit from a regular dividend. If it's acquired by another company or is listed on a public stock exchange, investors may receive a percentage of the purchase price as a lump-sum payment or sell their shares of the company on the open market for a profit.

SHARE THIS CONCEPT: http://book.personalmba.com/capital/

Hassle Premium

All human situations have their inconveniences.
—BENJAMIN FRANKLIN, EARLY AMERICAN POLITICAL LEADER, SCIENTIST,
AND POLYMATH

People are almost always willing to pay for things that they believe are too much of a pain to take care of themselves. Where there's a hassle, there's a business opportunity.

Hassles come in many forms. The project or task in question may:

▶ Take too much time to complete.

▶ Require too much effort to ensure a good result.

▶ Distract from other, more important priorities.

▶ Involve too much confusion, uncertainty, or complexity.

▶ Require costly or intimidating prior experience.

▶ Require specialized resources or equipment that's difficult to obtain.

The more hassle a project or task involves, the more people are generally willing to pay for an easy solution or for someone to complete the job on their behalf. Here's an example: a homeowner may be willing to pay a one-time fee of $50 for a pool cleaning kit, but they may be willing to pay a cleaning service $100 per *month* to have someone clean their pool for them.

The end result is a clean pool either way, but the cleaning service removes the hassle: the pool owner doesn't have to spend any time or effort to get the same desired result. As a result, the pool cleaning service benefits from the **Hassle Premium**: it's able to collect $1,200 per year—$1,150 more than the DIY option—by eliminating the hassle for the pool owner.

There is a limit, however: charging $10,000 a month for a pool cleaning service won't work—the vast majority of homeowners don't care about having a clean pool that much. To benefit from the Hassle Premium, you need to understand how much of a hassle the task is to the prospect. The greater the hassle, the higher the potential Hassle Premium.

If you're looking for a new business idea, start looking for hassles. Where there's hassle, there's opportunity. The more hassle you eliminate for your customers, the more you'll collect in revenue.

SHARE THIS CONCEPT: http://book.personalmba.com/hassle-premium/

Perceived Value

> People don't trade money for things when they value their money more highly than they value the things.
>
> —ROY H. WILLIAMS, *THE WIZARD OF ADS*

All forms of value are not created equal. "Value" is in the eye of the beholder.

Perceived Value determines how much your customers will be willing to pay for what you're offering. The more valuable a prospect believes your offer is, the more likely they'll be to buy it, and the more they'll be willing to pay.

The most valuable offers do one or more of the following:

▶ Satisfy one or more of the prospect's Core Human Drives.

▶ Offer an attractive and easy-to-visualize *End Result* (discussed later).

▶ Command the highest Hassle Premium by reducing end-user involvement as much as possible.

▶ Satisfy the prospect's Status Seeking tendency by providing desirable *Social Signals* (discussed later) that help them look good in the eyes of other people.

It's important to note that Perceived Value is a subjective matter and depends on your prospect's current situation, values, beliefs, and worldview. If your prospects don't believe your offer is valuable, they won't be *Receptive* (discussed later) to your offer.

Focus on providing the most significant benefits and the highest status in a way that requires the least amount of end-user effort and frustration, and you'll increase the Perceived Value of your offer.

SHARE THIS CONCEPT: http://book.personalmba.com/perceived-value/

Modularity

> Great things are not done by impulse, but by a series of small things brought together.
>
> —VINCENT VAN GOGH, ARTIST

Keep in mind that the *Twelve Standard Forms of Value* aren't mutually exclusive: you can offer any number or combination of these forms to your potential customers to see which ones they like best.

Most successful businesses offer value in multiple forms. Take the magazine industry, for example. Magazines charge a monthly or annual *Subscription* fee in exchange for a printed magazine delivered by mail on a periodic basis. Simultaneously, they use *Audience Aggregation* to sell access to their subscribers via advertising, which is included in the magazine alongside the content.

Travel Web sites like Orbitz sell **Products** (airplane tickets) alongside trip-cancellation **Insurance**, and display advertising (Audience Aggregation) to Web site visitors. Movie theaters combine movie showings (a **Shared Resource**) with tickets (an **Option**) and concession sales (**Products**).

In most companies, each of these offers is handled separately, and the customer can pick and choose which offers they want to take advantage of. By making offers **Modular**, the business can create and improve each offer in isolation, then mix and match offers as necessary to better serve their customers. It's like playing with LEGOS: once you have a set of pieces to work with, you can put them together in all sorts of interesting ways.

SHARE THIS CONCEPT: http://book.personalmba.com/modularity/

Bundling and Unbundling

A bit of this and a bit of that is how newness enters the world.
—SALMAN RUSHDIE, NOVELIST

The benefit of making your offers small and **Modular** is that it allows you to take advantage of a strategy called **Bundling**. Bundling allows you to repurpose value that you have already created to create even more value.

Bundling occurs when you combine multiple smaller offers into a single large offer. An example of Bundling occurs in the mobile phone industry, where a mobile phone (a physical **Product**) is bundled with a monthly service plan (a **Subscription**) for a single price. Similarly, buy-one-get-one-free offers at the grocery store are a form of Bundling.

Typically, the more offers contained in the bundle, the higher the **Perceived Value** of the offer, and the more the business can charge. That's why mobile phone providers add things like more minutes, unlimited text messaging, and Internet service onto the basic service plan. The more benefits provided, the more a customer is typically willing to pay on a monthly basis for the entire package.

Unbundling is the opposite of Bundling: it's taking one offer and splitting it up into multiple offers. A good example of Unbundling is selling MP3 downloads of a single album instead of the CD. Customers may not be willing to pay $10 for an entire album, but they may be willing to pay a dollar or two for the songs they particularly like. Unbundling the album into individual units opens the way to sales that wouldn't otherwise happen.

Bundling and Unbundling can help you create value for different types of customers without requiring the creation of something new. By combining offers and forms in various configurations, you can offer your customers exactly what they want.

SHARE THIS CONCEPT: http://book.personalmba.com/bundling-unbundling/

Prototype

It's this simple: if I never try anything, I never learn anything.
—HUGH PRATHER, AUTHOR OF *NOTES TO MYSELF*

The classic MBA product development model is shrouded in secrecy and mystique: develop the offering in private, make everyone involved sign non-disclosure agreements,[2] raise millions of dollars in venture capital, spend years making it perfect, then unveil your creation to the astonishment of the world and the thunderous sound of ringing cash registers.

Unfortunately, this mentality ruins careers and empties bank accounts. On their own, ideas are largely worthless—discovering whether or not you can actually make them work in reality is the most important job of any entrepreneur.

Don't be shy about showing potential customers your work in progress. Unless you work in an industry with unusually aggressive, competent, and well-funded competitors, you really don't have to worry about other people "stealing" your idea. Ideas are cheap—what counts is the ability to translate an idea into reality, which is much more difficult than recognizing a good idea.

"Stealth mode" diminishes your early learning opportunities, putting you at a huge early disadvantage. It's almost always better to focus on getting feedback from real customers as quickly as you possibly can.

A **Prototype** is an early representation of what your offering will look like. It may be a physical model, a computer rendering, a diagram, a flowchart, or a one-page paper that describes the major benefits and features. It doesn't have to be fancy: all your Prototype has to do is represent what you're offering in a tangible way, so that your potential customers can understand what you're doing well enough to give you good feedback.

For best results, create your prototype in the same form as the finished product. If you're creating a physical product, make a tangible model. If you're making a Web site, create a working Web page with the basic components. If you're creating a service, create a diagram or flowchart of everything that happens in the process, then act it out. The more realistic your Prototype is, the easier it'll be for people to understand what you're trying to do.

The Prototype is your first attempt at creating something useful, but it won't be your last. Your first will be embarrassingly poor and incomplete, and that's okay. Prototypes are valuable because they allow you to get good feedback from real people before you invest a huge amount of time, money, and effort into the project. The purpose of a Prototype is not to make it perfect: it's to quickly create a tangible focus for your efforts—something you and other people can see, evaluate, and improve.

As you show your Prototype to potential customers, you'll get a steady stream of ideas and **Feedback** (discussed later) that will help you make your offer even better.

SHARE THIS CONCEPT: http://book.personalmba.com/prototype/

The Iteration Cycle

I have not failed. I've just found 10,000 ways that won't work.
—THOMAS A. EDISON, PROLIFIC INVENTOR

Nobody—no matter how smart or talented they are—gets it right the first time.

For proof, consider any artistic masterpiece. Beneath the finished surface of the *Mona Lisa*, you'll find layer upon layer of draft sketches, false starts, and major alterations. The ceiling of the Sistine Chapel is covered with hundreds of millions of very small brushstrokes, each of which brought the resulting masterpiece one step closer to completion. It took Michelangelo millions of hammer strokes to turn a crude block of marble into the *David*.

The **Iteration Cycle** is a process you can use to make anything better over time. There's nothing wasteful about the inevitable changes and revisions that these artists made to their creations: every iteration brought the project one step closer to completion.

Iteration has six major steps, which I call the WIGWAM method:

1. *Watch*—What's happening? What's working and what's not?

2. *Ideate*—What could you improve? What are your options?

3. *Guess*—Based on what you've learned so far, which of your ideas do you think will make the biggest impact?

4. *Which?*—Decide which change to make.

5. *Act*—Actually make the change.

6. *Measure*—What happened? Was the change positive or negative? Should you keep the change, or go back to how things were before this iteration?

Iteration is a cycle—once you measure the results of the change and decide whether or not to keep it, you go back to the beginning to observe what's happening, and the cycle repeats.

For best results, clearly define what you're trying to accomplish with each iteration. Are you trying to make the offering more attractive or appealing? Are you trying to add a new feature people will value? Are you trying to make the offering cost less without detracting from its value? The more clearly you can define what you're after, the easier it'll be to understand the **Feedback** (discussed later) you're receiving and the more value you'll extract from each Iteration Cycle.

SHARE THIS CONCEPT: http://book.personalmba.com/iteration-cycle/

Iteration Velocity

Our goal is to have more at bats per unit of time and money than anyone else.

—ERIC SCHMIDT, CHAIRMAN AND CEO OF GOOGLE

When creating a new offering, your primary goal should be to work your way through each *Iteration Cycle* as quickly as possible. Iteration is a structured form of learning that helps you make your offering better; the faster you learn, the more quickly you'll be able to improve.

The faster you move through the Iteration Cycle, the better your offering will become. If you're really good, you can move through the process several times each day. The key is to keep each iteration small, clear, and quick, basing each iteration on what you learned via previous iterations.

The Iteration Cycle often feels like additional work because it *is* additional work. That's why so few people do it: it's very tempting to skip all of these "extra" steps and attempt to create the final offering outright.

The major problem with the direct approach is risk: you're sinking a great deal of time, energy, and resources into creating something that may not ultimately sell. If the idea's a dud, it's far better to figure that out quickly and inexpensively via a few quick Iteration Cycles than to bet the farm on an idea or market that just won't work.

Iteration may take some additional effort up front, but after you've gone through a few cycles, you'll have a deeper understanding of the market, direct knowledge of what people actually want enough to pay for, and a clear understanding of whether or not you have a viable offer to give them.

If you discover that you have what people want, great—full steam ahead. If there's no demand for what you're developing, you can quickly and cleanly move on to the next promising idea.

SHARE THIS CONCEPT: http://book.personalmba.com/iteration-velocity/

Feedback

> No business plan survives first contact with customers.
>
> —STEVEN GARY BLANK, SERIAL ENTREPRENEUR AND AUTHOR OF
> *THE FOUR STEPS TO THE EPIPHANY*

Getting useful **Feedback** from your potential customers is the core of the **Iteration Cycle**. Useful Feedback from real prospects helps you understand how well your offer meets their needs before development is complete, which allows you to make changes before you start selling.

Here are a few tips to maximize the value of the Feedback you receive:

1. *Get Feedback from real potential customers instead of friends and family.* Your inner circle typically wants you to succeed and wants to maintain a good relationship with you, so it's likely that they'll unintentionally sugarcoat their Feedback. For best results, be sure to get plenty of Feedback from people who aren't personally invested in you or your project.

2. *Ask open-ended questions.* When collecting Feedback, you should be listening more than you talk. Have a few open-ended questions prepared to give the conversation a bit of structure, but otherwise encourage the other person to do most of the talking. Short who/ what/when/where/why/how questions typically work best. Watch what they do, and compare their actions with what they say.

3. *Steady yourself, and keep calm.* Asking for genuine Feedback (the only useful kind) requires thick skin—no one likes hearing their baby is ugly. Try not to get offended or defensive if someone doesn't like what you've created; they're doing you a great service.

4. *Take what you hear with a grain of salt.* Even the most discouraging Feedback contains crucial pieces of information that can help you make your offering better. The worst response you can get when asking for Feedback isn't emphatic dislike: it's total apathy. If no one seems to care about what you've created, you don't have a viable business idea.

5. *Give potential customers the opportunity to preorder.* One of the most important pieces of Feedback you can receive during the iteration process is the other person's willingness to actually purchase what you're creating. It's one thing for a person to say that they'd purchase something and quite another for them to be willing to pull out their wallet or credit card and place a real order. You can do this even if the offer isn't ready yet—a tactic called **Shadow Testing** (discussed later).

Whenever possible, give the people who are giving you Feedback the opportunity to preorder the offering. If a significant number of people take you up on the offer, you're in good shape: you know that you have a solid offering *and* you immediately boost your cash flow.

If no one is willing to preorder, you know you have more work to do before you have a viable offer—by asking why they're not willing to purchase right now, you'll discover their major *Barriers to Purchase* (discussed later): what's holding them back.

SHARE THIS CONCEPT: http://book.personalmba.com/feedback/

Alternatives

> Until one is committed, there is hesitancy, the chance to draw back, always ineffectiveness. Concerning all acts of initiative and creation, there is one elementary truth the ignorance of which kills countless ideas and splendid plans: that the moment one definitely commits oneself, the providence moves too.
>
> —W. H. MURRAY, MOUNTAINEER AND WRITER

It's Friday night. You're hungry, and you're thinking about going out to eat. You've already decided that you value having food prepared for you enough to justify the extra expense. Where should you go for dinner?

If you go to the neighborhood diner, you'll have access to a large variety of decent food at a reasonable price. The place may not be very fancy, but you know you'll be served a pretty good meal quickly and without a lot of fuss or expense.

If you go to a swanky hot spot, you'll be treated to attractive décor, impeccable service, and sophisticated cuisine. You'll have an impressive story to tell your friends, as well as the anticipation and excitement of a big night on the town. You'll also have a heftier tab at the end of the evening.

Unless you're *really* hungry, you won't patronize both restaurants on the same evening—it's an either/or decision. At the same time, there's no "right" decision—in fact, you may choose to go to the diner one evening and the trendy restaurant the next. It all depends on what you value most at the moment you decide where to eat.

Now let's flip the situation. You're the owner of the diner, and you're looking for ways to serve your customers better and bring new people into the restaurant. What should you focus on improving? Would expanding your entrée selection, reducing the time it takes to serve customers, or remodeling the restaurant make the biggest difference to the bottom line?

In a perfect world, it would be best to do *all* of these things, but business has been lackluster recently, and you don't have an unlimited budget to work with. You know you need to do something, but it's not clear which improvements—if any—would make the cash register ring more often. What do you do?

As you develop your offering, you can't avoid making choices between competing **Alternatives**. Should you add a particular feature, or not? Should you optimize for market A, optimize for market B, or attempt to please both? If you invest more in the offering, will your customers be willing to pay more to defray the expense?

Examining the possible Alternatives and considering the customer's perspective results in better choices. As you make decisions about what to include and what to leave out, it's essential to appreciate the Alternatives that your potential customers face when they decide whether or not to purchase your offering. Once you're aware of the options, you can examine the combinations and permutations of those Alternatives to present an attractive offer.

SHARE THIS CONCEPT: http://book.personalmba.com/alternatives/

Trade-offs

> I can't give you a surefire formula for success, but I can give you a
> formula for failure: try to please everybody all the time.
>
> —HERBERT BAYARD SWOPE, PULITZER PRIZE–WINNING JOURNALIST

A **Trade-off** is a decision that places a higher value on one of several competing options. We live in a world where time, energy, and resources are finite. There are only twenty-four hours in a day, you only have so much available energy, and at any given time there's an upper limit on the amount of money you're able to spend. What do you do when you can't do everything you want?

You can't have everything you want all of the time. Even if your bank account is large enough to purchase a private island, you're still faced with the decision of *which* private island to buy. You may want it all, but you can't have it all, so you do the best you can by choosing the option with the characteristics that matter most to you at the moment you make the decision.

Every minute of every day, you and the people around you are making Trade-offs. Some of these Trade-offs are economic: which pair of pants should you purchase? Some of them are temporal: should you visit with friends or go to a movie? Some of them are about effort: should you go to the team meeting or complete the overdue TPS report?

Predicting how people will make certain Trade-offs is tricky—values change quickly, given the environment and context. Values are preferences— how much we want, desire, or place importance on one particular object, quality, or state of being versus another. What you value this morning may be different from what you value this afternoon or this evening. What you want today may be different from what you want tomorrow.

When making decisions about what to include in your offering, it pays to look for **Patterns**—how specific groups of people tend to value some characteristic in a certain context. The decisions you make about what to include and what to leave out will never make everyone happy, so perfection shouldn't be your goal. By paying attention to the Patterns behind what your *best* customers value, you'll be able to focus on improving your offering for *most* of your best potential customers *most* of the time.

SHARE THIS CONCEPT: http://book.personalmba.com/tradeoffs/

Economic Values

A successful business is either loved or needed.

—TED LEONSIS, FORMER EXECUTIVE AT AOL AND OWNER OF THE
WASHINGTON WIZARDS AND WASHINGTON CAPITALS

Every time your customers purchase from you, they're deciding that they value what you have to offer more than they value anything else their money could buy at that moment. As you develop your offering, one of your first priorities should be to find out what your potential customers value more than the buying power of the dollars in their wallets.

Everyone has slightly different values at any given time, but there are a few common patterns that appear when people evaluate a potential purchase. Assuming the promised benefits of the offering are appealing, there are nine common *Economic Values* that people typically consider when evaluating a potential purchase. They are:

1. *Efficacy*—How well does it work?

2. *Speed*—How quickly does it work?

3. *Reliability*—Can I depend on it to do what I want?

4. *Ease of Use*—How much effort does it require?

5. *Flexibility*—How many things does it do?

6. *Status*—How does this affect the way others perceive me?

7. *Aesthetic Appeal*—How attractive or otherwise aesthetically pleasing is it?

8. *Emotion*—How does it make me feel?

9. *Cost*—How much do I have to give up to get this?

In the book *Trade-Off: Why Some Things Catch On, and Others Don't*, Kevin Maney discusses these common values in terms of two primary characteristics: convenience and fidelity. Things that are quick, reliable, easy, and flexible are convenient. Things that offer quality, status, aesthetic appeal, or emotional impact are high-fidelity.

Almost every improvement you make to an offer can be thought of in terms of improving either convenience or fidelity. It's incredibly difficult to optimize for both fidelity and convenience at the same time, so the most successful offerings try to provide the most convenience or fidelity among all competing offerings. If you're craving pizza, a table at the original Pizzeria Uno in Chicago is high-fidelity; Domino's home delivery is convenient. Accordingly, Pizzeria Uno benefits more from making the dining experience remarkable, while Domino's benefits more from delivering decent pizza as quickly as possible.

The Trade-offs that are made in the development of new offerings are what give each option its unique identity. Here's an example from the apparel business: Old Navy, Banana Republic, and Gap are owned by the same company, Gap Inc. All three lines make the same types of clothing— shirts, pants, and so on—but offer different Trade-offs.

Instead of attempting to make a single clothing line that's designed to appeal to everyone (which is impossible, since everyone wants something different), the company focused each line around a specific Trade-off. Old Navy emphasizes functionality and low cost. Gap emphasizes style and fashion at a moderate cost. Banana Republic emphasizes aesthetics and status at a premium cost. Each line has its own identity and appeals to a different type of potential customer, even though the clothes may be manufactured using the same processes and the revenues end up in the coffers of the same company.

SHARE THIS CONCEPT: http://book.personalmba.com/economic-values/

Relative Importance Testing

> Things which matter most must never be at the mercy of things which matter least.
>
> —JOHANN WOLFGANG VON GOETHE, NINETEENTH-CENTURY DRAMATIST, POET, AND POLYMATH

The tricky thing about trying to figure out what people want is that people want everything. Here's proof: bring together a group of potential customers for a focus group. Ask each participant to rate the importance of each of the nine *Economic Values* for your offering on a scale of 0 to 10. What will the results look like?

Regardless of your product or service, the results will be the same: your customers want products that provide exceptional results instantly, every time, with absolutely no effort. Simultaneously, they want the offer to make them rich, famous, attractive, and eternally blissful. They also want it to be free. If you ask them what they'd be willing to give up, they'll answer that everything is critically important, and they won't be happy with less.

The reality outside of the focus group is always quite different. Shortly after the group adjourns, each of those participants will go out and purchase something that's not free and not perfect, and they'll be happy with their decision. Why?

As a rule, people never accept *Trade-offs* unless they're forced to make a *Decision*. If the perfect option existed, they'd buy it. Since there's no such thing as the perfect offering, people are happy to settle for the **Next Best Alternative** (discussed later).

The best way to discover what people actually value is to ask them to make explicit Trade-offs during the research process. The problem with the hypothetical focus group was that it didn't ask the participants to make any real Decisions—the participants could have everything, so they wanted everything.

Relative Importance Testing—a set of analysis techniques pioneered by statistician Jordan Louviere in the 1980s[3]—gives you a way to determine what people actually want by asking them a series of simple questions designed to simulate real-life Trade-offs. Here's how it works.

Let's assume we're conducting a Relative Importance Test for the diner previously mentioned. Instead of asking the participant to rank each benefit from 0 to 10, we show the participant something like the following:

A. Orders delivered to table in five minutes or less.

B. Most entrée prices under $20.

C. Appealing restaurant décor.

D. Large variety of menu options.

After this set is shown, the participant is asked the following questions:

1. Which of these items is most important?

2. Which of these items is least important?

Once the participant answers the questions, another set is shown:

E. Unique entrées I can't get anywhere else.

F. Knowing I can always order my favorite dishes.

G. People are impressed that I dine here.

H. Large portions.

Random question sets containing four or five criteria are provided until there are no more possible combinations or the participant's attention wanders, which will typically occur around the five- to ten-minute mark.

It won't take the participant long to provide a response to each of these simple questions, but the results are quite revealing. By asking the participant to make an actual choice, you're collecting more accurate information about how the participant would respond when faced with a similar choice in the real world. When the results are aggregated and statistically analyzed, the relative importance of each benefit becomes very clear. The more sets each participant completes, the more clearly you'll be able to judge the relative importance of each benefit.[4]

Relative Importance Testing can help you quickly determine which benefits you should focus on to make your offering maximally attractive.

SHARE THIS CONCEPT: http://book.personalmba.com/relative-importance-testing/

Critical Assumptions

It is better to be roughly right than precisely wrong.
—JOHN MAYNARD KEYNES, ECONOMIST

Imagine that you're interested in opening a yoga studio. The market opportunity looks good: you believe that you've identified an underserved neighborhood with significant demand and enough discretionary income to pay a $100-plus monthly membership fee. You've sketched out what the space would look like, and you have a rough idea of the different styles you'd like to offer and whom you'd bring in to teach classes.

You've found a suitable location that you can rent for around $10,000 per month (if you sign a twelve-month lease), and you estimate that you'll need an additional $12,000 per month to pay employee salaries and other monthly operating expenses. You'll also need to spend around $5,000 up front for equipment: mats, blocks, and a computer to handle membership records.

The commercial real estate agent you're working with is putting pressure on you to move quickly, saying the location you want may be snatched up by another tenant if you don't commit now. Your current life savings are enough to cover the start-up costs and three months of projected operating expenses. You're excited, but you want to ensure that you're making the right decision before you move forward. Should you sign the lease?

Stories like this are very common: an excited first-time entrepreneur has a dream of owning a restaurant, bar, or bookstore, so they invest their life savings and take on significant debt to open the new business. Sometimes these stories work out well. More often than not, in a few months the new entrepreneur is bankrupt and out of business, wondering how things went so terribly wrong.

Critical Assumptions are facts or characteristics that must be true in the real world for your business or offering to be successful. Every new business or offering has a set of Critical Assumptions, and if any Critical Assumptions turns out to be false, the business idea will be vastly less promising than it appears.

The previous yoga studio example has three primary Critical Assumptions:

1. Individuals in this neighborhood will be willing to commit to pay $100 or more per month for a yoga membership close to their home.

2. The business will be able to attract at least 220 members paying full price within three months.

3. Total monthly revenues will exceed $22,000 for the next twelve months, which is the minimum duration of the lease term.

Let's examine what would happen to the yoga studio if these Critical Assumptions turn out to be false:

1. Initial interest is high, but most of the people who tour the new studio balk at paying $100 per month, saying that they'd rather drive a few miles and pay $75. The studio lowers prices to $75, which means 300 members are now required to keep the studio afloat. After lowering prices, membership reaches the 220-member mark as planned, but it's not enough to keep the studio open.

2. The studio doesn't attract enough members to pay the bills because yoga enthusiasts in the neighborhood are already locked into twelve-month membership contracts with a studio a few miles away. The studio runs out of money quickly and closes.

3. A very nice competing studio opens up in the same neighborhood around the same time. After three months, the studio only has half of the members it needs to sustain itself. With nine more months on the lease, the financial outlook is bleak.

Every business or offering has a set of Critical Assumptions that will make or break its continued existence. The more accurately you can identify these assumptions in advance and actually test whether or not they're true, the less risk you'll be taking and the more confidence you'll have in the wisdom of your decisions.

SHARE THIS CONCEPT: http://book.personalmba.com/critical-assumptions/

Shadow Testing

Praemonitus praemunitus (forewarned is forearmed).
— ROMAN PROVERB

The best way to validate the truth of your *Critical Assumptions* is to test them directly, but going through the entire process of starting the business is needlessly risky and expensive. It's much smarter to minimize your risk by testing your offering with real paying customers before you fully commit to making it real.

Shadow Testing is the process of selling an offering before it actually exists. As long as you're completely up front with your potential customers that the offering is still in development, Shadow Testing is a very useful strategy you can use to actually test your Critical Assumptions with real customers quickly and inexpensively.

Real paying customers are always different from hypothetical customers. Shadow Testing allows you to get a critical piece of customer feedback you can get in no other way: whether or not people will actually pay for what you're developing. In order to minimize the risk you're taking on in committing to the project, your objective should be to start gathering data from real paying customers as soon as possible.

Fitbit is a company that knows the value of Shadow Testing. Founded by Eric Friedman and James Park in September 2008, Fitbit makes a small clip-on exercise and sleep data-gathering device. The Fitbit device tracks your activity levels throughout the day and night, then automatically uploads your data to the Web, where it analyzes your health, fitness, and sleep patterns.

It's a neat concept, but creating new hardware is time-consuming, expensive, and fraught with risk, so here's what Friedman and Park did. The same day they announced the Fitbit idea to the world, they started allowing customers to preorder a Fitbit on their Web site, based on little more than a description of what the device would do and a few renderings of what the product would look like. The billing system collected names, addresses, and verified credit card numbers, but no charges were actually processed until the product was ready to ship, which gave the company an out in case their plans fell through.

Orders started rolling in, and one month later, investors had the confidence to pony up $2 million dollars to make the Fitbit a reality. A year later, the first real Fitbit was shipped to customers. That's the power of Shadow Testing.

SHARE THIS CONCEPT: http://book.personalmba.com/shadow-testing/

Minimum Viable Offer

> If you're not embarrassed by the first version of your product, you've launched too late.
>
> —REID HOFFMAN, FOUNDER OF LINKEDIN

In order to conduct a *Shadow Test*, you need something to sell. Fortunately, you don't have to create the entire offer before you start selling.

A *Minimum Viable Offer* is an offer that promises and/or provides the smallest number of benefits necessary to produce an actual sale. A Minimum Viable Offer is essentially a *Prototype* that's been developed to the point that someone will actually pull out their wallet and commit to making a purchase. It doesn't have to be complicated: Fitbit's Minimum Viable Offer was a Prototype, a description, and a few computer renderings. All you need to do is convey enough information to convince a real potential customer to buy.

Creating a Minimum Viable Offer is useful because it's impossible to predict 100 percent accurately what will work in advance. You don't want to invest a ton of time and money in something that has no chance of working, and the faster you can figure out if your idea will work or not, the better off you'll be.

Since **Feedback** from prospective customers and paid-in-full orders are very different things, creating a Minimum Viable Offer allows you to start collecting data from real customers as quickly as possible, directly testing the idea's **Critical Assumptions** and reducing the risk of making a business-ending investment decision.

Here's how the hypothetical yoga studio we discussed earlier could use a Minimum Viable Offer and Shadow Testing to evaluate their Critical Assumptions:

Step 1: Create a simple Web site describing the studio in detail, including location, tentative schedule, teaching staff, sketches of the space, and membership fees. The site includes a sign-up form for visitors to preorder memberships by submitting their credit card information. By signing up, members commit to a twelve-month membership when the studio opens, but they have the opportunity to cancel within the first month if they don't like it. If the studio doesn't open, all preorders are canceled without charge. Total cost: a few hundred dollars.

Step 2: Direct prospective customers to the Web site. This can be done inexpensively in any number of ways: flyers, door-to-door inquiry, direct mail, and local search engine advertising. Total cost: a few hundred dollars.

Step 3: Track how many individuals sign up for preopening memberships at the full rate via the Web site or request additional information. Total cost: a few hours of analysis.

This method of testing is simple, fast, and inexpensive. Services like Kickstarter (www.kickstarter.com) are making tests like these easy: all it takes to allow potential customers to preorder is a video, a few sketches or renderings, and basic sales copy. Spending a few hours and a few hundred dollars testing your **Critical Assumptions** is a very good use of money, particularly if your findings indicate your business idea won't work.

The purpose of starting with a Minimum Viable Offer is to minimize your risk. By keeping the investments small, incremental, and learning oriented, you'll be able to quickly discover what works and what doesn't. If the idea is promising, you're in a great position to make it happen. If your assumptions don't hold true, you're able to cut your losses without losing your shirt or your dignity.

SHARE THIS CONCEPT: **http://book.personalmba.com/minimum-viable-offer/**

Incremental Augmentation

> Pick three key attributes or features, get those things very, very right, and then forget about everything else . . . By focusing on only a few core features in the first version, you are forced to find the true essence and value of the product.
>
> —PAUL BUCHHEIT, CREATOR OF GMAIL AND GOOGLE ADSENSE

Once your **Minimum Viable Offer** is selling and you've proven that your **Critical Assumptions** are valid, you're in good shape, but you're not finished. If you're committed to making your offer as good as it can be, you'll need to keep making small changes that improve the offer if you want to stay competitive and attract more customers.

Incremental Augmentation is the process of using the **Iteration Cycle** to add new benefits to an existing offer. The process is simple: keep making and testing additions to the core offer, continue doing what works, and stop doing what doesn't.

The process of customizing cars is an example of Incremental Augmentation. Starting with a stock car, the "tuner" steadily replaces and upgrades parts: a better engine, spoiler, tinted windows, and chrome hubcaps. The intent of every change is to make the car just a little bit better, until it's the best it can be. When the car is finished, it's a different machine.

Incremental Augmentation helps you improve your offering while minimizing the risk that any single iteration will fail catastrophically. If you're not careful, drastic changes after launch can eliminate the qualities that made your offer attractive or break the systems you use to create the value you're providing to your customers. By making and testing changes quickly and incrementally, you can continually improve your offer without betting the farm, helping you create even more value for your customers over time.

Keep in mind that Incremental Augmentation can only take you so far. In order to enter a new market or change the game, you may need to create something completely new. If that's the case, start over with a new **Prototype** and work your way through the value creation process from the beginning. When it's ready, get **Feedback** and use **Testing** (discussed later) to compare the new version with the old version to make sure it's actually better before you launch it.

SHARE THIS CONCEPT: http://book.personalmba.com/incremental-augmentation/

Field Testing

> Any engineer that doesn't need to wash his hands at least three times a day is a failure.
>
> —SHOICHIRO TOYODA, FORMER CHAIRMAN OF THE
> TOYOTA MOTOR CORPORATION

A hundred and fifty days a year, Patrick Smith lives in the Colorado wilderness, just as he has for the past fifty years. Smith is the founder of the Colorado School of Outdoor Living and two successful hunting/backpacking companies: Mountainsmith, which he sold in 1995, and Kifaru International, which he created in 1997.

Becoming a Kifaru customer is a quick way to overheat your credit card. Kifaru makes arguably the best hiking and hunting packs and shelters in the world—extremely rugged, lightweight, and well designed. Kifaru packs can carry two hundred pounds comfortably, will last for decades, and sell for hundreds of dollars.

It's not uncommon for avid sportsmen and soldiers to shell out thousands of dollars for custom-made Kifaru gear, then wait eagerly for six to eight weeks while the company makes it. Try as you might, it's extremely difficult to find a Kifaru customer who's disappointed in the quality of their gear. More often than not, a new Kifaru customer is a customer for life.

The secret behind Kifaru's quality is **Field Testing**. Smith personally creates, uses, and **Iterates** every single product Kifaru makes for *years* before offering it to customers. By the time the finished product is available, even the most demanding customers have a difficult time finding flaws.

Here's what Smith says about his personal approach to Field Testing:

The backcountry is definitely both my inspiration and my laboratory. I've figured out how to create designs out there [in the field]. I trust this technique. I get instant feedback about designs because I'm in the backcountry doing the things the design is for, and testing it right then, in the real world arena it's intended for . . . I really do think this is a better design process than sitting in front of a computer in an office in town. I think it's a win/win situation.[5]

Field Testing has a long and distinguished history in the creation of successful businesses. In 1923, W. H. Murphy, of the Protective Garment Corporation of New York, had an associate shoot him in the chest from ten feet away in front of a public audience to prove his product worked—a marketing stunt based on extensive Field Testing to verify that the vest was capable of stopping live rounds. Miguel Caballero, a Colombian suit manufacturer who has created bulletproof suits for heads of state like Barack Obama and Hugo Chávez, has continued the tradition by posting videos of people wearing his suits being shot point-blank in the stomach on YouTube.[6]

Most major automotive manufacturers put new car designs through on- and off-road obstacle courses to test performance and handling in real-world conditions. Software companies like Microsoft and Google extensively Field Test their new products internally with employees before releasing them to customers. Testing internally allows the company to eliminate any bugs before customers ever see the product.

Using what you make every day is the best way to improve the quality of what you're offering. Nothing will help you find ways to make your offer better than being its most avid and demanding customer.

SHARE THIS CONCEPT: http://book.personalmba.com/field-testing/

2

MARKETING

The cardinal marketing sin is being boring.

—DAN KENNEDY, MARKETING EXPERT

Offering value is not enough. If no one knows (or cares) about what you have to offer, it doesn't matter how much value you create. Without **Marketing**, no business can survive—people who don't know you exist can't purchase what you have to offer, and people who aren't interested in what you have to offer won't become paying customers.

Every successful business finds a way to attract the attention of the right people and make them interested in what's being offered. Without prospects, you won't sell anything, and without completing profitable transactions, your business will fail.

Marketing is the art and science of finding "prospects"—people who are actively interested in what you have to offer. The best businesses in the world find ways to attract the attention of qualified prospects quickly and inexpensively. The more prospects you entice, the better off your business will be.

Marketing is not the same thing as selling. While "direct marketing" strategies often try to minimize the time between attracting attention and asking for the sale, Marketing and selling are two different things.

Marketing is about getting noticed; **Sales,** which we'll discuss in chapter 3, is about closing the deal.

SHARE THIS CONCEPT: http://book.personalmba.com/marketing/

Attention

In an attention economy (like this one), marketers struggle for attention. If you don't have it, you lose.

—SETH GODIN, BEST-SELLING AUTHOR OF *PERMISSION MARKETING*, *PURPLE COW*, AND *TRIBES*

Modern life is overloaded with demands on your **Attention**. Think of all of the things that are competing for your attention right now: there's work to be done, people to call, e-mail to check, TV to watch, music to listen to, and countless Web sites to visit. Everyone has too many things to do, and too little time to do them all.

Rule #1 of **Marketing** is that your potential customer's available attention is limited. Keeping up with everything in your world would require *way* more attention than you actually have to work with. To compensate, you filter: you ration your attention, allocating more to things you care about and less to things you don't. So does everyone else, including your potential prospects. To get someone's attention, you have to find a way around their filters.

High-quality attention must be earned. When you're seeking someone's attention, it's useful to take a moment to remember that you're competing against everything else in their world. In order to be noticed, you need to find a way to earn that attention by being more interesting or useful than the competing alternatives.

Attention doesn't matter if people don't care about what you're doing. If all you're looking for is attention, don't bother with all of this business stuff: skipping down the street in a pink bunny suit while yelling at the top of your lungs will get you all the attention you'll ever want. When it comes to business, however, some kinds of attention aren't worth having. You want the attention of prospects who will ultimately *purchase* from you—otherwise, you're wasting your time.

It's nice to be the center of attention, but business is about making profitable sales, not winning a popularity contest. Being featured on national television or on a huge Web site is a wonderful thing, but very often this kind of broad publicity fails to deliver actual sales. Spending time and energy acting like a socialite reduces the amount of resources you can devote to creating real value for your customers, which doesn't help anyone.

Earn the attention of the people who are likely to buy from you, and you'll inevitably build your business. The mental models in this chapter will show you how.

SHARE THIS CONCEPT: http://book.personalmba.com/attention/

Receptivity

> They say it takes 7 exposures to a product ad before you'll want to buy it, but after 8,743 spam emails for Viagra, I still don't want it!
>
> —ERIN PAVLINA, INTUITIVE COUNSELOR AND BLOGGER AT ERINPAVLINA.COM

People ignore what they don't care about. One of the primary functions of the human brain is perceptual filtering: determining what to pay attention to and what to ignore. The fastest way to be ignored by anyone is to start talking about something they don't care about.

Receptivity is a measure of how open a person is to your message. Rabid fans of hit novels like Stephenie Meyer's *Twilight* books are paragons of Receptivity: they're interested in almost anything they can find about their obsession as soon as it's available. From a business perspective, that's ideal— it's difficult to offer something that this audience won't want immediately.

On the other hand, a committed ethical vegan isn't likely to be interested in hearing about the benefits of red meat consumption, regardless of how much disconfirming evidence there is or how compelling the presentation. The worldview mismatch is just too big, and even the largest publicity campaign won't be able to overcome the overwhelming urge to ignore.

Receptivity has two primary components: what and when. People tend to be receptive only to certain categories of things at certain times. I love hearing about great new business books, but I never want to be on the receiving end of a 3:00 a.m. phone call from a publicist.

If you want your message to be heard, the medium matters. The form of your message has a big influence on how receptive people are to the information that message contains. If the form of your message suggests that it was created just for them, you're far more likely to get your prospect's attention.

Here's an example: Almost everyone will ignore postal junk mail—if it looks blatantly commercial or mass-produced, there's a 99 percent chance the recipient will throw it away without a second thought. Change the form, however, and Receptivity changes as well.

Most people will at least open a hand-addressed envelope, since it's clear someone spent time and effort sending it to them. Taken to an extreme, almost everyone (including busy executives) will open and look through the contents of a large overnight hand-addressed FedEx envelope—it's big, expensive, and clearly requires effort to send. Even then, if the contents don't match what they're interested in, you'll lose their attention immediately.

SHARE THIS CONCEPT: http://book.personalmba.com/receptivity/

Remarkability

Advertising is the tax you pay for being unremarkable.
—ROBERT STEPHENS, FOUNDER OF GEEK SQUAD

Every time I go for a run, people ask me about my shoes. They don't ask me because they're fashionable: they ask me because they're weird.

Vibram FiveFingers are shoes that look like a cross between a sock and a glove. Wearing them makes you look a bit like a frog: each toe has its own little pocket, giving your feet a slightly amphibian look—odd enough to be noticed.

I picked up a pair of FiveFingers to experiment with barefoot running—the thin rubber sole protects your feet from rocks and glass without adding any unnecessary support, which lets your feet do what they're naturally designed to do. Running or walking in FiveFingers is surprisingly fun, which is why I keep wearing them.

FiveFingers are just strange enough that people can't help but notice your feet when you wear them—they violate expectations of what shoes are supposed to look like. As a result, people ask me about them constantly—even in as "unfriendly" a place as the streets of New York City. By the end of the conversation, I've inevitably told my new acquaintance what they are, why I'm wearing them, how much they cost, and where they can purchase them.

FiveFingers are designed to overcome the number one problem every new offering faces: if no one knows you exist, no one will buy what you have to sell. Every customer who wears a pair of FiveFingers inevitably provides Vibram all of the advertising they need to keep growing—for free.

From a business perspective, the **Attention**-grabbing design of FiveFingers is working beautifully. On the street, salespeople confirm that FiveFingers are flying off the shelves—new stock sells out almost immediately. According to the *New York Times* ("Wiggling Their Toes at the Shoe Giants," August 30, 2009), sales of the FiveFingers line have tripled every year since they were introduced in 2006, and in 2009 revenue crossed the $10 million mark in North America—without mass-market advertising. Not bad for funny-looking frog shoes.

Being **Remarkable** is the best way to attract Attention. In the classic marketing book *Purple Cow*, Seth Godin uses a wonderful metaphor to illustrate this principle. A field full of brown cows is boring. A purple cow violates the viewer's expectations, which naturally attracts Attention and interest.

If you design your offer to be Remarkable—unique enough to pique your prospect's curiosity—it'll be significantly easier to attract attention.

SHARE THIS CONCEPT: http://book.personalmba.com/remarkability/

Probable Purchaser

> There are 6 billion people on this planet. 99.999% of them would rather not give you their money.
>
> —HUGH MACLEOD, CARTOONIST AND AUTHOR OF *IGNORE EVERYBODY*

Assuming that everyone in the world cares about what you have to offer is a huge marketing mistake. You may think that what you have to offer is the greatest thing since sliced bread—in fact, I hope you do! That doesn't change the fact that it's not right for everyone. Whatever you're offering, I can guarantee you that most of the people in this world don't—and will never—care about what you're doing. Harsh but true.

Fortunately, you don't have to appeal to everyone in order to succeed. You just have to attract enough **Attention** to close enough sales to produce enough profit to keep going. To do that, it's best to focus on attracting the attention of the people who will actually care about what you're doing.

Skilled marketers don't try to get everyone's attention—they focus on getting the attention of the *right people* at the *right time*. If you're marketing Harley-Davidson motorcycles, trying to land an appearance on *Oprah* to show off this year's new models probably isn't the best strategy. Likewise, Oprah's core audience is not likely to include burly men in leather jackets with handlebar mustaches and tattoos, so don't expect her to pay for a marketing booth at a motorcycle trade show any time soon.

Your **Probable Purchaser** is the type of person who is perfectly suited to what you're offering. Harley's most profitable customer is the "weekend warrior"—middle-aged men with disposable income who want to feel powerful and dangerous while cruising around in their spare time. Oprah's Probable Purchasers are middle-aged women who want to improve themselves and enjoy listening to intimate confessions and emotional stories.

Harley doesn't try to appeal to Oprah's Probable Purchasers, and vice versa—they each focus on appealing to their specific core audience, to great effect.

Attempting to appeal to everyone is a waste of time and money: focus your marketing efforts on your Probable Purchaser. By spending your limited resources reaching out to people who are already interested in the types of things you offer, you'll maximize the effectiveness of your attention-grabbing activities.

SHARE THIS CONCEPT: http://book.personalmba.com/probable-purchaser/

Preoccupation

> You wouldn't worry so much about what others think of you if you realized how seldom they do.
>
> —ELEANOR ROOSEVELT, FORMER FIRST LADY OF THE UNITED STATES

In order to earn the **Attention** of a prospect, you must divert their attention from what they're already doing. That's not an easy task.

Preoccupation is a fact of life for modern marketers: at the beginning of the marketing process, your prospects are paying attention to something else, not you. In order to attract Attention to your offer, what you're doing must be more interesting than your prospect's current subject of attention.

The best way to break a potential prospect's Preoccupation is to provoke a feeling of curiosity, surprise, or concern. Our ancient brains pay close attention to opportunities and threats, scanning the environment for new stimuli that could help or harm us.

The stronger and more emotionally compelling the stimuli, the easier it is to attract Attention. There's a reason marketers use evocative imagery, words, and sounds: our brains are wired to stop what we're doing to evaluate them.

That's not to say that your marketing needs to be garish and loud: there are thousands of subtle ways to attract Attention that can work just as well. Depending on the prospect's environment or emotional state, the threshold of interest you need to generate may be low. If the prospect is bored, restless, or looking for entertainment or distraction, it'll be easier to attract their Attention.

It always pays to assume your prospects begin in a state of Preoccupation. Begin your marketing approach in a way that breaks their Preoccupation and earns their Attention.

SHARE THIS CONCEPT: **http://book.personalmba.com/preoccupation/**

End Result

People don't buy quarter-inch drills; they buy quarter-inch holes.

—THEODORE LEVITT, ECONOMIST AND FORMER PROFESSOR AT
HARVARD BUSINESS SCHOOL

Most business opportunity seekers aren't really interested in the day-to-day details and responsibilities of running a business. They buy business books and courses because they want to experience a more prosperous, abundant, and hopeful future.

Most drivers don't buy expensive off-road-capable vehicles because they actually drive off the road. They buy them because off-road capability makes them feel adventurous and bold, capable of meeting any driving challenge.

Most women don't buy a $20 tube of lipstick for its color alone. They buy it because they believe it will make them more beautiful and desirable.

Most college students don't pay hundreds of thousands of dollars to Harvard or Stanford or Yale just to sit in a class. They go (or, rather, their parents send them) because they believe they'll be perceived as sophisticated, intelligent, and powerful after they graduate.

Marketing is most effective when it focuses on the desired **End Result**, which is usually a distinctive experience or emotion related to a **Core Human Drive**. The actual function of the purchase is important, but the End Result is what the prospect is most interested in hearing about.

It's often far more comfortable to focus on the features: you know what your offer *does*. Even so, it's far more effective to focus on the benefits: what your offer will *provide* to customers.

The End Result is what matters most. By focusing on the End Result, you're homing in on what will cause your prospect to conclude, "This is for me."

SHARE THIS CONCEPT: http://book.personalmba.com/end-result/

Qualification

The product that will not sell without advertising will not sell profitably with advertising.

—ALBERT LASKER, FORMER CEO OF LORD & THOMAS AND PIONEER OF MODERN ADVERTISING

Believe it or not, it's often wise to turn away paying customers. Not every customer is a good customer: customers who require more time, energy, attention, or risk than they're worth to your bottom line aren't worth attracting in the first place.

Qualification is the process of determining whether or not a prospect is a good customer before they purchase from you. By evaluating a prospect before they buy, you can minimize the chance of wasting your time dealing with a customer who's not a good fit for your business.

Progressive Insurance has turned Qualification into a profitable business strategy. To see Qualification in action, go to the Progressive Insurance Web site (www.progressive.com) and request a quote for car insurance.

When you request a quote, Progressive asks you a set of basic questions:

1. What type of car do you have?

2. Do you own or lease it? If you own it, are you still making payments?

3. What's your ZIP code?

4. Are you married?

5. Did you go to college?

6. Have you had any at-fault accidents in the past five years?

Progressive then uses your answers to gather data from a series of databases to answer two questions:

(A) Are you the type of person Progressive wants to insure?

(B) If so, how much should they charge to insure you?

If you're the type of person Progressive wants as a customer, they'll quote you a price and encourage you to purchase an insurance policy immediately. If you're not, Progressive will tell you that you can get a better price elsewhere and *actively encourage you to purchase insurance from one of their competitors.*

Why in the world would a business encourage a hot prospect to purchase from the competition? As you recall from our previous discussion of **Insurance**, the profitability of an insurer depends on collecting as much money as possible in premiums while paying out as little money as possible in claims.

Progressive doesn't want to maximize its total client base: it wants to insure only people who are likely to drive safely and have few accidents, which means attracting customers who will pay premiums for a long time without making claims. Qualification allows Progressive to maximize the number of highly profitable customers it insures while funneling the "bad risks" directly to their competitors. It's good for customers as well—if they're "good risks," they get lower rates on their car insurance.

Screening your customers can help you filter out the bad customers before they do business with you. The more clearly you define your ideal customer, the better you can screen out the prospects who don't fit that description, and the more you'll be able to focus on serving your best customers well.

SHARE THIS CONCEPT: http://book.personalmba.com/qualification/

Point of Market Entry

There is nothing harder than the softness of indifference.

—JUAN MONTALVO, ESSAYIST

Assuming you don't have a small child and aren't expecting one any time soon, you probably don't care about diapers, strollers, cribs, infant toys, day care, and Baby Einstein DVDs. Any information you're exposed to about these things is likely to be filtered away by your brain, since it's not relevant to your life at the moment.

But once you're expecting a little bundle of joy to enter your life, you suddenly care a great deal about these things, and will probably start actively searching for information about them. Before hearing the news, you had no reason to care; now you do.

Certain markets have clearly defined entry and exit points. Learning a newborn is on the way is an example of a *Point of Market Entry*. Once you know you're expecting, you're suddenly *much* more receptive to information about products and services that will help you take care of a child. Attempting to attract the *Attention* of people who don't care about what you do is a waste of time, money, and energy, so it's best to find out *when* people are interested in hearing from you before you reach out.

Attracting your Probable Purchaser's Attention immediately after they've reached the Point of Market Entry is hugely valuable. Companies like Procter & Gamble, Kimberly-Clark, Johnson & Johnson, and Fisher-Price pay an enormous amount of attention to Points of Market Entry, since they have a huge impact on the effectiveness of every baby-product-related marketing activity. It's not uncommon for new moms and dads to come home from the hospital with a complimentary "care package" from one or more of these companies containing samples of diapers, diaper rash ointment, formula, and other new-born-care basics.

If you can get a prospective customer's attention as soon as they become interested in what you're offering, you become the standard by which competing offers are evaluated. That's a remarkably powerful position that increases the likelihood the prospect will ultimately purchase from you.

Discovering where Probable Purchasers start looking for information after crossing the interest threshold is extremely valuable. Before the advent of the Internet, most expecting parents immediately started devouring books and talking to more experienced family and friends. Today, newly minted moms and dads hit the Web first, which is why organic and paid search engine marketing is often so valuable. By optimizing for key words your prospective customers are likely to search for, you can ensure that they find you first.

SHARE THIS CONCEPT: http://book.personalmba.com/point-of-market-entry/

Addressability

Sometimes the road less traveled is less traveled for a reason.
—JERRY SEINFELD, COMEDIAN

A good salesman, as the old (and politically incorrect) saying goes, can sell a refrigerator to an Eskimo. It's a cliché, but there's some truth to it: Inuit who live above the Arctic Circle use insulated refrigerators to keep their food from freezing in subzero temperatures. The real barrier isn't need, it's finding these customers in the first place: making the sale involves traveling thousands of miles through brutally wild terrain just to get their attention, let alone land a sale and deliver the product.

Addressability is a measure of how easy it is to get in touch with people who might want what you're offering. A highly Addressable audience can be reached quickly and easily. A non-Addressable audience can only be reached with extreme hardship, or isn't **Receptive** and doesn't want to be reached at all.

Yoga is a good example of a highly Addressable market. It's relatively easy to find places where people are already paying attention to yoga-related information: studios, popular magazines like *Yoga Journal*, conferences, Web sites, etc. Yoga is an $8 billion industry worldwide, and you can tap into some or all of these outlets to help yogis and yoginis learn more about what you have to offer.

Sensitive or embarrassing topics tend to have low Addressability, even if there's a huge need. Chronic medical conditions are a good example: it's difficult to find and reach a large group of people who suffer from an uncomfortable and potentially embarrassing condition like psoriasis or ulcerative colitis. People suffering from these conditions typically don't gather in the same place or read the same things, and many will avoid being publicly identified as sufferers by joining organizations, so it's hard to find and talk to them directly.

Doctors, on the other hand, are more Addressable: they have publicly listed addresses and phone numbers and are willing and able to meet with drug company representatives about new offerings. Since each doctor sees many patients and acts as a gatekeeper for prescription medications, it's clear why pharmaceutical companies spend so much time and money marketing to MDs.

The Internet has dramatically improved the Addressability of many markets. People who have a sensitive medical condition are highly likely to search for information anonymously on the Internet, which is Addressable via advertising. Blogs, discussion boards, and databases like WebMD.com make it easier for people who don't know one another to share their experiences and knowledge, making these low-Addressability markets more accessible than ever before.

Addressability is a huge concern when you are developing a new offer. If you have a choice, it's far better to focus on building something for an Addressable audience than it is to go around and hand sell or try to address an audience that is not naturally Addressable or doesn't want to be addressed.

If you choose to serve an Addressable market before committing to an offer, it'll be significantly easier to market your offer without breaking the bank.

Desire

Effective marketing makes your prospect want what you have to offer. In order for a prospect to be willing to pay you perfectly good money for what you're offering, they must want what you have. If your marketing activities don't produce some visceral feeling of *Desire* in your prospects, you're wasting your time and money.

Provoking Desire is the part of marketing that makes most people uncomfortable. It's understandable: pop culture is enamored with the image of the marketer as a shadowy master manipulator, hypnotizing the masses into wanting things they don't really want or need. Nothing could be further from the truth.

Here's the reality: it's almost impossible to make someone want something they don't *already desire*. Yes, it's possible to be scammy and manipulative if you misrepresent what you're offering or promise something you can't deliver. Don't mistake that for brainwashing: the quickest way to waste a multimillion-dollar advertising budget is to try to force people to want something they don't already want. The human mind simply doesn't work that way—we only purchase what we already desire on some level.

The essence of effective marketing is discovering what people already want, then presenting your offer in a way that intersects with that preexisting Desire. The best marketing is similar to *Education-Based Selling* (discussed later): it shows the prospect how the offer will help them achieve what they desire. Your job as a marketer isn't to convince people to want what you're offering: it's to help your prospects *convince themselves* that what you're offering will help them get what they really want.

So what do people want? We've already covered that: the *Core Human Drives* are a starting point that will help you discover what your market wants at the most basic level. The more drives you can connect with your offering, the more effective your marketing activities will be.

SHARE THIS CONCEPT: http://book.personalmba.com/desire/

Visualization

As soon as you step onto the lot of a car dealership, the salesperson you work with has a single, clear objective: convince you to get behind the wheel of a vehicle for a test drive.

The test drive is used to sell cars all over the world for a very good reason: it works. The test drive is the most effective tool a salesperson has to convince you to purchase a car that day.

Until you're actually driving a car, it's much easier to treat a potential purchase in a detached way. You're capable of rationally comparing makes and models, features, and prices. You can convince yourself that you're "just looking," with no intention of purchasing anything just yet.

Once you're actually behind the wheel of a car, however, the emotional parts of your mind take control. You start to imagine what your life would be like if you owned this vehicle. Instead of dispassionately comparing horsepower and acceleration metrics, you can actually feel the power of the engine and the ease of handling, and you can imagine the respect (or envy) of your neighbors as you pull your attractive new vehicle into the driveway.

You've stopped comparing and started *wanting*. Once you start wanting, you'll probably buy—it's only a matter of time.

B&H Photo Video uses the same strategy in a different market. Roaming the aisles of their Manhattan superstore is an intense sensory experience. You can feel the weight of the camera you're considering, watch how quickly it focuses, and hear the snap of the shutter. Better yet, you can compare the feel of each camera to hundreds of others, all within arm's reach. It's little wonder B&H is one of the most successful photography retailers in the world—after test-driving a few cameras, it's extremely difficult to resist the urge to take one home.

The most effective way to get people to want something is to encourage them to **Visualize** what their life would be like once they've accepted your offer. As we'll discuss later in *Mental Simulation*, our minds are designed to automatically imagine the consequences of our actions. You can use this natural tendency to your advantage by helping your prospects imagine the positive experiences they'll have.

If you encourage your prospects to Visualize what their life will look like after purchasing, you increase the probability that they'll purchase from you. The best way to help your customers Visualize is to expose them to as much sensory information as possible—the information their mind uses to conclude, "I want this."

SHARE THIS CONCEPT: http://book.personalmba.com/visualization/

Framing

Everything we hear is an opinion, not a fact. Everything we see is a perspective, not the truth.

—MARCUS AURELIUS, ROMAN EMPEROR AND PHILOSOPHER

In a famous experiment conducted by psychologists Amos Tversky and Daniel Kahneman, participants were asked to make a decision about administering medical treatment to a sick population of six hundred people. Participants in the study were given two options: Treatment A would save two hundred lives. Treatment B had a 33 percent chance of saving all six hundred people and a 66 percent possibility of saving no one.

Treatment A and Treatment B are mathematically identical—statistically, there's no difference in the expected outcome. The results, however, revealed a clear psychological preference: 72 percent of participants chose Treatment A, while 28 percent of the participants chose Treatment B.

The experiment was then repeated with two different treatment options. Treatment C would result in four hundred deaths. Treatment D had a 33 percent chance that no one would die, but a 66 percent probability that all six hundred would die. Participants overwhelmingly preferred Treatment D, 78 percent to 22 percent.

What's interesting to note is that Treatments A and C are also statistically identical, but A was overwhelmingly preferred while C was not. Contemplating lives saved with fatalities significantly altered the preferences of the people making decisions, even though the expected outcomes were exactly the same. We'll explore one of the reasons for this preference in **Loss Aversion** (discussed later), but for now, let's focus on how the *emphasis* of the various messages changed the results.

Framing is the act of emphasizing the details that are critically important while de-emphasizing things that aren't, by either minimizing certain facts or leaving them out entirely. Proper use of Framing can help you present your offer persuasively while honoring your customer's time and attention.

Framing is a natural part of communication: some form of compression in any message is inevitable. It's simply not practical to include all of the facts and context when communicating with others—we emphasize some details and leave out others to save time. We Frame because we have to: otherwise, it would take a huge amount of time to communicate even the simplest information to other people. It would take two hours to order a pizza, as you told the person at the other end of the line not only the size and toppings you wanted, but how you got their phone number and why on this particular evening you were in the mood for a slice as opposed to, say, General Tso's chicken.

Since Framing is an ever-present part of communication, it pays to be conscious of it. By being mindful of what you're emphasizing and what you're minimizing, you can communicate the benefits of your offer to your prospects in a clear and concise way, which maximizes your persuasive power.

Framing is not the same as lying or being deceitful. Honesty is always the best policy, and not just from a moral perspective. Misrepresenting your offer may net a few more sales in the short term, but it dramatically increases the probability that your customer's expectations will be violated, decreasing their satisfaction and permanently harming your **Reputation**. (See the **Expectation Effect**.)

Using Framing to your advantage will allow you to communicate the benefits of your offer to your **Probable Purchasers** persuasively, as long as you don't leave out information that your customers have a right to know.

SHARE THIS CONCEPT: http://book.personalmba.com/framing/

Free

> To charge nobody nuthin' is a guarantee of no profit. Getting atten-
> tion is not the same as getting paid.
>
> —JOSEPH FERRARA, INTELLECTUAL PROPERTY ATTORNEY

If you want to attract **Attention** quickly, give something valuable away for
Free.

People love the promise of getting something for nothing. You've probably seen Free samples of food being given away at the supermarket, or
received an offer to try a product or service for a certain time at no obligation. Chances are, at least a few of those free offers have led you to purchase more. Offers of Free value continue to exist because they work—the
Free value is subsidized by the additional sales that are made because of the
offer.

I started my teaching and consulting business by giving away my research and writing for Free on my Web site. As a result, hundreds of thousands of people find (or are referred to) the Personal MBA, benefit from
the information, and come to trust me as a useful resource. More often than
not, they give me permission to continue providing even more useful Free
information via e-mail.

Periodically, I offer to meet with prospective consulting customers by
phone for Free—there's no obligation whatsoever on their part, and I don't
hold anything back. Every time I make this offer, I receive hundreds of in-
quiries and meet many new and interesting people. A good percentage of
the people who accept a "free sample" become paying customers, making
"Free" the foundation of my teaching and consulting business.

More often than not, offering genuine Free value is a quick and effective
way to attract attention. By giving your prospects something useful at no
cost up front, you earn their attention and give your potential customers a
chance to actually experience the value you provide. Done well, this strategy will net you sales you wouldn't have made otherwise.

Giving Free value attracts attention, but always remember that attention
alone doesn't pay the bills. The siren song of "going viral" encourages many
business owners to continually give away too much in an effort to chase
attention over establishing and improving the profit-generating parts of

their business. Attention is necessary to attract paying customers, but if that attention never leads to sales, it won't sustain your business.

For best results, focus on giving away real Free value that is likely to attract real paying customers.

SHARE THIS CONCEPT: http://book.personalmba.com/free/

Permission

Selling to people who actually want to hear from you is more effective than interrupting strangers who don't.

—SETH GODIN

I just did the unthinkable: I actually opened the spam folder in my e-mail account. The folder contained 1,555 unread messages, most of which were some variant of:

"Hot Russian babes want to chat with YOU!"

"Buy Viagra Online!"

"Eliminate hair loss instantly!"

I didn't ask for any of these e-mails—the spammers just sent them, without considering whether or not I wanted them. I have absolutely no interest in chatting with "hot Russian babes," I have no use for black-market Viagra, and I actually *like* being bald.

How likely am I to read these messages, let alone respond to them? Not likely at all—on the contrary, I'll go out of my way to *avoid* paying **Attention** to them, and it'll be a cold day in hell before I purchase what they're pushing.

Unfortunately, many businesspeople assume that the spam approach is the best way to get Attention. Unsolicited phone calls, press releases, mass-market advertising, and "resident"-addressed direct mail are the most common legal equivalents of spam: blanketing a huge, undifferentiated group of people with a standard message in the hopes that a tiny fraction will respond.

In the early days of television and radio advertising, commercial interruptions actually worked. When there were only three channels, people were more likely to actually pay Attention during the commercials. By purchasing a single thirty-second prime-time advertising slot on each of the three major networks, you could reach 90 percent of the television-watching population in a single day.

Now, people have the ability to filter out anything they don't want to pay Attention to, either by ignoring the offending message or by shifting their Attention to something else. The moment you start talking about something your prospects don't care about, they're gone.

Asking for **Permission** to follow up after providing **Free** value is more effective than interruption. Offering genuine value earns your prospect's Attention, and asking for Permission gives you the opportunity to focus on communicating with people you *know* are interested in what you have to offer.

Permission is a real asset. Reaching new people tends to be difficult and expensive. It's far easier to follow up with someone you already know—all it takes is an e-mail, a letter, or a phone call, all of which are easy and inexpensive. If you ask the new prospects you meet for Permission to follow up, you're making the most of your outreach activities.

The best way to get Permission is to ask for it. Whenever you provide value to people, ask them if it's okay to continue to give them more value in the future. Over time, your list of prospective customers will grow, and the larger it grows, the higher the likelihood you'll start landing more sales.

Use Permission once you have it, but don't abuse the privilege. Getting Permission to follow up never gives you carte blanche to send them anything you like. Before asking your prospects for Permission to follow up, make it clear what they'll be getting and how it'll benefit them.

If you honor your commitments by continually providing value and refraining from spamming your prospects with irrelevant information, you'll have a powerful asset that can help you build a deeper relationship with the people who are interested in what you're offering.

SHARE THIS CONCEPT: **http://book.personalmba.com/permission/**

Hook

If you can do it, it ain't braggin'.

—DIZZY DEAN, HALL OF FAME BASEBALL PLAYER

Complicated messages are ignored or forgotten. Your **Probable Purchasers** are busy—they don't have time to pay **Attention** to all of the information assaulting them every day. If you want people to remember who you are and what you're offering, you have to grab their Attention and hold it—all in a matter of seconds.

A **Hook** is a single phrase or sentence that describes an offer's primary benefit. Sometimes the Hook is a title, and sometimes it's a short tagline. Regardless, it conveys the reason someone would want what you're selling.

A classic example of a Hook in the publishing world is the title of Timothy Ferriss's book, *The 4-Hour Workweek*. This short title implies several intriguing benefits: (1) four hours is a lot less than most people work, and most people would like to work less; (2) you can potentially earn as much in four hours a week as in forty-plus hours a week; (3) if you're not working so much, you could do other cool things with your time. That's not bad at all for four short words. When paired with the book's cover image of a guy relaxing in a hammock on a tropical beach, the title goes a long way in convincing people to purchase and read the book.

Apple used a Hook for the launch of the iPod: "1,000 songs in your pocket." At the time, portable music players consisted of bulky CD and cassette players, and advertising for early MP3 players focused on geek-speak: megabytes of disk space. Apple's Hook highlighted the primary benefit: instead of carrying around hundreds of tapes or CDs, you could carry your entire music collection in one elegant device.

Apple's five-word tagline worked wonders. In a little under a year, 236,000 first-generation iPods were sold—an astounding start, considering this was the company's first foray into the portable music category. The Hook grabbed Attention, and the quality of the product closed the sale.

When creating a Hook, focus on the primary benefit or value your offer provides. Emphasize what's uniquely valuable about your offer and why the prospect should care. Brainstorm a list of words and phrases related to your primary benefit, then experiment with different ways to connect them in a short phrase. Crafting a Hook is a creative exercise—the more potential options you generate, the more quickly you'll find one that works.

Once you've created your Hook, use it! Place it on your Web site, your advertising, your business cards—make it one of the first things potential customers see. The Hook grabs Attention, and the remainder of your marketing and sales activities close the deal.

The better your Hook, the more Attention you'll grab, and the easier it'll be for your satisfied customers to tell their friends about you.

SHARE THIS CONCEPT: http://book.personalmba.com/hook/

Call-To-Action (CTA)

Don't make me think.

—STEVE KRUG, USABILITY EXPERT

Attracting a prospect's **Attention** doesn't help if they disappear: if you want to make a sale, you need to direct your prospects to take some kind of action.

Your prospects can't read your mind. If you want your prospects to take the next step you're encouraging, you need to tell them exactly what to do. The most effective marketing messages give the recipient or prospect a single, very clear, very short action to take next.

Think about a roadside billboard that says something like "Tony's Hamburgers are the best." What will people who see that message do? Nothing, probably. In all likelihood, the billboard is a waste of time and money.

Give them a **Call-To-Action** such as "Take exit 25 and turn right for the best burgers in town," and soon Tony will be serving more hamburgers to hungry travelers.

A Call-To-Action directs your prospects to take a single, simple, obvious action. Visit a Web site. Enter an e-mail address. Call a phone number. Mail a self-addressed stamped envelope. Click a button. Purchase a product. Tell a friend.

The key to presenting an effective Call-To-Action is to be as clear, simple, and obvious as you possibly can. The more clearly you present your proposal, the higher the probability your prospect will actually do what you suggest.

If you're encouraging someone to enter their e-mail address to sign up for a newsletter, say that verbatim multiple times, and make it immediately clear WHERE the e-mail address field is, WHY they should fill it out, WHAT to click once they've entered their e-mail, and WHAT they can expect to happen when they do. If you think you're being too obvious, you're doing it right.

The best Calls-To-Action ask directly either for the sale or for **Permission** to follow up. Making direct sales is optimal, since it makes it easy to figure out whether or not your marketing activities are cost-effective. Asking for Permission is the next best thing, since it allows you to follow up with your prospects over time, dramatically decreasing your marketing costs and increasing the probability of an eventual sale.

Ensure that every message you create has a clear Call-To-Action, and you'll dramatically increase the effectiveness of your marketing activities.

SHARE THIS CONCEPT: http://book.personalmba.com/call-to-action/

Narrative

A tale in everything.
—WILLIAM WORDSWORTH, POET

Since the dawn of history, people have been telling stories. Telling stories is a universal human experience, and stories have always been used in the conduct of trade. A good story will make even the best offer even better.

Most compelling **Narratives** around the world follow a common format. The world-renowned mythologist Joseph Campbell called this prototypical storyline "The Hero's Journey" or the "monomyth." People all over the world respond very strongly to this story motif, and you can use this basic format to craft and tell your own stories.

The Hero's Journey begins by introducing the Hero: a normal person who is experiencing the trials and tribulations of everyday life. The Hero then receives a "call to adventure": a challenge, quest, or responsibility that requires them to rise above their normal existence and hone their skills and abilities in order to prevail.

When the Hero accepts the call, they depart their normal experience and enter into a world of uncertainty and adventure. A series of remarkable experiences initiates them into the new world, and the Hero undergoes many trials and learns many secrets in the pursuit of ultimate success.

After persevering in the face of adversity and vanquishing the foe, the Hero receives a mighty gift or power, then returns to the normal world to share this knowledge, wisdom, or treasure with the people. In return, the Hero receives the respect and admiration of all.

Your customers want to be Heroes. They want to be respected and admired by all, to be powerful, successful, and determined in the face of adversity. They want to be inspired by the trials and tribulations of other people who have come before and vanquished the foe. Telling a story about people who have already walked the path your prospects are considering is a powerful way to make them interested in proceeding.

Testimonials, case studies, and other stories are extremely effective in encouraging your prospects to accept your "call to adventure." By telling stories about the customers who have come before, you grab your prospect's *Attention* and show them a path to achieve what they want. The more vivid, clear, and emotionally compelling the story, the more prospects you'll attract.

Tell your prospective customers the stories they're interested in hearing, and you'll inevitably grab their Attention.

SHARE THIS CONCEPT: http://book.personalmba.com/narratives/

Controversy

If you want an audience, start a fight.

—IRISH PROVERB

Controversy means publicly taking a position that not everyone will agree with, approve of, or support. Used constructively, Controversy can be an effective way to attract *Attention*: people start talking, engaging, and paying Attention to your position, which is a very good thing.

The Personal MBA itself is a good example of the power of positive Controversy. The Personal MBA is about fundamental business principles—what you need to understand about business in order to succeed. I firmly believe that anyone can learn whatever they need to know about business independently, without mortgaging their future earnings by enrolling in a traditional MBA program.

Some people vehemently disagree with that position—particularly graduates of Ivy League business school programs. MBA graduates and candidates are often quite vocal in their disagreement, which usually takes the form of denouncing the Personal MBA approach to business education on their own Web sites or publicly disagreeing with me by leaving comments on my Web site.

That's not a bad thing: this consistent level of mild Controversy has allowed the Personal MBA to grow year after year without paid advertising. By making their thoughts known, the Personal MBA's detractors are spreading the word to people who may not have been aware that there are alternatives to traditional business school programs.

The Controversy leads many new people to investigate and examine the Personal MBA and make up their own minds about its usefulness. More than a few of them stick around, read my *Free* content, then decide to purchase a book, take a course, or hire me as a consultant. As long as my detractors keep things civil, I welcome the disagreement.

It's okay to have an opinion and take a strong stand. Everyone has a natural tendency to want other people to like them, and disagreement is often uncomfortable. In an effort to be unobjectionable, it's easy to water down your opinions to the point where they offend no one. If your position is agreeable to everyone, it becomes so boring that no one will pay Attention to you.

It's okay to support a position that not everyone else supports. It's okay to disagree with someone, or to call someone out, or to position yourself against something, because Controversy provokes a discussion. Discussion is Attention, which is a very good thing if you want to attract people who will benefit from what you're doing.

That's not to say all Controversy is good Controversy: there's a fine line between being constructively controversial and creating a soap opera. Controversy with a purpose is valuable; Controversy for the sake of Controversy, or Controversy that belittles and demeans, is not. Controversy won't help you if you lose sight of the purpose behind your actions.

As long as you're able to maintain a sense of the bigger picture of how you're trying to help, creating a bit of Controversy can be a very effective tool in encouraging people to seek out more information about what you're doing.

SHARE THIS CONCEPT: http://book.personalmba.com/controversy/

Reputation

Like it or not, the market's perception becomes your reality.
—HOWARD MANN, ACTOR AND COMEDIAN

In my opinion, "branding" is one of the most overused and overhyped ideas in the modern business world. There's nothing magical or complex about building a brand: when business professionals say they want to "enhance their brand" or "build brand equity," they almost always mean "improve their reputation."

Reputation is what people generally think about a particular offer or company. Reputations naturally arise whenever people talk to one another. Some products and services are worth the price; others are not. Some experiences are worth having; others are not. Some people are good to work with; others are not. No one wants to waste their time or money, so people pay very close attention to what others say about things they're interested in.

Building a strong Reputation is hugely valuable: people are often willing to pay a premium for a good Reputation. One of the reasons well-known consumer brands like Tide and Crest can continue to charge premium prices in near-commodity categories is the strength of their Reputation. Potential customers want to feel certain that the purchase they're considering will benefit them, that others will think highly of their decision, and that they won't be wasting their money. As the venerable corporate saying goes, "no one ever got fired for buying IBM."

It's important to note that your Reputation is not directly under your control—it's the sum total of what others think about everything you do: the products you release, the advertising you promote, the customer service you provide. No matter how hard you try, you can't directly "manage" your Reputation—you can only try to improve it over time by making people glad they chose to do business with you.

Always remember that the marketplace is the final arbiter of your Reputation, and that it's always watching what you do. When you build a great Reputation, your customers will continue to do business with you and will refer you to others because they think highly of you (and because referring friends to good products and services is a way to build their own Reputations). Building your Reputation takes time and effort, but it's the most effective kind of marketing there is.

SHARE THIS CONCEPT: http://book.personalmba.com/reputation/

3

SALES

People don't like to be sold, but they love to buy.
—JEFFREY GITOMER, AUTHOR OF *THE SALES BIBLE*
AND *THE LITTLE RED BOOK OF SELLING*

Every successful business ultimately sells what it has to offer. Having millions of prospects isn't enough if no one ultimately pulls out their wallet and says, "I'll take one." The sales process begins with a prospect and ends with a paying customer. No sale, no business.

The best businesses in the world earn the trust of their prospects and help them understand why the offer is worth paying for. No one wants to make a bad decision or be taken advantage of, so sales mostly consists of helping the prospect understand what's important and convincing them you're capable of actually delivering on what you promise.

The end of the sales process is an excited new customer and more cash in the bank.

SHARE THIS CONCEPT: **http://book.personalmba.com/sales/**

Transaction

There is only one boss: the customer. And he can fire everybody in
the company from the chairman on down, simply by spending his
money somewhere else.

—SAM WALTON, FOUNDER OF WALMART

A **Transaction** is an exchange of value between two or more parties. If I have
something you want and you have something I want, we'd both be better
off if we agreed to trade.

The Transaction is the defining moment of every business. Sales are the
only point in the business cycle where resources flow into the business,
which makes completing Transactions critically important. Businesses survive by bringing in more money than they spend, and there's no way to do
that without completing Transactions.

You can only transact with things that are **Economically Valuable**. If you
don't have anything your prospective customers want, they won't buy from
you. This may seem obvious, but it's amazing how many prospective businesspeople enter the market without something the market wants. That's
why developing and testing a **Minimum Viable Offer** is so important: it's the
best way to determine whether or not you've created something valuable
enough to sell before you invest your life savings.

When you're starting a new business, the object is to get to the point
where you make your first profitable Transaction as quickly as you possibly
can, because that's the point where you transition from being a project to
being a business. The examples/concepts in this chapter will help you create
profitable Transactions that both parties are happy with.

SHARE THIS CONCEPT: http://book.personalmba.com/transaction/

Trust

> The secret of life is honesty and fair dealing. If you can fake that,
> you've got it made.
>
> —GROUCHO MARX

Here's a proposal: send me a certified bank check for $100,000 right now, and in ten years I'll give you the keys to a brand-new, ten-thousand-square-foot villa on Italy's Amalfi Coast. You can't see any example villas, you won't hear from me again until the villa is ready, and there are absolutely no refunds. Deal?

Unless you're an *extremely* trusting soul with cash to burn, probably not. After all, how can you be sure I can actually build you a seaside mansion for such a paltry sum? How can you be sure I won't just take the money and disappear?

You can't, which is why you shouldn't cut me (or anyone else) a check for a villa on the Mediterranean you've never seen.

Let's reverse the situation: let's assume I'm capable of building this villa, and you're interested in purchasing one. Would it be smart for me to purchase land, break ground, and start building before I'm sure you actually have the money to pay for it? Probably not—if the deal falls through, I'd have to find another customer or eat the cost.

Without a certain amount of **Trust** between parties, a **Transaction** will not take place. No matter what promises are made or how good the deal sounds, no customer is going to be willing to part with their hard-earned money unless they believe you're capable of delivering what you promise. Likewise, it's usually not smart to accept credit or IOUs from customers you don't know.

Building a trustworthy **Reputation** over time by dealing fairly and honestly is the best way to build Trust. You can also take steps to signal you're trustworthy: organizations like the Better Business Bureau, credit and background check services, and financial arrangements like escrow accounts exist to help overcome an initial lack of Trust between parties in a Transaction. These offerings break down an important mutual barrier to completing a sale: without these services, many Transactions would never take place.

The easier it is to demonstrate your trustworthiness and verify that the other party is trustworthy, the greater the chance of a successful Transaction.

SHARE THIS CONCEPT: http://book.personalmba.com/trust/

Common Ground

> A compromise is the art of dividing a cake in such a way that everyone believes he has the biggest piece.
>
> —LUDWIG ERHARD, POLITICIAN AND FORMER CHANCELLOR OF
> WEST GERMANY

Common Ground is a state of overlapping interests between two or more parties. Think of your available options as a circle that surrounds you. Your prospects have a circle of available options as well. Your job is to find exactly where those circles overlap, which is much easier if you understand what your **Probable Purchasers** want or need.

Consider the job you're currently in, or the last one you held. Chances are, you accepted that job because you were willing to take on certain responsibilities, and your employer was interested in having you do the work. You were interested in being paid a certain amount, and your employer was willing to pay you at least that much. Your interests overlapped, which resulted in a job offer and a paid position at the company. That's Common Ground.

The same thing happens every time you purchase something from a retailer. They have a product you want to own; you have a certain amount of money they are willing to accept for the product. If you don't want the product or the retailer wants more than you're willing to pay, no **Transaction** will take place.

Common Ground is a precondition of any type of Transaction. Without any areas of overlapping interest, there's no reason for a prospect to choose to work with you. After all, it wouldn't make sense to pay more for something than it's worth to you. Why expect your prospects to accept your offer if it's not in their best interest?

Aligning interests is critical to finding Common Ground. Sales isn't about convincing somebody to do something that's not in their best interest.

Ideally, you should want exactly what your prospects want: the satisfaction of their desire or the resolution of their problem. The more your interests are aligned with your prospect's, the more they'll *Trust* your ability to give them what they want.

There are always many paths to a successful Transaction, which is the essence of negotiation. Negotiation is the process of exploring different options to find Common Ground: the more potential paths you explore, the greater the chance you'll be able to find one in which your interests overlap. The more open you are to potential options, the higher the likelihood you'll find an area of Common Ground that's acceptable for all parties involved.

SHARE THIS CONCEPT: http://book.personalmba.com/common-ground/

Pricing Uncertainty Principle

> Everything you want in life has a price connected to it. There's a price to pay if you want to make things better, a price to pay just for leaving things as they are, a price for everything.
>
> —HARRY BROWNE, AUTHOR OF *FAIL-SAFE INVESTING*

One of the most fascinating parts of *Sales* is what I call the *Pricing Uncertainty Principle*: all prices are arbitrary and malleable. Pricing is always an executive decision. If you want to try to sell a small rock for $350 million, you can. If you want to quadruple that price or reduce it to $0.10 an hour later, there's absolutely nothing stopping you. *Any* price can be set to *any* level at *any* time, without limitation.

The Pricing Uncertainty Principle has an important corollary: you must be able to *support* your asking price before a customer will actually accept it. In general, people prefer to pay as little as possible to acquire the things they want (with some notable exceptions, which we'll discuss later in *Social Signaling*). If you expect people to pay you perfectly good money to buy what you're offering, you must be able to provide a *Reason Why* the offered price is worth paying.

It's difficult to support a price of $350 million for a rock—unless that rock is the Hope Diamond, a 45.5-carat deep-blue diamond with a long and distinguished history.

The Hope Diamond is currently owned by the Smithsonian National Museum of Natural History and is not for sale. If the Smithsonian decided to sell the Hope Diamond, however, they could easily set an asking price of $1 billion. What's to stop them?

Auctions are an example of the Pricing Uncertainty Principle at work—prices change constantly, rising in proportion to how many people are interested and how much they're each willing to spend.

By setting a low starting price and allowing potential buyers to bid against one another, auctions are typically an efficient way to establish a true market price for something that is difficult to reproduce and where no comparable items are already in the market. That's why rare items like the Hope Diamond—if they're sold—are typically sold at auction. The most expensive diamond ever sold was the rough 507.5-carat Cullinan Heritage diamond, which went for $35.3 million at auction.[1] Not bad for a rock.

SHARE THIS CONCEPT: http://book.personalmba.com/pricing-uncertainty-principle/

Four Pricing Methods

Money is better than poverty, if only for financial reasons.

—WOODY ALLEN, COMEDIAN, SCREENWRITER, AND DIRECTOR

Let's assume for a moment you own a house you're willing to sell. The *Pricing Uncertainty Principle* says the price could be anything—you have to set it yourself, since houses don't come with built-in price tags. Let's also assume you'd prefer to sell the house for as much as possible. How would you go about setting the largest price a customer will actually accept?

There are four ways to support a price on something of value: (1) replacement cost, (2) market comparison, (3) discounted cash flow/net present value, and (4) value comparison. These *Four Pricing Methods* will help you estimate just how much something is potentially worth to your customers.

The *Replacement Cost* method supports a price by answering the question "How much would it cost to replace?" In the case of the house, the question becomes "What would it cost to create or construct a house just like this one?"

Assume a meteorite scored a direct hit on the house, and there's nothing left—you have to rebuild the house from scratch. What would it take to purchase similar land, pay for an architect to draw up plans, acquire identical materials, and hire construction workers to create exactly the same house? Total up these costs, add a bit of margin to compensate for your time and effort, and you'll have a supportable estimate of how much your house is worth.

Applied to most offers, Replacement Cost is typically a "cost-plus" calculation: figure out how much it costs to create, add your desired markup, and set your price appropriately.

The **Market Comparison** method supports a price by answering the question "How much are other things like this selling for?" In the case of the house, this question becomes "How much have houses like this, in this general area, sold for recently?"

If you look at the surrounding area, there are probably a few other houses similar to the one you own that have been sold within the past year. They're probably not exactly the same (maybe they have an extra bedroom or bathroom, a little less square footage, etc.) but they're close enough. After you adjust for the differences, you can use the sale prices of those "comparable" houses to create a supportable estimate of how much your house is worth.

Market Comparison is a very common way to price offers: find a similar offer and set your price relatively close to what they're asking.

The **Discounted Cash Flow (DCF) / Net Present Value (NPV)** method supports a price by answering the question "How much is it worth if it can bring in money over time?" In the case of your house, the question becomes "How much would this house bring in each month if you rented it for a period of time, and how much is that series of cash flows worth as a lump sum today?"

Rent payments come in every month, which is quite handy: you can use the DCF/NPV formulas[2] to calculate what that series of payments over a certain period of time would be worth if you received it in one lump sum. By calculating the NPV of the house assuming you could rent it for $2,000 a month for a period of ten years with 95 percent occupancy and you could earn 7 percent interest on your money by choosing the **Next Best Alternative,** you'll have a supportable estimate of what the house is worth.

DCF/NPV is only used for pricing things that can produce an ongoing cash flow, which makes it a very common way to price businesses when they're sold or acquired—the more profit the business generates each month, the more valuable the business is to the purchaser.

The **Value Comparison** method supports a price by answering the question "Who is this particularly valuable to?" In the case of the house, this question becomes "What features of this house would make it valuable to certain types of people?"

Let's assume the house is in an attractive, safe neighborhood with a top-tier public school nearby. These characteristics would make the house more valuable to families who have school-age kids, particularly if they want to attend that school. To potential home buyers in the market, this particular house would be more valuable than the same house in an area with inferior schools.

Here's another example: assume Elvis Presley previously owned the house. To certain types of people—wealthy people who love Elvis—this house would be *extremely* valuable. Elvis's previous involvement with the property could easily triple or quadruple the price you'd be able to support via the replacement, market comparison, or DCF/NPV methods. By looking at the unique characteristics of what you're offering and the corresponding worth of those characteristics to certain individuals, you can often support much higher prices.

Value Comparison is typically the optimal way to price your offer, since the value of an offer to a specific group can be quite high, resulting in a much better price. Use the other methods as a baseline, but focus on discovering how much your offer is worth to the party you hope to sell it to, then set your price appropriately.

SHARE THIS CONCEPT: http://book.personalmba.com/4-pricing-methods/

Price Transition Shock

If you want to grow old as a pilot, you've got to know when to push it, and when to back off.

—CHUCK YEAGER, FIRST PILOT TO BREAK THE SOUND BARRIER

When you change the price of an offer, the effects aren't limited to your current target market. A change in prices can change your typical prospect overnight.

Most people who are new to business assume that the best way to increase sales is to reduce prices. That's not necessarily true. Often, raising your prices is an effective way to attract *more* customers.

Discounts attract customers when the offer is a commodity. If there's no difference between the gasoline at one gas station and another, the station that reduces its gas prices may bring in more customers. Since most service stations make more money from their convenience stores than they make selling gasoline, a gas discounting strategy may lead to higher profits.

In introductory economics courses, this idea is called "price elasticity." Offers with high price elasticity experience major changes in demand when prices go up or down. Offers with low price elasticity experience little fluctuation in demand when prices change. Economists love to draw downward-sloping pricing curves that show demand increasing as prices decrease.

The trouble with the traditional pricing curve is that it can be misleading when the offer isn't a commodity. In practice, raising your prices can *increase* demand by appealing to a more attractive type of customer.

Automobiles are a classic example of this type of price sensitivity: some cars are desirable *because they're expensive.* The typical customer who purchases a Bentley Continental GT is very different from the type of customer who purchases a Toyota Camry.

As you test different pricing strategies, you'll notice certain thresholds where you *stop* appealing to certain types of customers and *start* appealing to customers with very different characteristics. This **Price Transition Shock** can completely change the experience of operating your business, and you shouldn't take it lightly.

There are two major considerations when setting your prices with Price Transition Shock in mind: (1) potential profitability and (2) ideal customer characteristics. The best strategy is to set your prices to appeal to the prospects that will ensure you work with your most desirable customers in a way that results in the highest profits.

The ideal balance depends on your target market. In some markets, it's easy to serve customers who are attracted to low prices; in others, discount customers can be challenging and rude. Likewise, prospects that don't blink at high prices can be pleasant and cordial or demanding and snooty. The experience depends on the industry and the prospects' expectations.

One of the businesses I've been involved with over the years succeeded in doubling its average order value by eliminating low-priced offers. As a result, profits increased. As a *Second-Order Effect* (discussed later), the company's typical customer changed for the worse: prospects made unreasonable demands more often and acted in disrespectful ways when those demands weren't met. The short-term financial result was positive, but the change placed extraordinary stress on the staff.

On the other hand, a service business I advise decided to quadruple its typical service price and found that its new positioning appealed to its ideal customers: people who valued the firm's work and took the project seriously. Nonideal customers were turned off by the hike in prices, so they went away. As a result, the company filled its client roster with excellent customers and increased profits by more than 500 percent. The staff is thrilled with the change: they're doing more work for better clients and getting paid more for their expertise.

As you change your prices, the prospects attracted to your offer will also change. So long as you maintain *Sufficiency* (discussed later), you can choose to appeal to any type of customer you please.

SHARE THIS CONCEPT: http://book.personalmba.com/price-transition-shock/

Value-Based Selling

Price is what you pay. Value is what you get.

—WARREN BUFFETT

Imagine that you provide an ongoing service to a *Fortune* 500 corporation that increases their annual revenues by $100 million. Is your service worth $10 million a year? Sure—after all, what company would give up $90 million in ongoing revenue?

Does it matter if providing this valuable service doesn't cost you much money? Absolutely not—even if it only costs you a hundred dollars a year to provide the service, you're providing a huge amount of value, which supports the comparatively high price.

Does it matter if most business-to-business services cost $10,000 or less? Absolutely not—you're providing much more value than other services in the market, which completely justifies a higher price.

Value-Based Selling is the process of understanding and reinforcing the **Reasons Why** your offer is valuable to the purchaser. In the previous section, we discussed how the **Value Comparison** method is often the best way to support a high price on your offer. Value-Based Selling is *how* you support that price. By understanding and reinforcing the Reason Why a **Transaction** will be valuable to the customer, you simultaneously increase the likelihood of a Transaction as well as the price the buyer will be willing to pay.

Value-Based Selling is not about talking—it's about listening. When most people think of sales, they imagine a pushy, smooth-talking shyster whose sole priority is to "close the deal." Emulating shady used car dealers is the fastest way to destroy **Trust** and give your potential customers the impression that you care more about your bottom line than about what they want. In reality, the best salespeople are the ones who can listen intently for the things the customer really wants.

Asking good questions is the best way to identify what your offer is worth to your prospect. In the classic sales book *SPIN Selling*, Neil Rackham describes the four phases of successful selling: (1) understanding the situation, (2) defining the problem, (3) clarifying the short-term and long-term implications of that problem, and (4) quantifying the need-payoff, or the financial and emotional benefits the customer would experience after the resolution of their problem. Instead of barging in with a premature, boilerplate hard sell, successful salespeople focus on asking detailed questions to get to the root of what the prospect really wants.

By encouraging your prospects to tell you more about what they need, you reap two major benefits. First, you increase the prospect's confidence in your understanding of the situation, increasing their confidence in your ability to deliver a solution. Second, you'll discover information that will help you emphasize just how valuable your offer is, which helps you in *Framing* the price of your offer versus the value it will provide.

If you discover why, how, and how much your offer will benefit the customer, you'll be able to explain that value in terms they'll understand and appreciate. Understanding the value you can provide your customers is the golden path to a profitable sale.

SHARE THIS CONCEPT: http://book.personalmba.com/value-based-selling/

Education-Based Selling

> Upgrade your user, not your product. "Value" is less about the stuff and more about the stuff the stuff enables. Don't build better cameras—build better photographers.
>
> —KATHY SIERRA, AUTHOR AND COCREATOR OF THE *HEAD FIRST* SERIES OF BOOKS

Before moving to Colorado, my wife, Kelsey, was the sales manager of the Mark Ingram Bridal Atelier in New York City, the most prestigious bridal salon in the world. Her job was to help brides from around the world find "The One"—the perfect dress for their dream wedding.

Mark Ingram is the Martha Stewart of the bridal industry—his sense of style is legendary. Gowns by Oscar de la Renta, Monique Lhuillier, Lela Rose, and Vera Wang populate his collection. Mark's consultants are so skilled that one of the first three gowns they present is almost always the gown the bride chooses for her wedding. In addition, the shopping experience and customer service are superb—Mark doesn't discount, but brides would rather work with him than purchase their gown from a competitor, even though it'd be less expensive.

Compared with most bridal salons, the Mark Ingram Bridal Atelier sells very high-end gowns. The average sale price of a gown at Mark's atelier is $6,000—four times the national average. To make the sale, Mark's consultants must help the bride (and her parents, who often pay the bill) understand why the gown is worth the price.

It's certainly possible to purchase a less expensive gown from another salon, but cheaper gowns cut corners: they use lower-quality fabrics, skimp on construction, and use machined lace or beading. Also, alterations are necessary to ensure that the gown fits the bride perfectly. Mark's team of bridal seamstresses is the best in the world, and you can only work with them if you purchase a gown from Mark's atelier.

If you care about these things—and most fashion-conscious brides certainly do—it's easy to see why it's worth it to purchase a gown from Mark if you can afford to.

Education-Based Selling is the process of making your prospects better, more informed customers. As a sales consultant, Kelsey worked to do two things: (1) make the bride feel comfortable and relaxed, then (2) help the bride become more knowledgeable about gowns in terms of how they are made and what to look for when buying one.

Instead of pressuring the bride to "close the sale," Kelsey always took the time to explain the ins and outs of fabric, lace, beading, construction, and alterations to the bride and her family. She invested time in making her brides more knowledgeable, and this made them more likely to purchase an expensive dress from her, both because they had learned to fully appreciate the quality of what she was selling and because she had earned their *Trust*.

Education-Based Selling requires an up-front investment in your prospects, but it's worth it. By investing energy in making your prospects smarter, you simultaneously build Trust in your expertise and make them better customers. Be forewarned, however, that effective education requires your offer to be superior in some way to your competitors'—otherwise, you'll be sending customers away. All the more reason to ensure that you have an offer worth selling.

SHARE THIS CONCEPT: http://book.personalmba.com/education-based-selling/

Next Best Alternative

When others sense your willingness to walk away, your hand is
strengthened . . . Sometimes you are better off not getting to yes.

—ROBERT RUBIN, FORMER U.S. SECRETARY OF THE TREASURY

When negotiating, it's always useful to know what the other party is likely
to do in the event that an agreement can't be reached. Sometimes, it's just
not possible to reach an agreement—there's no **Common Ground**, so both parties agree to go their separate ways. What then?

Your **Next Best Alternative** is what you'll do in the event you can't find
Common Ground with the party you're negotiating with. Imagine you're
looking for a job, and there are three companies interested in hiring you.
You may prefer to work at Company A, but if you can't reach a mutually
acceptable agreement, it's easier to be a confident negotiator if you know
that Companies B and C are also interested in hiring you. If Company A
is your only option and they know it, you're not likely to get a good deal.

The other party always has a **Next Best Alternative** as well—that's what
you're negotiating against. If you're selling a product that costs $100, you
are selling against the next best thing that they could do with that $100:
saving, investing, or purchasing something else. If you're trying to hire an
employee, you're competing against the next best offer they have from another company. The more options the other party has, the weaker your
negotiating position.

Understanding the other party's Next Best Alternative gives you a major
sales advantage: you can structure your agreement so it's more attractive
than their next best option. The more you know about the other party's
alternatives, the more attractively you can **Frame** your total offer by **Bundling/
Unbundling** various options.

Having a strong Next Best Alternative keeps negotiations moving quickly.
Many professional sports players who are approaching free agency use the
opportunity to renegotiate or renew their contracts with their current teams,
particularly if other teams express interest in them. If the original team
doesn't want to lose the player, they have an incentive to reach an acceptable
deal quickly.

In every negotiation, the power lies with the party that is *able and will-*

ing to walk away from a bad deal. In almost every case, the more acceptable alternatives you have, the better your position. The more attractive your alternatives, the more willing you'll be to walk away from a deal that doesn't serve you, resulting in better deals.

SHARE THIS CONCEPT: http://book.personalmba.com/next-best-alternative/

Exclusivity

The best strategy is always to be very strong.
—CARL VON CLAUSEWITZ, MILITARY STRATEGIST

In most sales situations, it's in your best interest to maintain *Exclusivity*: creating a unique offer or quality that other firms can't match. If you're the only person or company that offers what your prospect wants, you're in a very strong position to negotiate on favorable terms.

If you want to purchase an iPhone, you have to buy it through Apple: it is the sole source. You may purchase the product directly or through a retailer: either way, Apple is paid. So long as you want an iPhone and aren't willing to settle for an alternative, Apple wins.

Exclusivity is beneficial for many reasons. Exclusive offers make it much easier to maintain high *Perceived Value*, since there's no direct competition. Substitutes or alternatives may exist, but if a prospect is set on your specific offer, they'll have to obtain it through you, making it far easier for you to set high prices and maintain healthy *Profit Margins*.

Exclusivity is easiest to maintain when you've created something new, which means an exclusivity strategy makes the most sense for *Products* and *Services*. Resellers typically find it difficult to establish exclusivity unless they play a role in the product's manufacture, which is why retailers often create "private label" brands. Costco's famous Kirkland Signature brand is a way of creating exclusivity, as is Trader Joe's strategy of negotiating with manufacturers to create unique products.

If you're the exclusive source for what your prospects want, you win.

SHARE THIS CONCEPT: http://book.personalmba.com/exclusivity/

Three Universal Currencies

Time will take your money, but money won't buy time.

—JAMES TAYLOR, MUSICIAN

In every negotiation, there are *Three Universal Currencies*: resources, time, and flexibility. Any one of these currencies can be traded for more or less of the others.

Resources are tangible items like money, gold, oil, etc. Resources are physical: you can hold them in your hand. If you want to buy some furniture, you can offer money in exchange. If you're selling your car, the purchaser could (with your agreement) give you a bar of gold or a mint first-edition issue of *Action Comics #1*, which features the first appearance of Superman in print. You're simply trading one resource for another.

Time is the second major currency. If you go to work as an hourly employee, you are trading a certain amount of time and effort for a certain amount of resources. You can also trade resources for time: you can offer to pay other people in exchange for their work, which is the essence of employment, contracting, and freelancing.

Flexibility is the third universal currency—one that is usually quite underrated. Becoming a salaried employee isn't a straightforward exchange of resources for effort—you're also giving up a certain amount of flexibility. There's an implicit agreement that you won't work on other things when you're supposed to be working for the company, which is a very real *Opportunity Cost*. While you're working, you're giving up the flexibility to do something else.

It's entirely possible to negotiate for a greater or lesser degree of flexibility by trading off effort or resources. For example, you can decrease your effort and increase your flexibility by working part time, in exchange for fewer resources—reduced salary and benefits. Purchasing a house requires less time if you agree to a thirty-year mortgage versus saving up to buy it outright, at the cost of additional resources (interest) and dramatically decreased flexibility.

It's possible to gain more of any of these desired currencies by finding appropriate *Trade-offs* between one or more of the others. If you'd like additional compensation in the form of a raise or larger contract, you can give up time or flexibility (such as the ability to use what you make for other purposes) as a Trade-off. If you'd like a bit more flexibility or time off in your working arrangements, you can negotiate a decrease in salary to compensate. If your employer or client wants you to work more or wants to benefit more from your work, you can ask them for more compensation in return.

Keep the Three Universal Currencies in mind when negotiating, and you'll be amazed at the range of potential options you'll be able to present to the other party, making it easier to find an option that works for all parties involved.

SHARE THIS CONCEPT: **http://book.personalmba.com/3-universal-currencies/**

Three Dimensions of Negotiation

> The first thing to decide before you walk into any negotiation is what to do if the other fellow says no.
>
> —ERNEST BEVIN, FORMER BRITISH SECRETARY OF STATE FOR
> FOREIGN AFFAIRS

Most people think of negotiation as sitting down across from the other party and presenting offers and counteroffers. But that's the last phase of the process; the other two happen well before you ever sit down at the negotiating table.

The **Three Dimensions of Negotiation** are setup, structure, and discussion. As David Lax and James Sebenius discuss in *3-D Negotiation*, each of these phases is critically important: by creating an **Environment** (discussed later) that's conducive to a deal and preparing your strategy in advance, you can dramatically increase the probability of finding a mutually acceptable solution.

The first phase of every negotiation is the **Setup**: setting the stage for a satisfying outcome to the negotiation. The more you can stack the odds in your favor before you start negotiating, the better the deal you'll be able to strike:

▶ Who is involved in the negotiation, and are they open to dealing with you?

▶ Who are you negotiating with, and do they know who you are and how you can help them?

▶ What are you proposing, and how does it benefit the other party?

▶ What's the setting—will you present your offer in person, by phone, or by some other means?

▶ What are all of the Environmental factors around the deal—do recent events make this deal more or less important to the other party?

Setup is the negotiation equivalent of *Guiding Structure* (discussed later)— the Environment surrounding the deal plays a huge role in the eventual outcome, so it pays to ensure that the Environment is conducive to getting a good deal before you ever reach the table. By thinking about the Setup, you can make sure you're negotiating with the right person—the person who has the *Power* (discussed later) to give you what you want. Research is what gives this dimension of negotiation its power—the more knowledge you gain about your negotiating partner during this phase, the more power you have in the entire negotiation, so do your homework before presenting an offer.

The second dimension of negotiation is *Structure*: the terms of the proposal. In this phase, you put together your draft proposal in a way they're likely to appreciate and accept:

▶ What exactly will you propose, and how will you *Frame* your proposal to the other party?

▶ What are the primary benefits of your proposal to the other party?

▶ What is the other party's *Next Best Alternative*, and how is your proposal better?

▶ How will you overcome the other party's objections and *Barriers to Purchase*?

▶ Are there *Trade-offs* or concessions you're willing to make to reach an agreement?

Remember, your goal in creating the proposal is to find *Common Ground*: an agreement that both parties will be happy to accept. By thinking through the Structure of your proposal in advance, you can prepare a few different options that you believe the other party will want, on terms you're willing to accept.

If you're expecting the other party to balk at the price, for instance, you can prepare arguments to overcome the objection, lower-cost options that provide less value, or alternative offers that would better fit their needs. When the time comes for you to discuss the deal with your negotiating partner, you'll be ready for anything.

The third dimension of negotiation is the *Discussion*: actually presenting the offer to the other party. The Discussion is where you actually talk through your proposal with the other party. Sometimes the Discussion happens the way you see it in the movies: in a mahogany-walled board-room, across the table, toe to toe with the CEO. Sometimes it happens over the phone. Sometimes it happens over e-mail. Whatever the setting, this is the point where you present your offer, discuss or clarify any issues the other party doesn't understand, answer objections and remove Barriers to Purchase, and ask for the sale.

Regardless of what happens during the Discussion phase, the end result of every round of Discussion is either (1) "Yes, we have a deal on these terms," (2) "We don't have a deal quite yet—here's a counteroffer or another option to consider," or (3) "No, we don't have a deal—there's clearly no Common Ground, so we'll suspend negotiations and reserve the right to talk to somebody else." Discussion continues until a final agreement is reached or the parties decide to quit negotiating, whichever happens first.

If you prepare the Three Dimensions of Negotiation (Setup, Structure, and Discussion) in advance, you'll be far more likely to settle on terms that benefit both parties.

SHARE THIS CONCEPT: http://book.personalmba.com/3-dimensions-of-negotiation/

Buffer

Zeal without knowledge is the sister of folly.

—SIR JOHN DAVIES, ELIZABETHAN POET AND LAWYER AND FORMER
ATTORNEY GENERAL OF IRELAND

In all but the most extenuating circumstances, *Common Ground* ensures that every deal is in the best interest of all parties involved. However, there may be parts of the agreement or discussion where one party's gain is the other's loss. If you're interviewing for a job and you attempt to negotiate a higher salary, any increase in your salary is necessarily the employer's loss.

Depending on the situation, these aspects of the negotiation can be tense. You want to push for as much as you possibly can, but if you push too hard, you risk torpedoing the deal and permanently harming your relationship with the other party. In these cases, it's helpful to work with someone who can help you negotiate a good deal without risking the relationship.

A *Buffer* is a third party empowered to negotiate on your behalf. *Agents*, attorneys, mediators, brokers, accountants, and other similar subject-matter experts are all examples of Buffers. Buffers who have expertise in specific types of negotiations can be extremely valuable in helping you get the best deal possible. You don't have to know everything about arcane topics like tort law and tax policy if you enlist the help of an honest and capable Buffer.

When a professional athlete is negotiating a contract to join a professional sports team, he or she typically enlists the help of both an agent and an attorney. The agent's job is to obtain the best possible compensation for the athlete, and the team's manager and owner know this. They can remain positive about hiring the athlete even while the agent plays hardball. In the end, the athlete's overall compensation is improved despite the agent's fees.

The same thing happens with the athlete's attorney, who can argue for the inclusion or exclusion of certain provisions in the proposed contract. An attorney can make these proposals with much greater force and effect based on their knowledge, experience, and expertise. Together with the agent, the attorney can work with the team owner and manager to ensure that the athlete gets the best deal the team is willing to accept, without adversely affecting the athlete's *Reputation* or goodwill.

Buffers can also be useful in order to add some time or space to a high-intensity negotiation. It's often quite useful not to be the party who has the final say. Being able to say, "I need to discuss this with my agent/accountant/attorney" before giving final approval on a deal is a valuable check-step that prevents hasty or unwise decisions.

Be very mindful of *Incentive-Caused Bias* (discussed later) when working with a Buffer. Depending on the arrangement, your Buffer's priorities may be very different from your own. For example, real estate agents act as Buffers between the sellers of property and potential purchasers. If you're looking to buy property, it's often useful to work with a buy-side agent, provided you're aware of how they're compensated.

Agents are typically compensated on a commission basis, so it pays to be wary if you're using them on the buy side of a deal. The Agent is compensated if and only if a *Transaction* actually occurs. Accordingly, their first priority is to complete a deal—any deal—regardless of whether or not it's actually a good deal for the buyer.

If at all possible, work with a Buffer who is willing to accept a flat fee in exchange for services rendered, whether or not the deal happens. If your Buffer will be paid regardless of what happens, their interests will be more closely aligned with getting you the best deal possible, which enhances their Reputation.

Don't let your Buffer replace your own informed judgment. One of the worst things you can do is relinquish control over your decisions to your Buffer, particularly if your interests aren't exactly aligned. Many unwary investors have found their savings depleted by giving carte blanche control to "investment professionals" who are compensated every time a security is bought or sold. By "churning" the account, the broker is legally able to rack up thousands of dollars in unnecessary fees. As a rule of thumb: don't give *anyone* unfettered control over decisions that directly affect your money.

Buffers can be a hugely valuable resource as long as you're clear about how they'll be rewarded, what they're responsible for, and how you intend to work together.

SHARE THIS CONCEPT: http://book.personalmba.com/buffer/

Persuasion Resistance

Sales are contingent upon the attitude of the salesman, not the attitude of the prospect.

—W. CLEMENT STONE, INSURANCE SALESMAN,
PHILANTHROPIST, AND AUTHOR

One of the things that makes prospects uncomfortable around salespeople is the feeling that they're going to get the "hard sell" or be tricked into agreeing to something that's not in their best interest. This experience is called **Persuasion Resistance**, and it's a major barrier to making sales.

When a prospect senses that someone is trying to convince or compel them to do something they're not sure about, they automatically resist and attempt to move away from the conversation. This is particularly true in situations where the salesperson is trying to force a choice or limit the prospect's available options in some way.

Psychologists call this *reactance*, and it appears in early childhood. Every parent has experienced the fallout of telling a child they "can't" or "have to" do something. Prospects react in much the same way when a salesperson attempts to pressure a sale, resisting out of an instinct to preserve their autonomy. The harder the salesperson pushes, the more the prospect resists. That's why hard-sell approaches usually fail to generate sustainable results.

The more effective strategy, in the words of the renowned sales expert Zig Ziglar, is to present yourself to the prospect as an "assistant buyer." Your job is not to sell the prospect a bill of goods: it's to help them make an informed decision about what's best for them. You're not pressuring them to give you their money: you're helping to ensure they invest their resources wisely. This basic **Reinterpretation** (discussed later) of your role in the sales process works: it eliminates the prospect's feeling of pressure by convincing them you're looking out for their best interests.

Salespeople need to be aware of two additional signals that can trigger Persuasion Resistance: *desperation* and *chasing*. Sending either signal during any part of the sales process will reduce the number and size of the **Transactions** you close.

If a prospect feels that you're *desperate* to make a sale, it diminishes their interest in a matter of seconds. Desperation is a subtle signal that other people don't find your offer desirable, and **Social Proof** (discussed later) starts working against you. In the same way that people don't want to date a person who desperately wants to be in a relationship, prospects don't want to do business with a person who desperately wants or needs their money.

It's much better to present yourself with confidence, in a way that signals your offer is valuable, is a good fit for the prospect, and will be a wise investment of the prospect's money. If you don't genuinely believe that, you need to find something else to sell.

If a prospect senses you're *chasing* them, their first impulse will be to move away from you. "Chasing" and "being chased" are evolutionary patterns that our primal minds recognize very quickly. For centuries, human beings have chased things that are desirable, and they have been chased by threats. Even if we wouldn't consciously label a situation as "chasing" or "being chased," our minds notice and respond automatically.

Chasing a prospect to make a sale is counterproductive, a waste of time and energy. Instead, find ways to **Frame** the situation in a way that encourages the prospect to feel like *they're chasing you*. If your prospect feels like they need to justify why they're good enough to work with you, you're in a very strong position to make a sale on favorable terms.

We'll discuss additional ways our primal minds process our modern environment in **Caveman Syndrome**. For now, it's important to remember that these social signals may seem silly at best or manipulative at worst, but that doesn't make them any less real or important. By understanding how your prospects evaluate offers, you can plan your pitch in a way that minimizes Persuasion Resistance and encourages the prospect to **Desire** what you have to offer.

If you're interested in exploring these signals in more detail, I recommend reading *Pitch Anything* by Oren Klaff.

SHARE THIS CONCEPT: http://book.personalmba.com/persuasion-resistance/

Reciprocation

> Gifts are never free: they bind the giver and receiver in a loop of reciprocity.
>
> —MARCEL MAUSS, SOCIOLOGIST AND ANTHROPOLOGIST

Reciprocation is the strong desire most people feel to "pay back" favors, gifts, benefits, and resources provided. If you've ever had the experience of receiving a holiday gift from someone you didn't send anything to, you know how uncomfortable this feels. If someone benefits us, we like to benefit them in return.

As a social force, Reciprocation is one of the primary psychological tendencies that underlie human cooperation. The "you scratch my back, I'll scratch yours" instinct is extremely powerful and forms the foundation of friendships and alliances. Historically, gift giving was how the powerful remained in **Power** (discussed later): by throwing lavish parties or generously awarding titles and land, leaders increased their influence by amassing a store of favors that could be called in during times of need.

Here's the tricky part: the desire to Reciprocate is not necessarily in proportion to the original benefit provided. In *Influence: The Psychology of Persuasion*, Robert Cialdini provides an example of reciprocation in car sales. Car salesmen typically offer prospects a small gift up front. "Can I get you a coffee? Would you like a soda? Some water? Cookies? Is there anything that I can do to make you more comfortable?"

It seems like a common gesture of hospitality. It's not. Accepting this small offer creates a psychological need to Reciprocate, subtly stacking the deck in the salesman's favor. Prospective car buyers who accepted this free offer were far more likely to purchase a vehicle, add optional accessories, and agree to less attractive financing terms. As a result, these customers spent thousands of dollars more than the people who did not accept anything from the salesman while negotiating. That doesn't make rational sense, because the coffee or cookies cost the dealer very little, but Reciprocation makes it more likely that the buyer will "pay back" the favor with a much larger concession.

The more legitimate value you can provide to others up front, the more receptive they'll be when it's time for your pitch. Providing **Free** value builds your social capital, making it more likely the people you benefit will Reciprocate when you make an offer down the road.

Being generous is one of the best things you can do to improve your results as a salesperson. By giving away value and helping others as much as you can, they'll respect you; it will build your **Reputation**, but it will also increase the probability that they will be interested enough when you *do* present your **Call-To-Action**.

SHARE THIS CONCEPT: http://book.personalmba.com/reciprocation/

Damaging Admission

> We confess our little faults to persuade people that we have no large ones.
>
> —FRANÇOIS DE LA ROCHEFOUCAULD, SEVENTEENTH-CENTURY FRENCH
> COURTIER AND APHORIST

When Kelsey and I moved from New York City to the mountains of northern Colorado, our new landlords, Ben and Betty, made sure to notify us of two important facts about our new home:

(1) Rock slides were a very real possibility.

(2) Black bears and mountain lions roamed nearby.

These facts didn't prevent us from leasing the apartment, but we were glad to know them in advance, and it increased our estimation of their integrity. We weighed the risks, increased our renter's insurance, purchased a can of Counter Assault bear pepper spray, and signed the lease.

Counterintuitively, making a **Damaging Admission** like this to your prospects can actually *increase* their **Trust** in your ability to deliver what you promise.

Since Kelsey and I didn't own a car when we lived in Manhattan, we had to purchase one when we moved to Colorado. We found a car we were interested in purchasing on eBay Motors, but it was uncomfortable to make such a big purchase without actually seeing the vehicle.

To help alleviate our concerns, the dealership that listed the car, Masters Auto Collection in Denver, went out of their way to photograph every detail—including a small chip in the paint on the left side, which wasn't a big deal. Because they were willing to include even the small flaws in their description before we purchased, we felt more confident that they had thoroughly described the vehicle. We purchased it, and everything was exactly as described. Without making a Damaging Admission, Masters Auto Collection wouldn't have made the sale.

Your prospects know you're not perfect, so don't pretend to be. People actually get suspicious when something appears to be "too good to be true." If an offer appears abnormally good, your prospects will start asking themselves, "What's the catch?"

Instead of making them wonder, tell them yourself. By being up front with your prospects regarding drawbacks and *Trade-offs*, you'll enhance your trustworthiness and close more sales.

SHARE THIS CONCEPT: http://book.personalmba.com/damaging-admission/

Barriers to Purchase

Selling begins when the prospect says no.

—SALES MAXIM

Assume for a moment you present an offer to a prospect, and their reply is something along the lines of "No—that doesn't work for me." Time to pack it in and move on?

There's always a reason a prospect says no. The fact that they're even talking with you implies that there's at least *some* interest—otherwise, the conversation would simply end. There's still hope of closing the sale, if you start asking the right questions.

Selling anything is largely the process of identifying and eliminating *Barriers to Purchase*: risks, unknowns, and concerns that prevent your prospects from buying what you offer. Your primary job as a salesperson is to identify and eliminate barriers standing in the way of completing the *Transaction*. Eliminate your prospect's objections and barriers, and you'll close the deal.

There are five standard objections that appear in sales of all kinds:

1. *It costs too much.* **Loss Aversion** (discussed later) makes spending money feel like a loss—by purchasing, the prospect is giving something up, and that naturally makes people hesitate. (Some people even experience this sense of loss after they make a purchase decision, a condition called "buyer's remorse.")

2. *It won't work.* If the prospect thinks that there's a chance the offer won't (or can't) provide the promised benefits, they won't purchase.

3. *It won't work for ME.* The prospect may believe that the offer is capable of providing benefits to other people but that they're different—a special case.

4. *I can wait.* The prospect may believe they don't have a problem worth addressing right now, even if it's very clear to you that they do.

5. *It's too difficult.* If the offer takes any effort whatsoever on their part, the prospect may believe that their contribution will be too hard to manage.

To overcome these objections as quickly as possible, it makes sense to build them into the structure of your initial offer. Since these objections are very common, anything that you can do to alleviate them before the prospect considers the offer will make the sales process much easier.

Objection #1 ("it costs too much") is best addressed via **Framing** and **Value-Based Selling**. If you're selling a piece of software to a business that can save them $10 million a year, and you're asking $1 million a year for a license, your software isn't expensive—it's effectively **Free**. If it's clear that the value of your offer far exceeds the asking price, this objection is moot.

Objections #2 and #3 ("it won't work" / "it won't work for me") are best addressed via **Social Proof**—showing the prospect how customers *just like them* are already benefiting from your offer. The more like your prospect your stories and testimonials are, the better. That's why **Referrals** are such a powerful sales tool—customers tend to refer people who have similar situations and needs, and the Referral itself helps break down these objections.

Objections #4 and #5 ("I can wait" / "it's too difficult") are best addressed via **Education-Based Selling**. Often, your prospects haven't fully realized they have a problem, particularly in the case of **Absence Blindness** (discussed later). If the business doesn't realize it's losing $10 million in the first place, it's difficult to convince them that you can help. The best way to get around this is to focus your early sales efforts on making your customers smarter by teaching them what you know about their business, then helping them **Visualize** what their involvement would look like if they decide to proceed.

Once you have the prospect's **Attention** and **Permission**, there are two possible tactics if they still have these objections: (1) convince the prospect that the objection isn't true, or (2) convince the prospect that the objection is irrelevant. The approach you'll use depends on the objection raised, but some combination of Framing, Value-Based Selling, Education-Based Selling, Social Proof, and Visualization will usually do the trick.

If the prospect still doesn't buy, that typically means there's a **Power** issue—your negotiating partner may not have the budget or the authority to agree to your proposal. Always try to negotiate directly with the decision maker—that way, if they refuse your offer, you know that it's because it wasn't a good fit for them, and you can move on to more promising prospects as quickly as possible.

SHARE THIS CONCEPT: http://book.personalmba.com/objections-barriers-to-purchase/

Risk Reversal

If you want a guarantee, buy a toaster.
—CLINT EASTWOOD, ACADEMY AWARD–WINNING ACTOR

People always hate to lose. They hate to feel stupid. They hate to make bad decisions or waste money. They hate to take risks.

When it comes to closing sales, *you* are that risk. In every transaction, the purchaser is taking on some risk. What if this doesn't work as promised? What if it doesn't meet their needs? What if purchasing from you is a waste of money?

These questions are always in the back of your prospect's mind as they're considering purchasing from you. If you don't eliminate these questions, it's very likely they'll ruin the sale.

Risk Reversal is a strategy that transfers some (or all) of the risk of a **Transaction** from the buyer to the seller. Instead of making the purchaser shoulder the risk of a bad Transaction, the seller agrees in advance to make things right if—for whatever reason—things don't turn out as the purchaser expected.

Take the bedding industry, for example. Look around, and you'll see a lot of over-the-top offers: twelve-month, 100 percent money-back guarantees, no questions asked! A customer could sleep on a bed for a year, decide they didn't like it, and call up the store to return it for a full refund. Crazy, right?

It's not crazy at all: this strategy completely eliminates the purchaser's perception of risk, which is a major **Barrier to Purchase**. If a customer makes a purchase and it doesn't work out, they don't have to feel stupid about wasting their money—and they don't have to feel angry at the company or at themselves for making a bad decision. All they need to do is take advantage of the guarantee and return it—no big deal. As a result, they'll go through with the Transaction—there's no downside, so why not?

Colloquially, this approach is sometimes called the "take the puppy home" strategy. If you visit a pet store and meet an adorable puppy, but you're not sure whether or not you're ready to commit, the pet store will tell you to take the puppy home on a trial basis. "If it doesn't work out," the salesman says, "you can always bring it back."

The puppy almost never comes back, of course. Without making this promise, though, the puppy might never go home in the first place.

Adopting a Risk Reversal strategy is naturally uncomfortable because sellers *also* hate to lose. No seller wants to feel used or taken advantage of, and it's often easy to feel that way if a customer obviously gets value from the offer and asks for a refund anyway.

The difference is that the purchaser is purchasing from one seller—the seller is selling to many purchasers. Your customers experience this risk with every purchase they make, and it's a big deal. Since you're serving many customers, you can spread the risk of a return among many customers.

Yes, you'll lose money on customers who are obviously taking advantage of your generosity, and that never feels good. In compensation, by eliminating the risk that every purchaser feels, you'll close many more sales and come out way ahead in terms of total revenue and profit.

If you want to maximize your sales, it almost always makes sense to offer a very strong Risk-Reversing guarantee and to extend the risk-free period as much as possible. If you don't already have a Risk-Reversal policy, implement one and you'll see your sales increase.

SHARE THIS CONCEPT: **http://book.personalmba.com/risk-reversal/**

Reactivation

Every company's greatest assets are its customers, because without customers there is no company.

—MICHAEL LEBOEUF, BUSINESS PROFESSOR AND AUTHOR OF *HOW TO WIN CUSTOMERS AND KEEP THEM FOR LIFE*

Sales is the process of convincing prospects to become customers. Winning new customers, however, is often costly and time intensive. What if there was another way to bring in more revenue at very little additional cost?

Reactivation is the process of convincing past customers to buy from you again. If you've been in business for a while, you'll inevitably have some "lapsed" customers—people who have already purchased from you but haven't purchased for quite some time. You know they're interested in what you have to offer, and you probably already have their contact information. Why not present them with a new offer to make them active customers once again?

Netflix is a company that uses Reactivation brilliantly. If you cancel a Netflix subscription, three to six months later you'll receive a postcard and/or e-mail from Netflix with an offer to resubscribe at a reduced rate. If you don't reply, they'll send another message every few months until you resubscribe or request to be removed completely from their system. Since Netflix is a **Subscription** business, every reactivated customer means a new monthly stream of income, which greatly enhances the **Lifetime Value** (discussed later) of each customer.

Reactivation is typically a quicker, simpler, and more effective approach to increasing revenue than attracting new customers. Your old customers already know and trust you, and they're aware of the value you provide. You have their information—you don't have to find them. Your cost of customer acquisition (a component of **Allowable Acquisition Cost**) is extremely low—all you have to do is contact them and present an attractive offer.

Reactivation is much simpler if you have **Permission** from your customers to follow up. Your list of prospective customers is a valuable asset, but your list of past customers is just as valuable. By obtaining Permission from your customers to follow up with them, you increase the probability of Reactivation if they—for whatever reason—stop buying from you.

Most point-of-sale (POS) systems keep track of customer data: who purchased and when the sale was made. It's relatively simple to extract a list of customers who haven't purchased from you in a while, then present them with a Reactivation offer directly via e-mail, phone call, or postal mail. Reactivation campaigns are consistently the easiest and most profitable marketing activities you'll ever try.

Make it a priority every three to six months to contact your lapsed customers with another offer to see if you can encourage them to start buying again, and you'll be amazed by the results.

SHARE THIS CONCEPT: http://book.personalmba.com/reactivation/

4

VALUE DELIVERY

A satisfied customer is the best business strategy of all.

—MICHAEL LEBOEUF, BUSINESS PROFESSOR AND AUTHOR OF
HOW TO WIN CUSTOMERS AND KEEP THEM FOR LIFE

Every successful business actually delivers what it promises to its customers. There's a term for a person who takes other people's money without delivering equivalent value: "scam artist."

Value Delivery involves everything necessary to ensure that every paying customer is a happy customer: order processing, inventory management, delivery/fulfillment, troubleshooting, customer support, etc. Without Value Delivery, you don't have a business.

The best businesses in the world deliver the value they've promised to their customers in a way that surpasses the customers' expectations. Customers like to get the benefits of their purchases quickly, reliably, and consistently.

The more happy customers a business creates, the more likely it is that those customers will purchase from the company again. Happy customers are also more likely to tell others about what you do, improving your *Reputation* and bringing in even more potential customers.

Successful businesses satisfy their customers most of the time in the midst of a changing environment. Unsuccessful businesses fail to make their customers happy, lose them, and eventually fail.

SHARE THIS CONCEPT: http://book.personalmba.com/value-delivery/

Value Stream

Great design is eliminating all unnecessary details.

—MINH D. TRAN, TECHNOLOGIST AND DESIGNER

When I worked at Procter & Gamble, one of the most fascinating things about my job was understanding how products were created and delivered. Here's a quick look at how a bottle of Dawn dishwashing detergent is made:

1. Raw materials are delivered to the factory.

2. The materials are combined to create dishwashing liquid, which is stored in large vats.

3. Plastic bottles are blown into shape using molds, then filled with the liquid and capped.

4. Adhesive labels are applied to each bottle.

5. Each bottle is inspected, boxed, then loaded onto a pallet.

It's a textbook example of a *Value Creation* process, which begins with raw materials and ends with finished *Products*, ready to be shipped. Here's what happens next:

6. Pallets are wrapped, stacked, and stored for shipment in a warehouse.

7. When orders from customers are placed, pallets are moved into position for loading onto a truck.

8. A truck picks up the pallets and delivers them to the customer's closest distribution center.

9. The customer puts the pallets on a delivery truck.

10. The truck delivers the pallet to a store that needs additional inventory.

11. The store unwraps the pallet, unboxes the product, and transfers it to the shelf, where it will remain until purchased by the consumer.

That's a lot of steps for a little bottle of dish soap. Those steps are worth studying.

A *Value Stream* is the set of all steps and all processes from the start of your Value Creation process all the way through the delivery of the end result to your customer. Understanding what your offer's Value Stream looks like is critically important if you want to be able to deliver value to your customers quickly, reliably, and consistently.

You can think of the Value Stream as a combination of your Value Creation and *Value Delivery* processes. Very often, your offer moves directly from the first into the second. Even though the purposes of these core processes are very different, treating them as one big process can help you improve your ability to deliver the value you create.

The Toyota Production System (TPS) was the first large-scale manufacturing operation to systematically examine its entire Value Stream on a regular basis. Analyzing the production system in great detail paved the way for an ongoing series of small, incremental improvements: Toyota engineers make over 1 million improvements to the TPS each year. As a result, the company consistently reaps huge rewards in speed, consistency, and reliability, which has greatly improved Toyota's *Reputation* as a company with very high-quality products—that is, until the *Paradox of Automation* (discussed later) destroyed that Reputation.

The best way to understand your Value Stream is to diagram it. Tracing the steps or transformations your offer goes through from the beginning to the end is an extremely enlightening process that can show you just how efficient your Value Delivery process is. It's very common for processes to contain unnecessary steps or awkward transitions. Creating a complete diagram of your entire Value Stream takes effort, but it can help you streamline your process, making the entire system perform better.[1]

In general, try to make your Value Stream as small and efficient as possible. As we'll examine later in the book when we discuss systems, the longer your process, the greater the risk of things going wrong. The shorter and more streamlined your Value Stream, the easier it is to manage and the more effectively you'll be able to deliver value.

SHARE THIS CONCEPT: http://book.personalmba.com/value-stream/

Distribution Channel

> Unless a person is a clam digger, a trapper, or an old-style pick-and-shovel prospector, it's virtually impossible these days to be a success all by oneself.
>
> —BENJAMIN F. FAIRLESS, FORMER HEAD OF U.S. STEEL

Once a sale is made, you must deliver what you promised to your customer. A **Distribution Channel** describes how your form of value is actually delivered to the end user.

There are two basic types of Distribution Channels: direct-to-user and intermediary.

Direct-to-user distribution works across a single channel: from the business directly to the end user. **Services** are a classic example: when you get a haircut, the value is provided by the business itself directly to you, with no intermediary.

Direct-to-user distribution is simple and effective, but it has limitations—you have full control of the entire process, but you can only serve as many customers as your time and energy allow. Once demand for your offer outpaces your ability to deliver it, you're risking disappointing your customers and diminishing your **Reputation**.

Intermediary distribution works across multiple channels. When you purchase a **Product** from a store, that store is acting as a **Reseller**. The store (in most cases) doesn't manufacture the Products—it purchases them from another business.

The business that created the Product can sell it to as many stores as it wants, a process called "securing distribution." The more distribution a Product has, the more sales the business is likely to make—the more stores selling the Product, the more opportunities for sales.

Intermediary distribution can increase sales, but it requires giving up a certain amount of control over your **Value Delivery** process. Trusting another business to deliver your offer to your customers frees up your limited time and energy, but it also increases **Counterparty Risk**—the risk that your partner will screw up and diminish your Reputation.

Imagine you're in the business of selling cookies, and you secure distribution at a local supermarket. The supermarket purchases cookies from you, places them on their shelves, and sells them to their shoppers at a premium. Instead of buying cookies from you directly, shoppers purchase them via the supermarket: classic intermediary distribution.

It's easy to see the benefits of this approach, but there are drawbacks. Let's say your cookies are damaged in the supermarket's truck on the way to the store: they break, crumble, and the box they're delivered in is crushed. The supermarket's shoppers won't know exactly what happened, but if it happens often, they'll assume that *you* create a low-quality product, damaging your reputation.

Securing distribution can be valuable, but keep an eye on your intermediaries. Distribution isn't a "set-it-and-forget-it" strategy—if you're working with multiple Distribution Channels, plan to devote time and energy to making sure they're representing your business well.

SHARE THIS CONCEPT: http://book.personalmba.com/distribution-channel/

The Expectation Effect

Never promise more than you can perform.

—PUBLILIUS SYRUS, FIRST-CENTURY B.C. SYRIAN APHORIST

Zappos has perfected the art of selling shoes online.

Selling shoes over the Internet is a tough business—customers can't try them on, and no one wants to be stuck with shoes they don't like and will never wear. To compensate, Zappos applies classic **Risk Reversal** to every order—they offer free shipping and free, no-questions-asked returns if you don't like the **Products** you order. Those two policies eliminate the risk of making a bad purchase, so customers are more willing to try Zappos out.

That's not, however, the reason Zappos has developed such a solid **Reputation** in this market. The secret lies in an unexpected benefit the company doesn't advertise.

When you order from Zappos, it's very likely that you'll receive a pleasant surprise: your shoes will arrive the next day, several days ahead of schedule.

Zappos could easily advertise "free expedited shipping," but they don't—the surprise is far more valuable.

A customer's perception of quality relies on two criteria: expectations and performance. You can characterize this relationship in the form of a quasi-equation, which I call the *Expectation Effect*: Quality = Performance - Expectations.

Customer expectations have to be high enough for a customer to purchase from you in the first place. After the purchase is made, however, the performance of the offering must *surpass* the customer's expectations in order for them to be satisfied. If performance is better than expectations, the customer's perception of quality will be high. If performance is lower than expectations, the perception of quality will be low—no matter how good the offer is in absolute terms.

Apple's first-generation iPhone was a massive success—customers expected something good, and they received a device that delivered benefits beyond their expectations. Apple's second-generation iPhone, the 3G, wasn't as well received—prelaunch expectations were so high that there was almost no way the company could surpass them, and a few glitches in the roll-out process quickly took center stage.

The iPhone 3G was a better phone in the absolute—it was faster and had several new features, more memory, and a lower price. To many customers, however, it didn't *feel* better—Apple failed to deliver on their expectations, and the company's Reputation suffered. The same thing happened again with the launch of the fourth-generation iPhone—a small antenna glitch soured many customers on the device, even though the new version was demonstrably better than the old.

The best way to consistently surpass expectations is to give your customers an unexpected bonus in addition to the value they expect. The purpose of the *Value Delivery* process is to ensure that your customers are happy and satisfied, and the best way to ensure customer satisfaction is to at least meet the customers' expectations, surpassing them whenever you possibly can.

Do whatever you can do to provide something that unexpectedly delights your customers. Zappos's free upgraded shipping is more valuable as a surprise—if it were part of the deal, it would lose its emotional punch.

When you perform well above your customers' expectations, they'll be satisfied with the experience.

SHARE THIS CONCEPT: http://book.personalmba.com/expectation-effect/

Predictability

I have always believed that for a product or service to thrive, it must deliver quality. A fine product or service is its own best selling point.

—VICTOR KIAM, FORMER OWNER OF REMINGTON AND THE NEW ENGLAND PATRIOTS FOOTBALL TEAM

Aaron Shira, one of my best friends growing up, *Bootstrapped* a painting company with his brother, Patrick, in Columbus, Ohio. Shira Sons Painting specializes in large-scale painting projects—they've painted universities, military bases, mega-churches, and multimillion-dollar homes. Starting from scratch, they're now the preferred painting company for several major general contractors in the Columbus area.

How did two young guys break into a competitive market against contractors who have been in business longer than they've been alive? Simple: when you hire Aaron and Pat, you can be *absolutely certain* the job will be done right and on time.

Contractors are notoriously unpredictable: they often show up late, take too long, do sloppy work, and have bad attitudes. The secret of Aaron and Pat's success is *Predictability*—they do great work every single time, deliver on schedule, and they're always pleasant to work with. As a result, they're booked solid—an impressive achievement, particularly in a soft construction market.

When purchasing something of value, customers want to know exactly what they can expect—they want their experience to be Predictable. Unexpected surprises can provide a customer with a great experience, but if you're not able to deliver what the customer expects in a Predictable manner, it doesn't matter how many bonuses you offer. People love pleasant surprises, but they hate to be caught off guard.

There are three primary factors that influence the Predictability of an offer: uniformity, consistency, and reliability.

Uniformity means delivering the same characteristics every time. Coca-Cola was one of the first large companies to combine solid marketing with large-scale product uniformity. Product uniformity in the beverage industry is an astounding feat: creating, bottling, and distributing soda is an incredibly complex logistical process. A little too much sugar or flavoring, slightly more air, or an introduction of bacteria can drastically alter the final product.

No one wants their favorite soda to taste different every time they drink it. When you open a can of Coke, you expect exactly the same product as you had the last time, no matter where you are in the world. If even 0.1 percent of the cans of Coca-Cola sold were flat or sour, people would quickly stop buying.

Consistency means delivering the same value over time. One of the reasons "New Coke" failed in the mid-1980s was that customers expected Coke to taste a certain way, and the company delivered something completely new under the same name. Violating consistency led to a swift decline in sales, followed by a swift increase when the Coca-Cola Company restored the original formula.

Violating the expectations of loyal customers is not the way to success—if you're offering something completely different, present it as something new.

Reliability means being able to count on delivery of the value without error or delay. Ask Microsoft Windows users what they hate most about their computers, and they'll always tell you, "System crashes." Unreliability is a huge frustration for a user, particularly when Predictability is at a premium. How would you feel if you were building a house and a contractor didn't show up on time?

Improving Predictability has major **Reputation** and value perception benefits. The more Predictable your standard offering is, the more you'll be able to increase the perceived quality of the **Products** and the **Services** that you offer.

SHARE THIS CONCEPT: http://book.personalmba.com/predictability/

Throughput

However beautiful the strategy, you should occasionally look at the results.

—WINSTON CHURCHILL, PRIME MINISTER OF GREAT BRITAIN DURING
WORLD WAR II

hroughput is the rate at which a system achieves its desired goal. By understanding and improving the process you use to actually create and deliver the value you've promised to your customers, you can improve quality and customer satisfaction.

Throughput is a measure of the effectiveness of your **Value Stream**. Throughput is measured in the formula [units/time]. The more results you create per unit of time, the higher the Throughput.

In order to measure Throughput, you need a clearly defined objective:

Dollar Throughput is a measure of how quickly your overall business system creates a dollar of profit. Assume a standard time unit, like an hour/day/week/month—how many dollars does your business system produce on average during that time? The faster your business produces dollars of profit, the better.

Unit Throughput is a measure of how much time it takes to create an additional unit for sale. How long does it take to go from raw materials to a finished unit rolling off the production line? The faster the unit Throughput, the more units you'll have available to sell, and the faster you'll be able to respond to new demand for those products.

Satisfaction Throughput is a measure of how much time it takes to create a happy, satisfied customer. It takes restaurants like Chipotle Mexican Grill approximately three minutes from the time the customer enters the restaurant to the time they receive their order. The less time that it takes to create a happy customer, the more customers you can serve in an hour and the more happy customers you can create every day. The longer customers have to wait, the fewer customers you can serve in an hour, and the less satisfied they will be with the experience.

The best way to begin increasing Throughput is to start measuring it. How long does it take for your business system to produce a dollar of profit? How long does it take to produce another unit to sell, or a new happy customer?

If you don't know your Throughput, make it a priority to find out—measuring Throughput is the first step toward improving it.

SHARE THIS CONCEPT: http://book.personalmba.com/throughput/

Duplication

The problems of this world are only truly solved in two ways: by extinction or duplication.

—SUSAN SONTAG, AUTHOR AND POLITICAL ACTIVIST

Duplication is the ability to reliably reproduce something of value. Factory production is the quintessential example of Duplication: one design, many copies. Instead of "reinventing the wheel" over and over again, Duplication allows you to design the wheel once, then make as many of them as you wish.

The better your ability to Duplicate your offer, the more value you can provide. The more time and effort it costs to make something, the less available it tends to be. Duplication allows you to make copies of your offer quickly and inexpensively, making it more widely available in a cost-effective way.

Consider this book. In the olden days, books used to be copied and bound by hand. It would take a scribe months (sometimes years[2]) of full-time work to copy a single book. As a result, books were extremely expensive and difficult to obtain.

How times have changed. This book was written only once, but via the wonder of large-scale printing equipment, it can be reproduced quickly, reliably, and inexpensively. As a result, tens of millions of copies can be made and distributed all over the world and can be purchased for a few dollars. That's the magic of Duplication.

The Internet has made Duplication of some forms of value even easier. As Kevin Kelly remarked in his essay "Better Than Free,"[3] the Internet is essentially an enormous, inexpensive copy machine. When I write a post for my Web site, it can be Duplicated by my Web server for next to nothing, and delivered to a reader on the other side of the world almost instantly.

Duplication of information—text, images, music, video—is essentially free. The value of this information, however, can be quite significant.

If you want to create something that you can sell without your direct involvement, the ability to Duplicate your offer is essential. If you have to be personally involved with every customer, there's an upper limit on the number of customers you can serve in a given amount of time. Combining Duplication with *Automation* allows you to deliver value to more people—and close more sales as a result.

SHARE THIS CONCEPT: http://book.personalmba.com/duplication/

Multiplication

> All growth depends upon activity. There is no development physically or intellectually without effort, and effort means work.
>
> —CALVIN COOLIDGE, THIRTIETH PRESIDENT OF THE UNITED STATES

McDonald's knows how to *Duplicate* Big Macs. Starbucks knows how to Duplicate triple soy vanilla lattes. Here's what McDonald's and Starbucks have in common: both businesses can Duplicate entire stores, which is why there are thousands of each all over the world.

Multiplication is Duplication for an entire process or *System*. McDonald's began as a single restaurant in California; Starbucks began as a single coffee shop in Seattle. By learning to Duplicate the entire business system that is a McDonald's or Starbucks store, each company opened new possibilities for growth.

Walmart did the same thing. Starting with a single store in Fayetteville, Arkansas, Walmart multiplied at an astounding rate, spreading rapidly across the Midwest, then nationally, then globally.

Walmart's success lies in Multiplying two interconnected systems: stores and distribution centers. Distribution centers Multiply the ability to receive inventory from suppliers and deliver it to stores. Stores replicate a proven system of receiving, displaying, and selling that inventory to paying customers.

Multiplication is what separates small businesses from huge businesses. There's an upper limit on what any single business system can produce. By creating more identical business systems based on a proven model, Multiplication can expand a business's ability to deliver value to more customers. That's the major benefit of franchising: instead of reinventing a business model, opening a franchise helps Multiply a model that already works.

The easier it is to Multiply your business system, the more value you can ultimately deliver.

SHARE THIS CONCEPT: http://book.personalmba.com/multiplication/

Scale

Ut sementem feceris, ita metes. (You reap what you sow.)
—MARCUS TULLIUS CICERO, ANCIENT ROMAN STATESMAN AND ORATOR

Think of a skilled quilter who specializes in creating quilts by hand. Assuming each quilt takes a week to produce, having one active customer a week is great: creating and delivering a single quilt to a single customer is no problem at all.

Having two customers at once is challenging: Customer #2 has to wait until Customer #1 is served. If the quilt maker receives a thousand orders in a single day, that's a huge issue—there's no way to keep up with the demand without keeping customers waiting, which creates an undesirable level of **Scarcity**.

Scale is the ability to reliably **Duplicate** or **Multiply** a process as volume increases. Scalability determines your maximum potential volume. The easier it is to Duplicate or Multiply the value provided, the more scalable the business.

Contrast the handmade quilt business with a Scalable business like Starbucks. Assume the average Starbucks has the capacity to serve a hundred beverages an hour—any demand above that, and the store starts getting overcrowded. The solution? Build another Starbucks—even if it's right across the street, not an uncommon sight in cities like New York.

Scalability is typically limited by the amount of required human involvement in a process. Starbucks is able to enhance their ability to Duplicate lattes via **Automation**. Starbucks employees are involved in making drinks, but the process is semiautomated: a machine actually makes the espresso, many of the ingredients are prepared ahead of time, and so on. The overall level of human attention or intervention that's required to make a good drink is actually quite small, which is why Starbucks can crank out so many drinks every hour.

If your goal is to create a business that doesn't require your direct daily involvement, Scalability should be a major consideration. **Products** are typically the easiest to **Duplicate**, while **Shared Resources** (like gyms, etc.) are easiest to **Multiply**.

Humans don't Scale. Individual people only have so much time and energy each day, which is a **Constraint** that doesn't change with the volume of work to be done. On the contrary—as we'll discuss later in **Performance Load**, a person's effectiveness usually goes down as the demands on them increase.

As a result, **Services** are typically difficult to Scale, since they tend to rely heavily on the direct involvement of people to deliver value. As a general rule, the less human involvement required to create and deliver value, the more Scalable the business.

SHARE THIS CONCEPT: http://book.personalmba.com/scale/

Accumulation

Sometimes when I consider what tremendous consequences come from little things, I am tempted to think: there are no little things.

—BRUCE BARTON, ADVERTISING EXECUTIVE BEST KNOWN FOR CREATING THE BETTY CROCKER BRAND

At this very moment, a Toyota engineer somewhere in the world is making a very small change to the Toyota Production System, one of the most efficient manufacturing **Systems** in the world.

Alone, the change may not look like much—a small tweak, a slight restructure, a bit of material or effort saved. Taken together, however, the effects are huge—Toyota employees implement over 1 million improvements to the Toyota Production System every year. It's little wonder that Toyota is now the world's largest and most valuable automotive manufacturer.[4]

Small helpful or harmful behaviors and inputs tend to **Accumulate** over time, producing huge results. According to *Lean Thinking* by James P.

Womack and Daniel T. Jones, Toyota's approach is based on the Japanese concept of *kaizen*, which emphasizes the continual improvement of a system by eliminating *muda* (waste) via a lot of very small changes. Many small improvements, consistently implemented, inevitably produce huge results.

Accumulation isn't always positive. Think of what would happen to your body if you consumed nothing but fast food, candy bars, and soda for a decade. Eating a single candy bar isn't a big deal, but eating hundreds of candy bars is. Fortunately, the opposite is true as well: small improvements in your diet, a little more exercise, and a little more sleep can have major effects on your health over time.

Incremental Augmentation is an example of the power of Accumulation. If your offer improves with every **Iteration Cycle**, it won't be long before your offer is many times more valuable to your customers than it was before. Small changes to your **Value Delivery** process can save you a ton of time and effort in the long run.

The more small improvements you make over time, the better your results.

SHARE THIS CONCEPT: http://book.personalmba.com/accumulation/

Amplification

In nature, there are neither rewards nor punishment—there are consequences.

—ROBERT G. INGERSOLL, POLITICAL LEADER AND ORATOR

Think of a typical can of soda. When cans were first used to sell beverages, they were cylindrical, flattopped, and made of steel. Over time, steel was phased out in favor of aluminum, pull tabs were introduced to make opening easier, and the can was "necked"—tapered slightly at the top.

"Necking" a can has two major effects—first, it makes it easier to drink from, which users like. Second, it reduces the amount of metal necessary to produce a structurally sound can: the walls of a typical beverage can are now around ninety micrometers thick (instead of about two millimeters), saving an enormous amount of raw materials.

According to the Can Manufacturers Institute, approximately 131 billion cans are manufactured every year in the United States. When you multiply the cost savings of modern can designs across billions of cans and several decades, a few very small changes have saved the beverage industry hundreds of billions of dollars.

That's **Amplification**: making a small change to a scalable **System** produces a huge result. The effect of any improvement or system optimization is Amplified by the size of the system. The larger the system, the larger the result.

When McDonald's comes up with a new sandwich, they're not limited to just selling it in one of their stores—they can start selling it in all of their stores around the world. When Starbucks comes up with a new drink, it can be made available to customers in every Starbucks location extremely quickly.

The best way to identify Amplification opportunities is to look for things that are constantly **Duplicated** or **Multiplied**. If Starbucks found a way to produce a shot of espresso using fewer coffee beans, it would make a huge difference in the amount of coffee they'd need to buy. If they discovered a way to make that espresso shot more quickly, it would reduce the time it takes to serve a customer and increase the number of customers a single store could serve in an hour.

Scalable systems amplify the results of small changes. Small changes to Scalable systems produce massive results.

SHARE THIS CONCEPT: http://book.personalmba.com/amplification/

Barrier to Competition

Don't compete with rivals—make them irrelevant.
—W. CHAN KIM, *BLUE OCEAN STRATEGY*

How much attention are you paying to what your competitors are doing? The more time and energy you spend following your competition, the less time and energy you have to actually build your business.

Think of a company like Apple—there's no other company in the technology world that focuses less on keeping up with what other companies are providing. Instead, they focus on building something completely new and **Remarkable**, then perfecting it as much as possible.

Apple's competitors, on the other hand, seem to be locked in a never-ending scramble to keep up. After Apple launched the iPhone in 2007, BlackBerry scrambled to create the Storm, which replicated many of the same features. By the time the Storm launched, the iPhone had already gone through several *Iteration Cycles*, making it very difficult for BlackBerry to compete. To date, Apple has sold over 50 million iPhones worldwide.

In the same vein, instead of trying to compete directly with commodity laptop manufacturers like Asus, HP, and Dell in the netbook category (small, low-powered computers designed for portability), Apple conspicuously avoided the market for years. That changed when the iPad was launched in 2010—an offer that redefined the market instead of competing directly with preexisting netbooks on features. In the first two months of its existence, the company sold over 2 million units. By choosing to innovate instead of compete, Apple successfully captured a leadership share of a very competitive market.

Every improvement you make to your *Value Stream* make it harder for potential competitors to keep up. By increasing your ability to create and deliver value efficiently and effectively, you're simultaneously making it more difficult for competitors to compete with you by doing what you're doing.

Every benefit you deliver and every customer you serve make it harder for competitors to replicate you. Don't focus on competing—focus on delivering even more value. Your competition will take care of itself.

SHARE THIS CONCEPT: http://book.personalmba.com/barrier-to-competition/

Force Multiplier

> Man is a tool-using animal. Without tools he is nothing, with tools he is all.
>
> —THOMAS CARLYLE, ESSAYIST AND HISTORIAN

One of the things that make humans unique is our ability to create and use tools. Tools are important because they *Multiply* the effect of physical force, thought, or attention. The more a tool *Amplifies* or concentrates your effort, the more effective the tool.

If you try pounding on a nail with your bare hands, you'll certainly be able to exert *some* force, but it won't be enough to drive the nail into something solid. (Besides, you'll probably hurt your hand.)

Using a hammer Multiplies the magnitude of the force you're exerting and concentrates that force into a small area, making it easy to drive a nail in a single stroke. Saws, screwdrivers, and other tools work the same way—they Amplify and concentrate the force you generate to produce more output.

The most effective tools Amplify force in the greatest magnitude. A power saw is far more effective at Multiplying force than a handsaw is. A dump truck can carry more than a wheelbarrow. A rocket can launch a payload farther than a slingshot.

Investing in **Force Multipliers** makes sense because you can get more done with the same amount of effort. If you need to dig the foundation to build a new house, a $10 shovel from your local hardware store will certainly work, but a backhoe will get the job done faster and easier. If building homes is your business, buying or leasing a backhoe is worth the cost.

Force Multipliers can be expensive—the more effective they are, the more expensive they tend to be. Factory production and distribution systems are examples of large-scale Force Multipliers—they make it possible to deliver value to thousands (or millions) of paying customers in a very short time. They may cost thousands (or millions) of dollars, but they can give you capabilities that would otherwise be out of reach.

As a general rule, the only good use of debt or outside capital in setting up a system is to give you access to Force Multipliers you would not be able to access any other way. If your business requires tooling up a factory, you probably don't have $10 million sitting in your bank account. Taking a **Loan** from a bank or accepting **Capital** from an outside investor may be your best option, provided you use those funds to purchase and maintain Force Multipliers, not to pay yourself or maintain rent on a fancy office.

Always choose the best tools that you can obtain and afford. Quality tools give you maximum output with a minimum of input. By investing in Force Multipliers, you free up your time, energy, and attention to focus on building your business instead of simply operating it.

SHARE THIS CONCEPT: http://book.personalmba.com/force-multiplier/

Systemization

If you can't describe what you are doing as a process, you don't
know what you're doing.

—W. EDWARDS DEMING, PRODUCTION MANAGEMENT EXPERT AND PIONEER
OF STATISTICAL PROCESS CONTROL

Even if you make everything up as you go along, there is still a process
involved, assuming that multiple steps are needed to get from point A to
point B. Instead of constantly "winging it," clarifying your process can provide a few major benefits.

A **System** is a process made explicit and repeatable—a series of steps that
has been formalized in some way. Systems can be written or diagrammed,
but they are *always* **Externalized** (discussed later) in some way.

The primary benefit of creating a system is that you can examine the
process and make improvements. By making each step in the process explicit, you can understand how the core processes work, how they're structured, how they affect other processes and systems, and how you can
improve the system over time.

Google is a great example of the power of systems. Every time you use
the Google search engine, thousands of computers automatically spring
into action to deliver your results. Google's search algorithm (a fancy programming word for system) defines how these computers work together,
and Google employees are constantly refining the details of how the system
works. Each year, Google engineers make over 550 improvements to the
primary search engine algorithm,[5] making it better able to point you to
what you're looking for.

As a result, the Google algorithm has become so efficient that your
search results are returned in approximately 0.2 seconds with zero human
intervention—an astounding achievement. If Google hadn't spent most of
their early time and energy defining and systemizing the search process, the
company simply wouldn't exist.

Systems also help teams of people stay on the same page. As we'll discuss in chapter 8, communication is necessary for people to work well together, and the more people you're working with, the more communication
you need. Developing systems and clear processes for certain events and

tasks can help everyone do what must be done with a minimum of misunderstanding and fuss.

If you can't systematize your process, you can't Automate it. Imagine what it would be like if Google relied on a team of human librarians to generate search results. It'd be a nightmare—you'd wait days (or weeks, or months) to get your results.

The key to Google's quality and speed is **Automation** (discussed later): by explicitly defining the rules of how the system operates, the search engine programmers are able to automate the day-to-day operation of the system. As a result, Google developers are free to focus their efforts on continually *improving* the system instead of on *operating* the system.

Most people resist creating business systems because it feels like extra work. We're all busy, and it's easy to feel like you don't have time to create and improve systems because there's already too much work to do. Actually, useful systems make your work easier—if you're feeling overloaded, the best thing you can do to solve the issue is spend time creating good systems.

Systemization and Automation have a few major drawbacks, which we'll explore in detail in chapters 10 and 11. For now, recognize that effective systems are the lifeblood of a business—they allow you to create, market, sell, and ultimately deliver what you have to offer.

The better your systems, the better your business.

SHARE THIS CONCEPT: http://book.personalmba.com/systemization/

5

FINANCE

He had heard people speak contemptuously of money: he wondered if they had ever tried to do without it.

—W. SOMERSET MAUGHAM, AUTHOR OF *OF HUMAN BONDAGE*

In my experience, people enjoy learning about *Value Creation*, *Marketing*, *Sales*, and *Value Delivery*—they're easy to understand and visualize.

When it comes to *Finance*, however, eyes glaze over. Finance conjures up associations of "bean counting," mathematical formulas, and spreadsheets overflowing with numbers. It doesn't have to be that way—finance is quite easy to understand if you focus on what's most important.

Finance is the art and science of watching the money flowing into and out of a business, then deciding how to allocate it and determining whether or not what you're doing is producing the results you want. Accounting is the process of ensuring the data you use to make financial decisions is as complete and accurate as possible. It's really not any more complicated than that. Yes, there can be fancy models and jargon, but ultimately you're simply using numbers to decide whether or not your business is operating the way you intended, and whether or not the results are enough.

Every successful business must bring in a certain amount of money to keep going. If you're creating value, marketing, selling, and delivering value, there's money flowing into and out of the business every day. In order to continue to exist, every business must bring in *Sufficient* revenue (discussed later) to justify all of the time and effort that goes into running the operation.

Everyone has bills to pay and groceries to buy, so the people involved in the business need to consistently make enough money to justify the time and energy they're investing, or they'll quit and do something else. Accordingly, every business must capture some amount of the value it creates as revenue, which is used to pay expenses and compensate the people who make the business run.

The very best businesses create a virtuous cycle: they create huge amounts of value while keeping their expenses consistently low, so they make more than enough money to keep going without capturing too much value. As a result, they're able to simultaneously pad their pocketbooks and improve the lives of their customers, since the continued existence of the business makes everyone involved better off.

Finance helps you watch your dollars in a way that makes sense.

SHARE THIS CONCEPT: http://book.personalmba.com/finance/

Profit

> Remind people that profit is the difference between revenue and expense. This makes you look smart.
>
> —SCOTT ADAMS, CARTOONIST AND CREATOR OF "DILBERT"

It doesn't matter if your business brings in $100,000,000 a year in revenue if you spend $100,000,001. Business is not about what you make—it's about what you keep.

Profit is a very simple concept: it's bringing in more money than you spend. In order for a business to continue to exist, the total revenue it collects must exceed the total expenses it accumulates at some point in the foreseeable future. If it doesn't, it'll cease to be a business—the operation will run out of resources and close or it'll become a project subsidized by the profits of another business. Nothing can operate at a loss forever.

Profit is important because it allows businesses to stay in operation. Without generating Profits, a business can't compensate its owners, who may be investing considerable time, money, and energy into the operation. If the owners don't find their investment worthwhile, they'll simply close the business.

Profit also provides a "cushion" that allows the business to weather unexpected events. If a business is barely generating enough revenue to cover its expenses and those expenses suddenly rise, the business is in a great deal of trouble. The more profitable the business, the better it will be able to handle *Uncertainty* and *Change*, and the more options it has to respond to the unforeseeable.

Profit is a very important consideration, but it's not the be-all and end-all of business. Some people believe that the purpose of a business is to maximize the amount of Profit generated, but that's not the only reason businesses are created. For some people (like me), business is more of a creative endeavor—a way to explore what's possible, help others, and support yourself at the same time. From this perspective, as long as you're making *enough* Profit, your business will continue to be successful.

The concepts you'll learn in this chapter will help you ensure that your business creates enough Profit to keep going.

SHARE THIS CONCEPT: http://book.personalmba.com/profit/

Profit Margin

> I never lost money by turning a profit.
> —BERNARD BARUCH, FINANCIER AND PHILANTHROPIST

Profit Margin (often abbreviated to "margin") is the difference between how much revenue you capture and how much you spend to capture it, expressed in percentage terms. Here's the formula for Profit Margin:

$$((\text{Revenue} - \text{Cost}) / \text{Revenue}) \times 100 = \% \text{ Profit Margin}$$

If you spend $1 to get $2, that's a 50 percent Profit Margin. If you're able to create a *Product* for $100 and sell it for $150, that's a *Profit* of $50 and a Profit Margin of 33 percent. If you're able to sell the same product for $300, that's a margin of 66 percent. The higher the price and the lower the cost, the higher the Profit Margin. In any case, your Profit Margin can never exceed 100 percent, which only happens if you're able to sell something that cost you nothing.

Profit Margin is not the same as *markup*, which represents how the price of an offer compares to its total cost. Here's the formula for markup:

$$((\text{Price} - \text{Cost}) / \text{Cost}) \times 100 = \% \text{ Markup}$$

If the cost of an offer is \$1 and you sell it for \$2, your markup is 100 percent, but your Profit Margin is only 50 percent. Margins can never be more than 100 percent, but markups can be 200 percent, 500 percent, or 10,000 percent, depending on the price and the total cost of the offer. The higher your price and the lower your cost, the higher your markup.

Most businesses try to keep each offer's Profit Margin as high as possible, which makes sense: the higher the margin, the more money the business gets to keep from each sale. Regardless, there are many market pressures that can lead to a decline in margins over time: aggressive pricing by competitors, new offers that decrease demand for older offers, and rising input costs.

Businesses often use Profit Margin as a way of comparing offers. If a company has more than one offer in the market, it tends to favor the offers with the highest margins. If a business needs to cut costs, it often starts by eliminating offers with the lowest margins.

When examining a business, pay close attention to Profit Margin. The higher the margin, the stronger the business.

SHARE THIS CONCEPT: http://book.personalmba.com/profit-margin/

Value Capture

> You can get anything you want in this life if you help enough other people get what they want.
>
> —ZIG ZIGLAR, SALES GURU

Every business must capture some percentage of the value it creates in the form of revenue as *Profit*. If it doesn't, the business will have a difficult time generating enough resources over time to continue operation.

Value Capture is the process of retaining some percentage of the value provided in every *Transaction*. If you're able to offer another business something that will allow them to bring in \$1 million of additional revenue and you charge \$100,000, you're capturing 10 percent of the value created by the Transaction.

Value Capture is tricky. In order to be successful, you need to capture enough value to make your investment of time and energy worthwhile, but not so much that there's no reason for your customers to do business with you. People buy because they believe they're getting more value in the Transaction than they're spending.

The more value you capture, the less attractive your offer becomes. Capture too much, and your prospects won't bother purchasing from you. Movies are great, but would you pay $5,000 for two hours of entertainment?

There are two dominant philosophies behind Value Capture: maximization and minimization.

Maximization (the approach taught in most business schools) means that a business should attempt to capture as much value as possible. Accordingly, the business should attempt to capture as much revenue in each Transaction as possible—capturing less than the maximum amount of value possible is unacceptable.

In the short run, it's easy to see the appeal of maximization—more Profit is a good thing for the owners of a company. Unfortunately, the maximization approach tends to erode the reason customers purchase from a business in the first place.

Would you spend $999,999 in order to make a million? It may be rational (after all, you'd be $1 ahead), but most people won't bother. Customers purchase from you because they're receiving more value than they're giving up in the purchase. The less they receive, the less they'll want to buy from you.

The minimization approach means that businesses should capture as little value as possible, as long as the business remains **Sufficient** (discussed later). While this approach may not bring in as much short-term revenue as maximization, it preserves the value customers see in doing business with the company, which is necessary for the business's long-term success.

When something is a "good deal," customers tend to continue to patronize the business and spread the word to other potential customers. When a business tries to maximize revenue by "nickel-and-diming" their customers or trying to capture too much value, customers flee.

As long as you're bringing in enough to keep doing what you're doing, there's no need to fight for every last penny. Create as much value as you possibly can, then capture enough of that value to make it worthwhile to keep operating.

SHARE THIS CONCEPT: http://book.personalmba.com/value-capture/

Sufficiency

Know contentment and you will suffer no disgrace; know when to stop and you will meet with no danger. You can then endure.

—LAO TZU, ANCIENT CHINESE PHILOSOPHER

Once, a powerful executive went on vacation—his first in fifteen years. As he was exploring a pier in a small coastal fishing village, a tuna fisherman docked his boat. As the Fisherman lashed his boat to the pier, the Executive complimented him on the size and quality of his fish.

"How long did it take you to catch these fish?" the Executive asked.

"Only a little while," the Fisherman replied.

"Why don't you stay out longer and catch more?" the Executive asked.

"I have enough to support my family's needs," said the Fisherman.

"But," asked the Executive, "what do you do with the rest of your time?"

The Fisherman replied, "I sleep late, fish a little, play with my children, take a siesta with my wife, and stroll into the village each evening, where I sip wine and play guitar with my friends. I have a full and busy life."

The Executive was flabbergasted. "I'm a Harvard MBA, and I can help you. You should spend more time fishing. With the proceeds, you could buy a bigger boat. A bigger boat would help you catch more fish, which you could sell to buy several boats. Eventually, you'd own an entire fleet.

"Instead of selling your catch to a middleman you could sell directly to the consumers, which would improve your margins. Eventually, you could open your own factory, so you'd control the product, the processing, and the distribution. Of course, you'd have to leave this village and move to the city so you could run your expanding enterprise."

The Fisherman was quiet for a moment, then asked, "How long would this take?"

"Fifteen, twenty years. Twenty-five, tops."

"Then what?"

The Executive laughed. "That's the best part. When the time is right, you'd take your company public and sell all of your stock. You'd make millions."

"Millions? What would I do then?"

The Executive paused for a moment. "You could retire, sleep late, fish a little, play with your children, take a siesta with your wife, and stroll into the village each evening to sip wine and play the guitar with your friends."

Shaking his head, the Executive bade the Fisherman farewell. Immediately after returning from vacation, the Executive resigned from his position.

I'm not sure where this parable originated, but the message is useful: business is not necessarily about maximizing **Profits**. Profits are important, but they're a means to an end: creating value, paying expenses, compensating the people who run the business, and supporting yourself and your loved ones. Dollars aren't an end in themselves: money is a tool, and the usefulness of that tool depends on what you intend to *do* with it.

Your business does not have to bring in millions or billions of dollars to be successful. If you have enough profit to do the things you need to do to keep the business running and make it worth your time, you're successful, no matter how much revenue your business brings in.

Sufficiency is the point where a business is bringing in enough profit that the people who are running the business find it worthwhile to keep going for the foreseeable future. Paul Graham, venture capitalist and founder of Y Combinator (an early-stage venture capital firm), calls the point of sufficiency "ramen profitable"—being profitable enough to pay your rent, keep the utilities running, and buy inexpensive food like ramen noodles. You may not be raking in millions of dollars, but you have enough revenue to keep building your venture without going under.

You can't create value if you can't pay the bills. If you're not bringing in sufficient revenue to cover the operating expenses, that's a major issue. In order to keep going, you must be able to pay the employees and the owners for the time, effort, and attention they're giving to the venture. If these people don't find their investment sufficiently worthwhile, they'll stop doing what they're doing and start doing something else.

You can track financial sufficiency using a number called "target monthly revenue" (TMR). Since employees, contractors, and vendors are typically paid on a monthly basis, it's relatively simple to calculate how much money you'll need to pay out each month. Your target monthly revenue helps you determine whether or not you've reached the point of Sufficiency: as long as you bring in more than your TMR, you're Sufficient. If not, you have work to do.

Sufficiency is subjective—how much is enough to continue what you're doing is a personal decision. If your financial needs are meager, you don't need that much revenue to keep going. If you're spending millions of dollars on payroll, office space, and expensive systems, you'll need much more revenue to maintain Sufficiency.

The more quickly you can reach the point of Sufficiency, the better the chance your business will survive and thrive. The more revenue you generate and the less money you spend, the quicker you will reach the point of Sufficiency.

Once you reach the point of Sufficiency, you're successful—no matter how much (or how little) money you make.

SHARE THIS CONCEPT: http://book.personalmba.com/sufficiency/

Valuation

The whole value of the dime is knowing what to do with it.

—RALPH WALDO EMERSON

We've talked about how to estimate the value of an offer, but how do you calculate the worth of a company?

Valuation is an estimate of the total worth of a company. The higher a business's revenues, the stronger the company's *Profit Margins*, the higher its bank balance, and the more promising its future, the higher its Valuation.

Many companies base their financial decisions on what will increase the business's Valuation. Higher estimates of value are beneficial for many reasons. If a company is private, having a high Valuation makes it easier to borrow money. If the company is public, a high Valuation leads to a high share price and a profit opportunity for the shareholders. If another business seeks to acquire the company, a high Valuation leads to a big payday for the business's owners or shareholders.

Valuation is also important if you intend to take on investors. The amount of **Capital** you raise, as well as the total amount of ownership you give to your investors in exchange, depends on the business's current Valuation at the time of investment. The higher the business's Valuation, the more money you'll be able to command for every share you sell to the investor. (If you're interested in how this works, I recommend *Venture Deals* by Brad Feld and Jason Mendelson.)

It's important to note that **Perceived Value** applies just as much to businesses as it does to individual offers. When people believe a company has bright future prospects, the company's Valuation increases. If people believe the company is in trouble, the Valuation decreases. This dynamic explains why some companies, like Amazon.com, have share prices equal to over one hundred times the company's most recent earnings per share report, while troubled companies sometimes sell for less than the liquidation value of their current assets.

Valuation is important to consider if you intend to sell shares of the company to investors or are positioning your business for future acquisition. If you own your own business and never intend to sell it, Valuation considerations become less important. If you're an executive of a public company, building a business you'd like to sell someday, or investing your capital in a company, Valuation may be on the top of your mind every day.

SHARE THIS CONCEPT: http://book.personalmba.com/valuation/

Cash Flow Statement

Lack of money is the root of all evil.
—MARK TWAIN

In order to understand how well a company is performing, it's useful to look at financial reports that track the business's performance. Where should you begin?

I recommend starting with the **Cash Flow Statement**. We'll examine the other basic types of financial statements in a moment, but examining the Cash Flow Statement is the best place to begin.

The Cash Flow Statement is straightforward: it's an examination of a company's bank account over a certain period of time. Think of it like a checking account ledger: deposits of cash flow in and withdrawals of cash flow out. Ideally, more money flows in than flows out, and the total never goes below zero.

Every Cash Flow Statement covers a specific period of time: a day, a week, a month, a year. The time period of the report depends on the purpose. Shorter periods, like days and weeks, are most useful for making sure the company doesn't run out of cash. Longer periods, like months and years, are more useful for tracking performance over time.

Cash tends to move in three primary areas: *operations* (selling offers and buying inputs), *investing* (collecting dividends and paying for capital expenses), and *financing* (borrowing money and paying it back). Cash Flow Statements usually track these sources separately to make it easy to see where the cash flows come from.

The nice thing about cash is that it doesn't lie. Barring outright fraud, cash is either in the bank account or it's not. If the company spends a lot of money, but less is coming in, the business's cash position will decrease over time. There's little room for "creative interpretation."

Many investors use a metric called "free cash flow" when evaluating companies. This metric comes from the Cash Flow Statement: it's the amount of cash a business collects from operations minus cash spent for capital equipment and assets, which are necessary to keep the company operating. The higher a company's free cash flow, the better: it means the business doesn't have to keep investing huge amounts of capital in order to continue bringing in money.

In every business, cash represents options: the option to create new offers, invest in marketing and sales, hire employees, purchase equipment, acquire another company, etc. As a general rule, the more cash your business has at its disposal, the more options it has, and the more *Resilient* (discussed later) the business becomes.

SHARE THIS CONCEPT: http://book.personalmba.com/cash-flow-statement/

Income Statement

> When I was young, I thought money was the most important thing in life. Now that I'm old, I know it is.
>
> —OSCAR WILDE

Cash is important, but it's not the whole picture. Cash is not *Profit*, and Profit is what we're after. It's possible to have a nice, comfortable cash position for a while, but lose money with every sale.

Imagine a *Retailer* that buys products from a manufacturer on credit: it receives inventory, but doesn't have to pay the manufacturer for ninety days. For three months, the sales roll in, and the retailer's cash position grows and grows. To the untrained eye, things look great.

After ninety days, the manufacturer's invoice comes due. When you total the cost of the products and the retailer's operating expenses, you discover the truth: the company lost money, even though the cash balance looked great for three months. If the retailer doesn't do something, it'll eventually run out of money and close. Businesses can't exist without Profits for long.

The retailer's error was relying on cash accounting without understanding the limitations. For many types of businesses, cash accounting is ideal: it's simple and easy to understand. As long as you bring in more cash than you spend, and you don't run out of money, life is good. I've run my businesses using cash accounting for years. I get paid immediately when I provide products and services, and I don't have an inventory to manage. My business isn't complicated, so my accounting and financial tracking don't need to be complicated.

For other businesses, relying on a *Cash Flow Statement* isn't enough. If the business manages an inventory or extends credit to customers, a simple cash flow analysis can be misleading. In order to determine whether or not your sales are profitable, you need to be able to track which sales and expenses are related. By matching each sale with the expenses incurred in the process of making that sale, it's possible to see if you're making a profit immediately, without unpleasant surprises.

First, the company must change the way it accounts for expenses. Instead of recording revenue when cash flows in, and an expense when cash flows out, the company begins tracking revenue and expenses on what's called an *accrual* basis.

In accrual accounting, revenue is recognized immediately when a sale is made (i.e., a product is purchased, a service is rendered, etc.), and the expenses associated with that sale are incurred in the same time period.

Accountants call this the "matching principle," and one of the primary jobs of an accountant is to match revenue and expenses as accurately as possible. This is harder than it sounds: an incredible amount of judgment is required, and ambiguous areas are common. (If you've ever wondered what accountants do all day, this is a big part of the job.)

The end result of this effort is an **Income Statement**, which is sometimes called a "Profit and Loss Statement," "Operating Statement," or "Earnings Statement." Regardless of the label, the Income Statement contains an estimate of the business's Profit over a certain period of time, once revenue is matched with the related expenses.

The general format for an Income Statement looks like this:

Revenue – Cost of Goods Sold – Expenses – Taxes = Net Profit

Income Statements are very useful: there's a reason businesses go to the trouble of creating them. By matching expenses with revenue, it's easier to look at the company's profitability and make decisions that will improve the company's bank account in the weeks and months to come.

That said, it's important to recognize that Income Statements, by nature, include many estimates and assumptions. They have to: large expenses like equipment purchases may involve a huge cash outlay, but the Income Statement attributes a small piece of the expense to each sales period, a practice called **Amortization** (discussed later). This practice helps match the expense to the associated revenue: looking at a huge negative cash flow statement for that period would be misleading.

The matching principle, for all of its benefits, introduces many sources of potential bias in the Income Statement. By changing when revenue is recognized and how expenses are matched to that revenue, accountants and finance professionals can make the "profit" line skyrocket or implode by changing a few assumptions or formulas.

Exploring every source of potential bias in the Income Statement is way beyond the scope of this book. If you're interested in more detail on this topic, I highly recommend *Financial Intelligence for Entrepreneurs* by Karen Berman and Joe Knight with John Case.

If you suspect your business needs accrual accounting to generate an accurate Income Statement, don't do it yourself: talk to a CPA or CFA as soon as possible. The more accurate and reliable your Income Statement is, the better you'll be able to manage your business: money well spent.

SHARE THIS CONCEPT: http://book.personalmba.com/income-statement/

Balance Sheet

If you would know the value of money, go try and borrow some.
—BENJAMIN FRANKLIN

A **Balance Sheet** is a snapshot of what a business owns and what it owes at a particular moment in time. You can think of it as an estimate of the company's net worth at the time the Balance Sheet was created.

Balance Sheets always cite a specific day and use this calculation:

Assets – Liabilities = Owner's Equity

Assets are things the company owns that have value: products, equipment, stock, etc. *Liabilities* are obligations the firm hasn't yet discharged: loans, financing, etc. What's left over when you discharge all of the business's liabilities is *Owner's Equity*, the company's "net worth."

For smaller businesses, the Balance Sheet is pretty straightforward: count your cash on hand, add the estimated market value of any assets you own, and subtract all debt and current obligations. Voilà: you've created a basic Balance Sheet.

For larger businesses, the Balance Sheet is more complicated and there are more entries to keep track of. Common assets include cash, *accounts receivable* (credit that you've extended to customers), inventory, equipment, and property. Common liabilities include long- and short-term debt, *accounts payable* (credit that other firms have extended to you), and other obligations. Owner's equity includes the value of the company's stock, capital from investors, and retained earnings (profit that hasn't been paid to the company's shareholders).

What makes the Balance Sheet "balance" is the secondary form of the calculation, which is a rearrangement of the first equation:

Assets = Liabilities + Owner's Equity

This calculation looks odd at first: why would you ever want to add Liabilities and Owner's Equity?

Here's why: when a business borrows money, it receives the amount of cash borrowed. That goes on the *Cash Flow Statement*, and the influx of money makes it look like the business had a very good month if you don't notice it's a loan. When you think about it, the company's financial picture didn't really change: the business now has more assets (more cash), but it also has a new liability (more debt). The company's "net worth" didn't change at all.

The second formula is useful because it reflects this relationship. Let's assume you're starting a business, and you borrow $10,000. Before you borrow the money, your Balance Sheet looks like this:

$0 = $0 + $0 (you have no assets, no liabilities, and no equity)

After you borrow the money, your Balance Sheet looks like this:

$10,000 = $10,000 + $0 (you have $10,000 in assets, $10,000 in liabilities, and no equity)

Both sides of the Balance Sheet are the same. The Balance Sheet always balances. If it doesn't balance, you've made an error.

Since Balance Sheets are snapshots of a moment in time, it's common to review several of them at a time. For example, a company might include Balance Sheets calculated on the last day of its fiscal year for the past two or three years. By comparing the balance sheets, it's easy to see how assets, liabilities, and owner's equity have changed over time.

Balance Sheets are valuable because they answer many important questions about the financial health of a business. By examining a company's Balance Sheet, you can determine whether or not the company is solvent (i.e., its assets are greater than its liabilities), if it's having trouble paying its bills, or how the company's value has changed over time.

Balance Sheets, just like Income Statements, are full of assumptions and estimates that can introduce bias in the numbers. What's the value of a brand name or reputation? What percentage of the company's accounts receivable will be paid? How valuable is the business's current inventory? Don't skip the footnotes: by examining the assumptions behind the entries on the Balance Sheet, you'll develop a more accurate picture of the strength of the business.

SHARE THIS CONCEPT: http://book.personalmba.com/balance-sheet/

Financial Ratios

In the real world, the tests are all open book, and your success is inexorably determined by the lessons you glean from the free market.

—JONATHAN ROSENBERG, FORMER SENIOR VICE PRESIDENT
OF PRODUCT MANAGEMENT AT GOOGLE

Once you've compiled your business's basic financial reports, you can examine them in many different ways. One of the most effective strategies is to calculate a *Financial Ratio*: a comparison of two important elements of your business.

Financial Ratios are beneficial because they allow you to make comparisons very quickly. Instead of poring through the data in the financial reports manually, looking at a Financial Ratio helps you decide at a glance whether or not certain parts of the business are healthy. Looking at how these ratios change over time helps you see how the business is changing over time. Comparing the ratios to industry averages makes it easy to see if the company is performing like a typical company in the industry or if something is odd.

Profitability ratios indicate a business's ability to generate *Profit*. The higher your revenue and the lower your costs, the higher your profitability ratios. We've already discussed *Profit Margin*, which is a very basic profitability ratio. "Return on Assets," which is calculated by dividing net profit by total assets, tells you what percentage of every dollar invested in the business was returned as profit.

Leverage ratios indicate how your company uses debt. "Debt-to-Equity" ratios, which are calculated by dividing total liabilities by shareholders' equity, tell you how many dollars a company has borrowed for every $1 in owner's equity. If the ratio is high, it's a signal the company is highly **Leveraged**, which could be a bad sign. Other ratios, like "Interest Coverage," calculate how much of the business's profit goes to pay off interest on debt.

Liquidity ratios indicate the ability of a business to pay its bills. Running out of cash is a serious issue, so ratios like the "Current Ratio" (current assets divided by current liabilities) and the "Quick Ratio" (current assets minus inventory divided by current liabilities) make it easy to determine how close a company is to bankruptcy, or if the business is sitting on cash instead of investing money in growth or improvement.

Efficiency ratios indicate how well a business is managing assets and liabilities. The most common use is inventory management: having too little inventory is a bad thing, but having too much is also bad. Calculating the average number of days an item is in inventory, how long it takes to sell out current inventory, and "Day Sales Outstanding," a measure of how long it takes to collect the cash from sales, are helpful when making changes in production, managing inventory on hand, and planning future capital investments.

There are thousands of different types of Financial Ratios, and covering them all is way beyond the scope of this book. Financial analysts tend to choose a small set of important ratios based on the industry: it makes no sense to calculate "inventory turns" for a barbershop. Every business has a small number of important ratios to consider; it's worthwhile to do a bit of research to see what they are for your industry.

We'll discuss other **Ratios** in chapter 10: the technique is useful in many areas outside of finance. For now, remember that Financial Ratios are useful for sanity-checking profit, debt, cash, and efficiency without spending too much time.

SHARE THIS CONCEPT: http://book.personalmba.com/financial-ratios/

Cost-Benefit Analysis

I must study the plain physical facts of the case, ascertain what is possible,
and learn what appears to be wise and right. The subject is difficult, and good
men do not agree.

—ABRAHAM LINCOLN

The purpose of financial analysis isn't to produce impressive-looking spreadsheets: it's to make better decisions. If the data you're examining doesn't lead to changes that improve your business, you're wasting your time. The core of finance is examining a potential action, consulting the data you have at your disposal, and deciding what (if anything) to do.

Cost-Benefit Analysis is the process of examining potential changes to your business to see if the benefits outweigh the costs. Instead of acting on a change the moment you think of it, you take a step back to evaluate the true cost of the action and whether or not you believe it's the best thing you can do with your limited time, energy, and resources.

When conducting a Cost-Benefit Analysis, it's important to include costs and benefits that aren't purely financial. Noneconomic costs, like enjoyment, can play a large role in whether or not a project is worth pursuing. Google's famous cafeteria benefits are a good example: the company provides free, high-quality food to employees around the clock. This policy looks like a huge cost until you consider the benefit: by providing breakfast, lunch, dinner, and snacks, the company is encouraging employees to be at work as much as possible. The cost is offset by the increase in productivity and team cohesion, which is very significant.

Removing chronic frustrations and small inefficiencies can be just as beneficial. I recently spent a few hundred dollars to upgrade my computer's hard disk to a solid-state drive that is six times faster. My applications and programs now launch instantly, instead of requiring a five- to ten-second wait. That doesn't sound like much, but small improvements **Accumulate** over time. I spend most of my work time on the computer, and it's a huge difference. I'm happier, and I'm getting more work done: money well spent.

Before making a decision, evaluate the total costs and benefits. A little evaluation will ensure you spend your money in the most effective ways.

SHARE THIS CONCEPT: http://book.personalmba.com/cost-benefit-analysis/

Four Methods to Increase Revenue

Money is plentiful for those who understand the simple laws which
govern its acquisition.

—GEORGE CLAYSON, AUTHOR OF *THE RICHEST MAN IN BABYLON*

Believe it or not, there are only four ways to increase your business's revenue:

▶ Increase the number of customers you serve.

▶ Increase the average size of each *Transaction* by selling more.

▶ Increase the frequency of transactions per customer.

▶ Raise your prices.

Imagine you're operating a restaurant, and you want to increase the amount of revenue that your restaurant brings in. Here's how to apply these strategies:

Increasing the number of customers means you're trying to bring more people in the door. This strategy is relatively straightforward: more visitors to your restaurant will equal more tabs, which (assuming the average transaction size stays the same) will bring in more money.

Increasing average transaction size means you're trying to get each customer to purchase more. This is typically done through a process called *upselling*. When a customer purchases an entrée, you offer them appetizers, drinks, and dessert. The more of these items the customer purchases, the more they spend, and the more revenue you collect.

Increasing the frequency of transactions per customer means encouraging people to purchase from you more often. If your average customer comes in once a month, convincing them to patronize your business once a week will increase your revenue. The more frequently they visit your establishment, the more revenue your restaurant will bring in, assuming the average transaction size stays the same.

Raising your prices means you'll collect more revenue from every purchase a customer makes. Assuming your volume, average transaction size, and frequency stay the same, raising your prices will bring in more revenue for the same amount of effort.

Remember the lesson of *Qualification*: not every customer is a good customer. Some customers will sap your time, energy, and resources without providing the results that you're looking for. If you're spending a lot of energy serving customers who don't come in often, have a low average transaction size, don't spread the word, and complain about the price, it doesn't make sense to attract more of those customers.

Always focus the majority of your efforts on serving your ideal customers. Your ideal customers buy early, buy often, spend the most, spread the word, and are willing to pay a premium for the value you provide.

The more ideal customers you can attract, the better your business.

SHARE THIS CONCEPT: http://book.personalmba.com/4-methods-to-increase-revenue/

Pricing Power

> The moment you make a mistake in pricing, you're eating into your reputation or your profits.
>
> —KATHARINE PAINE, FOUNDER OF THE DELAHAYE GROUP

Imagine doubling your current prices. If you'd lose less than half of your customers, it's probably a good move.

Pricing Power is your ability to raise the prices you're charging over time. The less value you're capturing, the greater your pricing power. Serving customers takes time, energy, and resources—the more you earn per customer served, the better your business. Changing your prices can help you maximize your results while minimizing your effort and investment.

Pricing Power is related to a concept economists call "price elasticity." If customers are very sensitive to the price of your offer, you'll lose many customers with even a slight increase in price, meaning demand is "elastic." Established semicommodity markets like toothpaste are good examples: unless you're able to create something new and unique that customers badly want, dramatically increasing your prices is a good way to ensure that everyone stops buying your product and starts buying from your competitor.

If your customers aren't price sensitive, you could quadruple the price with little change in sales. Take luxury goods, for example—customers purchase them because they're expensive **Social Signals** (discussed later) that are exclusive because they're costly. Increasing the price of designer handbags, clothing, and watches is likely to make those items *more* desirable, not less.

Economists like to spend time graphing and calculating price elasticity, but it's not necessary—unless you already have accurate **Norms**, you can't really know how much Pricing Power you have until you actually change your prices and watch what happens. Fortunately, unless you're an established player in a large and active market (in which case you'll have Norms to work with), changing your prices very rarely has permanent effects unless your prices are broadly publicized and scrutinized; you can **Experiment** to find what works.

Pricing Power is important because raising your prices allows you to overcome the adverse effects of inflation and increased costs. Historically, currency issued by any government tends to decrease in value over time—there are many strong incentives for officials to increase the supply of currency, which debases that currency's purchasing power.

As a result, it takes more currency to purchase the same products and services necessary to stay in business, increasing your business's **Sufficiency** needs. Without adequate Pricing Power, your business may not be able to remain Sufficient in the face of higher expenses.

The higher the prices you can command, the more reliably you'll be able to maintain profit Sufficiency. If you have a choice, choose a market in which you'll have Pricing Power—it'll be much easier to maintain Sufficiency over time.

Lifetime Value

> The purpose of a customer isn't to get a sale. The purpose of a sale is to get a customer.
>
> —BILL GLAZER, ADVERTISING EXPERT

Imagine operating a lemonade stand on the sidewalk of a popular tourist destination. Each cup of lemonade costs $1. You may be busy serving customers, but each customer you serve is just passing by—you'll probably never see them again.

Contrast that with the insurance business. Assume the average customer pays a premium of $200 per month for car insurance—that's $2,400 in premiums per year. If the average customer remains with the same insurance agency for ten years, each client is worth $24,000 in premium payments over the lifetime of their relationship with the company. That's a big difference.

Lifetime Value is the total value of a customer's business over the lifetime of their relationship with your company. The more a customer purchases from you and the longer they stay with you, the more valuable that customer is to your business.

One of the reasons **Subscriptions** are so profitable is that they naturally maximize Lifetime Value. Instead of making a single sale to a customer, Subscription businesses focus on providing value—and collecting revenue—for as long as possible. The longer a customer remains Subscribed and the higher the price they pay, the higher the Lifetime Value of that customer.

The higher your average customer's Lifetime Value, the better your business. By understanding how much your average customer purchases and how long they tend to buy from you, you can place a tangible value on each new customer, which helps you make good decisions. Losing a single lemonade stand customer isn't a huge deal—losing an insurance client is.

All told, it's much better to operate in markets where customers have a high Lifetime Value. The higher the Lifetime Value of your customer, the more you can do to keep them happy, and the more you can focus on serving customers well. Maintain a long-term relationship with profitable customers, and you win.

SHARE THIS CONCEPT: http://book.personalmba.com/lifetime-value/

Allowable Acquisition Cost (AAC)

> Any business can buy incremental unit sales at a negative profit margin, but it's simpler to stand on the corner handing out $20 bills until you go broke.
>
> —MORRIS ROSENTHAL, AUTHOR OF *PRINT-ON-DEMAND BOOK PUBLISHING*
> AND BLOGGER AT FONERBOOKS.COM

Think back to the lemonade stand: how much could you spend to attract a single paying customer? Not much—you're only earning $1 per cup of lemonade, so you can't afford to spend much on marketing to individuals.

Contrast that with the insurance agency: if the *Lifetime Value* of a customer is $24,000, how much could you spend to attract a new customer? Much more.

Getting people's attention and acquiring new prospects typically costs time and resources. Once you understand the Lifetime Value of a prospect, you can calculate the maximum amount of time and resources you're willing to spend to acquire a new prospect.

Allowable Acquisition Cost (AAC) is the marketing component of Lifetime Value. The higher the average customer's Lifetime Value, the more you can spend to attract a new customer, making it possible to spread the word about your offer in new ways.

Having a high Lifetime Value even allows you to lose money on the first sale. Guthy-Renker sells a topical acne treatment called Proactiv using long-form television infomercials, which are expensive—they hire celebrity endorsers like Jessica Simpson and spend millions to produce and air those commercials. At first glance, it doesn't make any sense: the first sale is for the "low, low price" of $20. How on earth are they not losing money hand over fist?

The answer is *Subscription*. When a customer purchases Proactiv, they aren't just buying a single bottle of face goo—they're signing up to receive a bottle every month in exchange for a recurring payment. The Lifetime Value of each new Proactiv customer is so high that it doesn't matter that Guthy-Renker "goes negative" on the initial sale—the company makes a ton of money, even if it loses money on a few customers who don't continue with the program.

The first sale is sometimes called a "loss leader"—an enticing offer intended to establish a relationship with a new customer. Many Subscription businesses use loss leaders to build their subscriber base. Magazines like *Sports Illustrated* offer gimmicks like football phones and spend a fortune on their annual Swimsuit Edition in an effort to attract new subscribers.

These enticements may absorb up to a year's worth of Subscription revenue, but the company comes out ahead when you consider the Lifetime Value of each customer. Each new subscriber allows *Sports Illustrated* to charge their advertisers higher prices, which provides the bulk of the company's revenue.

To calculate your market's Allowable Acquisition Cost, start with your

average customer's Lifetime Value, then subtract your *Value Stream* costs—
what it takes to create and deliver the value promised to that customer over
your entire relationship with them. Then subtract your *Overhead* (discussed
later) divided by your total customer base, which represents the *Fixed Costs*
(discussed later) you'll need to pay to stay in business over that period of
time. Multiply the result by 1 minus your desired *Profit Margin* (if you're
shooting for a 60 percent margin, you'd use 1.00 - 0.60 = 0.40), and that's
your Allowable Acquisition Cost.

Here's an example: if your average Lifetime Value is $2,000 over a five-
year period, and the cost of *Value Creation* and delivery is $500, that leaves
you with $1,500 in revenue per customer served. Assuming your Overhead
expenses are $500,000 over the same five-year period and you have 500
customers, your Fixed Costs are $1,000 per customer, which leaves you
with $500 in revenue before marketing expenses. Assuming you're shooting
for a minimum 60 percent profit margin, you can afford to spend 40 percent of that $500 on marketing, which gives you a maximum AAC of $200
per customer. Knowing that, you can test various forms of marketing to see
if they work—if your assumptions are correct, any customer you can attract
for $200 or less will be worth the investment.

The higher the Lifetime Value of your customers, the higher the Allowable Acquisition Cost. The more each new customer is worth to your business, the more you can spend to attract a new customer and keep them
happy.

SHARE THIS CONCEPT: http://book.personalmba.com/allowable-acquisition-cost/

Overhead

Beware of little expenses; a small leak will sink a great ship.
—BENJAMIN FRANKLIN, EARLY AMERICAN POLITICAL LEADER, SCIENTIST,
AND POLYMATH

The larger your rent or mortgage payment, the more money you need to
make each month to pay your expenses. The same general principle applies
to businesses.

Overhead represents the minimum ongoing resources required for a business to continue operation. This includes all of the things you need to run your business every month, regardless of whether you sell anything: salaries, rent, utilities, equipment repairs, and so on.

The lower your Overhead, the less revenue the business requires to continue operation, and the more quickly you'll reach your point of financial **Sufficiency**. If you don't spend much, you don't have to make much to cover your expenses.

Overhead is critically important if you are building your company on a fixed amount of **Capital**. Venture capitalists and other forms of investment can provide "seed capital"—a fixed amount of money you can use to start the business. The more money you raise in capital and the more slowly you spend it, the more time you have to make the business work.

The faster you "burn" through your capital, the more money you need to raise and the more quickly you need to start bringing in revenue. If you burn through all of your start-up capital and can't raise more, game over. That's why investors and savvy entrepreneurs watch the business's "burn rate" very closely—the slower the burn, the more time you have to create a successful business.

The lower your Overhead, the more flexibility you'll have and the easier it will be to sustain your business operations indefinitely.

SHARE THIS CONCEPT: http://book.personalmba.com/overhead/

Costs: Fixed and Variable

Watch the costs and the profits will take care of themselves.

—ANDREW CARNEGIE, NINETEENTH-CENTURY INDUSTRIALIST

There's an old business adage: you have to spend money to make money. There's some truth to that statement, but not all expenses are created equal.

Fixed Costs are incurred no matter how much value you create. Your **Overhead** is a Fixed Cost: no matter what you do in any given month, you still have to pay your salaried employees and the lease on your office space.

Variable Costs are directly related to how much value you create. If you're in the business of creating cotton T-shirts, the more T-shirts you produce, the more cotton fabric you'll need. Raw materials, usage-based utilities, and hourly workers are all Variable Costs.

Reductions in Fixed Costs *Accumulate*; reductions in Variable Costs are *Amplified* by volume. If you can save $50 per month on your phone bill, that savings Accumulates to $600 per year. If you can save $0.50 on each T-shirt you produce, you'll save $500 on every 1,000 T-shirts you make.

The better you understand your costs, the more likely you are to find ways of producing as much value as possible without spending everything you make.

SHARE THIS CONCEPT: http://book.personalmba.com/costs-fixed-variable/

Incremental Degradation

Quality, quality, quality: never waver from it, even when you don't see how you can afford to keep it up. When you compromise, you become a commodity and then you die.

—GARY HIRSHBERG, FOUNDER OF STONYFIELD FARM

Believe it or not, many of the chocolate products found in the candy aisles of grocery stores are no longer "milk chocolate"—they're "chocolate-flavored candies." What gives?

To make high-quality chocolate, you have to buy high-quality cocoa beans, which are ground up to make cocoa butter. Cocoa butter is then combined with sugar, water, and emulsifiers, which help the oils in the cocoa butter "stick" to the water-saturated sugar. The liquid chocolate is then heated, poured into molds, and cooled to produce solid chocolate.

Over the years, mass-market chocolate manufacturers decided to use cheaper ingredients to keep costs down and increase profitability. Instead of buying high-quality cocoa beans, they bought less expensive beans from mediocre sources—who would notice? Then they replaced cocoa butter with vegetable oils—so much that food regulatory bodies wouldn't allow them to call it "milk chocolate" anymore. They added more emulsifiers, preservatives, and other chemical additives to keep the zombified chocolate together and to make it last forever on the shelf.

Sounds appetizing, right?

Saving money doesn't help you if you degrade the quality of your offer. At the time, these "cost saving" measures didn't appear to have a huge impact on the chocolate's quality—they seemed to be a *Trade-off* worth making. Over time, however, the *Accumulated* effects undermined the taste and quality of the product. People noticed, and so did the manufacturers: you can now buy "premium" versions that contain the original high-quality ingredients.

Finance and accounting executives get their "bean counting" reputations from focusing primarily on cutting costs—reducing expenses in an effort to make an offer or business more profitable. Cutting costs can help you increase your *Profit Margin*, but it often comes at a steep price.

If your goal is to increase your profitability, cutting costs can only take you so far. Creating and delivering value will *always* cost at least some amount of money, so there is a lower limit to how much you can cut costs before the cuts begin to diminish the value you provide. Cutting costs that are wasteful or unnecessary is certainly a good idea, but *Diminishing Returns* (discussed later) always kick in—be careful not to throw the baby out with the bath water.

Creating and delivering more value is a much better way to enhance your bottom line. You can never spend less than nothing, but there's no upper limit on the amount of value you can provide or revenue you can collect.

Control your costs, but don't undermine the reason customers buy from you in the first place.

SHARE THIS CONCEPT: http://book.personalmba.com/incremental-degradation/

Breakeven

> It is unusual, and indeed abnormal, for a concern to make money during the first several years of its existence. The initial product and initial organization are never right.
>
> —HARVEY S. FIRESTONE, FOUNDER OF THE FIRESTONE TIRE AND
> RUBBER COMPANY

Assume your business is bringing in $100,000 per month, and you're spending $50,000 each month in operating expenses. Are you making money?

It depends.

When you create a new business, it typically takes a while before you're able to bring in more than you spend. **Systems** need to be created, employees hired and trained, and marketing efforts launched before revenue starts coming in. During your ramp-up period, those expenses add up.

Let's assume our hypothetical business took a year's worth of $50,000-per-month expenses to launch—that's $600,000. Now that the business is bringing in $50,000 per month more than it needs to cover operating expenses, it can start to recoup that initial investment.

Breakeven is the point where your business's total revenue to date is equal to its total expenses to date—it's the point where your business starts creating wealth instead of consuming it. Assuming the business keeps bringing in $100,000 each month and expenses stay the same, it'll take twelve months to pay down the initial investment. After that, the business will *really* be making money—before that, it just *looks* like the business is profitable.

Your Breakeven point will change constantly. Revenue naturally fluctuates, as do expenses. Keeping a running tally of how much you spend and how much revenue you collect from the start of your business's operations is the only way to figure out whether or not you've actually made money.

The more revenue you bring in and the less you spend on an ongoing basis, the more quickly you'll reach Breakeven, making your business truly self-sustaining.

SHARE THIS CONCEPT: http://book.personalmba.com/breakeven/

Amortization

> Before every action, ask yourself: Will this bring more monkeys on my back? Will the result of my action be a blessing or a heavy burden?
>
> —ALFRED A. MONTAPERT, AUTHOR OF *THE SUPREME PHILOSOPHY OF MAN: THE LAWS OF LIFE*

You've created the toy of the century: a stuffed animal that looks and acts exactly like a real dog but doesn't need to be fed, watered, or let out in the middle of the night. Kids go absolutely crazy for your **Prototype**, and parents are already throwing their credit cards at you to make sure they get one the minute it's available. It's a foregone conclusion that you'll sell millions.

There's only one problem: in order to make these faux dogs affordable, you'll have to tool up a major factory, which will cost at least $100 million. Your bank account has nowhere near $100 million in it—that's a heck of a lot of money. How can a business afford something as expensive as a factory and still make money?

Amortization is the process of spreading the cost of a resource investment over the estimated useful life of that investment. In the case of the faux dog factory, let's assume the factory is capable of producing 10 million units during its useful life. On a per-unit basis, that brings the cost per unit of the factory down to $10. If you sell every unit you produce for $100, that's a very healthy **Profit Margin**.

Amortization can help you determine whether or not a big expense is a good idea. As long as you have a reliable estimate of how much it will cost and how much you can produce, Amortization helps you figure out whether or not investing large amounts of **Capital** makes sense.

For example, a book designer may choose to purchase a copy of Adobe InDesign, the software commonly used by professionals to typeset books. Compared to most software packages, InDesign is pricey: a single-user license costs $700. Is it worth it?

The answer depends on how many books the designer uses the software to typeset. If they never complete a project, they've wasted their money. If they use it to typeset ten books for $1,000 each, they've earned $10,000 by making a $700 investment—not bad at all. Amortized across ten projects, the cost of the software is only $70 a project, or 7 percent of the revenue each project brings in. The designer's credit card may hurt when the purchase is made, but the tool offers the ability to earn more money than would be possible otherwise.

Amortization depends on an accurate assessment of useful life, which is a prediction. Amortization doesn't work well if you don't sell what you produce or if your equipment wears out more quickly than expected. Predictions are a tricky business—if you're wrong in your estimate, your investment may cost a lot more on a per-unit basis than you originally assumed.

Crocs makes funny-looking rubber shoes. After becoming an unexpected hit, the company ramped up for huge volumes: they opened a factory in

China and started producing millions of shoes in the expectation that they'd continue to sell each unit produced. As it turned out, Crocs were a fad—sales plummeted, and the company was stuck with a lot of expensive manufacturing capacity and huge amounts of inventory it couldn't sell. Amortization couldn't save the company from careening toward bankruptcy.

Using Amortization to figure out whether or not a big investment is worth it is smart—just remember you're making a prediction, and proceed accordingly.

SHARE THIS CONCEPT: http://book.personalmba.com/amortization/

Purchasing Power

> The job of the entrepreneur is to make sure the company doesn't run out of cash.
>
> —BILL SAHLMAN, PROFESSOR AT HARVARD BUSINESS SCHOOL

Here's an old business adage you may have heard: "Cash is king."

It's true. You can have millions of dollars in orders on the books, but without cash in the bank, it doesn't matter. IOUs don't pay the bills—if you can't pay your employees or keep the lights on, you're done.

Purchasing Power is the sum total of all liquid assets a business has at its disposal. That includes your cash, credit, and any outside financing that's available. More purchasing power is always better, as long as you use that power wisely.

Purchasing Power is what you use to pay your **Overhead** and your suppliers. As long as you continue to pay them, you're in business. As soon as you run out of Purchasing Power, you're finished. Game over.

Always keep track of how much Purchasing Power you have available. How much cash do you have in the bank? How much available credit do you have access to? The more Purchasing Power you have, the better off you are.

Keeping track of your available Purchasing Power makes it *much* easier to run a business. Instead of constantly worrying about paying the bills, Purchasing Power gives you room to breathe, secure in the knowledge that you're not going to suddenly run out of money. That frees up a great deal of mental and emotional energy you can put to better use—figuring out how to improve your business.

Always pay close attention to how much Purchasing Power you have left—it's the difference between a business that stays open and a business that fails.

SHARE THIS CONCEPT: http://book.personalmba.com/purchasing-power/

Cash Flow Cycle

All truth is found in the cash account.
—CHARLIE BAHR, MANAGEMENT CONSULTANT

Money flows through a business in predictable ways. If you understand how revenue, expenses, receivables, and credit work, you can ensure that you continue to have enough *Purchasing Power* on hand to continue operation and maximize your available options.

The *Cash Flow Cycle* describes how cash *Flows* (discussed later) through a business. Think of your business's bank account like a bathtub. If you want the water in the bathtub to rise, you add more water and keep it from leaking out via the drain. The more water that flows in and the less that flows out, the higher the level of water in the tub. Revenues and expenses work the same way.

Receivables are promises of payment you've accepted from others. Receivables are attractive, because they feel like a sale—someone has promised to give you money, which is great. There's a catch, however: Receivables don't translate into cash until the promise is fulfilled. IOUs are not cash—the more quickly that promise is translated into payment, the better your cash flow. Many businesses have closed with millions of dollars of "sales" on the books.

Debt is a promise you make to pay someone at a later date. Debt is attractive because you can benefit from a purchase now while holding on to your cash until later. The later you pay, the more cash you have at your disposal. Debt can be useful, but there's also a catch: Debts typically cost additional money in the form of interest. Very often, you'll also have to pay back a portion of your Debt over time, which is called "debt service," which you can treat as another type of expense. If you can't cover your debt service, you're in trouble.

Maximizing your cash tackles the issue directly: bring in more revenue and cut costs. Increasing your product margins, making more sales, and spending less of what you bring in will always improve your cash flow.

Deferring or negotiating a longer repayment period with your creditors can also help alleviate a cash crunch. If you have a supplier, vendor, or partner who is willing to let you pay later in exchange for receiving materials or capabilities now, that allows you to keep more cash in your bank account now. You must watch this carefully: Debts can easily get out of hand if you don't keep track of how much you owe and when it's due. When done properly, however, paying creditors later can be quite useful, particularly for marketing expenses. Borrowing $1 to make $10 is a good trade; it's even better if you're able to do that for months before the first bill comes due.

To bring cash in more quickly, it's best to speed up collections and reduce the extension of credit. The faster you get paid, the better your cash flow situation. Ideally, try to get paid immediately, even before buying raw materials and delivering value.

It's common in many industries to extend credit to customers, but that doesn't mean you have to as well. Always remember that you're a business, not a bank (unless your business involves *Loans*)—collect any outstanding payments as quickly as possible.

If necessary, you can increase your Purchasing Power by taking on additional Debt or opening lines of credit. It's best to avoid using Debt or lines of credit if you don't absolutely need to, but increasing available credit certainly increases your Purchasing Power. Think of these accounts as backup funding sources—for emergency use only.

The more Purchasing Power you have, the more *Resilient* (discussed later) your business is and the better your ability to handle the unexpected.

SHARE THIS CONCEPT: http://book.personalmba.com/cash-flow-cycle/

Opportunity Cost

Business, more than any other occupation, is a continual dealing
with the future; it is a continual calculation, an instinctive exercise
in foresight.

—HENRY R. LUCE, PUBLISHER AND FOUNDER OF TIME INC.

Let's say you decide to quit your $50,000-a-year job and start a business.
Starting the business will certainly have costs of its own, but it will also cost
you the $50,000 you would have made had you stayed at your job.

Opportunity Cost is the value you're giving up by making a *Decision*. We can't
do everything at once—we can't be in more than one place at a time or
spend the same dollar on two different things simultaneously.

Whenever you invest time, energy, or resources, you're implicitly choosing not to invest that time, energy, or resources in any other way. The value
that would have been created by your next best alternative is the Opportunity Cost of that decision.

Opportunity Cost is important because there are always other options.
If you're working for a company that's paying you $30,000 a year and you
have the option to move to a company that's paying $200,000 a year for the
same work, why would you stay? If you're paying your employees or contractors less than they could make elsewhere for the same work, why would
they work for you? If your customers can spend $20 to get something you're
charging $200 for, why would they buy from you?

Opportunity Cost is important because it's hidden. As we'll discuss later
in *Absence Blindness*, humans have a hard time paying attention to what's *not*
present. Paying attention to what you're giving up by making a Decision
helps you consider all of your options accurately before making a decision.

Obsessing over Opportunity Cost too much can make you needlessly
crazy, however. If you're a natural maximizer (like I am), it's tempting to
overanalyze every Decision to make sure you've chosen the very best option
available, which can easily go well past the point of *Diminishing Returns* (discussed later). Don't get bogged down with all of the options available—
consider only what appear to be the best alternatives at the time of your
decision.

If you pay attention to the Opportunity Costs of your decisions, you'll make much better use of the resources at your disposal.

SHARE THIS CONCEPT: http://book.personalmba.com/opportunity-cost/

Time Value of Money

> They always say time changes things, but you actually have to change them yourself.
>
> —ANDY WARHOL, ARTIST

Would you rather have a million dollars today or a million dollars five years from now?

The answer is obvious: why wait? Having the money now means you can spend it now, or invest it now. A million dollars, invested at a *Compounding* (discussed next) interest rate of 5 percent, will be $1,276,281.56 five years from now. Why give up the extra quarter of a million dollars if you don't need to?

A dollar today is worth more than a dollar tomorrow. How *much* more depends on what you choose to do with that dollar. The more profitable options you have to invest that dollar, the more valuable it is.

Calculating the *Time Value of Money* is a way of making *Decisions* in the face of *Opportunity Costs*. Assuming you have various options of investing funds with various returns, the Time Value of Money can help you determine which options to choose and how much you should spend, given the alternatives.

Let's go back to the million dollars example: Assume someone offers you an investment that will deliver $1 million risk free in one year's time. What's the maximum amount you should be willing to pay for it today?

Assuming your *Next Best Alternative* is another risk-free investment with a 5 percent interest rate, you shouldn't pay anything more than $952,380. Why? Because if you took that amount and invested it in your next best alternative, you'd have a million dollars: $1,000,000 divided by 1.05 (the 5 percent interest/discount rate) equals $952,380. If you can buy the first investment for less than that amount, you'll be ahead.

The Time Value of Money is a very old idea—it was first explained in the early sixteenth century by the Spanish theologian Martín de Azpilcueta. The central insight that a dollar today is worth more than a dollar tomorrow can be extended to apply to many common financial situations.

For example, the Time Value of Money can help you figure out the maximum you should be willing to pay for a business that earns $200,000 in profit each year. Assuming an interest rate of 5 percent, no growth, and a foreseeable future of ten years, the "present value" of that series of future cash flows is $1,544,347. If you pay less than that amount, you'll come out ahead as long as your assumptions are correct. (Note: this is the "discounted cash flow method" we discussed in the *Four Pricing Methods*.)

The Time Value of Money is an extremely versatile concept, and a full exploration is beyond the scope of this book. For a more in-depth examination, I recommend picking up *The McGraw-Hill 36-Hour Course in Finance for Nonfinancial Managers* by Robert A. Cooke.

Compounding

Improve by 1% a day, and in just 70 days, you're twice as good.

—ALAN WEISS, MANAGEMENT CONSULTANT AND AUTHOR OF *GETTING STARTED IN CONSULTING* AND *MILLION DOLLAR CONSULTING*

Here's a surefire way to become a millionaire: save $10 a day for forty years in a way that earns 8 percent interest. Saving $10 a day isn't difficult—you can save $300 a month by eliminating unnecessary expenses and earn 8 percent by investing that money simply and conservatively. (I recommend *Fail-Safe Investing* by Harry Browne and *I Will Teach You to Be Rich* by Ramit Sethi if you're interested in tactical, low-risk investment strategies.)

Here's what's even more amazing: you'll only contribute $146,110 over that forty-year span. How, then, do you end up with over a million dollars?

Compounding is the **Accumulation** of gains over time. Whenever you're able to reinvest gains, your investment will build upon itself exponentially—a positive **Feedback Loop** (discussed later).

A simple example of Compounding is a savings account. Let's say your bank account earns 5 percent interest. After a year, $1 in your bank account

is going to be worth $1.05. In year two, you don't start with $1—you start
with $1.05. In year three, you'll have $1.10. In year four, you'll have $1.15.
Fourteen years after you make the initial deposit, you'll have $2.

That doesn't sound like much until you consider that this relationship
Scales. If you start with $1 million, you'll have $2 million after fourteen
years. Not bad at all.

Compounding is important because it creates the possibility of huge
gains in surprisingly short periods of time. If you reinvest the revenue your
business generates and your business is growing rapidly, you can multiply
your original investment many times over. Compounding is the secret that
explains how small companies that reinvest their profits become large companies in a few short years.

Accumulating gains inevitably produces huge results over time. The
trick is to be patient enough to wait for the reward.

SHARE THIS CONCEPT: http://book.personalmba.com/compounding/

Leverage

> We've been criticized for not understanding what the word *leverage*
> means . . . We do know what *leverage* means, and having a few mil-
> lion dollars cash in the bank is much nicer than being heavily lever-
> aged.
>
> —KENNETH H. OLSEN, FOUNDER OF THE DIGITAL EQUIPMENT CORPORATION
> (DEC), WHICH WAS ACQUIRED BY COMPAQ IN 1998

Using "other people's money" sounds like a great way to make a fortune.
Borrow some money, make a fortune, pay back your lender, and keep
the rest. What could be better?

Making money by borrowing from others can be savvy, provided you're
aware of the risks.

Leverage is the practice of using borrowed money to magnify potential
gains. Here's an example: let's assume you have $20,000 you'd like to invest
in real estate. You could use that money as a 20 percent down payment on
a $100,000 property, borrowing $80,000, but that ties up all of your money
in a single investment.

Instead of using the $20,000 for a single down payment, you could take the same pool of money and invest in four $100,000 properties, each with a down payment of $5,000. That strategy requires borrowing $95,000 four times—a total of $380,000 in loans.

Here's where the magic happens. Let's assume all of the properties double in value, and you sell them. In the first scenario, you'd make $100,000 on a $20,000 investment—a 5x return on your $20,000 down payment. In the second scenario, you'd make $400,000 on the very same $20,000 down payment—a 20x return on investment. Leverage seems like a no-brainer, right?

Not so fast—what will happen if the value of each property drops dramatically, and you sell them all to get back as much money as possible? Assuming the property value drops by 50 percent, in the first scenario you'd lose $50,000. In the second scenario, the use of Leverage will magnify your losses to $200,000—four times as much.

Leverage is a form of financial *Amplification*—it magnifies the potential for both gains and losses. When your investment pays off, Leverage helps it pay off more. When your investment tanks, you lose more money than you would otherwise.

One of the major contributing factors of the recession of 2008–9 was the use of enormous amounts of Leverage by investment banks. It wasn't uncommon for banks to Leverage their investments by a factor of thirty or forty. Millions (or billions) of dollars were made or lost when the value of a particular stock went up or down by a single percentage point. When the market crashed, a bank's losses were magnified by the amount of Leverage they had taken on, which was more than enough to threaten the entire firm's existence.

Using Leverage is playing with fire—it can be a useful tool if used properly, but it can also burn you severely. Never use Leverage unless you're fully aware of the consequences and are prepared to accept them. Otherwise, you're putting your business and personal financial situation at risk.

Hierarchy of Funding

Money often costs too much.

—RALPH WALDO EMERSON, ESSAYIST AND POET

Imagine you've invented an antigravity device that can levitate solid objects without requiring much power. Your invention will revolutionize the transportation and manufacturing industries, making many new products possible. Demand for your invention is a given—all you need to do is create enough devices to fill the demand.

There's a problem, however—estimates indicate that tooling up a production line with the equipment you need to build these devices will cost $1 billion. Unfortunately, you don't have $1 billion to spare. Your device obviously solves a huge problem, but the next step is out of reach. What do you do?

Funding can help you do things that would otherwise be impossible with your current budget. If your business requires expensive equipment or many workers to create and deliver value, you'll probably need outside Funding. Few of us have enormous sums of money in our bank accounts waiting to be used, but it's surprisingly easy to reach out to those that do.

Funding is the business equivalent of rocket fuel. If your business needs additional capacity and is already pointed in the right direction, judicious use of financing can help you accelerate the operation's growth. If the business has structural issues, it will explode, and not in a good way.

In order to obtain access to Funding, it's often necessary to give up a certain amount of control over the business's operations. Businesspeople won't give you money for nothing—they always ask for something in return.

Remember, providing **Capital** is a form of value for many businesses. In exchange for resources, your lenders or investors are looking for value in return—interest, lease payments, or a share of your company's profits. They're also looking for a way to decrease their risk of losing everything if the business goes under. To alleviate this risk, they ask for control: the ability to influence the operations of the business. The more money you ask for, the more control they'll want.

I think it's useful to imagine a **Hierarchy of Funding**: a ladder of available options. Every businessperson starts on the bottom and climbs as far up the ladder as necessary. The higher you climb, the more Funding you get, and the more control you give up in exchange.

Let's examine the Hierarchy of Funding, starting at the bottom:

Personal Cash is by far the best form of financing. Investing cash you already own is quick, easy, and requires no approval or paperwork. Most entrepreneurs begin by financing themselves out of cash as much as possible.

Personal Credit is another low-cost method of financing. As long as your needs don't exceed a few thousand dollars, it's easy to finance expenses via Personal Credit. Approval is generally quick if you have good credit, and payment over time helps increase your cash flow. You risk ruining your personal credit rating (a form of **Reputation**) if you can't make your payments, but for many entrepreneurs, that's a risk worth taking.

I financed my entire business out of cash and personal credit. If your needs are modest, using personal credit to finance your start-up costs is a good option as long as you watch your budget.

Personal Loans are typically made by friends and family. If you need more money than you can cover via Personal Cash and Personal Credit, loans from friends and family are not uncommon. Just be wary: the risk that you won't be able to pay them back is very real and can have a devastating effect on important personal relationships. For that reason, I'd advise avoiding asking your parents or grandparents to gamble their life savings on your idea—there are better ways.

Unsecured Loans are typically made by banks and credit unions. You fill out an application, ask for a certain amount of money, and the bank will evaluate your ability to pay the loan back with interest over a certain time period. The loan can be either a lump sum or a line of credit that can be used at any time. The bank doesn't ask for collateral for smaller amounts (a few thousand dollars), so the interest rate will probably be a bit higher than a credit card or secured loan.

Secured Loans require collateral. Mortgages and automotive loans are good examples of secured loans: if you don't make the payments, the lender can legally seize the property promised as collateral. Because the lender can then sell that property to recoup their funds, Secured Loans are much larger than Unsecured Loans: tens or hundreds of thousands of dollars.

Bonds are debt sold to individual lenders. Instead of asking a bank for a loan directly, the business asks individuals or other companies to loan them money directly. Bond purchasers give money directly to the business, which is paid back at an agreed-upon rate for a certain amount of time. When the time expires (i.e., the Bond "matures"), the company must give back the original loan amount in addition to the payments already made. The legal and regulatory process that surrounds the Bond market can be extremely complicated, so Bond issues are typically conducted through an investment bank.

Receivables Financing is a special type of secured lending unique to businesses. Receivables Financing can make millions of dollars in credit available, but at a cost: the collateral for the loan is control over the business's receivables. Since the bank controls the receivables, they can ensure their loan is paid before anything else, including employee salaries and vendor commitments. Large amounts of funding are available, but you're giving up a great deal of control to the lender.

Angel Capital is where we shift from **Loans** to **Capital**. An "angel" is an individual private investor—someone who has excess wealth they'd like to invest in a private business, typically $10,000 to $1 million. In exchange, they'll own 1 to 10 percent of the business.

Taking on an angel investor is a bit like taking on a silent partner—they give you Capital, and in exchange you give them partial legal ownership of the business. Some angels offer advice and are available for consulting, but they generally don't have the power to make business decisions.

Venture Capital takes over where angels leave off. Venture Capitalists (VCs) are extremely wealthy investors (or groups of investors who pool their funds) with very large sums of Capital available: tens (or hundreds) of millions of dollars in a single investment. Funding via Venture Capital happens in "rounds" that start small, then grow as more Capital is needed. Later rounds can dilute the ownership percentage of current shareholders, so there's typically a great deal of negotiation involved. VCs also require large amounts of control in exchange for large amounts of Capital, which usually means seats on the company's board of directors.

A **Public Stock Offering** involves selling partial ownership of the company to investors on the open market. This is typically done via investment banks: companies that will provide a business with enormous amounts of Capital in exchange for the shares of that company to sell on the public stock market. The investment banks make money by selling the shares they've purchased at a premium to individual investors on the open market. An initial public offering (IPO) is simply the first Public Stock Offering a company offers on the open market.

Any investor who purchases shares is legally a partial owner of the company, which includes the right to participate in management decisions via electing the board of directors. Whoever owns the most shares in the company controls it, so "going public" creates the risk of a hostile takeover: the mass purchasing of shares in an effort to control the company.

Public Stock Offerings are typically used by angel and Venture Capital investors to exchange ownership for money. Investors can collect their returns in one of two ways: reaping dividends that distribute the *Profits* of the company or selling their shares to another investor. Public Stock Offerings enable investors to sell their shares in exchange for money, so it's common for angels and VCs to push successful companies to "go public" or be acquired by another company as quickly as possible in order to "cash out" of the investment.

The more control you must give up for each dollar of Funding obtained, the less attractive the source of Funding. The more people you're required to consult with before making decisions, the slower your company will operate. Investors increase *Communication Overhead* (discussed later), which can adversely affect your ability to get things done quickly.

It's also not uncommon for investors to remove executives of a company that's not performing well, even if those executives are the founders of the company. Even high-flying executives aren't immune: when Apple was performing poorly in the 1990s, the board of directors fired Steve Jobs from the company he cofounded. A word to the wise: before you take on large amounts of Capital, be aware of how much *Power* (discussed later) the business's board of directors will have over the operation of the company.

Funding can be useful, but be wary of giving up control over your business's operations—don't do it lightly or blindly.

SHARE THIS CONCEPT: http://book.personalmba.com/hierarchy-of-funding/

Bootstrapping

Felix qui nihil debet. (Happy is he who owes nothing.)

—ROMAN PROVERB

How much financing you need depends largely on what you're trying to do. If you're grasping for the brass ring—becoming obscenely wealthy by building a massive public company—you'll probably need financing. If your intent is to be self-sufficient and free to make your own decisions, it's much better to avoid financing in favor of retaining control.

Bootstrapping is the art of building and operating a business without **Funding**. Don't assume that the only way to create a successful business is by raising millions of dollars of **Venture Capital**—it's simply not true. By limiting yourself to the use of **Personal Cash, Personal Credit**, the business's revenue, and a little ingenuity, you can build extremely successful businesses without seeking Funding at all. My business operates via a checking account, a savings account, and a business credit card, and I like it that way.

Bootstrapping allows you to grow your business while maintaining 100 percent control over the business's operations. You don't have to get anyone else's approval to make the decisions you think are best. The drawback is that growing the business can take much longer—prudently used, Funding can help make things happen much more quickly than they'd happen otherwise.

If you accept Funding, make sure that you use it to do things that you couldn't do any other way. **Force Multipliers** are useful but expensive—taking on Funding in order to get access to critical capabilities can be smart. Otherwise, try to operate from cash and operating revenue as much as possible.

For best results, Bootstrap as far as you can go, then move up the **Hierarchy of Funding** only as needed. Having 100 percent ownership and control of a profitable, self-sustaining business is a beautiful thing.

SHARE THIS CONCEPT: http://book.personalmba.com/bootstrapping/

Return on Investment (ROI)

Wise are those who learn that the bottom line doesn't always have
to be the top priority.

—WILLIAM A. WARD, APHORIST

When you invest in something, you expect it to provide more value than
you paid for it. Knowing how to estimate how much you'll receive versus
how much you'd invest is a very useful skill.

Return on Investment (ROI) is the value created from an investment of time
or resources. Most people think of ROI in terms of currency: if you invest
$1,000 and you collect $100 in profit, that's a 10 percent return on your investment: ($1,000 + $100) / $1,000 = 1.10, or 10 percent. If your ROI is
100 percent, you've doubled your initial investment.

Return on Investment can help you decide between competing alternatives. If you deposit money in a savings account, the return on your investment will be equal to the interest rate that the bank gives you to hold your
money. Why put your money in an account that pays 1 percent interest if
you can deposit that money in an account that pays 2 percent, with no difference in fees?

The usefulness of Return on Investment extends far beyond money: you
can use it for other **Universal Currencies** as well. "Return on Invested Time" is
an extremely useful way to analyze the benefits of your effort. If you were
forced to work twenty-four hours a day nonstop for a year in exchange for
$1 million, would you do it? When you look at the return versus the cost
to your time and sanity, it's not worth it.

The return on every investment is always directly related to how much
the investment costs. The more you spend (in terms of both money and
time), the lower your return. Even "sure bets" like buying a house or getting
a college degree aren't wise if you pay too much for them. Every estimate
of return is speculative—you never know how it'll actually turn out. Calculating returns is an exercise in predicting the future, which is fundamentally impossible.

Every future ROI estimate is a semieducated guess. You can only know your
ROI for certain *after* the investment is made and the returns collected.
Nothing in this world is a sure bet—always take into account the risk of

something going wrong before making an investment, no matter how high the potential ROI appears to be.

SHARE THIS CONCEPT: http://book.personalmba.com/return-on-investment/

Sunk Cost

If at first you don't succeed, try, try again. Then quit. There's no point in being a damn fool about it.

—W. C. FIELDS, COMEDIAN

After returning from World War II, my grandfather started the Kaufman Construction Company, building storefronts, homes, union halls, and apartment buildings in Akron, Ohio. In 1965, after twenty-five years in the business, he kicked off his most ambitious project: a five-story, twenty-six-unit apartment building on Portage Path.

The "Baranel" was to be built on the lots of two older homes, which had been purchased and demolished for the job. Steel rebar and bricks were ordered, and excavation was proceeding as planned. The expected cost of the project was $300,000, roughly $2.4 million in 2010 dollars.

The project proceeded smoothly until the excavators found huge hidden deposits of blue clay, which could make the foundation extremely unstable. To continue the project, thousands of cubic feet of clay and dirt would have to be excavated to reach bedrock, and additional concrete and rebar would be required to fill the massive hole. Completing the building would cost far more than originally expected, but it was difficult to determine exactly how much.

Instead of walking away, Grandpa decided to finish the project—he'd already spent so much money on the land and excavation that it felt wrong to "waste it" without having something to show for the effort and investment. He found a few investors, put up another apartment building and the family home as collateral, and the project continued.

By the time the building was complete, they'd spent over three times as much money as originally planned: approximately $1 million, roughly $8 million in today's dollars when adjusted for inflation. It was more than the building was worth. Grandpa spent the rest of his career handling angry investors and lawyers. It's a sad story, but one worth learning from.

Sunk Costs are investments of time, energy, and money that can't be recovered once they've been made. No matter what you do, you can't get those resources back. Continuing to invest in a project to recoup lost resources doesn't make sense—all that matters is how much more investment is required versus the reward you expect to obtain.

Sunk Cost is easy to understand conceptually but much harder to put into practice. When you sink years of work into a career you realize you don't want, or millions of dollars into a project that unexpectedly requires millions more, it's difficult to walk away. You've invested so much that it feels wrong to "give it up for nothing." In reality, there's nothing you can do about your past investment—it's gone. All you can do is act based upon the information you have now.

Making mistakes is inevitable: no one is perfect. You *will* make a few decisions that, in retrospect, you'll wish you hadn't—count on it. If you could turn back time, you'd do things differently. Unfortunately, you can't. There will always be other projects, provided you don't double down on a risky project to recover your losses. "Throwing good money after bad" is not a winning strategy.

Don't continue to pour concrete into a bottomless pit—if it's not worth the additional investment, walk away. You never have to earn back money in the same way you lost it. If the reward isn't worth the investment required to obtain it or the risk, don't invest.

SHARE THIS CONCEPT: http://book.personalmba.com/sunk-cost/

Internal Controls

If something cannot go on forever, it will stop.
—HERBERT STEIN, ECONOMIST

One of the major benefits of tracking your financial and operations data over time is the ability to notice patterns in your revenue, costs, and **Value Chain**. Over time, these patterns become useful for budgeting, supervising operations, complying with laws and regulations, and preventing theft and fraud.

Internal Controls are a set of specific **Standard Operating Procedures** (discussed later) a business uses to collect accurate data, keep the business running smoothly, and spot trouble as quickly as possible. The better a company's internal controls, the more reliable its financial reports, and the more confidence you can have in the quality of the company's operations. Internal Controls are most useful in four areas:

Budgeting is the act of estimating future costs and taking steps to ensure that these estimates aren't exceeded without good reason. Budgets are very important in controlling **Profit Margins**, the **Cash Flow Cycle**, and **Leverage**. If part of your business breaks the budget in a given time period, you can take action to correct the situation.

Supervision is important in businesses that rely on employees or outside firms for important parts of its business process. By establishing controls related to delivery time, quality, cost, and systems failures, it's possible to conduct evaluations and make changes in operations if necessary if standards appear to slip or performance targets aren't met.

Compliance is necessary when a business operates in an industry affected by government regulations. The company may be obligated to collect and report certain data in the course of operations. Internal Controls ensure that this data is complete and accurate, preventing risks, significant losses, and potential legal issues.

Theft and Fraud Prevention is important to protect against the risk of financial loss by an unscrupulous party. Solid Internal Controls make it easier to notice something is amiss, identify the responsible party, and resolve the situation with a minimum of fuss.

In all of these areas, it's useful to have a dispassionate third party audit your data and control processes. Auditing is necessary to find and correct errors, particularly in large businesses with many moving parts. Auditing helps ensure the quality of the company's data and can increase the confidence of lenders, investors, shareholders, and regulatory bodies regarding the business's practices. In all cases, the auditing party should have no interest in the outcome: this "separation of concerns" helps ensure the results are accurate, particularly if they're not pretty.

Financial controls also help you to benchmark your company against other companies in your market. Every year, the Risk Management Association (RMA) compiles a huge amount of data from businesses in all industries. The RMA data set makes it easier to discover what solvent businesses of various sizes spend on marketing, sales, operations, and capital in a given period of time.

Banks and investors rely on RMA data to determine whether or not a business they're examining is typical. If the company's costs are in line with revenues, outside parties are likely to assume the business has a lower risk profile. If the company is spending three times the typical amount on sales and marketing, it can be a signal of trouble, inefficiency, or shady accounting.

Industry groups can also be a useful source of data. Many markets have trade associations that collect and share information about successful businesses. By comparing your business's data to that of other companies in your market, you can get a better picture of how well you're performing and where your business could use improvement.

SHARE THIS CONCEPT: http://book.personalmba.com/internal-controls/

6

THE HUMAN MIND

Ninety percent of this game is half mental.

—YOGI BERRA, FORMER PROFESSIONAL BASEBALL PLAYER AND MALAPROPIST

Now that we've covered the essentials of how businesses work, we're going to shift gears into understanding how people work.

Businesses are built *by* people *for* people. As we discussed in **Value Creation** and **Value Delivery**, if people didn't have needs and wants, businesses wouldn't exist. Likewise, if no one was able or willing to fulfill those needs and wants, businesses couldn't operate.

Understanding how we take in information, how we make decisions, and how we decide what to do or what not to do is critically important if you want to create and sustain a successful business venture. Once you have a clear picture of how the human mind works, it's easy to find better ways to get things done and work more effectively with others.

SHARE THIS CONCEPT: http://book.personalmba.com/human-mind/

Caveman Syndrome

Every man is a quotation from all his ancestors.

—RALPH WALDO EMERSON

Imagine for a moment what it would be like to have lived 100,000 years ago. Your senses are on full alert as you walk along the banks of a river, scanning for food: fish swimming in the stream, edible plants, or animals to catch. The sun is nearing its apex, and you've already walked six miles today—your callused feet will take you six miles more before the day is done.

In a few hours, you'll stop for some water and find shade: the mid-afternoon sun is blazingly hot, and rest will help you *Conserve Energy* (discussed later).

As you walk, your eyes settle on a small bush about twenty feet away. Your heart leaps—you recognize the pattern of the leaves, and you know that both the leaves and roots are good to eat. You start to dig at the earth around the base of the plant to expose the roots, intending to place the entire shrub into the simple woven basket you have strapped to your back.

Suddenly, you notice a movement out of the corner of your eye. Four feet away, a massive cobra has drawn itself up to strike, displaying its distinctive patterned hood and sharp fangs. There's no time to think—adrenaline surges, your pulse races, and you quickly jump out of the way and run away as fast as you're able, leaving the food behind.

You run until it's clear that the threat is gone, and then you spend a few minutes recovering, trembling from the exertion and the stress as the adrenaline wears off. You're disappointed about losing the food, but it wasn't worth risking your life.

Once you recover, you resume your search for food and shelter from the midday sun. Tonight, you'll return to your tribe to share what food you've found.

You know everyone well, since there are only forty or so people in the tight-knit group. You've banded together primarily for protection from wild animals and other tribes, who periodically attempt to seize your tribe's resources via raids.

Together, you make spears and nets to catch fish, turn flint into knives and axes for hunting and defense, and create baskets and clay pots to store food. On the fire, an antelope is roasting—a group of hunters in your tribe literally chased it to death, a technique called persistence hunting.

In the evening, you'll sit around the fire the group has built to cook food and keep predators away, and you'll discuss the day and tell stories until you drift off to sleep. Tomorrow, you'll do it all over again.

Human biology is optimized for conditions that existed 100,000 years ago, not for the world in which we actually live today. Food is everywhere; predators are not. You no longer have to be in constant motion; instead, you probably spend most of your time occupied by sedentary activities, like sitting behind a desk at a computer. As a result, we face many new threats to our brains and bodies, like obesity, heart disease, diabetes, Alzheimer's disease, and chronically low energy.

Your brain and body simply aren't optimized for the modern world. Part of the challenge of working in the modern world is that our brains and bodies are tuned for physical and social survival, not sixteen-hour workdays. Business hasn't been around long enough for our biology to adapt to the new demands we're placing upon ourselves.

Don't be too hard on yourself—you simply weren't built for the type of work you're currently responsible for. No one is—we're all running demanding new software on ancient hardware.

SHARE THIS CONCEPT: http://book.personalmba.com/caveman-syndrome/

Performance Requirements

> Now no joy but lacks salt / That is not dashed with pain / And weariness and fault
>
> —ROBERT FROST, POET

Pounding Red Bull and pulling all-nighters can only take you so far. If you want to do good work, taking care of yourself isn't optional. If you don't give your body what it needs to run, you'll run out of gas long before you reach your goals.

Your mind is first and foremost a physical system. Oftentimes, what we experience as mental fatigue or emotional distress is simply a signal from our body that we're not getting enough of something we physically need: nutrients, exercise, or rest.

If you want to get things done, you can't run on "empty"—the human body has **Performance Requirements**. Just as a car can't run with an empty gas tank or a broken spark plug, your body can't operate for long without a few necessary inputs. When you have a lot of work to do, it's common to think that taking care of yourself is a secondary concern. It's not—taking care of yourself should be your *primary* concern if you want to get important things done without burning out.

Nutrition, exercise, and rest are the inputs your body converts into productive energy. Poor (or too little) input inevitably reduces the quantity and quality of your output. Here are a few basic guidelines to help you get the most out of each day:

Eat high-quality food. **Garbage In, Garbage Out** (discussed later)—pay attention to what you put into your body. If you eat meat, eggs, or dairy, avoid sources that contain antibiotics or hormones. Also avoid refined sugar and processed foods as much as possible—if your great-grandparents wouldn't immediately recognize it as food, don't eat it.

Eating a small snack or meal every 2.5 hours or so helps keep your blood sugar stable, so you don't crash during the day. I'm the kind of guy who sometimes forgets to eat, so I try to keep things simple—a handful of almonds or a piece of fruit works best for me. Use caffeine in moderation—herbal tea is a good substitute for soda, and carrying a water bottle makes it much easier to stay hydrated.

Exercise regularly. According to *Brain Rules* by John Medina, even low-intensity physical activity increases energy, improves mental performance, and enhances your ability to focus. Going for a walk or run, jumping rope, or doing a bit of yoga can help clear the cobwebs in your mind and give you more energy for the rest of the day. I often swing around a fourteen-pound sledgehammer to get my blood pumping—it's a cheap and effective weight-lifting tool that doesn't take up much space. (Just don't hit anything.)[1]

Get at least seven to eight hours of sleep each night. Sleep helps consolidate the results of **Pattern Matching** and **Mental Simulation**, as well as reverse the effects of **Willpower Depletion** (all discussed later)—so don't skimp on rest. I find it useful to set an alarm to remind me to *go to bed*, giving me enough time to wind down before retiring for the night. Going to bed early helps you get up early, which is very useful if you do creative work—I find it's best to write or do other creative tasks before the day begins, so you don't get distracted and run out of time.

Get enough sun, but not too much. Vitamin D is an important part of many chemical reactions in your body, and your body can only synthesize it if your skin is exposed to direct, nonfiltered sunlight. (Light through windows doesn't count.) Just don't get too much—sunburns and skin cancer aren't fun.

Light helps set your circadian rhythm, which affects your sleeping patterns. I regularly use a light therapy device[2] to ensure that I'm getting enough light, particularly in the winter months. Getting as little as ten minutes of sunlight in the morning is a very easy way to improve both your sleep and your mood.

Feed your brain the raw materials it needs to run. If you've ever felt angry, sad, apathetic, or lethargic for no reason, your body may not be getting enough of the raw materials necessary to build the neurotransmitters responsible for making you feel good. In *The Mood Cure*, Julia Ross explains that your brain needs certain compounds to produce critical mood-altering neurotransmitters like dopamine and serotonin. Without the materials necessary to build these mood-altering chemicals, you'll feel off, even if everything in your world is going just fine.

Changes in our modern diet make it necessary to get some of these substances in supplement form. A good multivitamin supplement, fish oil, magnesium, and essential amino acids can go a long way to ensure your brain has what it needs to function effectively. Just make sure whatever you buy is highly bioavailable—supplements won't help you if they pass through your body undigested.[3]

I constantly **Experiment** with new ways to improve my energy, productivity, and mood—I recommend you do the same. **Guiding Structure** can help make these lifestyle changes much easier—changing the structure of my environment has helped me make many changes almost effortlessly, including three years on a vegan diet (no animal products). Don't be afraid to try something new to see if you notice an improvement—just be safe.

When in doubt, consider how your ancient ancestors lived, and act accordingly.

SHARE THIS CONCEPT: http://book.personalmba.com/performance-requirements/

The Onion Brain

The views expressed here do not necessarily represent the unani-
mous view of all parts of my mind.

—MALCOLM MCMAHON, BISHOP OF NOTTINGHAM

Most of us identify with the voice inside our head that's constantly commenting about the world around us. That voice is sometimes electric with
excitement, but more often it's uncertain, concerned, or scared.

Fortunately, "you" are not that voice.

"You" are only a small part of your brain. The voice in your head is just
a radio announcer, commenting on what your brain is doing automatically.
It is not *you*—your consciousness is actually what your brain uses to solve
problems it can't handle on autopilot.

Since human behavior has its roots in the brain, it's very useful to understand how your brain is actually constructed. Here's a brief (and massively oversimplified) look at how your brain works.

Think of the **Brain as an Onion**—it has several layers, which sit on top of
one another. At the core is a structure called the *hindbrain*, which is essentially responsible for keeping you alive. The hindbrain is responsible for
all of the physiological functions necessary for survival: heart rate, sleeping,
waking, reflexes, muscle movements, and biological urges.

Located at the base of the brain, the hindbrain is sometimes called the
"lizard brain" because this basic neurological structure appears in all of our
biological precursors, including reptiles and amphibians. The hindbrain is
primarily responsible for generating signals that are passed down through
your spinal cord and nerves to every part of your body, resulting in your
physical actions.

Above your hindbrain is the *midbrain*, which is responsible for processing
sensory data, emotion, memory, and **Pattern Matching** (discussed later). Our
midbrains are constantly (and automatically) predicting what will happen
next, then sending that information to the hindbrain, which readies our
body for immediate action. The midbrain is the radio announcer, and the
hindbrain is the radio.

Sitting just above the midbrain is a thin, folded layer of tissue—the *forebrain.* This small sheet of neural matter is responsible for the cognitive capabilities that make us distinctly human: self-awareness, logic, deliberation, **Inhibition**, and **Decision**.

Developmentally speaking, the forebrain is very new, and likely evolved to help us handle ambiguity. Most of the time, our midbrain and hindbrain run the show—we're operating on instinct and autopilot. That changes, however, when we face something unexpected or unfamiliar, which confounds the midbrain's ability to predict what will happen next. That's when the forebrain kicks into gear, gathering data and considering options.

After some deliberation and analysis, the forebrain decides what to do based on what appears to be best at the time. Once a Decision is made, the midbrain and hindbrain assume normal operation and carry out the decision.

Neuroscientists are probably ready to shoot me at this point, but this very basic model of the brain is accurate enough to be useful.[4] P. J. Eby, my "mind hacking" friend and mentor, uses a great analogy to explain the relationship between the different parts of your mind: your brain is a horse, and "you" are the rider. Your "horse" is intelligent—it moves on its own, can identify challenges, and will balk at things that appear dangerous or scary. "You," the rider, are there to set a direction and reassure the "horse" that it's safe to proceed.

One of the best things you can do to get more done is to dissociate yourself from the voice in your head. The radio announcer has the attention span of a two-year-old after drinking a triple espresso. Its job is to highlight things in your environment you may be interested in paying attention to—things that may fulfill one of your **Core Human Drives** or present some danger. That doesn't mean the voice is always right, or that you must take everything it says as gospel truth.

Meditation is a simple practice that can help you separate "you" from the voice in your head. There's nothing mystical or magical about meditation—you simply breathe and watch what your "monkey mind" does without associating yourself with it. After a while, the voice becomes quieter, improving your ability to keep yourself on the course you choose.

A few moments of quiet meditation every day can be the difference between feeling scared and overwhelmed and feeling in control of your destiny. If you're interested in learning to meditate, I recommend *Mindful-*

ness in Plain English by Bhante Henepola Gunaratana and *Wherever You Go, There You Are* by Jon Kabat-Zinn.

SHARE THIS CONCEPT: http://book.personalmba.com/onion-brain/

Perceptual Control

> The behavior of an organism is the output of control systems, and is performed with the purpose of controlling perceptions at desired reference values. Behavior is the control of perception.
>
> —WILLIAM T. POWERS, CONTROL SYSTEMS THEORIST AND AUTHOR OF
> *MAKING SENSE OF BEHAVIOR: THE MEANING OF CONTROL*

In the hallowed halls of businesses (and business schools) around the world, B. F. Skinner is the hidden king.

Skinner was one of the major intellectual forces behind the behaviorist movement in psychology—the idea that biological systems always respond a certain way to certain stimuli. Control the stimuli, and you can control the behavior. "Condition" the organism with rewards and punishments, and the organism will learn exactly how to behave.

Over the decades, behaviorism has fallen out of vogue in psychology—research has made it clear that there's *far* more to behavior than the carrot and the stick. Unfortunately, that hasn't extended to business practice—in corporations and business school classrooms around the world, the search continues for the magic incentive that will make people do exactly what businesses want.

In reality, human behavior is much more like a thermostat. A thermostat is a very simple system: all it consists of is a sensor, a set point, and a switch. The sensor measures the temperature of the surrounding environment. When the temperature is within a given range, the thermostat does nothing. When the temperature is below the set point, the switch turns the heater on. Once the temperature is above the set point, the switch turns the heater off.

This relationship is called *Perceptual Control*—the thermostat controls the temperature of the room by comparing the perceived temperature against the set point, then taking an action if and only if that perception is "out of control." Once the action brings the perception under control, the system stops acting until the set point is violated once again.

Living organisms—including human beings—are essentially very complex Perceptual Control systems: we act in ways to keep our perceptions of the world within acceptable boundaries. We don't put on a coat because cold weather *forces* us to—we put on a coat *because we feel cold* and we don't *want* to feel cold. If the light entering our eyes is too bright, we find shade, pull down the blinds on the windows, or put on sunglasses—the action controls the perception, and the action we ultimately take depends on the **Environment** (discussed later) we find ourselves in at the time.

In *Making Sense of Behavior: The Meaning of Control*, William T. Powers uses the following example to explain how control systems account for the wide range of behaviors human beings exhibit: imagine a ship in the middle of an ocean during a wild storm. The ship is rising and falling randomly, pitching back and forth as it's buffeted by the waves.

A rock on the deck of the ship is not a control system. The rock doesn't *want* anything, so it has nothing to control—it just tumbles wherever the forces of physics take it. A human being on the deck of the ship, however, *wants* to stay upright, and will therefore take many different actions to continue to stay standing: changing balance, moving, holding on to handrails, etc. If the human stumbles and falls, they'll take whatever actions they can to get back on their feet once more.

The Environment dictates which actions are possible to bring the perception under control. Control is not planning—it's adjusting to changes in the Environment as they actually happen. The human in the storm doesn't have the capability to predetermine what actions they'll take to stay on their feet—as the Environment changes, their actions will change in response, depending on the resources and options available at the moment.

Perceptual Control explains why the same stimulus often produces different responses. A good example of why the stimulus/response model doesn't paint the whole picture is the classic incentive of many employers: paid overtime. If you want your hourly employees to work more, you should pay more overtime, right?

Not necessarily. Workers who are controlling for income (i.e., they don't have enough and want more) will probably work more overtime, but what about workers who already feel they're making enough money or have priorities that are more important than work? A few of those workers will work exactly the same amount of time, and some will actually work *less*—they're controlling for a certain amount of income, then spending their time doing other things that are important to them, like being with their family or pursuing a side project. Raising overtime pay will allow them to reach that point more quickly, so they'll spend *less* time at work.

The overtime incentive produces three different results, two of which are complete opposites—working more and working less. So much for behaviorism.

Perceptual Control represents a fundamental shift in understanding why people do the things they do. Once you understand that people act to control their *perceptions*, you'll be better equipped to influence how they act.

SHARE THIS CONCEPT: http://book.personalmba.com/perceptual-control/

Reference Level

Action comes about if and only if we find a discrepancy between what we are experiencing and what we want to experience.

—PHILIP J. RUNKEL, PROFESSOR OF PSYCHOLOGY AND EDUCATION,
UNIVERSITY OF OREGON

At the heart of every **Perceptual Control** system is a **Reference Level**—a range of perceptions that indicate the system is "under control." When a perception is within the system's Reference Level, nothing happens. When the perception violates the Reference Level by being too high or too low, the system will act to bring the perception back under control.

There are three kinds of Reference Levels: set points, ranges, and errors.

A *set point* is a minimum or maximum value. The thermostat is an example of a set point—whenever the temperature falls below a certain value, the heater kicks on. Your body's production of melatonin is another set point—once it reaches a particular threshold, you'll start falling asleep.

Business financial controls are managed as set points: as long as your revenue is above a certain set point and your expenses are below a certain set point, you're okay. If you suddenly spend three times what you normally spend or your revenue falls below your point of **Sufficiency**, that triggers action—you want to find out why you overspent and how to bring your expenses back under control.

A *range* is a spread of acceptable values. The difference between a range and a set point is the existence of an upper *and* lower limit to the perception being controlled. With a set point, the perception must be above or below a certain level to be under control; with a range, the perception must be between *two* set points to be under control.

For example, your body has a system for regulating the level of glucose in your blood, which it uses for energy. Too much or too little blood glucose can be life threatening, so your body works to keep the level within an acceptable range by releasing insulin, which causes extra glucose to move into (or out of) the cells in your body. As long as your blood glucose is within the acceptable range, nothing happens. When the reference range is violated, your body starts working to bring the situation back under control.

An *error* is a set point defined as zero—any perception that's not zero is out of control. Think of the pain receptors in your skin. Most of the time, they do nothing, which means everything is under control. If you cut or burn yourself, however, the receptors send a signal that something is wrong, and you'll act to remedy the situation. Customer service complaints are a business example—if you don't receive any, everything is under control. If your in-box is filling with complaints, you know something needs to be fixed.

If you want to change a behavior, you must either change the system's Reference Level or change the **Environment** in which the system is operating. Think back to the thermostat—if you want to turn the heater off, you can change the set point to a lower temperature. If you're aware that your expenses will be three times what they were last month because you're launching a huge marketing campaign, your finances are no longer out of control. If you're in the process of getting a tattoo, pain receptors firing is an acceptable situation.

The perceptions themselves haven't changed, but you'll no longer act to bring the perception under control because *it already is under control*. Changing the Reference Level changes the behavior of the system.

Consciously defining and redefining Reference Levels can help you change your behavior. If you're worried that your spending is out of control, you can create a budget that will give you information on what your Target Monthly Revenue needs to be in order to stay **Sufficient**. If you're worried that your weight is too high or low, a visit to your doctor can help you calibrate your expectations and self-perception against medical data. If you're consistently working twelve-hour days and you decide that no more than eight is acceptable, your work habits will change.

Change the Reference Level, and your behavior will change automatically.

SHARE THIS CONCEPT: http://book.personalmba.com/reference-level/

Conservation of Energy

> The fundamental principle of human action is that men seek to gratify their desires with the least exertion.
>
> —HENRY GEORGE, AUTHOR OF *THE SCIENCE OF POLITICAL ECONOMY*, 1898

Here's a universal truth of human nature: people are generally lazy. The critical insight is that being lazy is a feature, not a bug.

Think what would happen if one of your ancient ancestors ran around all day for no good reason until they collapsed from exhaustion? If a predator or enemy appeared, they'd have no reserves left to respond to the threat—a very bad situation. As a result, we've evolved to avoid expending energy unless absolutely necessary, which I call *Conservation of Energy*.

Over the past several decades, researchers have studied marathoners and ultramarathoners (people who regularly run fifty to one hundred miles at a stretch) to learn more about how the body responds to pain. Here's what they've found: when you're so tired that it feels like you're about to kick the bucket any second, physiologically, you're *not even remotely close to actually dying*. The signals your brain is sending to your body are a ruse that serves as a warning, prompting you to keep some energy in reserve, just in case energy is needed later.

Unless a *Reference Level* is violated, people generally will Conserve Energy by not acting. Think of two roommates who share different standards of household cleanliness. To one, the presence of dirty dishes in the sink is a problem—in his mind, any dishes at all is "out of control," which prompts action to fix the situation. To the other roommate, the situation may not be out of control until the sink is overflowing, at which point he'll expend some energy washing dishes. Different Reference Levels, different actions.

If you think your weight, health, and physique are just fine, you probably won't change your diet or start exercising spontaneously. If you're comfortable with your social circle and confidence, you probably won't do much to improve your social skills or expand your circle of acquaintances. If you think you're making enough money, you probably won't do much to earn more.

Conservation of Energy explains why some people stay in dead-end jobs for decades, even though they know the position isn't great. If the work is okay, the bills get paid, and the job never becomes stressful or frustrating enough to violate expectations, people generally won't go out of their way to get a promotion, find another job, or start a new business. People only start to expend effort if their Reference Levels are violated in some way, so if their expectations aren't violated, they simply don't act.

Sources of information that change your Reference Levels are valuable in prompting action. One of the things that prompted me to build courses and offer consulting was the knowledge that some business authors and coaches were able to spend all day learning and helping others, and be paid very well for their expertise. That was enough to violate my Reference Levels about work at the time—if they could get paid for doing what I loved to do, why should I have to spend all day in a day job that was just "okay"? The more I learned about what people did to make this possible, the more I wanted to do to make it a reality for myself.

Before Roger Bannister's record-breaking performance in 1954, running a mile in under four minutes was considered beyond the physical limitations of the human body. After Bannister proved it was possible, the psychological barrier was broken: by the end of 1957, sixteen runners had accomplished the feat. The only thing that changed was the Reference Level: these athletes knew it was possible and wanted to do it, so they did.

Good books, magazines, blogs, documentaries, and even competitors are valuable if they violate your expectations about what's possible. When you discover that other people are actually doing something you previously considered unrealistic or impossible, it changes your Reference Levels in a very useful way. All you need to know is that something you want is possible, and you'll find a way to get it.

SHARE THIS CONCEPT: http://book.personalmba.com/conservation-of-energy/

Guiding Structure

Your environment will eat your goals and plans for breakfast.

—STEVE PAVLINA, AUTHOR OF *PERSONAL DEVELOPMENT FOR SMART PEOPLE*
AND BLOGGER AT STEVEPAVLINA.COM

For three years, Kelsey and I experimented with a vegan diet—no animal products whatsoever. No meat, no eggs, no cheese, no milk.

Most of our friends and family had two responses: "Are you crazy?" and "That must be very difficult—I could never do that." It was such a drastic lifestyle change that people marveled at our willpower.

I'd like to make a confession: it wasn't difficult at all. There was very little effort or willpower involved. Here's the secret: instead of relying on willpower to resist the urge to cook a steak or order a pepperoni pizza, we changed the structure of our **Environment** to support our choices.

We threw out all of the food we didn't want to eat and replaced it with healthier options that still tasted good. We changed where we shopped—instead of going to the supermarket, we went to a small natural food store. We stopped going to steakhouses and started going to restaurants that specialized in serving vegetarian/vegan food.

As a result, we didn't have to use much willpower to act consistently with our choice. When I got hungry, I ate an apple or carrots and hummus—that's what was in the refrigerator. Ordering a pizza or buying and cooking a steak took more effort, so I didn't do it. By changing the structure of our Environment, Kelsey and I made it easier to act the way we had decided to act.

Guiding Structure means the structure of your Environment is the largest determinant of your behavior. If you want to successfully change a behavior, *don't try to change the behavior directly*. Change the structure that influences or supports the behavior, and the behavior will change automatically. If you don't want to eat ice cream, don't buy it in the first place.

In Homer's *Odyssey*, Odysseus and his crew prepare to sail past the island of the Sirens—bird women who sang so beautifully that unwitting sailors would lose all reason and shipwreck themselves. Instead of relying on strength of will to resist the temptation of the Sirens, Odysseus changed the structure of the Environment, plugging his men's ears with beeswax and tying himself to the ship's mast. Temptation thus avoided, the ship made safe passage.

Change the structure of your Environment, and your behavior will change automatically. Add a bit of *Friction* (discussed later) or eliminate certain options completely, and you'll find it much easier to focus on what you're trying to accomplish.

A great example of Guiding Structure is the "Sterile Cockpit Rule" that the Federal Aviation Administration (FAA) instituted in 1981. Most airline accidents happen below ten thousand feet, where distractions can be deadly. Above ten thousand feet, pilots can talk about anything they want, but below ten thousand feet, the only discussion permitted is about information directly related to the flight in progress. By eliminating distractions, the Sterile Cockpit Rule reduces errors and accidents.

Change the structure of your Environment, and you'll be amazed at how drastically your behavior will change in response.

SHARE THIS CONCEPT: http://book.personalmba.com/guiding-structure/

Reorganization

Not all those who wander are lost.

— J. R. R. TOLKIEN, AUTHOR OF *THE LORD OF THE RINGS*

Whenever a perception violates the system's *Reference Level*, action will occur to bring the perception back under control. Sometimes that response is well defined—as we discussed earlier, your body knows exactly what it needs to do to regulate blood glucose. Often, however, you don't know exactly what is wrong—or how to fix it.

Think of a perception as abstract as "job satisfaction"—there's a set point in your mind that stands for "how happy I should be at work," and your perception of job satisfaction is an average of your actual experiences at work. Pleasant experiences move the average higher, and unpleasant experiences move the average lower.

If your perception of "job satisfaction" is lower than you think it should be (your Reference Level), your brain will kick into action—"I'm not as happy as I should be . . . *Something* needs to change."

Here's the problem: you may not know what that "something" is. Would you be happier if you changed assignments, worked for a new boss, left the company, or started working for yourself? Who knows? That's where **Reorganization** comes in.

Reorganization is random action that occurs when a Reference Level is violated but you don't know what to do to bring the perception back under control. The "quarter-life" or midlife crisis many people experience is a perfect example of Reorganization. You don't quite know what to do to eliminate the angst you're feeling, so you start doing things that aren't normal for you, like quitting your job to backpack across Europe or getting a tattoo and buying a motorcycle.

Reorganization feels like you're lost, depressed, or crazy—that's completely normal. Your brain starts spitting out all kinds of off-the-wall things in an effort to find something to fix the situation. Sometimes, when I'm really stressed out, I'll start to think that being a janitor sounds appealing—the work's not difficult, you don't have to think so much, and you still get paid. That doesn't mean it's a good idea, but this type of thought process is absolutely normal—my brain is just trying out random ideas to bring certain systems back under control.

Reorganization is the neurological basis of learning. As we'll discuss in **Pattern Matching**, our minds are learning machines that associate specific causes with specific effects. If your mind hasn't already learned what to do in a certain situation, the best way to solve the problem is to try new things in an effort to gather data. That's what Reorganization is for—it's the impulse to consider or try new things to see what works.

One of the most important things to understand about Reorganization is that it's best not to fight it. Even though it's sometimes tempting to try to convince yourself that everything is okay, resisting or repressing the impulse to try something different slows down your learning.

There's nothing odd or abnormal about "dark nights of the soul"—they're a signal that some perception about your life is out of control, and Reorganization is required to gather more data about how to fix it. Once you learn how to bring the perception back under control, Reorganization stops naturally.

When you're feeling lost, take heart—it's just your brain gathering the information it needs to make good decisions. Embracing the impulse to try something new will help you exit Reorganization more quickly.

SHARE THIS CONCEPT: http://book.personalmba.com/reorganization/

Conflict

The significant problems we face cannot be solved at the same level of thinking we were at when we created them.

—ALBERT EINSTEIN, RENOWNED PHYSICIST

Let's take a moment to examine everyone's favorite character flaw: procrastination.

Everyone procrastinates to a certain extent: with too many things to do, putting off tasks until they feel urgent is a natural response. How can you focus on something due in the future when there's something that needs to be done *now*?

What's particularly frustrating are the times we know we have time to get something done in advance, but we just don't feel like doing it *right now*. Part of us wants to work, and part of us wants to *not* work. If you try to force yourself to work, you find that you're so easily distracted that not much gets done. If you try to rest, part of you feels bad that you're not working, which means you're not really resting.

Entire days can pass where you neither really work nor really rest, but you feel exhausted from the effort of getting nothing done. What gives?

Conflicts occur when two control systems try to change the same perception. When you're procrastinating, one of your brain's subsystems is trying to control "getting things done," while another is trying to control "getting enough rest." Since both systems are trying to control the same perception—physical action—the systems fight to move the perception in the way they want it to go.

The situation is akin to a heater and an air conditioner fighting to control the temperature in a single room. As long as their respective reference levels are mutually exclusive, neither system will ever be under control—they'll continue to expend effort to move the system in the direction they're controlling for. Even if one system brings their perception back under control temporarily, it won't be long before the other system ensures it's out of control once more.

Procrastination is an example of an inner Conflict, but Conflicts happen *between* people as well. Conflicts occur when people are controlling for different outputs that require the same input. Think of two children fighting over the same toy. It's the procrastination/temperature battle all over again, only the control systems are people. As long as one child has the toy, the other will be upset. As a result, the toy moves back and forth constantly, and both children are upset.

Think about senior leaders in a large company squabbling over how a limited budget will be allocated, and you'll have a good idea of where Conflicts come from. If $1 million is allocated to one VP, that means all of the other VPs can't use it, so they protest—corporate politics at its best.

One of the things that make interpersonal Conflict challenging is that we can never truly control the actions of another human being. We can influence, persuade, inspire, or negotiate, but we can never directly act upon another person's perceptions or directly change their **Reference Levels**.

Conflicts can only be resolved by changing Reference Levels—how success is defined by the parties involved. Attempting to resolve a Conflict by simply calling attention to unacceptable behavior is ineffective in the same way that willpower can't change behavior directly—it's not addressing the root cause of the Conflict.

Each party in the Conflict has a different Reference Level, which is primarily influenced by the situation or **Environment**. The only way to resolve the conflict is to change each party's Reference Level, which is best done by changing the structure of the situation.

In the case of procrastination, Conflict can be ended by scheduling firm times for work and rest, ensuring enough of each. In *The Now Habit*, Neil Fiore recommends creating an "unschedule" that prioritizes rest over work. When your brain is sure that you'll be receiving all of the relaxation and enjoyment you need, and that you only have a certain amount of time to get things done, it's easier to focus on doing productive work.

In the case of the competing heater and air conditioner, the situation can only exist as long as you maintain the conflicting temperatures on the thermostats. Change the Reference Levels, and you resolve the Conflict.

In the case of squabbling children (or vice presidents), you can change the situation by ensuring that each combatant gets roughly the same toy, gets no toy at all, or changes their measure of success from "getting mine" to "working together."

Change the situation that creates the Reference Levels each party is using to measure success, and you'll eliminate the Conflict.

SHARE THIS CONCEPT: http://book.personalmba.com/conflict/

Pattern Matching

> Your memory is a monster; you forget—it doesn't. It simply files things away. It keeps things for you, or hides things from you—and summons them to your recall with a will of its own. You think you have a memory; but it has you!
>
> —JOHN IRVING, NOVELIST AND ACADEMY AWARD–WINNING SCREENWRITER

Long before you knew what gravity was, you knew that a ball would move toward the ground if you released it. The first few times you let go of a ball, it would always fall to the ground. It didn't take many such experiences for you to learn that any object you released would fall. Gravity is just a name for something your brain learned by itself.

One of the most interesting things about the brain is its ability to automatically learn and recognize patterns. Think of Pavlov's famous dogs: ring a bell, and they'll start to salivate. Pavlov taught them a pattern: every time the bell rings, food is on the way. It didn't take long for the dogs to learn the pattern, so they'd respond even before the food appeared.

Our brains are natural *Pattern Matching* machines. The brain is constantly busy trying to find patterns in what we perceive, then associating new patterns with other patterns that are stored in memory. This Pattern Matching process happens automatically, without conscious effort. Simply by paying attention to the world around you, your brain is collecting new patterns and adding them to memory.

Humans learn patterns primarily via *Experimentation*. If a small child wants to be held by its mother, it doesn't take long to try several different approaches and learn which response produces the desired result, typically

"If I cry, Mom is going to pick me up and hold me." From then on, the child will rely on the pattern whenever it desires the result.

You can think of your memory as the database of patterns you've learned via past experience. Patterns get stored in our long-term memory, waiting to be used to determine responses to new or uncommon situations. Recall is optimized for speed, not accuracy—the brain stores information contextually, which helps you recall related patterns quickly when you need them. That's why the best way to find a set of lost keys is to mentally walk through all of the places you've been recently—the context makes it easier to recall the information.

The more accurate patterns you've learned, the more options you have when solving new problems. Pattern Matching is one of the primary reasons experienced people tend to make better decisions than inexperienced people—they've learned more accurate patterns via their experience. Having a larger mental database to draw from is what gives experts their expertise.

Pattern Matching is one of the foundational capabilities of our mind and how it works. The more accurate patterns you have stored in your memory, the more quickly and accurately you can respond to whatever life throws at you.

SHARE THIS CONCEPT: **http://book.personalmba.com/pattern-matching/**

Mental Simulation

I saw the angel in the marble and carved until I set him free.
—MICHELANGELO, SCULPTOR AND ARTIST

Quick: imagine jumping into the middle of an active volcano. Is it a good idea?

Answering this question took you only a few fractions of a second, even though you've never personally jumped into a volcano or seen anyone who has. What you've done is quite extraordinary: how is it possible to immediately know the answer to something you've never considered before?

Mental Simulation is our mind's ability to imagine taking a specific action, then simulating the probable result before acting. Our minds are constantly trying to predict what will happen in the future, based on what's happening around us and what actions we're considering. Anticipating the results of our actions is a significant advantage: it dramatically enhances our ability to solve novel problems.

Mental Simulation relies on our memory—the database of **Patterns** we've learned via perception and experience. When you imagined jumping into a volcano, your brain couldn't find any personal experiences, but it did find relevant **Associations**: lava is hot, hot things burn, burns are painful and dangerous, painful and dangerous things are bad. This set of Associations is used to simulate the probable result in the blink of an eye, resulting in a snap judgment: VERY BAD IDEA.

Mental Simulation is extremely powerful and versatile—it can be used to test even the most arbitrary actions without risk. Given any goal or scenario, Mental Simulation is what your brain uses to connect point A to point B, where point A is where you are now and point B is what you're imagining. The only limitation on what you can simulate is your imagination.

For example, how would you go about visiting Antarctica? It's a random question, but by holding the **End Result** in mind for a few seconds, your brain automatically starts connecting the dots, based on the Patterns you've learned. "I could call a travel agent . . . Cruises go to Antarctica all the time . . . I'd have to fly to Argentina . . . I'd have to buy a really warm coat," etc. All of this thinking just happens, without much effort on your part—it's what your brain is designed to do.

Mental Simulation only works if you supply a "point B," even if the action or goal is completely arbitrary—you can simulate the path to even the most unrealistic and absurd destination you can imagine. Think of using a service like Google Maps or a vehicle GPS system—the system can give you accurate directions, but it won't work unless you enter a destination. That destination can be your best friend's house or someplace random, like Albuquerque, New Mexico. Either way, without supplying a **Goal** (discussed later), the system can't operate. The same rule applies to Mental Simulation—no destination, no simulation.

Mental Simulation is particularly powerful if you learn how to harness it consciously, which we'll explore in detail in **Counterfactual Simulation**.

Interpretation and Reinterpretation

We don't see things as they are. We see things as we are.

—ANAÏS NIN, AUTHOR AND DIARIST

Have you ever received an e-mail from someone that made you very angry, only to find out later that you misunderstood the tone or intent of the message? Your mind reached a conclusion that wasn't true based on what you thought you perceived, only to discover there was a different way of interpreting the message that also made sense.

Our minds are always simulating different courses of action, but sometimes there's not enough information to ensure that a *Pattern* is completely accurate. Since you're not omniscient, your mind never has complete data, so it automatically fills in missing pieces by interpreting what you sense via the Patterns you have stored in memory. In the absence of any other information to the contrary, you'll "jump to conclusions" by relying on the interpretation your mind creates.

This capacity to fill in the blanks even happens on the physiological level. In our field of vision we have two complete blind spots—the points where our optic nerves connect to our eyes. We literally cannot see in those spots, but our brains automatically take in all of the surrounding information and seamlessly fill in the blanks. As a result, we appear to have a solid field of vision, even though it's an illusion created by our brain's ability to interpret information.

The human brain constantly relies on prior Patterns and information to make *Interpretations* in the absence of information. Think of the spam folder in your e-mail account—it uses a collection of previous spam messages (called "priors") to estimate the probability that any new incoming message is also spam, using a process called Bayesian inference. The messages don't self-identify as spam, but the computer's Bayesian spam filter can spot them anyway.

Your brain does roughly the same thing every time you decide you like someone right after meeting them—your brain is relying on Patterns you've learned via past experiences with other people to make a snap judgment.

These snap Interpretations can also be altered—a process called *Reinterpretation*. Think of meeting an attractive person who consistently becomes quiet and aloof whenever you're around. At first glance, their behavior may signal that they're shy or don't like you very much. If one of your friends tells you that they're romantically interested in you, however, your Interpretation of that person's past behavior can change in an instant.

Reinterpretation is possible because your memory is fundamentally impermanent. Our memories aren't like computer disks—every time we recall a memory, it doesn't simply resave to the same location in the same state. Every time we recall something, the memory is saved in a different location, with a twist: the new memory will *include any alterations we've made to it*.

It's possible to change your beliefs and **Mental Simulations** consciously by recalling and actively Reinterpreting past events. Mental Simulation and Interpretation rely on Patterns stored in memory, so if you want to change the results of your brain's simulations, the best way to go about doing that is to alter the mental database of information those simulations are based on. Reinterpretation is how you change the database.

In *Re-Create Your Life*, Morty Lefkoe teaches a process that can be used to Reinterpret past events in a simple and useful way:

1. Identify the undesirable pattern.

2. Name the underlying belief.

3. Identify the source of the belief in memory, including as much sensory detail as possible.

4. Describe possible alternate interpretations of the memory.

5. Realize that your original belief is an interpretation, not reality.

6. Consciously choose to reject the original belief as "false."

7. Consciously choose to accept your reinterpretation as "true."

Here's an example of how I personally used Lefkoe's process: one possible way of Interpreting my brand management career at P&G is that I was a miserable failure—I was on the management fast track, and I couldn't "cut it," so I "washed out." For a while, I believed that was true, but that belief didn't serve me very well. When I tried to explore alternate paths, my mind naturally simulated that my "failure" would extend to my new projects as well. As long as my mind relied on this Interpretation to simulate the future, I was stuck in a self-defeating cycle.

There's another way of Interpreting my previous career at P&G: my experience taught me a lot about how large corporations work, and I learned more about what I'm good at, what I don't particularly enjoy doing, and how I want to invest my time. Working at P&G helped me discover a path that didn't work for me, so I stopped following that path and tried other things that better fit my strengths and desires until I found one I loved—a major victory and a huge life improvement.

Which Interpretation is "true"? Both are valid Interpretations. My mind wasn't malfunctioning when it created the first Interpretation, but that Interpretation didn't serve me very well. Reinterpreting the situation and accepting the second version as "true" was much more useful—without it, you probably wouldn't be reading this book.

Reinterpret your past, and you'll enhance your ability to make great things happen in the present.

SHARE THIS CONCEPT: http://book.personalmba.com/interpretation/

Motivation

BUT I DON'T WANNA!!!
—TWO-YEAR-OLD CHILDREN EVERYWHERE

Motivation is something that you probably think about all the time, using phrases like "I'm feeling really motivated to get this done" or "I'm not feeling very motivated to do this right now." Since so many of us rely on the term to explain our daily experience, it's worthwhile to understand what we're actually talking about.

Motivation is an emotional state that links the parts of our brain that feel with the parts that are responsible for action. Using the **Onion Brain** as a basic model, Motivation is the link between the midbrain (which perceives the world) and the hindbrain (which sends the signals to our body to take action). In most cases, Motivation is automatic—our mind perceives a difference between the way things are and the way we want them to be, and the body automatically acts to eliminate the difference.

You can break down the experience of Motivation into two basic desires: moving *toward* things that are desirable and moving *away* from things that aren't. Things that fulfill our *Core Human Drives* appear desirable, so we experience an impulse to move toward them. Things that appear dangerous, scary, or threatening are undesirable, so we naturally experience an impulse to move away from them.

In general, "moving away" takes priority over "moving toward." The reason comes back to *Caveman Syndrome*—running away from a lion automatically takes priority over cooking lunch.

Let's say you have an exciting opportunity to start a new business. A feeling of excitement may cause you to move toward that opportunity. At the same time, if the opportunity requires you to leave a high-paying job, which feels risky, you may be compelled to move away from the very same opportunity, resulting in Conflict. As long as the risk outweighs the excitement, you'll hesitate, even if there's very little chance you'll ever be in danger if you take the leap. This safety mechanism in our minds developed for very good reasons, but today, most of the decisions we make don't have life-and-death consequences.

Motivation is an emotion—NOT a logical, rational activity. Just because your forebrain *thinks* you should be motivated to do something does not mean you'll automatically become motivated to do that thing. (If only it were that easy, right?) Very often, *Mental Simulations*, *Patterns*, *Conflicts*, and *Interpretations* hidden in the midbrain can get in the way of making progress toward what we want to accomplish. As long as there are "move away from" signals being sent, you'll have a hard time feeling motivated to move toward what you want.

In the same vein, you can't "motivate" other people by yelling at them to work faster—all the drill-sergeant approach accomplishes is making them want to move away from you. They may comply with you temporarily if they perceive some threat to themselves if they don't, but you can bet that they'll move away from working with you at the first available opportunity.

Eliminate the inner conflicts that compel you to move away from potential threats, and you'll find yourself experiencing a feeling of Motivation to move toward what you really want.

SHARE THIS CONCEPT: http://book.personalmba.com/motivation/

Inhibition

Inhibition is the ability to stop: to delay our response until we are adequately prepared to make it.

—MICHAEL GELB, AUTHOR OF *BODY LEARNING: AN INTRODUCTION TO THE ALEXANDER TECHNIQUE* AND *HOW TO THINK LIKE LEONARDO DA VINCI*

Believe it or not, most of your daily actions require very little conscious thought.

Most of the time, our bodies and minds are on autopilot—our minds sense the world around us, compare our *Environment* and actions against internal *Reference Levels*, and act accordingly. Think about driving a car: with practice, your body does everything necessary to keep the car on the road, without requiring much conscious thought.

Every once in a while, however, it pays to ignore the autopilot and do something different. If you stumble across a bear in the woods, the last thing you want to do is run, even though that's what your instincts may be telling you to do. If you run, the bear is likely to decide you look like lunch and chase you down.

Instead of running, it's actually more effective to stand your ground and make yourself appear as big and loud and threatening as you can. Appearing to be a threat requires you to consciously inhibit your natural response, but it'll cause the bear to see *you* as a threat and decide to leave you alone.

Inhibition is the ability to temporarily override our natural inclinations. If you've ever put up with one of your siblings (or colleagues) acting immature, obnoxious, or annoying, Inhibition prevented you from doing something you would have regretted later.

Willpower is the fuel of inhibition. As we discussed in the section on the *Onion Brain*, the forebrain's job is ambiguity resolution, decision making, and Inhibition. Whenever we inhibit our natural responses to our Environment, Willpower is at work. Our midbrain and hindbrain are the autopilot, and the forebrain is the override. In that sense, "free will" is a bit misleading—"free won't" is a more accurate description.

Inhibiting certain decisions or responses can be beneficial, but our ability to inhibit has limitations, which we'll discuss next.

SHARE THIS CONCEPT: http://book.personalmba.com/inhibition/

Willpower Depletion

If you don't want to slip, don't go where it's slippery.

—ALCOHOLICS ANONYMOUS MAXIM

In the 1960s, Dr. Walter Mischel, a researcher at Columbia University, systematically tortured small children.

Here's how he did it: Dr. Mischel placed the child in a small room with a table and a chair. In the middle of the table, Dr. Mischel would place a big, fluffy marshmallow, then tell the child, "If you wait until I come back, you can have two." Then he'd leave.

Here's what happened: some kids would gobble up the marshmallow seconds after the researcher left. Others made heroic efforts to distract themselves from temptation, forcing themselves to pay attention to something other than the marshmallow in an agonizing attempt to hold out long enough to get the bigger reward.

Dr. Mischel found a correlation between **Willpower** and success: kids with a greater ability to "defer gratification" were more successful in school, as well as later on in life. Overriding our instincts can often make it possible to collect larger rewards later—spending is easy, but saving is not, even if the latter is more beneficial over time.

Willpower can be thought of as instinctual override—it's a way to interrupt our automatic processing in order to do something else. Whenever we experience a situation in which it's useful to inhibit our natural inclinations, Willpower is required to keep us from responding. As such, Willpower is a useful tool, but it has certain inherent limitations.

Our reserves of Willpower are very limited and become **Depleted** with use. Dr. Roy Baumeister, a researcher at Florida State University, found that our ability to successfully use Willpower for self-control tasks is dependent on a physiological fuel: blood glucose. Acts of Willpower Deplete relatively large amounts of glucose, and when those stores run low, we have a hard time using Willpower to inhibit behavior. That's why it's difficult to resist dishing up a bowl of ice cream at 8:30 p.m. when you're on a diet—by then, your stores of Willpower are long gone.

The best way to use your limited reserves of Willpower is to use **Guiding**

Structure to change the structure of your ***Environment*** instead of your behavior.
For example, if you decide you want to quit eating ice cream, it doesn't
make sense to keep a tub in your freezer, then rely on your Willpower to
resist the temptation to eat it. That situation is a recipe for disappointment,
and when your Willpower inevitably fails, it's easy to misinterpret the lapse
as a fundamental character flaw, an example of the ***Attribution Error*** (discussed
later).

Instead, it's much more effective to use a little Willpower to remove the
ice cream from your freezer entirely, by either giving it to someone else or
throwing it away. By removing the ice cream from your Environment, no
Willpower is required—you'd actually have to go somewhere to get it,
which takes more effort. The path of least resistance changes accordingly,
so if you're hungry, you'll eat something else—an apple, perhaps.

The Internet is a massive temptation to me—I love learning new things,
and the Web contains enough interesting information to keep me endlessly
occupied. It's easier for me to spend time reading rather than writing, but
I write on a computer, which is the equivalent of keeping ice cream in my
freezer—it's always there, tempting me away from writing.

Instead of constantly relying on my Willpower to get this book done, I
used a small amount of Willpower to alter my Environment by installing
an application called Freedom[5] on my Mac. The program temporarily dis-
ables Internet connectivity on my laptop, making it impossible for me to
connect to the Internet for a few hours. (Windows users can accomplish
the same result using a program called LeechBlock.[6]) Temptation thus
obliterated, I write. It's safe to say that, without Freedom, you wouldn't be
reading this right now.

Save your Willpower: focus on using it to change your Environment,
and you'll have more available to use whenever ***Inhibition*** is necessary.

SHARE THIS CONCEPT: http://book.personalmba.com/willpower-depletion/

Loss Aversion

Our doubts are traitors, and make us lose the good we oft might win,
by fearing to attempt.

—WILLIAM SHAKESPEARE, *MEASURE FOR MEASURE*

Recently, my wife, Kelsey, decided to withdraw some funds from an investment account. When the brokerage deposited the money into her bank account, they deposited an additional $10,000 by mistake.

Rationally, it shouldn't have been a big deal—it was a simple mistake that was easily corrected. Emotionally, however, Kelsey felt like she was "losing" the extra money, even though it wasn't really hers at all.

Loss Aversion is the idea that people hate to lose things more than they like to gain them. There are very few relationships that psychology is able to quantify, but this is one of them: people respond twice as strongly to potential loss as they do to the opportunity of an equivalent gain. If you look at your investment portfolio and notice that it's increased by 100 percent, you'll feel pretty good. If you notice that your portfolio went down 100 percent, you'll feel *horrible*.

Loss Aversion explains why threats typically take precedence over opportunities when it comes to **Motivation**. The threat of loss used to require immediate attention, because losses were extremely costly—even life threatening. Dying or losing a loved one to a predator, sickness, exposure, or starvation is universally a horrible experience, so we're built to do everything in our power to prevent that from happening. The potential losses we typically face now are rarely as serious, but our minds still give them automatic priority.

Loss Aversion also explains why uncertainty appears risky. Depending on the study you look at, anywhere between 80 and 90 percent of adults think it would be great to own their own business and work for themselves. If that's true, why don't more people start businesses? Loss Aversion keeps them from acting: the threat of losing a steady (and somewhat predictable) job commands more **Attention** than the opportunity to create a new self-sustaining business. Starting a business involves the specter of potential loss, which prevents people from getting started in the first place.

Loss Aversion is particularly pronounced in recessions and depressions.

Losing a job, a home, or a significant percentage of your retirement fund isn't life threatening, but it feels horrible all the same. As a result, people tend to become more conservative, avoiding risks that could make things worse. Unfortunately, some of those risks—like starting a new business—may actually present a major opportunity to make things better.

The best way to overcome Loss Aversion is to **Reinterpret** the risk of loss as "no big deal." Casinos are in the business of overcoming Loss Aversion every single day—in a sense, the ostentatious buildings on the Las Vegas Strip are enormous monuments to human stupidity. If Loss Aversion is such a big deal, how do casinos encourage people to play games in which they're *mathematically certain* to lose money?

Casinos win by abstracting the loss. Instead of having players gamble with currency, which is perceived as valuable, the casino converts currency into chips or debit cards, which don't *feel* as valuable. As the player loses this "fake" money over time, the casino will provide "rewards" like free drinks, T-shirts, room upgrades, or other benefits to alleviate any remaining sense of loss. As a result, losing becomes "no big deal," so players continue to play—and continue to lose money night after night.

Loss Aversion is why **Risk Reversal** is so important if you're presenting an offer to a potential customer. People hate to lose, which makes them feel stupid and taken advantage of. As a result, they'll go to great lengths to ensure that they don't lose, and the best way to ensure that they don't make a stupid decision is to not buy your offer in the first place. If you're in the business of making sales, that's a big problem. Eliminate this perception of risk by offering a money-back guarantee or similar Risk Reversal offer, and people will feel the decision is less risky, resulting in more sales.

SHARE THIS CONCEPT: http://book.personalmba.com/loss-aversion/

Threat Lockdown

How little can be done under the spirit of fear.

—FLORENCE NIGHTINGALE, PIONEER OF PROFESSIONAL NURSING

You're fast asleep when something goes bump in the night. Almost immediately, you're alert—your heart rate increases, your pupils dilate to take

in more light and detail, and stress hormones like adrenaline and corti-
sol flood your bloodstream. Your mind automatically identifies the likely
source of the noise, escape routes, and potential defensive weapons. In the
blink of an eye, you're ready to defend yourself against the threat, whatever
it might be.

When your mind perceives a potential threat—real or imaginary—your
body immediately prepares to respond. This automatic physiological response is designed to help you do one of three things to eliminate the
threat: fight, flee, or freeze. As long as you're in "protection mode," it's difficult to do anything other than fixate on the threat. Until you search the
house, there's no way you'll be able to go back to sleep—your body will only
come out of protective mode after you're sure there's no threat to face.

The subconscious choice to fight, flee, or freeze is largely dependent
on your brain's automatic **Mental Simulation** of the situation. If your brain
predicts you can win if you fight, you'll fight. If your brain predicts you
can "win" by getting away, you'll flee. If your brain predicts you can't get
away, you'll freeze in the hope that the threat will pass you by. Freezing
makes your brain go into **Threat Lockdown**—protection mode—which makes
it difficult to do anything other than fixate on the threat.

Threat Lockdown is a constructive response designed to help you defend yourself, but like many ancient instincts, it often malfunctions in our
modern environment. The threats you face are far less acute today, but they
are often chronic.

In the olden days, when the threat was a predator or an angry tribal
chief, the lockdown response was constructive, since it focused our energy on
staying alive and/or part of the tribe. Even though the thoughts that run
through our heads on a daily basis have little in common with those of our
ancient ancestors, the hardware those thoughts are running on—our brains—
is still largely the same and is constantly on the lookout for very old threats
in a very new environment. As a result, we eat too much and exercise too
little, and the instinctive behaviors of fighting like hell, freezing, or running
away aren't very constructive when dealing with an angry boss or an overdue
mortgage payment.

The recent turmoil in the stock market is an excellent example of Threat
Lockdown in action. The stock market crash in late 2008 sparked a flurry

of panic and hand-wringing, even among people who were in no danger of losing their homes or jobs. The mere *possibility* of bad things happening grinds businesses to a halt at the very time increased productivity is needed to keep the firm in good shape. Instead of focusing on doing good work, employees spend most of their time and energy worrying about what the future holds and gossiping about who's next on the chopping block, decreasing the overall amount of value created and increasing the likelihood that the firm's future will get worse.

Threat Lockdown can easily become a vicious cycle. If you're ever in the unfortunate situation of having to lay off workers, it's best to do it quickly, cleanly, and all at once. It's best to make cuts swiftly, then reassure remaining employees that no more cuts will be made. Rumors of layoffs or workers constantly wondering "if I'll be next" is a recipe for Threat Lockdown.

If you're experiencing Threat Lockdown, *don't try to repress the threat signal*. Many studies have shown that active repression doesn't make a perception go away—instead, it makes the signals progressively stronger. Think of what a small child does when they want to get your attention, but you ignore them—they'll continuously increase the commotion they make until they're sure you've noticed them. Your brain does the same thing—repression only makes the threat signals stronger. Consciously sending a mental "message received, safe to proceed" signal to your brain is a simple and surprisingly effective way to make yourself stop fixating on the issue so you can consider appropriate responses.

The key to dealing with Threat Lockdown is to convince your mind that the threat no longer exists. You can do that in one of two ways: (1) you can convince your mind there was never actually any threat, or (2) you can convince your mind the threat has passed. Convincing your mind there was never a threat is the equivalent of searching your house in the dark at midnight—the search proves that no threats exist, so it's safe to leave protective mode. Convincing your mind that the threat has passed does the same thing—the threat is gone and can no longer harm you, so it's safe to carry on.

Sometimes it's difficult to defuse Threat Lockdown, particularly if you've been in it for a long time. Because protective mode is physiological, it's often best to use physiological means to calm yourself down. Exercise, sleep, and meditation can help calm your mind by metabolizing or counteracting the stress hormones that have been flooding your body. When you're feeling overwhelmed, going for a quick run or lifting weights can do wonders for your state of mind.

Notice the threat signal, then do what you can to prove to your mind the threat no longer exists, and you'll break yourself out of Threat Lockdown.

SHARE THIS CONCEPT: http://book.personalmba.com/threat-lockdown/

Cognitive Scope Limitation

One death is a tragedy. A million deaths is a statistic.
—KURT TUCHOLSKY, GERMAN SATIRIST

If you ever have a chance to walk through the middle of Times Square in New York City during tourist season, you'll quickly realize that, to most of the people moving toward you, *you are not a person*. Instead of being a human being, you are an object—an obstacle standing between where they are and where they want to go. As a result, they'll run you over with impunity.

No matter how intelligent a person is, there's an upper bound on the amount of information a single mind can process, store, and respond to. Above that limit, information may be stored in abstract terms, but it's processed differently from information related to that individual's personal experience or concerns.

"Dunbar's number" is a theoretical cognitive limit on the number of stable social relationships humans can maintain at one time. According to Robin Dunbar, a British anthropologist, humans have the cognitive capacity to keep track of somewhere around 150 close personal connections. Beyond this limited circle, we start treating people less like individuals and more like objects, and groups of people beyond this limit are likely to splinter off into subgroups over time.

If you've ever wondered why you don't write letters to your elementary school classmates, Dunbar's number is a decent hypothesis—you're too busy maintaining your ties to people who are in your immediate social circle.

There's some controversy regarding the actual quantity of connections where *Cognitive Scope Limitation* kicks in (the Bernard-Killworth median, a competing estimate, is 231), but there's little doubt that such a limit exists. When a disaster strikes somewhere around the world that affects millions of people, we may feel bad, but we don't feel a *million times* what we would feel if that disaster directly affected a close friend or family member. The more remote the connection, the less such an impact affects us individually.

The tourists in Times Square aren't evil—they're just overwhelmed. Over 364,000 people pass through Times Square every day,[7] and our minds simply aren't capable of handling that much information at once. Abstractly, these people still realize that you're a human being, but there's so much going on in the area that it's difficult to treat you like one. The mind gets overwhelmed, so it starts simplifying reality to compensate.

The same thing happens to executives of large companies. Rationally, they may be aware that they're responsible for hundreds of thousands of employees and millions of shareholders, but no matter how intelligent they are, their brains simply aren't capable of processing the magnitude of that reality. As a result, executives can hurt a lot of people without even realizing it. The CEO of a large company may not particularly care if thousands of frontline workers are laid off—after all, they may not know any frontline workers personally.

Whenever you see an executive making a boneheaded decision like dumping toxic waste into a river millions of people drink from, or downsizing thousands of jobs while handing out millions of dollars in bonuses, it's probably *not* because they're rotten to the core. As scary as it sounds, it's probably because they simply *haven't thought too much about it*—the scope and scale of what they're managing is too complex to handle, so their mind processes the decision abstractly instead of viscerally.

Personalizing an issue is a way to hack this universal limitation. In the absence of brain upgrades, it's not possible to directly expand the scope of information our minds are capable of processing. In order to get around this limitation, it's useful to personalize decisions and issues by imagining they affect someone close to us.

In the case of the boneheaded executive, they'd feel very different about their decision if their *mother's* water was polluted, or their *child's* job was downsized. Instead of abstractly considering the issue, personalizing it makes it easier to feel the effects of the decision viscerally, which makes it easier to make better decisions.

In *Green to Gold*, Daniel Esty and Andrew Winston describe several ways of making it easier to internalize the results of large decisions. The "newspaper rule" and "grandchild rule" are effective ways of personalizing the results of your decisions. The "newspaper rule" is a simulation of the following: assume your decision was publicized on the front page of tomorrow's *New York Times*, and your parents and/or significant other read it. What would they think? Imagining the personal consequences of your decisions in this way is a much more accurate way to evaluate the impact of short-term decisions.

The "grandchild rule" is a way of evaluating decisions with long-term consequences. Imagine that, thirty or forty years from now, your grandchild gives you feedback on the results of your decision. Will they laud you for your wisdom or reprimand you for your stupidity?

Personalize the results of your decisions and actions, and you'll be far less likely to run afoul of Cognitive Scope Limitation.

SHARE THIS CONCEPT: http://book.personalmba.com/cognitive-scope-limitation/

Association

> In general, we are least aware of what our minds do best.
> —MARVIN MINSKY, COGNITIVE SCIENTIST AND ARTIFICIAL INTELLIGENCE
> RESEARCHER AT MIT

Who cares which golf clubs Tiger Woods uses? Who cares which shoes Michael Jordan wears? Who cares which purse Paris Hilton is carrying?

Your mind cares. Remember, your brain is taking in information all the time and is using it to create **Patterns** that describe how the world works. Rationally, these things may not matter—you probably know that using the same golf clubs Tiger Woods uses won't magically correct your atrocious slice. When it comes time to buy golf clubs, however, your mind will be drawn to the clubs that make you feel good, and more likely than not, you'll find the clubs Tiger uses quite appealing.

The human mind stores information contextually, including cues like

Environment and correlation. Because the brain is a *Pattern Matching* machine, it's constantly trying to figure out what's associated with what. As a result, your mind effortlessly forms *Associations*—even between things that aren't logically connected.

For decades, the Coca-Cola Company has been associating Coke with a single emotion: happiness. Do a quick search for Coke commercials on YouTube: you won't find any images of layoffs or funerals. What you will find is a litany of happy moments: Adrien Brody cruising in his car, parades of whimsical creatures celebrating as a bottle of Coke exits a vending machine, and Charlie Brown winning the race for a runaway Coke bottle balloon in the Macy's Thanksgiving parade. Even holidays aren't immune: the company largely invented the modern image of Santa Claus, who just so happened to be holding a bottle of Coke.

It's possible to influence behavior by using associative cues, even Associations that make no logical sense. Coca-Cola's advertisements don't convince soda consumers that Coke is better in some functional respect *("Now with 37 percent more sugar!")*, but they do make people feel good whenever they think about Coke. When a customer is standing in the supermarket deciding which soft drink to buy, those feelings make a big difference in each customer's final choice.

Consider beer commercials, which usually feature attractive women and confident men. Your rational mind knows that drinking a certain type of beer won't make you more attractive or confident, but *Correlation* is powerful—your brain will make the Association anyway. As a result, beer ads influence behavior, even though no one takes the images they contain seriously.

Presenting your prospects with positive Associations can influence how they think about what you offer. Celebrity endorsements work because they tie into strong Associations people already have with the endorsers, associations that rub off on the product or service being endorsed. Everyone knows James Bond is a fictional character, but when Daniel Craig is featured wearing a tuxedo in a watch advertisement, the "sophisticated international spy" Association is automatically transferred to the timepiece.

Cultivate the right Associations, and potential customers will want what you have even more.

SHARE THIS CONCEPT: http://book.personalmba.com/association/

Absence Blindness

Facts do not cease to exist because they are ignored.

—ALDOUS HUXLEY, ESSAYIST AND AUTHOR OF *BRAVE NEW WORLD*

Here's a curious fact about human beings: we have a really hard time realizing that something isn't there.

When I worked in P&G's Home Care division, one of my first projects was testing the viability of a **Product** that *prevented things from getting dirty*. You still had to clean, but it took more time for things to get dirty again, so the Product saved the user significant time and effort.

Once the Product went into testing, however, it was apparent that the idea wasn't feasible. The Product genuinely worked, but users didn't realize it—they had a hard time believing the Product worked, since they couldn't see anything happening. After the test phase was complete, the project was canceled.

Absence Blindness is a cognitive bias that prevents us from identifying what we can't observe. Our perceptual faculties evolved to detect objects that are present in the **Environment**. It's far more difficult for people to notice or identify what's missing.

Examples of Absence Blindness are everywhere. Here's a common example: great management is boring—and often unrewarding. The hallmark of an effective manager is anticipating likely issues and resolving them in advance, *before* they become an issue. Some of the best managers in the world look like they're not doing much, but everything gets done on time and under budget.

The problem is, no one sees all of the bad things that the great manager *prevents*. Less skilled managers are actually more likely to be rewarded, since everyone can see them "making things happen" and "moving heaven and earth" to resolve issues—issues they may have created themselves via poor management.

Make a note to remind yourself to handsomely reward the low-drama manager who quietly and effectively gets things done. It may not seem like their job is particularly difficult, but you'll miss them when they're gone.

Absence Blindness makes prevention grossly underappreciated. In the case of the Product I was working on, people had a hard time believing that something they couldn't see working was actually effective. If you're trying to sell the absence or prevention of something, you're fighting an uphill battle, even if your Product is great. Always state benefits in positive, immediate, concrete, and specific terms by focusing on things the user can directly experience.

Absence Blindness also makes it uncomfortable for people to "do nothing" when something bad happens, *even if doing nothing is the best course of action*. Often, the best course of action is to choose not to act, but that's often difficult for humans to accept emotionally.

The economic "boom and bust" cycle most markets experience is partially a consequence of Absence Blindness. According to Ludwig von Mises in *Human Action*, economic "bubbles" are created when a government tries to encourage an economy to grow by artificially reducing interest rates, making it easier to borrow money. By making access to **Capital** abnormally easy,[8] this policy leads investors to speculate by paying abnormally high prices for assets they'd otherwise avoid, like tulips,[9] dot-com companies with no revenue,[10] and risky mortgage-backed securities.[11] Eventually, the bubble "pops" when investors realize that the assets they've been speculating on aren't worth what they paid, leading to a sudden crash in the price of the overvalued asset.

Because of **Loss Aversion**, people start freaking out and start clamoring for an immediate solution to the collapsing market. More often than not, the "solution" is to reduce interest rates even more to encourage the economy to start growing again—a self-reinforcing **Feedback Loop** (discussed later) that ultimately does nothing but exacerbate the issue by creating the conditions necessary for an even larger bubble to form down the road.

To fix the issue, the best course of action is to stop artificially manipulating interest rates, which caused the issue in the first place. Unfortunately, Absence Blindness makes doing nothing psychologically uncomfortable—after all, "we can't sit here and do nothing while the world burns!" As a result, people typically prefer the government to act, even if the action the government takes ultimately makes things *worse*.

Experience makes it easier to avoid Absence Blindness. Experience is valuable primarily because the expert has a larger mental database of related **Patterns**, and thus a higher chance of noticing an absence. By noticing violations of expected Patterns, experienced people are more likely to get an "odd feeling" that things "aren't quite right," which is often enough warning to find an issue before it becomes serious.

In *Sources of Power: How People Make Decisions*, researcher Gary Klein tells the story of a team of firefighters putting out a fire on the first floor of a house. When water was sprayed at the base of the fire, the fire didn't respond as expected—it didn't diminish at all. The chief noticed and ordered everyone out—something just didn't feel right. A few minutes later, the house collapsed—the fire had started in the basement, destroying the foundation. If the team had stayed inside, they would have died. That's the power and benefit of experience.

The only reliable way I've found to overcome Absence Blindness is **Check-listing** (discussed later). By thinking in advance what you want something to look like and translating that into visible reminders you can refer to while making decisions, checklists can help you remember to look for the absence of qualities in the moment. (We'll discuss creating **Checklists** in great detail in chapter 11.)

SHARE THIS CONCEPT: http://book.personalmba.com/absence-blindness/

Contrast

> The world is full of obvious things which nobody by any chance ever observes.
>
> —SIR ARTHUR CONAN DOYLE, AUTHOR OF THE SHERLOCK HOLMES BOOKS

If you walk into a department store to buy a business suit, you're likely to notice a few options that appear to be abnormally expensive. The store will very rarely sell these suits—that's not their purpose. Compared to a $3,000 suit, a $400 suit doesn't sound like a lot of money—even if the same suit could be purchased at another store for $200.

The same principle applies to the order in which products are presented by the salesperson. After choosing a suit, you'll be directed to shirts, shoes, and accessories. Compared to a $400 suit, what's another $100 on shoes?

$80 for a belt? $60 for a few shirts? $50 for a few ties? $40 for a set of cuff links? Compared to the suit, the accessories seem inexpensive, so why not?

Here's what Jordan Smart, one of my clients, reported:

> I went shopping last year on Black Friday, looking to get some slightly more formal clothes . . . I went out with the intent of buying a set of shirts and two blazers. I thought for a while on buying ties to go with it, and decided that the one or two I had in my closet already would suffice.
>
> I went shopping at two stores. In the first, I picked out a set of shirts, and as I was leaving, the salesman asked if I needed ties to go with them. I politely told him no, and privately congratulated myself on sticking to my resolution.
>
> At the second store, I tried on a few blazers and decided to purchase them. Again, the salesman asked if I needed ties to go with my blazers. At that point, I very clearly remember thinking about the price of the blazers and thinking to myself, "Well, I'm spending this much money anyway," and proceeded to buy a set of ties.
>
> I didn't think anything of it until I learned about Contrast. Looking back at the receipt, I realized I'd spent more on the ties than I had spent on the blazers.

Our perceptions are influenced by information gathered from the surrounding environment. Is $10,000 a lot of money? It depends on your circumstances. If you have $10 in your bank account, $10,000 is an enormous sum. If you have $100,000,000, it's a rounding error.

Our perceptual faculties are optimized to notice **Contrast**, not to compare what we perceive with things that aren't there, which is the root of **Absence Blindness**. Everything we notice and every decision we make is based on information gathered from the surrounding **Environment**. That's why camouflage works—it reduces the contrast between an object and its surrounding Environment, which makes it harder to notice.

Contrast is often used to influence buying decisions. In the business world, contrast is often used as pricing camouflage. In the case of the $60 shirt, it may be possible to buy the exact same shirt at another retailer for $40, but the less expensive shirt *isn't present in the store where the comparison is taking place.* What *is* present is the $400 suit, which makes the $60 shirt look like a bargain.

Compared with a $2,000 computer, a $300 extended warranty appears inexpensive, even though it increases the total purchase price by 15 percent. Compared with a $30,000 vehicle, spending $1,000 for leather seats feels like a bargain. Compared with buying a $400,000 house, spending $20,000 to remodel the kitchen feels like no big deal.

Framing is a way to control the perception of Contrast. For example, I often use the phrase "$149,000 less than a top-tier business program" when marketing my business courses. Compared with buying a book, my course looks expensive; compared with the cost of an MBA program, it's a bargain.

Take advantage of Contrast when presenting your offer, and you'll increase the odds that your potential customers will view your offer favorably.

SHARE THIS CONCEPT: http://book.personalmba.com/contrast/

Scarcity

The way to love anything is to realize it might be lost.
—G. K. CHESTERTON, ENGLISH WRITER AND CHRISTIAN APOLOGIST

Because of **Conservation of Energy**, people have a natural tendency to decide to "do things later" unless there's a compelling reason to act immediately. As a businessperson, "later" is a big issue, because "later" turns into "never" if the customer forgets about you. How can you encourage your customers to act immediately?

Scarcity encourages people to make decisions quickly. Scarcity is one of the things that naturally overcomes our tendency to conserve—if you want something that's scarce, you can't afford to wait without the risk of losing what you want. **Loss Aversion** ensures that this possibility feels bad enough to prompt us to take action *now*.

As a result, adding a Scarcity element to your offer is a great way to encourage people to take action. Scarcity makes people understand that they'll lose something valuable if they wait, making it more likely they'll choose to act immediately if they desire what is being offered.

The more scarce the value, the more intense the desire. In 1996, Tickle

Me Elmo was the hot toy of the Christmas season. Elmo was already a popular character, but limited quantities of the toy drove parents into a buying frenzy. Normally rational people started spending hundreds of dollars on eBay for the toy and mobbing retailers when new stock became available.

Here are a few ways you can add an element of Scarcity to your offer:

1. *Limited Quantities*—inform prospects that you're offering a limited number of units for sale.

2. *Price Increases*—inform prospects that the price will go up in the near future.

3. *Price Decreases*—inform prospects that a current discount will end in the near future.

4. *Deadlines*—inform prospects that the offer is only good for a limited period of time.

Scarcity that appears blatantly artificial can backfire. For example, putting an artificial limit on sales of e-books, downloadable software, or electronic music files makes no sense—everyone knows electronic files can be **Duplicated** infinitely at essentially no cost, so the scarcity feels manipulative, which makes people want to buy from you less. Price increases with deadlines, on the other hand, tend to work well—raising the price after a certain number of orders or a certain amount of time is a reasonable policy and is less likely to come across to the customer as unreasonable or manipulative.

Add an element of Scarcity to your offer, and you'll encourage people to buy now instead of "later."

SHARE THIS CONCEPT: http://book.personalmba.com/scarcity/

Novelty

Why is it that when I ask for a pair of hands, a brain comes attached?

—HENRY FORD

At the height of World War II, Norman Mackworth took Royal Air Force radar operators away from their jobs for a special mission: staring at a clock for two hours at a time.

Mackworth was a psychologist who specialized in studies of vigilance—the ability to maintain high levels of **Attention** on a single object for long periods of time. Radar operators were natural test subjects—their job mostly consisted of looking at blips on a radar screen in a dark room for hours on end.

Most of the time, very little on the radar screen changed. When something abnormal appeared on the screen, however, it could be critically important: inbound enemy airplanes on a bombing mission. The radar operator's job was to be alert enough to notice anomalies immediately, but the task was extremely difficult—boredom often led to mistakes that cost lives.

To simulate this challenging environment, Mackworth created the "Mackworth Clock," a device designed to test how well people pay attention over time. The "clock" featured a second hand that worked like a normal clock, with a twist—it would randomly skip a second, ticking two notches instead of one. The test subject's job was to press a button every time they noticed the skip.

Here's what Mackworth found: after ten minutes of staring at the clock, the quality of the subject's attention went down dramatically. The maximum period of sustained attention even highly motivated operators (who were given substantial bonuses for performance) were able to sustain was thirty minutes—any longer, and they'd inevitably zone out.

Novelty—the presence of new sensory data—is critical if you want to attract and maintain attention over a long period of time. One of the reasons people can focus on playing games or surfing the Internet for hours at a time is novelty—every new viral video, blog post, Facebook update, Twitter post, and news report reengages our ability to pay attention.

In *Brain Rules*, John Medina shares how he's able to keep the attention of his students effectively in classes that last more than an hour: he plans his class in modules that last no more than ten minutes. Each module starts with a **Hook**—an interesting story or anecdote, followed by a brief explanation of the key concept. Following this format ensures that his audience retains more information and doesn't zone out. (That's the primary reason this book is organized in short sections that take less than ten minutes to read.)

Even the most **Remarkable** object of attention gets boring over time. Human attention requires novelty to sustain itself. Continue to offer something new, and people will pay attention to what you have to offer.

SHARE THIS CONCEPT: http://book.personalmba.com/novelty/

7

WORKING WITH YOURSELF

Your body and mind are the tools you use to get things done. Learning how to work effectively with yourself makes accomplishing what you set out to achieve easier and more enjoyable.

In today's busy business environment, it's easy to get stressed about everything that needs to be done. Learning how to work effectively and efficiently can be the difference between a fulfilling career and a draining one.

In this chapter, we'll discuss how to decide what to do, set and achieve goals, track your daily tasks, overcome resistance, and consistently get more productive work done without burning out.

SHARE THIS CONCEPT: http://book.personalmba.com/working-with-yourself/

Akrasia

In one of his most famous stand-up comedy routines, Jerry Seinfeld describes his difficulties going to bed:

I never get enough sleep. I stay up late at night, 'cause I'm Night Guy. Night Guy wants to stay up late. "What about getting up after five hours' sleep?" That's Morning Guy's problem. That's not my problem, I'm Night Guy. I stay up as late as I want. So you get up in the morning, you're exhausted, groggy. . . . Night Guy always screws Morning Guy. There's nothing Morning Guy can do. The only thing Morning Guy can do is try and oversleep often enough so that Day Guy loses his job and Night Guy has no money to go out anymore.

The routine is funny because it's so familiar. All of us have had the experience of knowing or feeling that we should do something or that an action would be in our best interest . . . but we don't do it. The term for that experience is *Akrasia* (pronounced "ah-KRAH-see-ah").

Akrasia and procrastination are related, but they're not the same thing. Procrastination occurs when you've decided to complete a task, but you keep putting it off until later without consciously deciding to do it later. If you have "answer e-mail" on your to-do list, but you browse the Internet for hours without answering any e-mail, that's procrastination.

Akrasia is a deeper issue: it's a general feeling that you "should" do something, without necessarily deciding to do it. The "should" feeling doesn't lead to decision or action, even if the action seems to be in your best interest. Most people experience Akrasia when considering changing *Habits* they no longer want ("I should quit smoking"), taking a new action ("I should donate to that nonprofit"), or contemplating an uncomfortable topic ("I should look into life insurance and talk to a lawyer to write a will"). The "should" feeling sticks around, but never leads to action, generating intense frustration.

Akrasia is a very old problem: discussions about the source of Akrasia go back to Socrates, Plato, and Aristotle. The term comes from the Greek ἀκρασία, which means "lacking command (over oneself)." Socrates and Plato believed that Akrasia was a moral defect, while Aristotle argued that it stems from a mistaken opinion about what a person "should" do. Even though philosophers have been debating the topic for centuries, they haven't discovered a cure.

Akrasia is one of the most widespread and persistent barriers to getting things done. In order to spend your time making progress, instead of fighting both sides in a battle of wills, it's useful to have a strategy for recognizing and combating Akrasia when you recognize it.

In my experience, Akrasia has four general parts: a task, a desire/want, a "should," and an emotional experience of resistance. Within this framework, there can be many potential sources of resistance:

▶ You can't define what you want.

▶ You believe the task will bring you closer to something you don't want.

▶ You can't figure out how you're going to get from where you are right now to where you want to be.

▶ You idealize the desired **End Result** to the point that your mind estimates a low probability of achievement, resulting in **Loss Aversion**.

▶ The "should" was established by someone else, not you, prompting **Persuasion Resistance**.

▶ A competing action in the current **Environment** promises immediate gratification, while the reward of the task in question will come much later. (Psychologists call this "hyperbolic discounting.")

▶ The benefits of the action are abstract and distant, while other possible actions will provide concrete and immediate benefits. (Psychologists call this "construal level theory" or "near/far" thinking.)

Akratic situations can take many forms: eating a cookie versus "becoming healthier" by sticking to a diet. Browsing the Web versus exercising. Staying in a bad relationship versus moving on. Dreaming about a new business idea versus testing it. Whenever you "should" do something, but resist doing it, you're experiencing Akrasia.

Akrasia is a slippery problem, and there's no easy, universal solution. That said, there are many strategies and techniques that are useful in preventing and resolving akratic situations. We'll discuss them in this chapter.

SHARE THIS CONCEPT: http://book.personalmba.com/akrasia/

Monoidealism

Just do it.

—NIKE BRAND SLOGAN

Much has been written in the past few years about the subject of productivity—how to get more done. Books like *Getting Things Done*, *The Power of Less*, and *Master Your Workday Now!* all propose different methods of achieving work-flow nirvana.

When we're trying to "be productive," what exactly are we shooting for? Ideally, you want to focus the full powers of your energy and *Attention* on a single subject at a time.

Monoidealism is the state of focusing your energy and attention on only one thing, without conflicts. Monoidealism is often called a "flow" state, a term coined by psychologist Mihaly Csikszentmihalyi. This is the state of human attention at its most productive: clear, focused Attention and effort directed at one (and only one) subject for an extended period of time.

P. J. Eby, a former computer programmer who specializes in helping people use their minds more productively, defines Monoidealism this way:

> *When somebody says "just do it," they are trying to communicate that you should not do anything else. It might better be phrased as, "Do it, without thinking about anything, not even about what you're doing. In fact, don't even do it, just watch yourself doing it, but don't actually try to do anything."*
>
> *Properly, "monoidealism" is simply the state in which you have exactly one thing on your mind, with no conflicts. It's a condition that results in one naturally taking action in relation to the thought, rather than a technique in and of itself . . . The usefulness of a particular [productivity] technique for a particular individual will largely depend on whether it addresses their particular stumbling blocks in achieving a monoideal state.*

When you're "just doing it," you're in "flow"—a Monoideal state. There are no distractions, no interruptions, no self-judgments, no doubts. When your mind is in 100 percent "do" mode, you inevitably get a lot done.

So how exactly do you get yourself into a Monoideal state?

First, eliminate potential distractions and interruptions. Depending on the level of cognitive activity required to complete your work, it'll take ten to thirty minutes before your mind becomes absorbed in what you're doing. Phone calls, coworkers "dropping by to pick your brain," and other unanticipated demands on your Attention will break your Monoideal state, so priority number one is ensuring that you don't get distracted. I often use earplugs or play instrumental music to eliminate background noise, and disconnect the phone when I don't want to be interrupted.

Turning off my Internet connection (see *Willpower Depletion*) while I'm writing also makes it much easier for me to maintain a Monoideal state. Otherwise, I'm way too likely to browse the Web when the going gets tough. Using similar *Guiding Structure* techniques is a good way to prevent your Attention from straying.

Second, eliminate inner *Conflicts*. Sometimes it's difficult to get started because you're experiencing a Conflict between two control systems in your mind. Eliminating these Conflicts before you start working helps you achieve a Monoideal state much more quickly. If you feel resistance to getting started, it's useful to spend some time and energy exploring that Conflict more deeply *before* you keep working.

While writing this book, I experienced several periods of frustrating resistance. Instead of trying to ignore the resistance or push through it (a surefire way to experience Willpower Depletion), exploring that resistance using *Mental Simulation* and *Reinterpretation* helped me uncover a hidden Conflict: I wasn't happy with how my work was turning out, and doing more of what wasn't working would be a waste. Spending some time revising the structure of the book resolved that Conflict, simultaneously making the book better and eliminating the source of the resistance.

Third, kick-start the Attention process by doing a "dash." Since it can take ten to thirty minutes to get into the zone, setting aside ten to thirty minutes for a quick burst of focused work can make it much easier to get into the zone quickly. If you're not productive by the time the dash is over, you have permission to stop and do something else. That's rarely the case: once you get started, it's easy to keep going.

One technique I often use is called the Pomodoro Technique,[1] named by its creator, Francesco Cirillo, after those funny little kitchen timers shaped like a tomato (*pomodoro* in Italian). Here's how the technique works: Set a kitchen timer for twenty-five minutes. Your job is to focus on a single task for the entire duration—if you get stuck, just keep focusing until the timer goes off. After the twenty-five-minute work period is over, you can take a five-minute break, bringing the total duration to half an hour—a block of time any of us can fit into our schedule here and there.

What I love about the Pomodoro Technique is that it accomplishes two goals at once: it makes it easy to get started, and it gives you permission to ignore distractions. Even if you're not excited about what you need to do, saying to yourself "it's only twenty-five minutes" is a great way to overcome the initial resistance to getting started. The Pomodoro Technique is also a good excuse to ignore distractions: if the phone rings, reminding yourself that "a Pomodoro is indivisible" is an effective way to give yourself permission to ignore it, maintaining your Monoideal state.

If you eliminate distractions and Conflicts before you start your dash, you'll naturally transition into a Monoideal state a few minutes into the work period.

Meditation is a form of Monoidealism "resistance training." Simple meditations like focusing on your breathing, then consciously (and nonjudgmentally) bringing your focus back to your breath if and when your Attention strays is a way to consciously practice the skills used to maintain your Attention in the face of distractions. As little as ten minutes of simple meditation every day can dramatically improve your ability to focus.

SHARE THIS CONCEPT: http://book.personalmba.com/monoidealism/

Cognitive Switching Penalty

Rule your mind or it will rule you.

—HORACE, FIRST-CENTURY B.C. ROMAN POET

Every project and every task that you decide to work on takes a certain amount of **Attention**, energy, and focus to get it done. The question is: how can you accomplish everything you need to do most effectively?

Many people rely on multitasking: trying to do more than one thing at the same time. While many people assume this makes them more efficient,

Monoidealism and multitasking are complete opposites. Neurologically, it's impossible for your brain to multitask. When you're trying to do more than one thing at a time, you're not really parallel processing—you're rapidly switching your Attention from one thing to another. While you're paying Attention to Task A, you're ignoring Task B until you switch back to it.

As a result, productive multitasking is a myth. According to several recent neurological studies,[2] the more things you try to pay Attention to at any given time, the more your performance at all of them suffers. That's why it's never a good idea to talk on a cell phone while driving—by trying to focus on two things at once, you decrease your reaction times to the same level as someone who's driving while intoxicated.[3]

Every time you switch the focus of your Attention from one subject to another, you incur the **Cognitive Switching Penalty**. In order to take action, your brain has to "load" the context of what you're doing into working memory. If you constantly switch the focus of your Attention, you're forcing your brain to spend time and effort thrashing, loading and reloading contexts over and over again. That's why it's possible to spend an entire day multi-tasking, get nothing done, and feel exhausted at the end—you've burned all of your energy context-switching instead of making progress.

The Cognitive Switching Penalty is a **Friction** cost (discussed later): the less you switch, the lower the cost. That's why Monoidealism is so efficient—by focusing your Attention on only one thing at a time, you're allowing your brain to load the context into working memory *once*, which means you can focus your energy on actually accomplishing the task at hand.

To avoid unproductive context switching, a batching strategy is best. Eliminating distractions can help prevent unnecessary interruptions, but it's entirely possible to waste energy mentally thrashing even if you have the entire day free. The best approach to avoid unnecessary cognitive switching is to group similar tasks together.

For example, I find it difficult to make progress on creative tasks (like writing or shooting training videos) between client calls. Instead of attempting to juggle both responsibilities at the same time, I batch them together. I typically focus on writing for a few uninterrupted hours in the morning, then batch my calls and meetings in the afternoon. As a result, I can focus on both responsibilities with my full Attention.

I use a similar strategy when doing chores, updating financial reports, or running errands: I'll dedicate a few hours solely to finishing those tasks. As a result, I accomplish everything I need to do in very little time.

Paul Graham, a venture capitalist, programmer, and essayist, calls this batching strategy "Maker's Schedule/Manager's Schedule."[4] If you're trying to create something, the worst thing you can possibly do is to try to fit creative tasks in between administrative tasks—context switching will kill your productivity. The "Maker's Schedule" consists of large blocks of uninterrupted time; the "Manager's Schedule" is broken up into many small chunks for meetings. Both schedules serve different purposes—just don't try to combine them if your goal is to get useful work done.

A simple rule of thumb I use to plan my day is the 3-10-20 method: in one day, I have the capacity to finish three major tasks and ten minor tasks. A major task is any activity that requires more than twenty minutes of focused concentration; all other tasks are minor. If a major task is interrupted, restarting it counts as a new task.

For example, one day's major tasks might be writing a proposal, consulting with a client, and reviewing a book. Between these major tasks, I might make a short phone call, process and answer incoming e-mails, read a few articles, do the dishes, and clean my office.

As long as I set aside large chunks of time for my major tasks, I can accomplish everything in a single day. If I'm interrupted in the middle of a major task, that task won't be done that day, or another major task will have to slip. Keeping in mind that there's a limit to what I can accomplish in a single day makes it easier to keep *Stress and Recovery* in balance.

Eliminate unproductive context switching, and you'll get more done with less effort.

SHARE THIS CONCEPT: http://book.personalmba.com/cognitive-switching-penalty/

Four Methods of Completion

I am only one, but I am one. I cannot do everything, but I can do
something. And because I cannot do everything, I will not refuse to
do the something I can do. What I can do, I should do. And what I
should do, by the grace of God, I will do.

—EDWARD EVERETT HALE, NINETEENTH-CENTURY UNITARIAN CLERGYMAN
AND WRITER

There are really only four ways to "do" something: completion, deletion,
delegation, and deferment.

Completion—doing the task—is the option most people think about. If
you keep a to-do list, you're probably assuming that those tasks are all your
responsibility to get done. That's not quite true—completion is best for
important tasks that only you can do particularly well. Everything else can
be handled in another manner.

Deletion—eliminating the task—is effective for anything that's unimportant or unnecessary. If something on your task list is unimportant, don't
feel bad about eliminating it. If it's not worth doing, it's not worth doing
well or quickly—don't hesitate to get rid of it.

Delegation—assigning the task to someone else—is effective for anything another person can do 80 percent as well as you can. In order to
delegate, you must have someone to delegate *to*. Employees, contractors, or
outsourcers can all help you get more things done by completing tasks on
your behalf.

In preparing my online Personal MBA business course,[5] Kelsey and I
shot the videos, but we enlisted Kelsey's grandmother—an insanely fast
typist—to help us create transcripts of each of the videos. As a result, we
were able to complete the entire course in record time, without feeling
overwhelmed.

If you don't have anyone to delegate routine tasks to, working with a
virtual assistant company can be quite useful. For less than $100 a month,
you can enlist the help of a team of professionals to help you get things
done. If you have little experience with delegation, it's an experiment worth
trying.[6]

Deferment—putting the task off until later—is effective for tasks that
aren't critical or time dependent. Don't feel bad about putting some things

off—the best way to bog yourself down is to try to handle too many things at the same time. Saving noncritical tasks for later is a good way to keep your attention and energy focused on what's most important.

In *Getting Things Done*, David Allen recommends keeping a "someday/maybe" list of things you'd like to do someday but that aren't that important right now. Creativity researcher Scott Belsky recommends a similar approach in *Making Ideas Happen*: create a "back burner" list of tasks you want to get to eventually but that aren't a priority right now. Periodically reviewing this list when you're looking for something new or exciting to do is quite useful.

Use all four options when processing your to-do list, and you'll get more done than you ever thought possible.

SHARE THIS CONCEPT: http://book.personalmba.com/4-methods-of-completion/

Most Important Tasks

> You've got to think about the big things while you're doing small things, so that all the small things go in the right direction.
>
> —ALVIN TOFFLER, TECHNOLOGY RESEARCHER AND FUTURIST

Not all tasks are created equal—some are more important than others.

You only have so much time and energy to get things done each day. Of all of the things that are on your to-do list right now, some of them are really important, and some of them really aren't important. If you want to make the most of your limited time and energy, it pays to focus on completing the tasks that will make the biggest difference first, before spending your time and energy on anything else.

A *Most Important Task (MIT)* is a critical task that will create the most important results you're looking to achieve. Everything on your plate is not critically important, so don't treat everything on your task list equally. By taking a few minutes to identify a few tasks as particularly important, you'll make it easier to focus on achieving them first.

At the beginning of every day, create a list of two or three MITs, then focus on getting them done as quickly as possible. Keep this list separate from your general to-do list or task tracking system. I typically use a 3 × 5 index card or David Seah's "Emergent Task Planner,"[7] a free downloadable PDF that makes it easy to plan your day.

When creating your list of MITs, it's useful to ask a **Self-Elicitation** question: "What are the two or three most important things that I need to do today? What are the things that—if I got them done today—would make a huge difference?" Write only those tasks on your MIT list, then try to get them done first thing in the morning.

Combining this technique with **Parkinson's Law** (discussed later) by setting an artificial deadline is extremely effective. If you set a goal to have all of your MITs done by 10:00 a.m., you'll be amazed at how quickly you can complete the day's most important tasks.

Having a list of two or three MITs helps you maintain a **Monoideal** state by giving you permission to say no to interruptions that aren't as important. If you're working on your MITs and someone calls you, it's easier to ignore the call or tell the caller, "I'm working under deadline—I'll get back to you later." By definition, everything that's not an MIT is not as important, so it's easier to say no to noncritical interruptions.

Achieve your MITs as quickly as possible, and then you'll have the rest of the day to handle anything else that comes up.

SHARE THIS CONCEPT: http://book.personalmba.com/most-important-tasks/

Goals

> Setting a vague goal is like walking into a restaurant and saying, "I'm hungry. I want some food." You'll stay hungry until you order something.
>
> —STEVE PAVLINA, AUTHOR OF *PERSONAL DEVELOPMENT FOR SMART PEOPLE* AND BLOGGER AT STEVEPAVLINA.COM

Much has been made in business literature about the importance of having **Goals**. Well-formed Goals accomplish two things: they help you visualize what you want and make you excited about achieving it. A Goal is a statement that clarifies *precisely* what you want to achieve, which makes it easy for your brain to use **Mental Simulation** to **Visualize** what achieving that Goal looks like. If the **End Result** you're looking for is vague or fuzzy, you're making it difficult for your mind's automatic planning systems to find ways to get what you want. Well-formed Goals also play a key role in **Motivation**—the more clearly defined your Goal, the easier it is to get excited about doing the things required to get what you want.

Fuzzy Goals like: "I want to climb a mountain" aren't very helpful, because they don't give your brain any material to work with. Which mountain? Where? When? Why? Without answers to these questions, you probably won't do anything at all.

Well-formed Goals pass the "Everest Test." Useful Goals look like this: "I want to climb to the summit of Mount Everest before my fortieth birthday, and take a panoramic picture to frame on my wall as a trophy." This Goal is easy for your brain to simulate—Mount Everest is in Nepal, so you'll have to arrange travel. You'll also have to improve your climbing skills, find a guide, buy equipment, purchase a suitable panoramic camera, etc. Once you make a conscious **Decision** to achieve the Goal, your mind automatically starts finding ways to get it done.

Goals are most useful if they're **Framed** in a Positive, Immediate, Concrete, Specific (PICS) format:

▶ *Positive* refers to Motivation—your Goal should be something you move *toward*, not away from. Goals like "I don't want to be fat anymore" are a recipe for **Threat Lockdown**—you're reinforcing the negative instead of using **Reinterpretation** to change your mind's prediction to get excited about improving. For best results, eliminate **Conflicts** first, then move toward what you want to achieve.

▶ *Immediate* refers to time scale: your Goals should be things that you decide to make progress on now, not "someday" or "eventually." If you don't want to commit to working on a particular Goal now, put it on your someday/maybe list and focus on something else.

▶ *Concrete* means you're able to see the results in the real world. Goals are achievements—you should know when you've accomplished what you set out to achieve. Setting Goals like "I want to be happy" won't work because they're not concrete—how would you know when you're done? When you reach the top of Mount Everest, you've achieved something concrete in the real world—that's concrete.

▶ *Specific* means you're able to define exactly what, when, and where you're going to achieve your Goal. Climbing Mount Everest on a certain date in the near future is specific, which makes it easy for your mind to plan exactly how you'll go about accomplishing it.

For best effect, your Goals should be under your control. Goals like "losing twenty pounds" are soul crushing because they're *not* directly under your control—losing weight is a result, not an effort. If your weight randomly moves up a few pounds on a given day, it's easy to feel defeated, even though you had no choice in the matter. For best results, make your Goals actions that are within your *Locus of Control* (discussed later), like doing a minimum of thirty minutes of exercise every day and controlling the number of calories you consume.

To track your Goals, any simple notebook or reference system will do. Personally, I capture all of my Goals in a simple text file, which I print out and keep in my to-do notebook. Whenever I'm thinking about what I need to do, I have my list of Goals handy for easy reference, which makes it easy to determine which tasks are most important.

It's perfectly okay to change your Goals. Sometimes we think we want something, only to find out later that we don't want it so much anymore. Don't feel bad about that—it's called learning. If you find yourself working toward a Goal you no longer feel good about, work on something else.

SHARE THIS CONCEPT: http://book.personalmba.com/goals/

States of Being

I may not have gone where I intended to go, but I think I have ended up where I intended to be.

—DOUGLAS ADAMS, HUMORIST AND AUTHOR OF THE HITCHHIKER'S GUIDE SERIES

One of the mistakes I constantly see people making when setting *Goals* is assuming everything is an achievement.

Think of statements like "I want to be happy," "I want to feel excited," and "I want to be successful." How do you know if you've achieved what you set out to do? Can you really achieve happiness, excitement, or success if your day-to-day experience changes?

A **State of Being** is a quality of your present experience. Emotional experiences aren't achievements because they fluctuate over time—you can be happy right now and upset an hour from now. Accordingly, "being happy" is not an achievement—it's a quality of your present experience.

States of Being are *decision criteria*, not Goals. It's okay to want to "be happy" or "be successful," but treating these desires as Goals is a recipe for frustration. Instead of treating these states as achievements, it's far better to think of them as decision criteria—ways of understanding whether or not your actions are leading to your desired results.

States of Being help you answer the question "Is what I'm doing right now working?" For example, if you want to feel happy, you may notice that spending time with close friends and family members creates the experience you want, so making time for those things is obviously important. If you want to feel calm, but your job is making you stressed out all the time, it's clear the situation needs to change—what you're doing isn't working.

Breaking down complex States of Being into smaller parts is even more useful. Instead of using complex States of Being like "success" and "happiness" as decision criteria, it's far better to decide what these states actually mean to you. For example, I define "being successful" as "working on things I enjoy with people I like," "feeling free to choose what I work on," and "having enough money to live without financial stress." Together, these States of Being provide a much more useful definition of success—if that's how I'm experiencing the world, I'm "successful."

The same goes for "happiness." Instead of being a single State of Being, "being happy" is a combination of "having fun," "spending time with people I enjoy," "feeling calm," and "feeling free." When those States of Being describe my experience in the present moment, I'm "happy." Breaking down "happiness" into its component parts helps me ensure I'm doing things that will help me experience it more fully and more often.

Decide what States of Being you want to experience, and you'll have a powerful set of decision criteria you can use to evaluate the results of your actions in an entirely new and useful way.

SHARE THIS CONCEPT: http://book.personalmba.com/states-of-being/

Habits

We are what we repeatedly do. Excellence, then, is not an act, but a habit.

—WILL DURANT, HISTORIAN, PARAPHRASING ARISTOTLE, ANCIENT GREEK PHILOSOPHER

What about things you want to do on a daily basis, like exercising? Is that a *Goal* or a *State of Being*? Neither, actually.

Habits are regular actions that support us. Exercising, brushing your teeth, taking vitamins, following a particular diet, or keeping in touch with friends and family are all examples of Habits that keep us happy and healthy. Due to the power of *Accumulation*, small Habits can add up to huge results over time.

Most Habits take on one of four common forms: things you want to *start* doing, things you want to *stop* doing, things you want to do *more*, and things you want to do *less*. For example, you might want to start exercising regularly, stop watching television, drink more water, or spend less money.

Habits typically require a certain amount of *Willpower* to create. Therefore it's best to use the techniques we discussed in the section on *Guiding Structure* to make it easier to instill the Habits you want to adopt. If you want to go to the gym first thing in the morning, packing your gym bag and laying out workout clothing the night before makes it easier to go, since you've structured your environment to require less effort to act.

Habits are easier to install if you look for *triggers* that signal when it's time to act. For example, if you want to take vitamins, it's easier to remember to take them if you use another habitual action as a trigger for the action. Instead of relying on your mind to remember to take your vitamins in the middle of the day, you can use brushing your teeth in the morning or evening as a reminder.

For best results, focus on installing *one* Habit at a time. Remember, you only have so much Willpower to use each day, and overriding your default mode of action depletes it quickly. If you try to install too many Habits at the same time, you probably won't succeed at adopting any of them for

long. Focus on installing one Habit until taking action feels automatic, then
move on to the next.

SHARE THIS CONCEPT: http://book.personalmba.com/habits/

Priming

Many an object is not seen, though it falls within the range of
our visual ray, because it does not come within the range
of our intellectual ray, i.e., we are not looking for it. So, in
the largest sense, we find only the world we look for.

—HENRY DAVID THOREAU, *JOURNAL*, 1837–1861

Have you ever been interested in a particular type of car, only to start noticing them *everywhere*? I certainly have—it feels like someone suddenly un-
loaded hundreds of the exact make and model of the car you like all over
the highway.

That's not true, of course—the universe isn't playing tricks on you. The
cars were always there; you just never noticed them before. Before you
decided you were interested in a particular type of car, your brain filtered
those cars out of your awareness.

Once you became interested, however, your brain stopped filtering out
that information, and you started noticing every time that particular car
drove by. In a sense, you programmed your brain to notice certain things
about the *Environment* around you. All it took was becoming interested in
something specific to remove the filter.

Priming is a method of consciously programming your brain to alert
you when particular information is present in your Environment. One of
the fascinating ramifications of our brain's *Pattern Matching* function is that
we're constantly scanning the Environment for useful information. If you
tell your mind specifically what you want to find, it will alert you whenever
your senses notice it.

Priming is a way to consciously influence your brain's Pattern Matching
capabilities. By taking a few moments to consciously decide what you're interested in and what you're looking for, you can program your mind to alert
you when it notices something relevant. Some people call this *intuition*—
Priming is how you consciously put your intuition to productive use.

Here's an example of how I use Priming: in the book *10 Days to Faster Reading*, Abby Marks-Beale recommends a technique I refer to as *purpose setting*: taking a few minutes before you start reading to figure out (1) why you want to read this material and (2) what kind of information you're looking for. Jotting down a few notes before picking up the book reinforces exactly what you're looking to find.

After defining your purpose, you then pick up the book and flip through it quickly, paying particular **Attention** to the table of contents, section headings, and index—condensed sources of information about what the book contains and how the material is structured. Jotting down terms and concepts that appear to be particularly important helps prime your brain to notice them when they appear later.

This process only takes a few minutes, but the impact it has on your reading speed is profound. Once you've Primed your mind to notice important concepts, you can work your way through the entire book at lightning speed. As you read, your brain automatically filters out unimportant material and homes in on the material you're particularly interested in learning.

As a result, it's possible to extract most of the useful content in almost any nonfiction book in less than twenty minutes. When I go to a library or bookstore, this technique allows me to read several books in less than an hour. Without using this method, there's no way I could have created the Personal MBA reading list as it exists today, let alone written this book.

One of the ways people "get lucky" when they're working toward a particular **Goal** is via Priming. One of the reasons Goal setting is useful is because it's an easy way to Prime your brain to look for things that will help you get what you want. If your goal is to climb Mount Everest, you're far more likely to notice when tickets to Nepal are 70 percent off while browsing a travel Web site. If you read the same thing before setting the Goal, you'd probably filter it out—you'd have no reason to pay Attention.

Take some time to consciously Prime your brain to notice what's important to you, and you'll inevitably find it.

SHARE THIS CONCEPT: **http://book.personalmba.com/priming/**

Decision

> At the moment of every day I must decide what I am going to do the
> next moment; and no one can make this decision for me, or take my
> place in this.
>
> —JOSÉ ORTEGA Y GASSET, PHILOSOPHER AND ESSAYIST

A **Decision** is the act of committing to a specific plan of action. The word
"decide" comes from the Latin *decidere*, which means "to cut off." When
you make a decision, you're cutting off the other possible avenues that you
could explore, leaving only the path you're committing to. If you're not cutting off viable options, you're not really making a Decision.

No matter how good your personal productivity system is, it can't make
decisions for you. No matter how sophisticated your task-tracking system is,
it will never be able to tell you the best thing to do at any given moment.
Constructing a system to make decisions for you is a pipe dream—all systems
can do is help provide information you can use to make *better* decisions.
Making the decision will always be your responsibility.

No Decision, large or small, is *ever* made with complete information.
Since we can't predict the future, we often attribute the feeling of inde-
cisiveness to a lack of information. What's really happening is mental
thrashing—your forebrain's job is to resolve ambiguities and make decisions,
so your midbrain will continue to send signals until your forebrain does its
job. Once a decision is made—whatever it is—the thrashing stops.

Don't feel you need to have all of the information before you decide—
the world is too complicated to make accurate predictions. Retired general Colin Powell famously advocates collecting half of the information
available, then making a decision, even though your information is clearly
incomplete. "Don't wait until you have enough facts to be 100 percent sure,
because by then it is almost always too late . . . Once [you've acquired 40
to 70 percent of the available information], go with your gut."[8]

If that's a winning strategy for life-and-death battle decisions, it'll work
for life's daily decisions as well. Collect just enough information to make
an informed decision, then make your Decision and move forward.

Failure to make a Decision is itself a decision. Life doesn't stop if you refuse to choose—the world will keep moving forward, and you may be forced to take action by default. Abdicating responsibility for your Decisions doesn't mean you're not making them—you're just allowing yourself to be a victim of circumstance.

For best results, make your Decisions clearly and consciously. In my experience, many people have difficulty figuring out what to do because they hesitate to actually make a decision—**Loss Aversion** prompts them to leave all of their options open, "just in case." Without a decision, however, their brain can't use **Mental Simulation** to figure out how to get from where they are now to where they think they want to be, so their minds thrash around unproductively.

Simply saying to yourself, "I am deciding to do X right now," makes it much easier to proceed. Once a Decision is finally made, your brain's Mental Simulation planning circuits will kick into gear, and you'll start moving again.

If you're having difficulties making a Decision, Steve Pavlina, the author of *Personal Development for Smart People*, recommends using this question as the tiebreaker: "Out of the available options, which experience do I want to have?" If you're having a difficult time making a particular decision, it's probably because your brain is having a hard time figuring out which one is best. It's an uncomfortable situation, but what it really means is that *it doesn't really matter which one you choose.* If that's true, you can simply choose the experience you find more interesting.

When Kelsey received an enticing job offer in New York City, we spent weeks torn between staying in Cincinnati and moving to the big city. There were many uncertainties involved with moving: Where would we live? Could we afford it? What about my job? It was enough to give us both a bad case of **Threat Lockdown**.

In the end, we realized there wasn't a clear winner, so it didn't really matter which one we chose. Living in New York was an experience we both wanted to have, so we decided to move. Almost immediately, we felt a sense of clarity and relief. Instead of continuing to thrash, making a Decision allowed us to move forward, even in the face of **Uncertainty**.

SHARE THIS CONCEPT: http://book.personalmba.com/decision/

Five-Fold Why

> Ask the next question, and the one that follows that, and the one that follows that.
>
> —THEODORE STURGEON, AUTHOR OF *MORE THAN HUMAN*

Very often, we're not consciously aware of *why* we want what we want. Conducting a "root cause analysis" is a useful way to discover the motivations behind our desires.

The **Five-Fold Why** is a technique to help you discover what you *actually* want. Instead of taking your desires at face value, examining the root cause of what you want can help you define your core desires more accurately.

Applying the Five-Fold Why is easy: whenever you set a **Goal** or objective, ask yourself *why* you want it. If you want to become a millionaire, ask yourself why you want to have a million dollars.

Don't try to force an answer—just ask yourself the question in a spirit of curiosity, and wait until your mind generates a response on its own. When your mind provides an answer, ask "why?" again. Continue to ask yourself why until you get a "because I want it" response, which indicates you've reached the root cause of your original Goal.

Here's an example of how to apply the Five-Fold Why to the classic Goal, "I want to be a millionaire":

1. *Why do I want a million dollars?* Because I don't want to be stressed about money.

2. *Why don't you want to be stressed about money?* So I don't feel anxious.

3. *Why don't you want to feel anxious?* So I feel secure.

4. *Why do you want to feel secure?* So I feel free.

5. *Why do you want to feel free?* Because I want to feel free.

The root desire isn't having a million dollars—it's feeling free. Is it possible to feel free without having a million dollars? Absolutely—there are many ways to feel free that have absolutely nothing to do with money. Taking an alternate approach that addresses the real desire may be more effective than your original Goal.

Discover the root causes behind your Goals, and you'll discover new ways to get what you *actually* want.

SHARE THIS CONCEPT: http://book.personalmba.com/five-fold-why/

Five-Fold How

> Go as far as you can see; when you get there you'll be able to see farther.
>
> —THOMAS CARLYLE, ESSAYIST AND HISTORIAN

After applying the **Five-Fold Why**, you'll probably discover that what you actually want is quite different from what you thought you wanted. Now that you've identified the root cause of your original **Goals**, it's time to figure out how to get what you actually want.

The **Five-Fold How** is a way to connect your core desires to physical actions. Let's use the previous example: the core desire is to feel free. How would you go about doing that?

1. Paying off an outstanding debt

2. Reducing your work hours, finding another position, or becoming an entrepreneur

3. Moving to a new city or country

4. Breaking off a restricting personal relationship

Once you find a "how" that looks like a good idea, ask "how" again. Let's say that quitting your job and starting a business would give you the greatest sense of freedom. How would you go about doing that? Fill in the details, and what was at first a fuzzy idea becomes more and more clearly defined.

Continue asking "how" until you've clearly defined your plan in terms of **Next Actions** (discussed next). The purpose of the Five-Fold How is to create a complete chain of actions from your big idea all the way down to things that you can do *right now*.

Done properly, each action gives you an experience of what you want as you do it. If paying off a debt would make you feel free, connecting the dots in this way enables you to feel more and more free *every time you make a payment*, which makes it much easier to keep going.

Connect your big Goals to small actions you can take now, and you'll inevitably achieve what you set out to accomplish.

SHARE THIS CONCEPT: http://book.personalmba.com/five-fold-how/

Next Action

If we attend continually and promptly to the little that we can do, we shall ere long be surprised to find how little remains that we cannot do.

—SAMUEL BUTLER, NINETEENTH-CENTURY NOVELIST

Often, what we want to achieve can't be done in a single sitting. Projects are *Goals* that take more than one action to complete, and the larger the project is, the more difficult it is to anticipate all of the actions that must be done.

Climbing Mount Everest is a project—one fraught with complexity and *Uncertainty*. How do you work on a project so large it threatens to overwhelm you?

Simple: focus only on the action you need to take next to move toward your Goal.

The *Next Action* is the next specific, concrete thing you can do right away to move a project forward. You don't have to know everything that must be done to make progress on a project—all you need to know is the very next thing you can do to move the project forward.

David Allen, the author of *Getting Things Done*, coined the term to describe one of the core steps of his "fundamental process":

1. Write down a project or situation that is most on your mind at this moment.

2. Now describe in a single written sentence your intended desired outcome for this problem or situation. What needs to happen to mark this "done"?

3. Next, write down the very next physical action step required to move the situation forward.

4. Put those answers in a system you trust.

According to Allen, these questions help you clarify exactly what "done" and "doing" look like. If you define what "done" looks like, you can focus your attention and energy on "doing" the things that will get you to "done."

Writing this book was a massive undertaking—it took me years to compile the research and a little over a year to actually write the text. "Write the book" is not an action—it's a project. There's no way I could've finished the manuscript in one sitting, but it *was* possible to write a small section of the book in less than an hour. After breaking up the book into well-defined sections, it was much easier to make progress, since each individual task was less overwhelming.

To keep yourself from feeling overwhelmed, track your projects and tasks separately. Here's what I do: I always carry around a notebook that contains a 3 × 5 index card.[9] The card contains a short list of my active projects. The notebook contains my to-do list: the next actions that will move my projects forward, which I process using a system called "Autofocus," which was created by Mark Forster.[10] The system helps me use my intuition to identify what I can do *right now* to make progress. As long as my projects are tied to my Goals and are aligned with my preferred **States of Being**, it's only a matter of time before I complete them.

Focus on completing the Next Action, and you'll inevitably complete the entire project.

SHARE THIS CONCEPT: http://book.personalmba.com/next-action/

Externalization

Words are a lens to focus one's mind.

—AYN RAND, PHILOSOPHER AND AUTHOR OF *ATLAS SHRUGGED* AND *THE FOUNTAINHEAD*

One of the quirks about how your mind works is that it handles information from *outside* your head better than the thoughts that are rattling around *inside* your head.

If you've ever worked with a personal trainer or coach, you know what I mean. When exercising by yourself, it's very easy to listen to the little voice inside your head that says, "This really hurts—you should stop"— even if you'll get better results by continuing.

When working with someone else, the little voice goes away, since there's a person in your *Environment* who's encouraging you to push yourself just a little bit more. As a result, you get a better workout.

Since we respond more easily to stimuli in our Environment than our own internal thoughts, there's a simple method we can use to improve our productivity—we can convert our internal thoughts into an external form our minds can use more effectively.

Externalization takes advantage of our perceptual abilities in a very intelligent way. By converting our internal thought processes into an external form, Externalization essentially gives us the ability to reinput information into our own brains via a different channel, which gives us access to additional cognitive resources we can use to process the same information in a different way.

There are two primary ways to Externalize your thoughts: writing and speaking. Writing (or drawing, if you prefer) is the best way to capture ideas, plans, and tasks. Not only does writing give you the ability to store information in a form you can reference later, it gives your mind the opportunity to examine what you know from a different angle. Challenges and issues that seem insurmountable while they're bouncing around in your frontal lobe can often be solved surprisingly quickly after they're put on paper.

Capturing your ideas on paper makes them easier to share with others, in addition to archiving your thoughts for later reference and review. As the saying goes, "The palest ink is clearer than the fondest memory." Notebooks and journals, regularly used, are worth their weight in gold.

Speaking—to yourself or to another person—is another effective method of Externalization. Vocal Externalization explains why most of us have had the experience of solving our own problems while talking with a friend or colleague. By the time you're done talking, you're likely to have more insight into your problem—even if your listener didn't say a word.

The key to vocal Externalization is to find an audience who is willing to listen patiently and avoid interrupting you as you talk through an issue.

Even talking to yourself or an inanimate object can help: explaining your problem to a rubber duck, teddy bear, action figure, or other anthropomorphic object sitting on your desk can work if you can get over the initial awkwardness. More often than not, "rubberducking" the problem makes it easier to solve.

However you choose to Externalize your thoughts, don't keep them locked up in your head. *Experiment* with different approaches to find which method works best for you. To help keep your mind clear during the day, schedule a small amount of dedicated time to Externalize. Early mornings or late evenings typically work best for this purpose.

However you do it, the more you Externalize, the clearer your thoughts will become, and the faster you'll make progress toward your goals.

SHARE THIS CONCEPT: http://book.personalmba.com/externalization/

Self-Elicitation

> How do I know what I think until I hear what I say?
> —E. M. FORSTER, NOVELIST AND SOCIAL ACTIVIST

Externalization is most useful if you use it as a tool to examine your plans, goals, and actions. Jotting down the events of the day in a diary format is useful for later review, but using a journal or confidant as a problem-solving tool is even more useful.

Self-Elicitation is the practice of asking yourself questions, then answering them. By asking yourself good questions (or working with someone who asks good questions), you can grasp important insights or generate new ideas very quickly.

The *Five-Fold How* and *Five-Fold Why* are specific examples of Self-Elicitation. Simply by asking yourself questions, you're exploring options you previously didn't consider and *Priming* your brain to notice related information.

In *Self-Directed Behavior*, David Watson and Roland Tharp explain a very useful self-questioning technique you can use to discover the reasons behind behaviors that don't serve you. The ABC Method (Antecedent, Behavior, Consequences) is a set of questions to ask yourself whenever you notice a behavior you want to change.

By recording answers to the following questions in a journal, logging when specific behaviors occur, and noting the frequency or duration of those behaviors, it's possible to discover patterns in your behavior or thought processes. Once you know the pattern, it's easier to change the behavior.

ANTECEDENT

—*When did it happen?*

—*Whom were you with?*

—*What were you doing?*

—*Where were you?*

—*What were you saying to yourself?*

—*What thoughts were you having?*

—*What feelings were you having?*

BEHAVIOR

—*What were you saying to yourself?*

—*What thoughts did you have?*

—*What feelings were you having?*

—*What actions were you performing?*

CONSEQUENCES

—*What happened as a result?*

—*Was it pleasant or unpleasant?*

When you don't know where to begin, it's often difficult to know with certainty which questions are important. The solution is simple: ask yourself, "What are the best questions I could ask myself about this situation?" This meta-question applies in every situation and will help you generate a working list of relevant issues to explore. Once you have a working list of questions, you can follow up with related questions that will help you find answers, like "Who can I ask?" "What could I read?" and "What could I try?"

Asking yourself good questions helps you discover good answers. Make it a *Habit* to consistently ask yourself good questions, and you'll be surprised how easy it is to overcome the challenges you face.

SHARE THIS CONCEPT: **http://book.personalmba.com/self-elicitation/**

Counterfactual Simulation

> To be able to ask a question clearly is two-thirds of the way to getting it answered.
>
> —JOHN RUSKIN, NINETEENTH-CENTURY ART CRITIC AND SOCIAL THEORIST

As we discussed in the section on *Mental Simulation,* our minds are constantly trying to predict the future. Now it's time to learn how to simulate potential courses of action *intentionally.*

Counterfactual—"what if"—questions allow you to directly access your brain's simulation capabilities. You can think of *Counterfactual Simulation* as applied imagination—you're consciously posing a "what if" or "what would happen if" question to your mind, then sitting back and letting your brain do what it does best.

Based on the *Patterns, Associations,* and *Interpretations* you have stored in memory, your brain will produce what it believes to be the most likely result. All you have to do is suspend judgment, pose the question, and wait for the answer.

Counterfactual Simulation is one of our most powerful (and underused) capabilities. Instead of waiting for your brain to simulate a potential course of action, Counterfactual Simulation allows you to "force" your brain to run the simulations you want it to run.

One of the reasons Counterfactual Simulation is useful is because of its flexibility: you can simulate *anything you want.* The subject of your simulation can be completely arbitrary: the only limit to the things you can simulate is your imagination. If you want to simulate what would happen if you suddenly quit your job and moved to Tahiti, there's nothing stopping you. You could even simulate what would happen if you lived ten thousand years in the future or set up shop on Jupiter.

Counterfactual Simulation can help you discover hidden opportunities you may have previously assumed weren't possible. While I was working at P&G, I often dreamed of working for myself and developing the Personal MBA full-time, but I always assumed it was "a year or two away." A year later, it was still "a year or two away." Working for myself was a pleasant daydream, but I simply assumed it wasn't realistic without really examining the possibilities.

That changed shortly after I discovered Counterfactual Simulation. While traveling on business in September of 2008, I ran a simulation: "What would have to be true if I left my job at P&G by my birthday?" (It's in early November.) I didn't think this question was realistic, but it was ambitious enough to be interesting, so I **Inhibited** my judgment and simulated the question anyway.

When you run a Counterfactual Simulation, you assume the event or end state you're simulating *is already true*. By supplying your mind with an artificial destination, it will automatically start to fill in the blanks between point A and point B. When I ran the simulation on leaving P&G, I assumed that it was *definitely going to happen*, then figured out how it would be possible.

As I ran the simulation, other questions naturally presented themselves. How much revenue was coming in? How many clients would I need to have? What other projects would I work on, and how much money would I need to bring in to be financially **Sufficient**? As these questions presented themselves, I answered them as best I could, scribbling my answers in a notebook.

By the time I was finished simulating, I had discovered it was possible for me to leave my job at P&G *immediately*, instead of "in a year or two." When I returned to work the following Monday, I resigned. My last day of corporate work was four days before my twenty-eighth birthday.

In my experience, time spent examining counterfactuals is never wasted. Instead of simply assuming what you want isn't realistic or possible, Counterfactual Simulation allows you to actually figure out what it would take to make what you want real. After doing a simulation, you'll always come away with a greater understanding of what it takes to do something, or what would need to be true in order to make something work.

Apply your mind to Counterfactual Simulation, and you'll be absolutely astounded at how easy it is to accomplish some of the things that you assumed were simply dreams.

SHARE THIS CONCEPT: http://book.personalmba.com/counterfactual-simulation/

Parkinson's Law

Work expands so as to fill the time available for its completion.

—CYRIL NORTHCOTE PARKINSON, NAVAL HISTORIAN AND
MANAGEMENT THEORIST

In 1955, Cyril Northcote Parkinson wrote a humorous essay in the *Economist* based on his experience in the British civil service. In that essay, Parkinson proposed what became his eponymous law: "Work expands so as to fill the time available for its completion."

If something must be done in a year, it'll be done in a year. If something must be done next week, it'll be done next week. If something must be done tomorrow, it'll be done tomorrow. We plan based on how much time we have, and when the deadline approaches, we start to make *Choices* and *Trade-offs* to do what must be done to complete the task by the deadline.

Parkinson's Law should not be considered carte blanche to set unreasonable deadlines. All projects take time—you certainly can't build a skyscraper in a day or a factory in a week. The more complex the project, the more time it typically takes—to a point.

Parkinson's Law is best used as a *Counterfactual Simulation* question. What would it look like if you finished the project on a very aggressive time scale? If you had to build a skyscraper in a day, how would you go about doing it? Answer the question the way you would a counterfactual, and you'll discover techniques or approaches you can use to get the work done in less time.

Ingvar Kamprad, the founder of IKEA, once said, "If you split your day into ten-minute increments, and you try to waste as few of those ten-minute increments as possible, you'll be amazed at what you can get done." For small tasks, use what I call Ingvar's Rule—assume each task will take no more than ten minutes to complete, then begin. This includes meetings and phone calls: for some reason, the default time period for meetings is an hour—whether you need it or not. Often you can get just as much, if not more, done if you assume that the basic unit of time for a meeting is ten minutes. Ingvar's Rule is a counterfactual—what would you do if you only had ten minutes to get something done? Act accordingly.

SHARE THIS CONCEPT: http://book.personalmba.com/parkinsons-law/

Doomsday Scenario

What looks large from a distance, close up ain't never that big.
—BOB DYLAN, SONGWRITER AND MUSICIAN

If you're in *Threat Lockdown*, it's hard to get anything done—your mind is fixated on the threat, imagining scenes that would fit right into a bad horror movie.

Let's say you're thinking of starting a business, but you lock up with anxiety whenever you think about striking out on your own. You imagine quitting your job, and your mind immediately pictures investing a lot of money building something that doesn't work, going bankrupt, and becoming homeless. You won't be able to get another job, everyone will hate you, and you'll spend the rest of your days living in a van down by the river.

How do you encourage your brain to stop trying to protect you if it's clearly overreacting?

A *Doomsday Scenario* is a *Counterfactual Simulation* where you assume everything that can go wrong does go wrong. What if you don't complete the project on time? What if your plan doesn't work? What if you lose everything? What if they all laugh at you?

Doomsday Scenarios are pessimistic for a reason—they help you realize that, in most circumstances, you're going to be okay. *Caveman Syndrome* makes our ancient brains overdramatic, so they assume every potential threat is a life-or-death situation. The reason we get so stressed out is that our brains *Interpret* losing resources, diminishing in status, or being rejected as threats to our survival. That may have been true a long time ago, but it's not anymore. Now you can lose money, screw up, or be rejected hundreds of times a day—and live to tell the tale.

When you actually examine your worst fears, you'll discover that things won't be as bad as you fear. Creating a Doomsday Scenario is the equivalent of giving a small child who is afraid of monsters under their bed a flashlight—by shedding some light on the subject of their fears, they realize there's nothing to be afraid of.

By intentionally *Externalizing* and defining your worst fears, you're exposing them as what they really are: irrational overreactions. More often than not, you'll discover that you were scared of something that doesn't really matter. Even if something bad goes wrong, it's not really going to be as bad you think. As soon as you realize you're not going to die, you're free to do much more than you previously dared to do.

Once you've imagined your Doomsday Scenario, you can start doing things to improve upon the worst case. If you're starting a business, you can begin defining the actual risks and make plans to mitigate them. Instead of being a victim of your fears, you can use them constructively.

Construct your Doomsday Scenario, and you can make your overdramatic brain work with you, instead of against you.

SHARE THIS CONCEPT: http://book.personalmba.com/doomsday-scenario/

Excessive Self-Regard Tendency

I haven't been wrong since 1961, when I thought I made a mistake.

—BOB HUDSON, POLITICIAN

Every few months, television viewers around the world cringe while delusional contestants on *American Idol* show the world how horrible they are at singing.

The most fascinating part of this spectacle isn't the epic display of tone-deafness—it's the fact that many of the people auditioning *believe they're talented singers.* The contrast is astounding—how could anyone be so horribly wrong about something so obvious?

Excessive Self-Regard Tendency is the natural tendency to overestimate your own abilities, particularly if you have little experience with the matter at hand. Being optimistic about our capabilities has benefits—it increases the probability we'll try something new. That's how novices sometimes accomplish great things—they do them before realizing how risky or difficult their objective was.

Steve Wozniak, who cofounded Apple Computer with Steve Jobs, built the world's first personal computer. Here's what he had to say about the experience: "I never had done any of this stuff before, I never built a computer, I never built a company, I had no idea what I was doing. But I was going to do it, and so I did it." Woz didn't know what he was doing, but he thought he could, so he did.

Unfortunately, our natural confidence also comes with a cost—the potential for harmful self-delusion.

The Excessive Self-Regard Tendency is even more pronounced if you don't know much about the subject at hand. The more incompetent a person is, the *less they realize they're incompetent*. The more a person actually knows, the better their ability to self-assess their capabilities, and the more likely they are to doubt their capabilities until they have enough experience to know they've mastered the subject.

According to David Dunning and Justin Kruger of Cornell University, Charles Darwin's famous quip "Ignorance more frequently begets confidence than does knowledge" is literally true. They explain the "Dunning-Kruger effect" as follows:

1. Incompetent individuals tend to overestimate their own level of skill.

2. Incompetent individuals fail to recognize genuine skill in others.

3. Incompetent individuals fail to recognize the extremity of their inadequacy.

4. If they can be trained to substantially improve their own skill level, these individuals can recognize and acknowledge their own previous lack of skill.

People who are "unconsciously incompetent" don't know they're incompetent—they know so little about the subject that they can't fully appreciate how little they actually know. That's why every barber and taxi driver you meet is an expert on the economy and international politics.

Once you learn a bit more about a new subject, you become "consciously incompetent"—you *know you don't know* what you're doing. As a result, most individuals become less confident in their abilities shortly after learning more about a topic—more knowledge makes it easier to fully appreciate the limits of their knowledge and capabilities.

Developing "conscious competence"—the state of knowing what you're doing—takes experience, knowledge, and practice. When you're consciously competent, you regain your confidence: you know the limits of your knowledge and can accurately assess your abilities.

A certain amount of humility is a valuable self-correcting quality. Overconfidence sometimes produces greatness, but it's a high-risk bet—without guidance, you're far more likely to find yourself in a bad situation. Cultivating a healthy amount of humility can keep you from assuming you know everything there is to know about everything, then painfully discovering otherwise.

The Excessive Self-Regard Tendency is universal (be very wary if your first impulse is to think *you're* immune to it), so it's important to have trusted advisers who aren't afraid to tell you if you're making a mistake. One of the easiest ways to get yourself in trouble via the Excessive Self-Regard Tendency is estimating deadlines—overconfidence is a major cause of the *Planning Fallacy* (discussed later). When I agreed to write this book, I thought it would take about six months—but I'd never written a book before, so I really had no idea. Several of my more experienced friends and advisers counseled that it would probably take a year, and I'm very glad I listened—they were right.

All of us are prone to overestimating our abilities. Padding your team with yes-men is deadly because people who always agree with you can't help you correct for this tendency—people who always support your decisions won't prevent you from making huge mistakes.

Cultivate relationships with people who aren't afraid to tell you when you're making questionable assumptions or going down the wrong path—they're valuable friends indeed.

SHARE THIS CONCEPT: http://book.personalmba.com/excessive-self-regard-tendency/

Confirmation Bias

It ain't what you don't know that gets you into trouble. It's what you
know for sure that just ain't so.

—MARK TWAIN

Paradoxically, one of the best ways to figure out whether or not you're right
is to actively look for information that *proves you're wrong*.

Confirmation Bias is the general tendency for people to pay **Attention** to
information that supports their conclusions and ignore information that
doesn't. No one particularly likes to learn they've made a bad decision, so
we tend to filter the information we pay Attention to.

The more strongly held the opinion or belief, the more we ignore sources
of information that challenge that position. That's why you won't find many
political conservatives reading politically liberal sources of news, and vice
versa—they already know they don't agree, so why bother? Unfortunately,
this makes both positions more and more extreme, since neither side seeks
information that may challenge their convictions.

The best way to counteract Confirmation Bias is to intentionally seek
out sources of information that challenge your current hypothesis or belief. When Kelsey and I adopted a vegan diet for a number of years, it was
easy to also adopt the mind-set that we were clearly making the optimal
choice—for our health, for our animal friends, and for the planet. This
worldview naturally made it difficult to pay attention to any source of information that argued the contrary.

Ultimately, we changed our minds as a result of finding disconfirming
evidence. After reading *The Vegetarian Myth* by Lierre Keith, we discovered
that vegetarianism isn't as healthy or environmentally friendly as we had
originally believed. *Protein Power* by Michael R. and Mary Dan Eades
taught us more about how our bodies biochemically process the food we
eat, and about how the **Feedback Loops** (discussed later) that exist in our
metabolism actually function. As a result, we learned that a few persistent
health issues (low energy, slow digestion, etc.) we were experiencing were
actually a consequence of our diet.

Both books provided evidence that contradicted our original position—
and they changed our minds. We learned a great deal from the experience—

both about diet and about the importance of paying Attention to disconfirming evidence.

Paying Attention to disconfirming evidence is naturally difficult—it means intentionally looking for reasons you might be wrong, and we usually hate to be wrong. Seeking disconfirming evidence will either show you the error of your ways or provide additional evidence for why your position is actually correct—as long as you suspend judgment long enough to learn from the experience.

Looking for disconfirming information is uncomfortable, but it's useful, whatever you ultimately decide.

SHARE THIS CONCEPT: http://book.personalmba.com/confirmation-bias/

Hindsight Bias

> Finish each day and be done with it. You have done what you could. Some blunders and absurdities no doubt crept in; forget them as soon as you can. Tomorrow is a new day; begin it well and serenely and with too high a spirit to be encumbered with your old nonsense.
>
> —RALPH WALDO EMERSON, ESSAYIST AND POET

How do you feel when you realize that you've made a mistake?

Hindsight Bias is the natural tendency to kick yourself for things you "should have known." If you lose your job, you "should have known it was coming." If the price of a particular stock you own drops 80 percent overnight, you "should have sold it." If you launch a product and no one buys it, you "should have known it wouldn't work."

Baloney. If you knew then what you know now, you wouldn't have done what you did.

Every decision you ever make will be based on incomplete information—we have to use **Interpretation** to fill in the blanks. Since you're not omniscient, you'll always have more information when you evaluate the results of your actions than you had when you actually made the decision.

As a result, it's very easy to feel stupid if things don't turn out the way you expected. It's important to realize that these feelings are irrational—your decisions were based on the best information you had at the time, and there's nothing you can do now to change them.

Don't feel bad about things that you "should have seen" or "should have done." Changing the past is outside of your *Locus of Control* (discussed later), so there's no sense in wasting energy on self-doubt, wondering what might have been. Hindsight Bias becomes destructive if you negatively judge yourself or others for not knowing the unknowable.

As the saying goes, "Hindsight is 20-20." *Reinterpret* your past mistakes in a constructive light, and focus your energy on what you can do right now to move in a positive direction.

SHARE THIS CONCEPT: http://book.personalmba.com/hindsight-bias/

Performance Load

If not controlled, work will flow to the competent man until he submerges.

—CHARLES BOYLE, FORMER U.S. CONGRESSIONAL LIAISON FOR THE
NATIONAL AERONAUTICS AND SPACE ADMINISTRATION (NASA)

Being busy is better than being bored, but it's possible to be too busy for your own good.

Performance Load is a concept that explains what happens when you have too many things to do. Above a certain point, the more tasks a person has to do, the more their performance on all of those tasks decreases.

Imagine juggling bowling pins. If you're skilled, you may be able to juggle three or four without making a mistake. The more pins that must be juggled at once, the more likely you are to make a mistake and drop them all.

If you want to be productive, *you must set limits*. Juggling hundreds of active tasks across scores of projects is not sustainable: you're risking failure, subpar work, and burnout. Remember *Parkinson's Law*: if you don't set a limit on your available time, your work will expand to fill it all. If you don't draw the line somewhere, work will consume all of your energy, and you'll inevitably burn out.

Limits always have consequences—if you're not prepared to handle the consequences, it's not really a limit. If you're working for a manager who expects you to work twenty hours a day, seven days a week, telling them no by setting limits on your working hours may cost you your job. Working that pace is completely unrealistic, but if you're not willing to accept the possibility of losing the job, you haven't really set the limit.

In order to handle the unexpected, you must have unscheduled time to respond to new inputs. The default mind-set of many modern businesses is that "downtime" is inefficient and wasteful—workers should be busy all the time. Unfortunately, this philosophy ignores the necessity of handling unexpected events, which always occur. Everyone only has so many hours in a day, and if your agenda is constantly booked solid, it'll always be difficult to keep up with new and unexpected demands on your time and energy.

You can't perform at 110 percent of your capacity at all times—use the **Four Methods of Completion** to eliminate, defer, or delegate marginally valuable work that contributes to Performance Load. By keeping some capacity in reserve, you'll be ready to handle the **Most Important Tasks** immediately.

SHARE THIS CONCEPT: http://book.personalmba.com/performance-load/

Energy Cycles

We all have times when we think more effectively, and times when we should not be thinking at all.

—DANIEL COHEN, CHILDREN'S AUTHOR

Here's the problem with "time management": time is not what needs to be managed. No matter what you choose to do, time will inevitably pass.

The implicit assumption of time management systems is that every hour is fungible—equivalent to any other. Nothing could be further from the truth: all people are created equal, but all hours are most definitely not.

Throughout the day, your energy level naturally cycles up and down. Your body has natural rhythms during the day, which I call **Energy Cycles**. Most people are familiar with the twenty-four-hour circadian rhythm, which wakes you up in the morning and makes you feel tired at night. Lesser known is the ninety-minute ultradian rhythm, which is described in *The Power of Full Engagement* by Jim Loehr and Tony Schwartz.

The ultradian rhythm influences bodily systems, controlling the flow of hormones throughout your body. When your energy is on an upswing, you're capable of focusing deeply and getting a lot accomplished. When it's on a downswing, all your mind and body want to do is rest and recover. There's nothing abnormal about these changes in energy during the day, but we often act as though being on a downswing is somehow a problem that needs to be fixed.

Nowadays, it's popular to try to "hack" this cycle to get more done by resting less. Attempting to work eight to twelve hours without a break is not uncommon in highly competitive workplaces. Most of us try to over-clock our brains with large doses of sugar and caffeine. Some people even resort to abusing prescription or illegal drugs to work a little bit longer or faster.

Like all biological organisms, humans need to rest and recover for peak performance. Taking a break isn't a sign of laziness or weakness—it's a recognition of a fundamental human need. Paying attention to your natural Energy Cycle will help you consistently perform at your best over long periods of time.

Here are four simple ways to work with your body instead of against it:

1. *Learn Your Patterns*—Use a notebook or calendar to track how much energy you have during different parts of the day, as well as what you're eating and drinking. If you do this for a few days, you'll notice patterns in how your energy waxes and wanes, allowing you to plan your work accordingly.[11]

2. *Maximize Your Peak Cycles*—When you're in an up cycle, you're capable of getting a lot accomplished, so plan your day to take advantage of that energy. If you're doing creative work, carve out a three- to four-hour block of time during an up cycle to get it done. If your work consists of attending a lot of meetings, plan the most important meetings during the up cycle.

3. *Take a Break*—When you're in a down cycle, it's better to rest than attempt to power through it. Rest and recovery are not optional—if you don't rest now, your body will force you to rest later, by either cycling down longer than usual or by getting sick. During a down cycle, go for a walk, meditate, or take a twenty-minute nap. Relaxing

on the down cycle can restore your energy, allowing you to take full advantage of the next up cycle.

4. *Get Enough Sleep*—Sleep deprivation results in a prolonged down cycle, which gets in the way of getting things done. To ensure you get enough sleep each evening, set a timer to go off an hour before you'd ideally be in bed sleeping. When the timer goes off, turn off the computer and/or TV, go through your evening routine, make a cup of noncaffeinated tea, and spend some time with a book you enjoy. When your reading comprehension starts to go down, you'll know it's time for bed.

Paying attention to your Energy Cycles during the day will help you get the most out of the time you have available. Take maximum advantage of your up cycles and rest on your down cycles, and you'll be amazed at what you can accomplish in a day.

SHARE THIS CONCEPT: http://book.personalmba.com/energy-cycles/

Stress and Recovery

Only those who will risk going too far can possibly find out how far one can go.

—T. S. ELIOT, POET AND PLAYWRIGHT

During my last semester of college—around the time I created the Personal MBA—I pushed myself to the breaking point.

I was taking twenty-two credit hours of classes across three subjects: business information systems, real estate, and philosophy. Every class I took had some kind of capstone project on top of the final exam. Two of the courses I was taking were at the graduate level, and each required a twenty-plus-page paper on an extremely complex topic to pass. I had far too much work to do in the time available.

By the last two weeks of the quarter, I was an absolute wreck: sleep deprived, exhausted, and stressed beyond belief. Everything got done on time, but the workload took its toll, and it took me a few weeks of doing nothing after graduation to fully recover.

Even though it wasn't pleasant, I'm glad I found my breaking point. Here's why: now I know how much I'm capable of doing, and how much is too much. I know more about how my mind and body react to stress, and I'm better able to identify the warning signs of taking on too much before things get out of hand.

As a result, I've learned to keep myself running at about 90 percent capacity, which is enough to get a lot done without burning out. At any given time, I'm writing, consulting, and working on a few interesting side projects. Paying attention to *Stress and Recovery* ensures that I don't take on too much to handle. Learning my breaking point has made it much easier to know when to push and when to slow down.

It's impossible to know how much you're capable of until you decide to push your limits. As long as you stay safe by limiting your *Experimentation* to things that won't kill you or do permanent damage, you can learn a ton about how you work by stretching yourself to the limit. The knowledge you gain will help you make better choices in the future about which projects to take on and how much is too much.

That said, our bodies are not machines that are designed to operate at maximum capacity at all times. It's remarkably easy to fall into the trap of comparing your output to an idealized version of yourself who can build Rome in a day, then build the Great Wall of China as a fun side project. If that's your vision of personal effectiveness, you'll always come up short.

You are not a machine—the ideal of human productivity is not acting like a robot. Humans need rest, relaxation, sleep, and play in order to function effectively. Too little of any of these things can seriously diminish your capacity to do good work and impact how much you enjoy your life.

So how do you rest and recover? It's simple: spend time doing something completely different from your normal activities and responsibilities. The less overlap between your hobby and your work, the better.

During World War II, Winston Churchill was under as much stress as a person can withstand. As prime minister of the United Kingdom, he was responsible for leading in the defense of Great Britain from 1940 until the end of the war in 1945. The fate of a country and the freedom of its people depended upon his fortitude and persistence for five long years.

How did Churchill keep from collapsing under such a heavy burden?

In *Painting as a Pastime*, Churchill explains how spending time painting helped him recover from the demands of war and politics:

> *Many remedies are suggested for the avoidance of worry and mental overstrain by persons who, over prolonged periods, have to bear exceptional responsibilities and discharge duties upon a very large scale. Some advise travel, and others, retreat. Some praise solitude, and others, gaiety. No doubt all these may play their part according to the individual temperament. But the element which is constant and common in all of them is Change.*
>
> *Change is the master key. A man can wear out a particular part of his mind by continually using it and tiring it, just in the same way as he can wear out the elbows of his coat. There is, however, this difference between the living cells of the brain and inanimate articles: one cannot mend the frayed elbows of a coat by rubbing the sleeves or shoulders; but the tired parts of the mind can be rested and strengthened, not merely by rest, but by using other parts. It is not enough to merely switch off the lights which play upon the main and ordinary field of interest; a new field of interest must be illuminated.*
>
> *It is no use saying to the tired mental muscles—if one may coin such an expression—"I will give you a good rest," "I will go for a long walk," or "I will lie down and think of nothing." The mind keeps busy just the same. If it has been weighing and measuring, it goes on weighing and measuring. If it has been worrying, it goes on worrying. It is only when new cells are called into activity, when new stars become the lords of the ascendant, that relief, repose, refreshment are afforded.*

If Churchill could find time to paint in the middle of a world war, you can find time in your busy schedule to rest and recover doing something you enjoy. Dedicating guilt-free time to rest and recovery can simultaneously make your life more enjoyable and more productive.

SHARE THIS CONCEPT: http://book.personalmba.com/stress-recovery/

Testing

Discoveries are often made by not following instructions, by going
off the main road, by trying the untried.

—FRANK TYGER, POLITICAL CARTOONIST AND COLUMNIST

I write best early in the morning, after eight hours of sleep. After waking up I drink two mugs of coffee, each containing one tablespoon of unsalted, grass-fed butter and MCT (refined coconut) oil,[12] and turn on a bright blue LED lamp that simulates morning sunlight. Once I'm nourished and alert, I open up my computer, turn off my Internet connection, and start writing. Once I get started, I can concentrate on writing for up to six hours without stopping if I'm not interrupted.

Writing is important to me, so this is what I do every day. I've Tested *many* different approaches, Testing many different variables. This is what works best for me, so I've made it a *Habit*.

Will this be my method forever? I doubt it—I'll eventually find other methods that work even better. My *Experimentation* never stops.

Testing is the act of trying something new—a way of applying the scientific method and the *Iteration Cycle* to your own life. The most happy and productive people I know all have something in common: they're always trying new things to see what works. You can't make positive discoveries that make your life better if you never try anything new.

Testing doesn't have to be complicated. All that's required is choosing some part of your life to focus on, then trying new ways to get what you want. You can Test random approaches or read about what works for others, then test the approach yourself. *Externalizing* your results in a notebook can help you keep track of what you've tried, what works, and what doesn't.

Here's a simple structure that will help you plan and track your Experiments:

▶ *Observations*—What are you observing in your life or business that you want to improve?

▶ *Knowns*—What have you learned from past Experiments that might be related to your observations?

▶ *Hypotheses*—Based on what you've observed, what situations or factors might cause or contribute to your observations?

▶ *Tests*—What will you try or change to improve your situation? Which hypotheses will this experiment Test?

▶ *Results*—What happened after each Test? Does it support or disconfirm the hypothesis?

Here are a few questions to help you discover things worth Testing:

▶ How much sleep do you need to feel rested and alert?

▶ Which foods make you feel energetic after eating? Which foods make you feel ill or lethargic?

▶ When do you do your most productive work? Are there any patterns in your productivity?

▶ When do you get your best ideas? What are you doing when they occur to you?

▶ What is your biggest source of stress or concern? When do you start worrying, and why?

Once you've found a **Pattern** in one of these areas, it's time to start Experimenting. Consciously change your approach to one of these areas of your life and Externalize your results. If you find a change useful, keep doing it—if not, stop doing it and try something else.

Testing is the best way to ensure that your life gets better over time. By constantly trying new things, you're learning what works for you and what doesn't. Over time, you'll discover Patterns—things that make your life better and things that make your life worse. The results of your Experiments **Accumulate**, until they inevitably produce the results you want.

You never know until you try.

SHARE THIS CONCEPT: http://book.personalmba.com/testing/

Mystique

What grief we'd avoid if we knew how to transfer emotional experience across generations, as we do money or scientific knowledge.

—ALAIN DE BOTTON, PHILOSOPHER AND ESSAYIST

There's a big difference between liking the idea of being/doing something and *liking the actual being/doing*.

It's easy to like the idea of being the CEO of a *Fortune* 500 company. It's harder to like the hours, the responsibility, and the pressure that comes with the top job.

It's easy to like the idea of being a manager. It's harder to like the demands from C-level execs, surprises from your direct reports, and the necessity of defending your turf in a political environment.

It's easy to like the idea of having an Ivy League MBA or law degree. It's harder to like the six-figure debt and the corresponding necessity of getting a stressful 60-plus-hour-a-week job to make the investment "worth it."

It's easy to like the idea of being self-employed. It's harder to like the fact that 100 percent of your income comes from your own effort, and that if you screw up, you're the one who will face the consequences.

It's easy to like the idea of raising millions of dollars of venture capital. It's harder to like the fact that you've given up control over the project you're investing your life in.

It's easy to like the idea of being an author. It's harder to like the solitude, self-doubt, and long hours of "butt in chair, hands on keyboard" that consistent writing requires.

It's easy to like the idea of being a celebrity. It's harder to like the inevitable scrutiny, loss of privacy, and constant fear that people will direct their attention away from you in favor of the "next big thing."

Mystique is a powerful force—a little mystery makes most things appear to be a lot more attractive than they actually are. Fortunately, there's an easy way to counteract the rose-colored glasses of Mystique: have a real, human conversation with someone who's actually done what you're interested in doing.

Here's what to ask: "I really respect what you're doing, but I imagine it has high points and low points. Could you share them with me? Knowing what you know now, is it worth the effort?"

This conversation will only take a few minutes, but you'll be amazed by what you learn, on both the positive and the negative side.

No job, project, or position is flawless—every course of action has **Trade-offs**. Learning what they are in advance gives you a major advantage: you can examine an option without idealizing it, then choose if it's really what you want to do *before you start*. That kind of knowledge is priceless.

SHARE THIS CONCEPT: http://book.personalmba.com/mystique/

Hedonic Treadmill

> If thou wilt make a man happy, add not unto his riches but take away from his desires.
>
> —EPICURUS, ANCIENT GREEK PHILOSOPHER

Let's assume that you believe buying a fancy new car will make you happy. In the short term, it might: for the first week or so, you'll probably experience great pleasure when you drive. Over time, however, your joy will fade, a phenomenon psychologists call "hedonic adaptation." Before long, your new car will blend into your surroundings and your mind will fixate on something else to pursue in the quest for happiness.

This cycle is called the **Hedonic Treadmill**: we pursue pleasurable things because we think they'll make us happy. When we finally achieve or acquire what we're seeking, we adapt to our success in a very short period of time, and our success no longer gives us pleasure. As a result, we begin seeking something new, and the cycle repeats.

The Hedonic Treadmill explains why people who achieve wealth, status, and fame continue to seek more. Since we're not satisfied with what we have for very long, it's only a matter of time before we fixate on something else to achieve or possess.

The Hedonic Treadmill is a major problem if you'd like to experience a feeling of success or achievement for an extended period of time. It's possible to work hard, invest, sacrifice, and push your way to the top of your field, only to find yourself restless and despondent. You'd be surprised at how many "successful" people aren't happy with their lives, even after they've achieved everything they set out to do.

Short-circuiting the Hedonic Treadmill is tricky: it's a side effect of **Caveman Syndrome.** There are, however, a few things we can focus on that tend to lead to sustained levels of life satisfaction. Based on the available research, here are five priorities that will contribute to your long-term happiness in a way that minimizes hedonic adaptation:

1. *Work to make "enough" money.* Money contributes to happiness, but only to a certain point. According to a 2010 study by Daniel Kahneman and Angus Deaton, money has a positive correlation with reported levels of happiness up to an annual household income of approximately $75,000 per year, which represents an income in the top third of U.S. households in 2008–09, the years of the study. Reaching this level of income requires effort, but it's very achievable: average U.S. household income during the years of the study was $71,500.

Once you have enough money to cover the necessities and a few luxuries, you reach a point of **Diminishing Returns** (discussed later): every additional dollar you earn doesn't provide the same amount of utility. Beyond the point of Diminishing Returns, having more money doesn't increase happiness and may actually decrease it by becoming a source of stress and worry. (For examples of how money can decrease happiness, read *Fables of Fortune: What Rich People Have That You Don't Want* by Richard Watts.)

Knowing your monetary point of Diminishing Returns is useful: by consciously limiting your consumption beyond a certain point and establishing long-term savings, you can reap the benefits of financial security and **Resilience** (discussed later) without spending every waking moment working to pay for pleasures you'll adapt to in less than a month.

As a general rule: experiences contribute more to happiness than material goods. Beyond the point where your needs are met, you'll get a higher emotional return for your dollar by traveling with people you like than by purchasing an expensive luxury item.

2. *Focus on improving your health and energy.* Health is a major contributing factor to happiness: when you feel great, you're more likely to feel happy. The converse is also true: when you feel ill, you tend to experience less pleasure, enjoyment, and life satisfaction.

Experimenting with ways to improve your typical level of health and energy can result in huge improvements in your quality of life. Remember, the human body has **Performance Requirements**: food, exercise, and rest are not optional. If you make it a priority to give your body what it needs to thrive, you'll reap the rewards over the years to come.

3. *Spend time with people you enjoy.* One of the single biggest predictors of happiness is the amount of time you spend with people you enjoy: family, friends, and like-minded acquaintances. The context and environment are less important than the people you spend time with.

Different people need different levels of social contact to feel happy. Extroverted people feel energized by social contact and need to be around others on a regular basis. Introverted people (like me) can go days or weeks with little social contact and generally get their energy from spending time alone. Still, introverted people benefit from spending time with people they like: regular social time with friends is highly correlated with major sustained increases in life satisfaction. Long meals and trips with friends are a great use of time.

According to George Vaillant, the project's director, the results of the Harvard Study of Adult Development (the longest-running longitudinal study of mental health) boil down to this: "the only thing that really matters in life are your relationships with other people."[13]

4. *Remove chronic annoyances.* There are many things in life that can wear on your nerves. Examining ways to reduce or eliminate chronic stresses or annoyances can generate significant improvements in life satisfaction.

If you find driving in rush-hour traffic stressful, moving closer to work is a good solution. If you don't like your current job, start looking for another. If you find working with a particular client annoying, fire them. If you always forget to pack your laptop's power cable when you travel, buy a second cable that stays in your travel bag. By finding simple ways to remove unnecessary stress and frustration, you'll spend less time and energy feeling bad and more time feeling good.

5. *Pursue a new challenge.* Most people assume retirees feel overjoyed, but that's often not the case. It's common for people to derive a sense of purpose and enjoyment from their work, and retirees can feel empty and lost when their former career is no longer a priority. Left unresolved, this sense of loss can spiral into depression.

The solution is to take on an exciting new challenge. This challenge can be anything: mastering a new skill, completing a big project, or pursuing a major accomplishment. Whether it's learning a new language, playing an instrument, building something from scratch, or completing a marathon, striving for new achievement is the best way to experience happiness and growth over long periods of time.

Focusing on experiences over material goods goes a long way if you want to step off the Hedonic Treadmill. In the immortal words of Charles Kingsley, a nineteenth-century historian and clergyman: "We act as though comfort and luxury were the chief requirements of life, when all we need to make us happy is something to be enthusiastic about."

SHARE THIS CONCEPT: http://book.personalmba.com/hedonic-treadmill/

Comparison Fallacy

Never compare your inside with someone else's outside.
—HUGH MACLEOD, AUTHOR OF *IGNORE EVERYBODY*

In business and in life, it's easy to compare our situation to others'. **Status Seeking** ensures that we spend energy tracking our relative status to our peers, and most of the time our conclusions aren't favorable.

We tend to fixate on what other people are accomplishing instead of what we need to do next to achieve our **Goals**. When other people we know accomplish big things, it's easy to feel sad for ourselves instead of happy for their achievements . . . as if their success diminishes us in some way. It doesn't.

The Comparison Fallacy is a simple idea: other people are not you, and you are not other people. You have unique skills, goals, and priorities. In the end, comparing yourself to other people is silly, and there's little to be gained by it.

Here's an example: one of my friends is very successful in business and makes about ten times what I make each year. He has received a lot of public recognition for his work. His products sell well, and he enjoys his success. There's a lot to envy.

Here's the other side of the coin: my friend works twelve hours a day, sometimes more. He doesn't have a family. He has a large staff that requires constant attention, and his business's **Overhead** is more than ten times mine. He's overwhelmed with e-mail, phone calls, and meetings. He's under tremendous stress almost all the time.

It's easy to see the benefits of my friend's life, and just as easy to overlook the **Trade-offs**. That's the trick: he is successful in certain areas because he works very hard, and he's willing to pay the price of his success.

If I could swap lives with my friend, I wouldn't: I'd be miserable. His life doesn't mesh with my priorities or how I prefer to live and work. The benefits he enjoys appeal to me, but I'm not willing to pay the price he's paid for achieving them. Remembering the Comparison Fallacy allows me to wish him well and stay focused on achieving the Goals that are most important to me. I can be genuinely happy for his success and not waste my energy on pointless envy.

The same trick works in any situation that has the potential of inflaming feelings of envy or inferiority. Whenever you're tempted to compare yourself to an acquaintance, colleague, classmate, or celebrity, it always helps to keep in mind that your goals, preferences, and priorities are completely different. You've lived different lives, and you've each paid a different price for what you've accomplished. Any comparison you make instantly renders itself invalid, so you can relax.

The only metric of success that matters is this: are you spending your time doing work you like, with people you enjoy, in a way that keeps you financially **Sufficient**? If so, don't worry about what other people are doing. If not, focus on making changes that are within your **Locus of Control**, so you can start moving in the direction you desire. Remember the Comparison Fallacy, and keep moving closer to what you want.

SHARE THIS CONCEPT: http://book.personalmba.com/comparison-fallacy/

Locus of Control

Grant me the serenity to accept the things I cannot change, the courage to change the things I can, and the wisdom to know the difference.

—THE SERENITY PRAYER

No matter how much you want a particular job, after the interview is over, you can't control whether or not you get the job—you've done what you could.

No matter how intently you watch the stock market, you can't will the stock price of a particular company to go up.

No matter how much you'd like to retain a key employee or make a personal relationship work, you can't prevent them from leaving if they want to.

Understanding your **Locus of Control** is being able to separate what you can control (or strongly influence) from what you can't. Trying to control things that aren't actually under your control is a recipe for eternal frustration.

As much as we'd like to, we can't control everything that happens to us. Natural disasters are a perfect example: if a tornado or earthquake destroys your home, there's nothing you can do about it. As uncomfortable as it is to imagine, the **Environment** contains many things we can't control. It's a fundamental aspect of life that we can't change, no matter how much we might want to.

Focusing on your efforts helps you stay sane—turning results you don't directly control into **Goals** is a recipe for frustration. One of the reasons that diets drive people crazy is that they involve trying to control a result—weight—that is not directly under their control. If you focus on efforts—

eating healthy food, exercising, and doing what you can to manage related medical conditions—your weight will handle itself.

Worrying about things you can't influence or control is a waste of time and energy. One of the best things I've ever done was choose to stop paying **Attention** to the news—99.9 percent of the information you'll find in a newspaper or television newscast is completely outside of your Locus of Control. Instead of fruitlessly worrying about "what the world is coming to," ignoring the news helps me spend more of my time doing what I can to actually make things better.

The better you're able to separate what you can control from what you can't, the happier and more productive you'll be. Focus most of your energy on things that you can influence, and let everything else go. Keep your Attention on what you're doing to build the life you want to live, and it's only a matter of time before you get there.

SHARE THIS CONCEPT: http://book.personalmba.com/locus-of-control/

Attachment

> If thou wilt make a man happy, add not unto his riches but take away from his desires.
>
> —EPICURUS, ANCIENT GREEK PHILOSOPHER

Imagine you're on your way up Mount Everest, on the way to achieving your **Goal**. The night before you plan to summit, a massive storm appears without warning. Visibility is zero, the temperature is steadily dropping, and conditions are so bad you risk falling or freezing to death if you continue climbing.

Have you failed?

When something outside of our **Locus of Control** affects our plans or Goals, it's easy to take it personally. If you have your heart set on summiting Mount Everest *today*, you'll likely meet your doom. Far better to change your plans and live to climb the mountain another day.

The more **Attached** you are to a particular idea or plan, the more you limit your flexibility and reduce your chances of finding a better solution. It's good to be dedicated to the pursuit of your goals, but only to a point. If you become too Attached to the visions you have in your head, you'll have a hard time adjusting to the inevitable twists and turns of life.

Acceptance requires applying the concept of **Sunk Cost** to yourself. Imagine losing millions of dollars in the stock market—a horrible situation. No matter how much you rail against greedy bankers, corrupt politicians, or the unfairness of life, it's not going to bring that money back. Spending time feeling down for not "knowing better" or being omniscient won't improve your situation.

The solution to Attachment is accepting that your idea or plan is no longer feasible or useful. The less Attached you are to your plans, Goals, status, and position, the easier it will be to respond appropriately to inevitable change or unforeseen circumstances.

If you suddenly lose your job, remaining Attached to your previous position is a hindrance, not a help. It's better to spend your energy doing what needs to be done to bring in more income.

The more you focus and accept the things that have happened and choose to work on things that you can do to make things better, the happier you'll be.

SHARE THIS CONCEPT: http://book.personalmba.com/attachment/

Personal Research and Development (R&D)

If a man empties his purse into his head, no one can take it from him.
An investment in knowledge always pays the highest return.

—BENJAMIN FRANKLIN

Every successful business dedicates a certain amount of resources to trying new things. **Research and Development (R&D)** is what business leaders around the world count on to determine what the company should work on next. Large companies spend millions (sometimes billions) of dollars in speculative research every year, experimenting with new techniques and processes in order to enhance their capabilities.

R&D exists because it works—companies that make Research and Development a priority often discover new products to offer their customers or process improvements that meaningfully contribute to the bottom line. If it works for them, it can work for you.

What would it look like if you set aside a few hundred dollars a month as a *Personal R&D* budget? Using the techniques discussed in *I Will Teach You to Be Rich* by Ramit Sethi, it's remarkably easy to automatically divert a certain amount of your monthly income into an account earmarked for Personal R&D. That money can then be used—guilt free—for purchasing books, taking courses, acquiring equipment, or attending conferences: anything that will improve your skills and capabilities.

Personal finance gurus might disagree with me here, but I think having a robust Personal R&D budget is more important than maximizing your savings. I'm all for having a well-funded emergency account and saving enough for future needs, but savings can only get you so far.

Investments in improving your personal skills and capabilities can simultaneously enrich your life and open doors to additional income sources. New skills create new opportunities, and new opportunities often translate into more income. Your ability to save is limited; your ability to earn is not.

Here's a simple planning exercise that will help you establish your own Personal R&D budget: what would have to change to be able to dedicate at least 5 percent of your monthly income to personal development and *Experimentation,* assuming your current income stays the same?

Any money-saving tip you find in good personal finance books or blogs can be used to fund your Personal R&D account: for details, I recommend reading *Your Money or Your Life* by Vicki Robin and Joe Dominguez, as well as following Get Rich Slowly (getrichslowly.org) and The Simple Dollar (thesimpledollar.com) online. All it takes is a little creativity and budgeting, and you'll be well on your way to funding your own self-directed Research and Development laboratory.

SHARE THIS CONCEPT: **http://book.personalmba.com/personal-research-and-development/**

Limiting Belief

Intelligent discontent is the mainspring of civilization.

—EUGENE V. DEBS, LABOR UNION ACTIVIST

In general, there are two primary ways of looking at the world—two mind-sets that influence your response to new experiences.

The first basic mind-set is that your skills and abilities are fixed. If you try something and it doesn't work, it's because you're "not good at that," and you never will be. You were born with innate skills and abilities that will never change.

Using this mind-set, if you experience a challenge or difficulty, you're likely to stop—you're obviously not good at it, so why bother?

The second basic mind-set is that your skills and abilities are malleable. If you try something and it doesn't work, it's because you haven't worked on it very much, but if you keep trying, you'll inevitably get better. Your skills and abilities are like muscles—they strengthen with use. If you experience a challenge or difficulty, you're likely to keep going—you might not be good at it yet, but you're always getting better.

These two mind-sets color how you experience everything in the world. In *Mindset: The New Psychology of Success*, Dr. Carol Dweck calls these mind-sets the "fixed" and "growth" theories of intelligence. If you have a "fixed" mind-set, challenges are a commentary on your worth as a person—you've been tried and found wanting, which makes trying new things feel threatening. If you have a "growth" mind-set, challenges are simply an obstacle to be overcome by working harder. The fixed mind-set is an example of a *Limiting Belief*: something you believe is true about the world that holds you back from achieving a *Goal* you value. The fixed mind-set isn't true, but it's capable of holding you back if you choose to believe it.

Some Limiting Beliefs are the result of errors in *Pattern Matching*. Here's a common example: if you believe that wealthy people are superficial, unethical, or corrupt, you'll find it difficult to make money. If you make more money than you make now, you'll become one of "those people," and the thought will make you uncomfortable anytime money is an issue.

If you don't identify the *Conflict* and resolve it, money matters will always make you uncomfortable. Your mind is not malfunctioning: part of your brain is anticipating the future and trying to protect you from something you don't want, but it's going about the task in a counterproductive way. To make progress, you have to identify and eliminate the beliefs that are holding you back.

Everyone has Limiting Beliefs in certain areas. Anytime you use the words "I can't," "I have to," or "I'm not good at," you've discovered a potential Limiting Belief. Most of the time, taking a moment to consciously question the belief is all you need to do to break it. "Is that really true?" and "How do I know that's true?" are very powerful and versatile *Self-Elicitation* questions.

Limiting Beliefs may also appear when you consider doing things that make you uncomfortable, like applying for a new job or selling an offer to a new prospect. Images of rejection and disapproval start flashing through your mind, and your first impulse is to conclude "this won't work" before conducting a single test or gathering real feedback.

Here's a useful rule of thumb for these types of situations: make the other party tell you no. This is a *Habit* worth installing: you may believe you're going to be turned down when you make a request or propose an idea, but make the other party say it instead of assuming it's a given. You'll be surprised at how often you get what you want, even when you believe the odds are slim.

The way you choose to respond to challenges determines how successful you ultimately will become. It's important to realize that you have no "fundamental defects"—there's nothing that you're fundamentally incapable of learning or doing. It may take time and effort, but you'll improve eventually if you make the effort.

Viewing your mind as a muscle is the best way to help it grow.

SHARE THIS CONCEPT: **http://book.personalmba.com/limiting-belief/**

8

WORKING WITH OTHERS

Take away my people but leave my factories, and soon grass will grow on factory floors. Take away my factories but leave my people, and soon we will have a new and better factory.

—ANDREW CARNEGIE, NINETEENTH-CENTURY INDUSTRIALIST

Working with other people is an ever-present part of business and life: you can't escape it, even if you want to. Customers, employees, contractors, and partners are all individuals with their own unique motivations and desires. If you want to do well in this world, it pays to understand how to get things done with and through other people.

In this chapter, we'll discuss how to work effectively with others. You'll learn how to communicate more effectively, earn the respect and trust of others, recognize the limitations and pitfalls of group interactions, and lead or manage a team of people effectively.

SHARE THIS CONCEPT: http://book.personalmba.com/working-with-others/

Power

> Force is all-conquering, but its victories are short-lived . . . Nearly all
> men can stand adversity, but if you want to test a man's character,
> give him power.
>
> —ABRAHAM LINCOLN, SIXTEENTH PRESIDENT OF THE UNITED STATES

All human relationships are based on **Power**—the ability to influence the
actions of other people. We can never control people in the sense that we've
discussed in the section on **Perceptual Control**—we don't have direct access to
the inner processes that make people do the things they do. All we can really do is act in ways that encourage people to do what we suggest.

The use of Power typically takes one of two fundamental forms: influence or compulsion. Influence is the ability to encourage someone else to
want what you suggest. Compulsion is the ability to force someone else to
do what you command.

Encouraging an employee to "go the extra mile" out of a sense of loyalty
or craftsmanship is influence. Forcing the employee to work over the weekend by threatening to fire them if they refuse is compulsion. The actions
that employee takes may be exactly the same, but how they *feel* about taking
those actions will be quite different.

On the whole, influence is much more effective than compulsion. The vast
majority of people naturally resist being forced to do something against their
will or better judgment, so constantly relying on compulsion to get things
done is a poor strategy. Bossing people around only serves to make them
dislike you, and they'll find ways to retaliate or quit working with you at the
earliest available opportunity. Influence, on the other hand, is sustainable—
encouraging people to want what you want gets you the results you're looking
for without provoking unnecessary ill will.

Like it or not, everyone relies on Power to get things done. In *The 48
Laws of Power*, Robert Greene argues that no one is completely exempt
from dealing with others, which inevitably involves Power.

Power is a neutral tool—one that can be used for good or ill. Power represents your ability to get things done through other people—the more
power you have, the more things you can do. Accordingly, there's nothing

morally wrong with consciously seeking to increase your Power, provided you respect the rights of other people. The more Power you have, the more you can ultimately accomplish, but with great Power comes great responsibility.

The reason that interactions among large groups of people inevitably become political is the ever-present nature of Power. If you don't have a plan, your actions will be determined by someone else. By refusing to make the effort to move in the direction you think is best, you're ceding Power to those who *do* have plans. Refuse to understand that Power is important, and you're likely to find that any influence you have rapidly disappears. The only way to win is to decide to play.

The best way to increase your Power is to do things that increase your influence and **Reputation**. The more people know your capabilities and re-spect the Reputation you've built, the more Power you will have.

SHARE THIS CONCEPT: **http://book.personalmba.com/power/**

Comparative Advantage

Be a first-rate version of yourself, not a second-rate version of someone else.

—JUDY GARLAND, ACTRESS AND SINGER

Essential to the idea of working with other people is the question, Why work with other people in the first place? If you can't control them and get them to do exactly what you want them to do all the time, why bother?

The answer is **Comparative Advantage**, a concept that originated in the "dis-mal science" of economics. Attributed to David Ricardo's 1817 text *On the Principles of Political Economy and Taxation*, "Ricardo's Law of Comparative Advantage" provided an answer to a question of international politics: is it better for the economies of countries to be self-sufficient and produce ev-erything themselves, or specialize in producing certain goods, then trade with one another?

Using Portugal and England as examples, Ricardo calculated that even if both countries were capable of producing cloth and wine, England could produce cloth with much less effort, and Portugal was much better at producing wine. As a result, instead of wasting time and money struggling to do something they weren't good at, Portugal and England would both be better off if they specialized, then traded with each other.

Comparative Advantage means it's better to capitalize on your strengths than to shore up your weaknesses. In *First, Break All The Rules* by Marcus Buckingham and Curt Coffman, and *StrengthsFinder 2.0* by Tom Rath, the authors share the results of the Gallup Organization's comprehensive research on human productivity. As it turns out, Comparative Advantage applies as much to individuals as it does to countries: businesses work better if the individuals who operate them focus on what they're best at, working with other specialists to accomplish everything else they need. "Strengths-Based Management" is simply another term for Comparative Advantage.

Comparative Advantage explains why it often makes sense to work with contractors or outsourcers rather than try to do everything yourself. If you want to build a house, it's probably more efficient to hire a general contractor and specialists who do the kind of work the project requires every day. You could certainly try to do it yourself, but unless you know what you're doing, it'll probably take longer, and the results won't be as good.

Comparative Advantage also explains why diverse teams consistently outperform homogenous teams. Having a wide variety of team members with different skills and backgrounds is a major asset: it increases the probability that one of your teammates will know what to do in any given circumstance. If every team member has the same skills and the same background, it's far more likely the team will get stuck or make a preventable error.

Self-reliance naturally improves your flexibility and knowledge over time, but too much self-reliance is a mistake. I'm a huge advocate of self-education and learning how to do things yourself, but taking the DIY ethic to an extreme can do more harm than good. Working with others can help you get more done, faster, and improve the quality of the end result. Even Thoreau left Walden Pond every once in a while to buy things in town.

The major benefit of self-education when working with others is knowing what skill looks like. You may be able to hire a programmer halfway around the world via Elance.com or oDesk.com, but if you've never done any programming yourself, you're going to have a difficult time figuring out whether or not their work is actually good. Learn a little programming, however, and your ability to identify good programmers will increase, making you more likely to identify skilled colleagues and partners.

In the immortal words of John Donne: "No man is an island." Focus on what you can do well, and work with others to accomplish the rest.

SHARE THIS CONCEPT: http://book.personalmba.com/comparative-advantage/

Communication Overhead

> If you had to identify, in one word, the reason why the human race
> has not achieved, and never will achieve, its full potential, that word
> would be: "meetings."
>
> —DAVE BARRY, COMEDIAN AND NEWSPAPER COLUMNIST

There's a reason high-performing surgical teams, military units, and sports teams tend to be small and focused: too much time spent in communication and coordination can kill a team's effectiveness.

Communication Overhead is the proportion of time you spend communicating with members of your team instead of getting productive work done. In order to keep everyone on the same page, communication is absolutely necessary. The more team members you have to work with, the more you have to communicate with them to coordinate action.

As the number of people you work with increases, Communication Overhead increases geometrically until the total percentage of time each individual must devote to group communication approaches 100 percent. After a certain threshold, each additional team member diminishes the capacity of the group to do anything other than communicate.

Large companies are slow because they suffer from Communication Overhead. If you're responsible for working with a group of more than five to eight people, at least 80 percent of your job will inevitably be communicating effectively with the people you work with. Objectives, plans, and ideas are worthless unless everyone involved understands them well enough to take action.

I experienced this daily while working at P&G—one of my primary projects consisted of creating a company-wide strategy on how to measure certain marketing tactics. Because it was a global project, my recommendation required input and/or approval from dozens of individuals across the company before anything could be implemented.

Naturally, everyone involved had different ideas, argued endlessly over various approaches, and wanted a share of the credit without having to commit to too much work or expense. I spent three months of full-time effort simply putting together a workable proposal. In the meantime, *no actual work was being accomplished*—99 percent of my time was spent doing little more than communicating with other members of the group. That's Communication Overhead.

In the book *Beyond Bureaucracy*,[1] Derek Sheane proposed "8 Symptoms of Bureaucratic Breakdown" that appear in teams suffering from Communication Overhead:

1. *The Invisible Decision*—No one knows how or where decisions are made, and there is no transparency in the decision-making process.

2. *Unfinished Business*—Too many tasks are started but very few are carried through to the end.

3. *Coordination Paralysis*—Nothing can be done without checking with a host of interconnected units.

4. *Nothing New*—There are no radical ideas, inventions, or lateral thinking—a general lack of initiative.

5. *Pseudo-Problems*—Minor issues become magnified out of all proportion.

6. *Embattled Center*—The center battles for consistency and control against local/regional units.

7. *Negative Deadlines*—The deadlines for work become more important than the quality of the work being done.

8. *Input Domination*—Individuals react to inputs—i.e., whatever gets put in their in-tray—as opposed to using their own initiative.

If any of these qualities describe your daily work experience, your team is probably suffering from a case of Communication Overhead.

The solution to Communication Overhead is simple but not easy: make your team as small as possible. You'll be leaving people out, but that's the point—including them is causing more work than it's creating in benefits. Removing unnecessary people from the team will save everyone's time and produce better results.

Studies of effective teamwork usually recommend working in groups of three to eight people. In *Peopleware*, project managers Tom DeMarco and Timothy Lister recommend keeping teams "elite and surgical." Small groups tend to be more effective than large groups because Communication Overhead is reduced—each team member adds more networking capacity to the team than they require in communication to be effective. Once group size expands above eight, each additional team member requires more investment in communication than they add in productive capacity.

If you want your team to perform at its best, make your teams as small and autonomous as possible.

SHARE THIS CONCEPT: http://book.personalmba.com/communication-overhead/

Importance

The deepest principle in human nature is the craving to be appreciated.
—WILLIAM JAMES, DOCTOR AND PIONEERING PSYCHOLOGIST

Everyone has a fundamental need to feel *Important*. It doesn't matter if you're dealing with a customer, an employee, an acquaintance, or a friend. The more Important you make them feel, the more they'll value their relationship with you.

Make someone feel small or unimportant, and you'll earn their enmity in record time. How do you feel when you're talking with someone who's checking their BlackBerry, or interrupts your conversation to take a phone call?

The more interest you take in other people, the more Important they will feel. The reason you don't feel valued when a sleazy car salesman asks "how you're doing" is that you know the question doesn't indicate genuine interest—it's clearly a means to close the deal. People want to feel Important even if they don't buy from you, which is where canned sales scripts fail.

Fortunately, making others feel Important is not particularly difficult if you make an effort to be present and curious. It mostly has to do with undivided focus: paying attention, listening intently, expressing interest, and asking questions. Being the complete focus of someone's attention is so rare in today's world that it makes a memorable impact almost immediately.

Cultivating a genuine interest in other people goes a very long way. The more Important you make people feel when they're around you, the more they'll like you and want to be around you.

SHARE THIS CONCEPT: http://book.personalmba.com/importance/

Safety

> You can't operate a company by fear, because the way to eliminate fear is to avoid criticism, and the best way to avoid criticism is to do nothing.
>
> —STEVE ROSS, FORMER CEO OF TIME WARNER

"That's the stupidest thing I've ever heard! Seriously—did you even think that through before you opened your mouth?"

Ever had a meeting like that? I have.

Unfortunately, this type of interaction happens all the time. In *What Got You Here Won't Get You There*, veteran executive coach Marshall Goldsmith explains that high-level executives often subtly (and sometimes blatantly) put down their peers and subordinates to make themselves feel smarter or more *Important*. What putting others down actually accomplishes is shutting down effective communication.

Effective communication can only occur when both parties feel safe. As soon as people start to feel unimportant or threatened in a conversation, they start "stonewalling," shutting down communication. The threatened party may continue to interact, but mentally and emotionally, they've withdrawn from the conversation.

The only way to prevent stonewalling is to make the person you're communicating with feel safe being open and honest with you. Just as people have a fundamental need to feel Important, people also have a need to feel safe when expressing what's on their minds and talking about things that are Important to them. The moment they begin to sense they're being judged, evaluated, or looked down upon because of an idea they have or a position they hold, they'll shut down.

In *Crucial Conversations*, a book about maintaining a sense of **Safety** while discussing important issues with colleagues and loved ones, authors Kerry Patterson, Joseph Grenny, Ron McMillan, and Al Switzler recommend using the STATE model to communicate without provoking anger or defensiveness:

1. *Share your facts*—Facts are less controversial, more persuasive, and less insulting than conclusions, so lead with them first.

2. *Tell your story*—Explain the situation from your point of view, taking care to avoid insulting or judging, which makes the other person feel less safe.

3. *Ask for others' paths*—Ask for the other person's side of the situation, what they intended, and what they want.

4. *Talk tentatively*—Avoid conclusions, judgments, and ultimatums.

5. *Encourage testing*—Make suggestions, ask for input, and discuss until you reach a productive and mutually satisfactory course of action.

Some people are more sensitive than others. Becoming more aware of your words and actions and how they might be interpreted by people with different attitudes is half the battle. If you want to communicate with someone in a way that you both benefit from the conversation and get something done, both parties need to feel safe. The best way to make that happen is to avoid passing judgment and focus on making the other party feel Important. Books like *Crucial Conversations, How to Win Friends and Influence People* by Dale Carnegie, and *Emotional Intelligence* by Daniel Goleman can help you learn how.

SHARE THIS CONCEPT: http://book.personalmba.com/safety/

Golden Trifecta

Any fool can criticize, condemn, and complain—and most fools do.

—DALE CARNEGIE, AUTHOR OF *HOW TO WIN FRIENDS AND*
INFLUENCE PEOPLE

If people have a fundamental need to feel **Important** and **Safe,** how do you go about making that happen?

The **Golden Trifecta** is my personal three-word summary of *How to Win Friends and Influence People.* If you want to make others feel Important and safe around you, always remember to treat people with appreciation, courtesy, and respect.

Appreciation means expressing your gratitude for what others are doing for you, even if it's not quite perfect. Imagine that you're designing a product, and your lead designer shows you some mockups that you believe won't work. Bluntly responding, "This is totally wrong—do it again," is a good way to make your colleague feel unimportant and insecure. Instead, express Appreciation: "Thanks—it's clear you worked hard on this and I appreciate that. I'm not sure if we're there yet, so here are a few ideas that may help. . . " It's the same content, but delivered in a very different tone.

Courtesy is politeness, pure and simple. I once heard Courtesy defined as "accepting small inconveniences on behalf of another person," and I think that's a very useful definition. Opening the door for another person is a small inconvenience, but it can have a major impact on how they perceive you. There's no need to make every petty issue a big deal.

Respect is a matter of honoring the other person's status. No matter how you relate to the person you're communicating with, Respecting them as an individual is critical if you want to make them feel Important or safe, no matter how high or low their social status.

It's important to apply the Golden Trifecta to all of your interactions with other people, not just the people you're particularly interested in. If you've ever had lunch or dinner with someone who was nice to you but rude to the waitstaff, you know what I mean. Treating other people poorly sends a clear signal to everyone that you can't be trusted.

If you make it a policy to treat people with Appreciation, Courtesy, and

Respect in all circumstances, other people will feel Important and safe in your presence.

SHARE THIS CONCEPT: http://book.personalmba.com/golden-trifecta/

Reason Why

Civilization advances by extending the number of operations we can perform without thinking.

—ALFRED NORTH WHITEHEAD, MATHEMATICIAN AND PHILOSOPHER

Here's a fascinating quirk about asking people to do something: they'll be far more likely to comply with your request if you give them a reason to do what you ask. In *Influence: The Psychology of Persuasion*, Dr. Robert Cialdini describes an ingenious experiment that demonstrates this principle in action.

In the 1970s, Ellen Langer, a psychologist at Harvard University, conducted a set of famous experiments about compliance—what makes people agree to a request. The experiments centered around a busy copy machine on the Harvard campus.

Langer's students asked people waiting in line to use the copy machine if they could move to the front of the line, using various approaches. A straightforward request was honored 60 percent of the time, but Langer found that adding a *reason* for the request increased the compliance rate to 95 percent—an astounding improvement. The technique worked even if the reason was vacuous—"because I have to make copies" worked just as well as "because I'm late for class" or "because I'm in a rush." All the reason had to do was supply a "because," and it was enough to make people agree to the request.

Humans are predisposed to look for behavioral causes. People will be more receptive to any request if you give them a reason why. Any reason will do.

SHARE THIS CONCEPT: http://book.personalmba.com/reason-why/

Commander's Intent

Never tell people how to do things. Tell them what to do, and they
will surprise you with their ingenuity.

—GENERAL GEORGE S. PATTON

Almost universally, people hate to be told exactly what to do. "Micromanagement" is the bane of any worker's existence—if you're a competent professional, nothing is more demeaning than someone else defining and
scrutinizing your work to the last detail.

Micromanagement isn't simply annoying—it's extremely inefficient.
Not only does spelling out every single detail make people feel less *Important*,
it actually impairs their effectiveness. No set of instructions, no matter how
detailed, is capable of covering every contingency. When something inevitably changes, micromanagement fails.

Think of how overwhelmed a CEO who insists on micromanagement
will inevitably become—remember, human beings don't *Scale*. The more
people who work for the company, the more directions the CEO must give
to keep everything moving. If you have ten employees, micromanagement
is a hassle. If you have hundreds or thousands, it's a nightmare.

Commander's Intent is a much better method of delegating tasks: whenever
you assign a task to someone, tell them *why* it must be done. The more your
agent understands the purpose behind your actions, the better they'll be
able to respond appropriately when the situation changes.

Commander's Intent originated on the battlefield. If a general tells a
field commander precisely how to capture a hill and the situation changes,
the field commander is forced to return to the general for new orders,
which is slow and inefficient. If the general explains the strategy to the field
commander and explains *why* that particular hill is important and how it
will support the overall strategy, the field commander is free to use his
knowledge of the *Goal* and fresh intelligence to act in a new way that supports the original intent.

Commander's Intent alleviates *Communication Overhead*. By communicating the intent behind a certain plan, a leader can make constant communication less critical for the success of the entire team. If everyone understands

the purpose of the plan, everyone can act in ways that support the intent without requiring constant attention.

When you communicate the intent behind your plans, you allow the people you work with to intelligently respond to changes as they happen.

SHARE THIS CONCEPT: http://book.personalmba.com/commanders-intent/

Bystander Apathy

> Accountability is about one person taking responsibility. If two people
> are accountable for the same decision, no one is really accountable.
>
> —GLYN HOLTON, INVESTMENT RISK MANAGEMENT CONSULTANT

Growing up, I was very active in the Boy Scouts. The standard Scout program covers first aid, CPR, and emergency management—basic training that prepares you to handle the most common emergencies you're likely to face.

Outside of specific techniques, I remember two useful principles from this training: (1) always personally step up and take responsibility, unless relieved by a more experienced professional, and (2) always direct commands or requests very clearly to *one specific individual at a time.*

If someone appears to be experiencing a heart attack in a crowded store and you yell, "Someone call 911," it's likely that no one will actually call—the more people around, the more likely everyone will assume that someone else is taking action. It's far more effective to single someone out, make eye contact, point, and say very clearly, "YOU—CALL 911." They will.

Bystander Apathy is an inverse relationship between the number of people who *could* take action and the number of people who *actually choose to act.* The more people available, the less responsibility each member of the crowd feels to do anything about the situation.

The 1964 murder of Kitty Genovese and the 2009 shooting of Petru Barladeanu are dramatic, well-known examples of Bystander Apathy. In both cases, the victims were attacked in the presence of many bystanders, none of whom offered assistance. There's some controversy over exactly how many people witnessed the Genovese murder, but there's no doubt about the Barladeanu case—it was captured on video. As Barladeanu bled to death from a gunshot wound on the floor of a metro station, scores of people who could clearly see what was going on simply walked by.

Bystander Apathy explains why anything assigned to a committee never gets done. If you've ever worked with a group of people who have no **Power** over one another, you know what I'm talking about. Unless someone steps up and takes individual responsibility for actually making things happen and holding individuals accountable for progress, a committee can deliberate for years without getting anything done. Each member of the committee simply assumes someone else is working on it.

The best way to eliminate Bystander Apathy in project management is to ensure that all tasks have single, clear owners and deadlines. Unless every individual on your team knows exactly what they're responsible for and when it must be done, it's very unlikely that they'll actually do it.

When delegating responsibilities, *always assign tasks to a single owner with a clear deadline*. Only then will people feel responsible for getting things done.

SHARE THIS CONCEPT: http://book.personalmba.com/bystander-apathy/

Planning Fallacy

Hofstadter's Law: it always takes longer than you expect, even when you take into account Hofstadter's Law.

—DOUGLAS HOFSTADTER, COGNITIVE SCIENTIST AND PULITZER PRIZE–
WINNING AUTHOR OF *GÖDEL, ESCHER, BACH: AN ETERNAL GOLDEN BRAID*

People are consistently and uniformly horrendous at planning. As uncomfortable as this sounds, any plan created by even the most intelligent and skilled CEO or project manager is very likely to be grossly inaccurate.

As Jason Fried and David Heinemeier Hansson memorably quip in their book *Rework*, "Planning is guessing." The reason we're so bad at planning is because we're not omniscient—unforeseen events or circumstances can dramatically impact even the most detailed plans. When we create plans, we're simply guessing and using **Interpretation** to fill in the blanks, no matter how much we cloak that uncomfortable reality in official-sounding language and fancy-looking charts.

The *Planning Fallacy* means that people have a persistent tendency to underestimate completion times. The more complex the project, the more *Interdependencies* (discussed later) the project contains. The more Interdependencies there are, the more likely it is that something at some time will not go according to plan.

When planning, we naturally tend to imagine a scenario in which everything goes well. As a result, we tend to underestimate the likelihood of things that could impact the plan, as well as how much those contingencies will affect the project. Rare is the project plan that contains a line item that says, "Project manager contracts mononucleosis: out for a month."

Most plans drastically underestimate the amount of *Slack* (discussed later) necessary to make the plan accurate. If you're responsible for completing a complex project, including a few months of Slack time is appropriate—unexpected delays, vacations, sicknesses, and other unforeseen events are likely to make things take longer than expected.

The challenge is that including significant Slack time is almost never seen as acceptable or appropriate. If you go to a CEO, customer, or partner with a plan that involves three months of Slack time, the most common response is, "That's not acceptable—get it done faster." The Slack is eliminated, and as a result, almost every project plan is very likely to be completely wrong.

The inaccuracy of plans doesn't make planning worthless. Plans aren't useful because they help you predict with better accuracy—they're useful because the act of creating the plan helps you understand requirements, dependencies, and risks more thoroughly than when you started. In the immortal words of Dwight D. Eisenhower: "No battle was ever won according to plan, but no battle was ever won without one . . . Plans are useless, but planning is indispensable." The value of planning is in *Mental Simulation*: the thought process required to create the plan itself.

Use plans, but don't depend on them—as long as you keep working as quickly and effectively as possible, the project will be done as soon as it's feasible.

SHARE THIS CONCEPT: http://book.personalmba.com/planning-fallacy/

Referrals

The way to get on in the world is to make people believe it's to their
advantage to help you.

—JEAN DE LA BRUYÈRE, SEVENTEENTH-CENTURY ESSAYIST
AND MORALIST

When your car breaks down, whom would you rather take it to—a mechanic who's a friend of a friend, or a random operation you found in the
phone directory?

Given the choice, people always prefer to interact with people they
know and like. **Referrals** make it far easier for people to **Decide** to work with
someone they don't know.

Referrals are effective because they transfer the qualities of being known
and liked. The reason you're more likely to go to a mechanic your friend
recommends is that you know and like your friend, and your friend knows
and likes that mechanic. Even if the competing mechanic in the phone
book is highly qualified, that doesn't matter as much as being known and
liked. The Referral transfers the knowing/liking effect to the recipient—
instead of being a risky unknown quantity, they're suddenly a friend.

Cold calling doesn't work very well because the caller is unknown. Remember, our minds tend to treat unknown people and situations as potential threats, which activates our natural defenses. If someone doesn't already
know or like you, you're going to have a tough time convincing them to do
what you want.

Even the most obscure commonalities can significantly warm up a cold
connection. If someone mentions they're from the same area as you, or that
they went to the same college, or know the same person, you'll automatically start to like them more—even though the connection may be very
tenuous.

The last year Kelsey sold wedding gowns in Manhattan, over 70 percent
of her sales came from Referrals. When you're considering spending $10,000
or more on a designer dress, you want to work with someone you know and
like—and Kelsey's previous customers *really* liked working with her. Before
they entered the salon, most of Kelsey's prospective customers already knew
and liked her—and she closed many more sales as a result.

The more people who know, like, and trust you, the better off you are. Referrals are the best way to expand your network of personal connections.

SHARE THIS CONCEPT: http://book.personalmba.com/referrals/

Clanning

> It is a more inspiring battle cry to scream, "Die, vicious scum!" instead of "Die, people who could have been just like me but grew up in a different environment!"
>
> —ELIEZER YUDKOWSKY, ARTIFICIAL INTELLIGENCE RESEARCHER AND FOUNDER OF LESSWRONG.COM

In 1954, twenty-two twelve-year-old boys were selected to attend a special summer camp in Robbers Cave State Park in Oklahoma. Here's what made the summer camp special: the camp was actually a psychology experiment, operated under the direction of Drs. Muzafer and Carolyn Sherif.

Each of the boys was intentionally selected to be as similar to the rest of the group as possible—the psychologists ensured that all of the boys had similar IQs, families, and childhood experiences. Before the experiment started, the group of twenty-two was split into two groups and placed on opposite sides of the park. By design, neither group knew the other existed.

The original plan was to let each group coalesce for a while, then make them aware that the other group existed to see what would happen. The camp counselors were psychologists and graduate students, who would be watching the events unfold up close and personal.

Here's what happened: the groups accidentally discovered each other earlier than planned, and hostilities started immediately. As soon as the boys discovered there was another group in "their camp," they rallied together in preparation and defense.

Humans naturally tend to form distinct groups, a process called *Clanning*. One group of boys began calling themselves "the Eagles," while the other group self-identified as "the Rattlers." Distinct group identities formed to help members identify "insiders" and "outsiders." The Eagles created an image of themselves as the heroic good guys, while the Rattlers took on the persona of misfits and rebels.

With surprising speed, minor provocations like put-downs and stealing the other group's flag turned into chaos: campsite raids and dining hall fist fights. Competitive activities like sports were a disaster. For the safety of the campers, the researchers quickly tried to find a way to resolve the conflict.

The psychologists introduced challenges and goals that required both groups to work together: solving a water shortage, deciding on a movie to watch, and pushing a broken-down truck back to camp. When the campers started feeling like part of a larger group, the conflicts subsided.

Clanning is a natural human tendency—we're automatically and profoundly influenced by the people around us. Identifying ourselves as part of a group and distinguishing ourselves from other groups is an instinct that explains many of the ongoing wars and conflicts featured in the news every day.

Think of sports fans. The players, coaches, and even stadiums and uniforms change so often it's difficult to understand what exactly the fans are cheering for—the life of a rabid New York Yankees fan will go on unchanged, regardless of whether their team wins or loses. While that may be true, it doesn't feel that way to the fan—when the Yanks win, the fans feel like winners too.

Sports rivalries happen for the same reason. I grew up in northern Ohio, where the Ohio State–Michigan State rivalry is alive and well. Where I come from, during certain parts of the year, Michigan is *evil* in the eyes of Ohio State fans. If you look at the situation from a distance, it's absolutely silly—college kids scrambling for a little oblong brown ball while hundreds of thousands of people scream themselves hoarse. In the moment, however, for those two groups the enmity is everything.

Groups naturally form around important issues, positions, or events. Understand the group dynamic, or you're likely to be caught up in it.

SHARE THIS CONCEPT: http://book.personalmba.com/clanning/

Convergence and Divergence

> The individual has always had to struggle to keep from being over-
> whelmed by the tribe. If you try it, you will be lonely often, and some-
> times frightened. But no price is too high to pay for the privilege of
> owning yourself.
>
> —FRIEDRICH NIETZSCHE

Over time, you become more and more like those whom you spend time with, and less like people in other groups.

Convergence is the tendency of group members to become more alike over time. In business, this is sometimes called a company "culture," in the sense that people who work there tend to have similar characteristics, behaviors, and philosophies.

Convergence also means that groups have a tendency to police themselves. The **Norms** (discussed later) of the group work like gravity—if they are violated, others will exert an influence on the rebel to bring them back in line. As the proverb goes: "The tallest blade of grass is the first to be cut."

If you've ever worked for a company with a workaholic culture, you know how powerful Convergence can be. If it's normal for workers to come in at 6:00 in the morning and stay until 10:30 at night, it can be difficult to keep shorter working hours, since violating the Norms is a **Social Signal** that you don't belong in the group. One of my clients, who works for a major medical research institution, often has conflicts with coworkers who believe he's not "pulling his weight" because he leaves work at 5:00 p.m. instead of 7:30 p.m., even though he does great work and gets everything done. Instead of being viewed as "working smart," going home at a reasonable hour is seen as a form of treason. Sad, but common.

Divergence is the tendency for groups to become less like other groups over time. Since group behavior often evolves to clearly distinguish members of one group from another, the Norms of most groups constantly change to resist being confused with another group or imitator.

Divergence explains why fashions among the socialite class in New York City change so quickly and dramatically. In certain social circles, dress is a way to signal your wealth or status. When the latest fashions start appearing in Target so people can imitate the look, fashions change to compensate. This constant Divergence keeps the group affiliation signal valid.

The groups you spend time with automatically and profoundly influence your behavior. According to the late Jim Rohn, author of *The Art of Exceptional Living*, "You are the average of the five people you spend the most time with." The values and behaviors of the people you interact with on a daily basis exert constant pressures on you to adopt the same values and behaviors.

Convergence can be useful if you consciously choose to spend time with people you'd like to become more like over time. If you'd like to become less shy and more outgoing, spending time with social people in social situations can't help but influence your behavior. You won't become a social butterfly overnight, but you will naturally start to adopt the behaviors and Norms of the people you're spending time with.

This approach works for anything—if you want to test a raw-food diet for a while, spend more time hanging out with people who eat that way. Used consciously, you can use convergence to make habit change easier.

Breaking away from groups that aren't serving you is painful but necessary to grow. People who want to quit smoking or drinking often find it extremely difficult to quit because a large portion of their social network engages in those behaviors. Taking a smoke break at 3:00 p.m. or attending a 6:00 p.m. happy hour is a very significant social event—if your friends are expecting you, the temptation is even harder to resist. To make significant changes, it's often necessary to leave one group and find another that's more supportive of where you want to go, which is why joining support groups like Alcoholics Anonymous is a very effective way to change specific behaviors.

Once you realize how powerful Convergence and Divergence are, you can use them to your advantage. If your social circle isn't supporting your goals, change your social circle.

SHARE THIS CONCEPT: http://book.personalmba.com/convergence-divergence/

Social Signals

The only rule is don't be boring and dress cute wherever you go. Life
is too short to blend in.

—PARIS HILTON, SOCIALITE

A Rolex doesn't tell time any better than a Timex. That's not the point.

People will expend huge amounts of money and energy to send Social
Signals. A Gucci handbag doesn't carry items any better than a JanSport
backpack, and a Porsche 911 won't (legally) get you from point A to point
B any faster than a Honda Civic. "Luxury" items can cost many times more
than their more functional counterparts, but function is not the purpose.
The benefit lies in sending a message to other people.

Social Signals are tangible indicators of some intangible quality that increases a person's social status or group affiliation. People don't wear sports
jerseys because they're stylish—they're ugly by any aesthetic measure. People wear them because they want to clearly affiliate themselves with their
favorite team—it's a statement of identity.

Signals sometimes have little or nothing to do with the reality of what
the signal is supposed to communicate. In *The Millionaire Next Door*,
Thomas Stanley and William Danko describe the lives and habits of people
who have a net worth of over $1 million. More often than not, they live in
modest houses, drive used cars, and buy inexpensive clothing. If you think
about it, that makes sense—the best way to build wealth is to earn a lot of
money *without spending it*.

People who want to signal they're well off, on the other hand, tend to
spend their money on items that communicate wealth and status—large
houses, luxury cars, designer clothing, expensive vacations. These purchases
are often financed with debt—if you look at the bank statements of the seem-
ingly well-to-do, you'll often find they're in a precarious financial position.

Social signals have real **Economic Value**, so it pays to build them into your
offer if you can. Part of building a signaling value into something is understanding what people want to signal to others. Since signals go back to the
Core Human Drives (acquisition, bonding, learning, defending, and feeling),
people want to signal that they're wealthy, attractive, intelligent, high status,
interesting, and confident. Connecting your offer to one of these qualities

via **Association** is a surefire way to make people **Desire** your offer more strongly.

Use Social Signals to your advantage, and you'll make people want what you have to offer.

SHARE THIS CONCEPT: http://book.personalmba.com/social-signals/

Social Proof

> If fifty million people say a foolish thing, it is still a foolish thing.
>
> —ANATOLE FRANCE, NOBEL PRIZE–WINNING NOVELIST AND POET

Have you ever stood waiting for a stoplight to change before crossing the street when the person standing next to you suddenly started walking? Chances are, you unconsciously started moving too, unless you used **Willpower** to consciously **Inhibit** the response.

In most situations, the actions of other individuals in our situation are a very strong indication that it's okay to behave in a certain way. When a situation is ambiguous, we learn by watching the behavior of others. If you don't know how to act in Rome, doing what the Romans do is a pretty safe bet.

Social Proof can take on a life of its own. Fads often form when one person takes an action, others perceive it as a **Social Signal**, then act the same way, creating a social **Feedback Loop** (discussed later). Pet rocks, yellow Lance Armstrong "Live Strong" bracelets, viral videos, and stock market bubbles all gain power via social proof—if so many other people are doing it, it's easy to come to the conclusion that you should probably do it too.

Testimonials are an effective form of Social Proof often used in business to close more sales. There's a reason why Amazon.com and other online retailers prominently feature user reviews: stories about people who have been pleased with a purchase send a clear signal that an item is safe to buy, so more people purchase.

The best testimonials don't necessarily contain superlatives: *amazing*, *best*, *life-changing*, and *revolutionary* have been so overused that people expect them and discount their expectations accordingly. The most effective testimonials tend to follow this format: "*I was interested in this offer, but skeptical. I decided to purchase anyway, and I'm very pleased with the end result."*

The reason this format is more effective than a litany of people gushing about your offer is that it more closely matches how your prospects are feeling: interested but uncertain. By signaling that the decision was a good one, testimonials tell your prospects that it's safe to buy.

Add a bit of Social Proof to your offers, and your sales will soar.

SHARE THIS CONCEPT: http://book.personalmba.com/social-proof/

Authority

Show respect to all men, but grovel to none.

—TECUMSEH, EIGHTEENTH-CENTURY LEADER OF THE SHAWNEE TRIBE

In the 1970s, Sanka (a popular mass-market coffee brand) hired Robert Young, an actor, to promote the health benefits of decaffeinated coffee. Young was better known to the public as Dr. Marcus Welby, the lead character of the popular television show *Marcus Welby, M.D.*

Even though Young wasn't an expert on the medical effects of caffeine, people still perceived him as an authority—and bought Sanka. The approach worked so well that Sanka used "Dr. Welby" to promote their product for decades.

People have an inherent tendency to comply with **Authority** figures. This tendency begins in childhood—we wouldn't survive very long if we didn't obey our parents most of the time. As we grow up, we're socialized to respect and obey other Authority figures: teachers, police officers, government officials, and clergy. As a result, when an Authority figure asks us to do something, we're very likely to comply—even if the request isn't appropriate or doesn't make sense.

People tend to comply with Authority figures even if they'd refuse to take the same action under normal circumstances. In a famously disturbing social psychology experiment, Stanley Milgram proved that most individuals will comply with Authority figures to a surprising degree—even if the request appears to be morally wrong.

In a series of experiments that began in 1961, Milgram placed test subjects in a room with a "scientist" in a white lab coat and another individual, both of whom were actors. The subject was told the study was about the effect of punishment on learning, and one of the participants was "randomly" selected to be the "learner"—the actor. The "learner" was taken to an adjacent room, strapped into a chair, and attached to electrodes.

The test subject's job as the "teacher" was to read the learner questions, then "shock" the learner if they responded incorrectly. The shocks weren't real, but the actor would scream, cry, and beg to be released from the study. Every few minutes, the "scientist" would instruct the teacher to raise the voltage of the shocks. The intent of the study was to see how long the test subject would obey the scientist before refusing to continue.

The results were disturbing: 80 percent of participants continued past the point where the learner begged to stop, and 65 percent continued all the way to the maximum level of 450 volts, which was clearly marked as deadly. Throughout the study, the subjects were clearly uncomfortable and uncertain, but the scientist told them to continue, so they obeyed.

Authority figures are automatically and strongly persuasive. In the presence of an Authority figure, people will do things they'd otherwise view as reprehensible, or wouldn't consider in the first place—the source of many a scandal involving famous and powerful people.

If you're in a position of Authority, your Authority will change the way others interact with you. Simply because you express an opinion, your subordinates will be far more likely to Interpret your position as a truth or as a command. As a result, people will begin to filter the information they give you based on what they think you want to hear—which may not be what you *need* to hear. This filtering behavior is how Authority figures often end up "living in a bubble"—the combination of Authority and **Confirmation Bias** shelters them from information that contradicts their opinions. As a result, it's difficult for Authority figures to compensate for the **Excessive Self-Regard Tendency**.

Developing a strong **Reputation** in a certain area confers the benefits of Authority. Not all parts of Authority are insidious—if people respect your knowledge and experience, they're more likely to do what you suggest. As a result, developing clear expertise and a strong Reputation can be beneficial—it increases your own influence. Work to establish yourself as an Authority on what you're offering, and people will be more likely to accept your offer.

SHARE THIS CONCEPT: http://book.personalmba.com/authority/

Commitment and Consistency

A foolish consistency is the hobgoblin of little minds.
—RALPH WALDO EMERSON

A few months ago, Kelsey received a phone call from our alma mater, asking for a donation. Here's the twist: they didn't ask for the donation outright. Instead, they asked if she'd be "willing to donate money to the university in the future."Thinking nothing of it, she agreed—and promptly forgot about the call.

Shortly before we moved from New York to Colorado, an official-looking "invoice" for $150 from the university appeared in the mail. It said, "Here is your $150 commitment—you can send your check via the enclosed envelope."

Money was tight, since we were paying for movers, buying cars, and purchasing furniture—but Kelsey sent the check anyway. After all, she had promised, right?

No one wants to be considered an "oath breaker." **Commitments** have been used throughout history as a way of binding groups together. Breaking a promise or Commitment can often have a negative impact on social status and **Reputation,** so most people will do whatever they can to act in ways that are **Consistent** with previous positions and promises.

Even small Commitments make it more likely that individuals will take actions Consistent with those Commitments in the future. One of my favorite stories about Commitment comes from Michael Masterson, the author of *Ready, Fire, Aim*.[2] On a trip to India, Masterson visited a rug merchant. He entered the shop with a healthy level of skepticism and absolutely no intention of buying anything—he was just interested in the experience.

The rug merchant was an excellent salesman and relied on two primary strategies. To break down Masterson's skepticism, he used stories (*Narrative*) of past sales to encourage Masterson to like and *Trust* him before the selling began. Then he used Commitment: whenever Masterson so much as looked at a rug, the proprietor would have his staff take it down off the racks to examine it closely. The rugs were heavy, and it was clear that the sales staff was working hard on his behalf. By making a small Commitment—expressing interest in a particular rug—Masterson provoked a flurry of action.

As the minutes passed, it became difficult for Masterson to imagine leaving without purchasing a rug—it would be inconsistent with the interest he'd expressed and the work the proprietor's staff were doing for him. The least he could do was *Reciprocate*—how could he tell them no?

In the end, he purchased a rug for $8,200 and walked away a happy customer.

Obtaining small Commitments makes it more likely people will choose to act Consistently with them later. Salespeople are often taught to do what they can to encourage their customers to start saying yes as soon as possible. By getting a "foot in the door," they increase the probability that their prospect will take further action.

That's why so many activists use opening questions like "Do you care about child safety?" or "Do you care about the environment?" when telemarketing or collecting signatures on a petition. Most people *do* care about these things, so the reply is automatic and swift. Once you've said you care about something, however, it would be rude of you to refuse their request—it's inconsistent with your previous statement.

Obtain a small Commitment, and you'll make it far more likely that others will comply with your request.

SHARE THIS CONCEPT: http://book.personalmba.com/commitment-consistency/

Incentive-Caused Bias

It is difficult to get a man to understand something when his salary depends upon his not understanding it.

—UPTON SINCLAIR, PULITZER PRIZE–WINNING AUTHOR OF *THE JUNGLE*

If you're working with a real estate agent or mortgage broker, they're primarily interested in convincing you to buy a house. Accordingly, most agents won't tell you it's in your best interest to rent,[3] even if it's true.

Incentive-Caused Bias explains why people with a vested interest in something will tend to guide you in the direction of their interest. We touched on the idea of Incentive-Caused Bias when talking about **Buffers**. If you're working with an agent who's paid on commission, it's not necessarily in their best interest to tell you that purchasing something is not a good idea. As the saying goes: don't ask the barber if you need a haircut.

Incentives automatically influence the way people act, based on how they're rewarded. As a result, the structure of the incentives people are exposed to has a significant impact on behavior. Assuming that the things people are controlling for stay the same, changing the incentives is also likely to change behavior.

In *The Knack*, Norm Brodsky and Bo Burlingham describe how they compensate their salespeople. Most companies compensate salespeople on a commission basis: closing more sales nets the salesperson more money. Under this incentive structure, their salespeople were hyperfocused on closing sales—even if those sales weren't profitable or in the long-term interest of the company. By compensating their salespeople on a salary basis and giving generous bonuses based on long-term performance, Brodsky and Burlingham encouraged them to focus on making *profitable* sales versus sales at any cost.

Sometimes incentives create unintended **Second-Order Effects** (discussed later). Stock options were created under the theory that executives who had an interest in the company's stock price would act in ways to make the stock go up in value over time, which was in the best interest of the shareholders. That's true, but only to a point: the actual interest of those executives is in making the stock price go up *right before they intend to sell*. Once the options are sold, they no longer care so much, leading to policies that sacrifice long-term stability for short-term gains.

Incentives are tricky because they inevitably interact with our **Perceptual Control** systems. For example, giving an employee a bonus or raise for doing something good can create a curious result—they stop doing what got them the reward.

That makes no sense until you realize there was always a reward—they did what they did because they *wanted* to, so the reward was internal. Paying them makes the action part of their job, which reduces their inner drive to complete it for its own sake. In the case of **Conflict**, Perceptual Controls win over incentives every time.

Incentives can be useful if used appropriately, but tread cautiously. If the incentives of the people you work with aren't aligned with your interests, you're bound to have problems.

SHARE THIS CONCEPT: http://book.personalmba.com/incentive-caused-bias/

Modal Bias

> We find comfort among those who agree with us, and growth among those who don't.
>
> —FRANK A. CLARK, MINISTER AND NEWSPAPER COLUMNIST

A few years ago, I was traveling on business with a colleague who was amazed that I was carrying a shoulder bag instead of a rolling suitcase. It was an overnight trip, so I didn't need much—a change of clothes, my computer, and a book. I had everything I needed and the bag wasn't heavy, so my solution worked just fine.

My colleague thought my solution was absurd and spent the next ten minutes telling me so: "It's much better to carry a rolling suitcase! It would be more comfortable, and there'd be less weight. You should *always* carry a rolling suitcase . . ."

Modal Bias is the automatic assumption that *our* idea or approach is best. Most of us like to assume we have everything together—that we know what we're talking about, we know what we're doing, and that our way of doing things is best. Very often, we are quite mistaken. There is always more than one way to get something done, and good ideas can come from anywhere.

In the absence of evidence to the contrary, the HiPPO rules—decisions are made according to the "Highest Paid Person's Opinion." HiPPO is a term coined by Avinash Kaushik in *Web Analytics: An Hour a Day* to explain why it's critically important to support business proposals and decisions with data. In the absence of data, you'll ultimately be forced to do things the boss's way: Modal Bias ensures that the bosses think that their way is best, unless you can prove otherwise. In a battle of opinions, the HiPPO always wins.

The best way to avoid Modal Bias is to use *Inhibition* to temporarily suspend judgment. Part of the value of understanding cognitive biases is the knowledge that you're not immune to them, and simply knowing they exist doesn't make them any less influential. Modal Bias is automatic—we have to use *Willpower* to overcome it.

If you're a leader or manager, it pays to consciously suspend your judgment long enough to thoroughly consider the perspectives and suggestions of the people you work with. Otherwise, you're very likely to miss important information. Remind yourself to keep an open mind, and you'll enhance your ability to make wise decisions.

SHARE THIS CONCEPT: http://book.personalmba.com/modal-bias/

Pygmalion Effect

High achievement always takes place in the framework of high expectation.

—CHARLES KETTERING, PROLIFIC INVENTOR AND FORMER HEAD OF
RESEARCH FOR GENERAL MOTORS

Individuals tend to rise to the level of other people's expectations of them. In general, people tend to perform up to the level that others expect them to perform. If you don't expect much from the people you work with, it's likely you won't inspire them to perform to the limits of their capabilities. Let them know you expect great things from them, and more often than not, you'll find that they perform well.

The **Pygmalion Effect** is a tendency named after the protagonist of a Greek myth. Pygmalion was a gifted sculptor who created a statue of a woman so perfect that he fell in love with his creation. After Pygmalion desperately prayed to Aphrodite, the goddess of love, she took pity on him by bringing the statue to life.

The Pygmalion Effect explains why all of our relationships are, in a very real sense, self-fulfilling prophecies. The effect was first verified in studies that examined the relationship between teachers and students. If a teacher believed a student was "gifted" or "smart," the teacher would act in ways that encouraged the student to live up to that assessment. If the teacher believed a student was "difficult" or "challenged," they wouldn't receive as much support and wouldn't perform as well—a self-fulfilling prophecy.

In *How to Win Friends and Influence People*, Dale Carnegie recommends "Giving others a great reputation to live up to." He was a wise man—raise your expectations of others, and they'll naturally do their best to satisfy those expectations.

The Pygmalion Effect isn't an excuse to have unrealistic expectations of other people. Even the best builder on earth couldn't replicate the pyramids of Egypt in an afternoon, so expecting that level of performance from anyone is a recipe for disappointment and frustration. Expecting quality and performance is one thing—expecting miracles is unrealistic.

The Pygmalion Effect also features a paradox: having high expectations of people will produce better results, but it also increases the probability that you'll be disappointed. The **Expectation Effect** means that our perception of the quality of someone's work is a function of our original expectations. The higher our expectations are to begin with, the higher their performance will generally be, but the risk that our expectations will be violated is also much higher. If you're doing a formal assessment of someone's performance, remember to judge performance objectively and quantitatively as much as possible.

Let others know you expect great work from them, and they'll do their best to live up to your expectations.

SHARE THIS CONCEPT: http://book.personalmba.com/pygmalion-effect/

Attribution Error

Rare is the person who can weigh the faults of others without putting
his thumb on the scales.

—BYRON J. LANGENFELD, WORLD WAR I AVIATOR

Let's assume you hire a contractor to build a house and give him a clear
deadline for completion. The deadline comes and goes, and the project isn't
done. Three months go by before the house is complete.

Unless you're feeling particularly charitable, you're likely to think the
contractor is unprofessional, lazy, or inexperienced. You tell all of your
friends who are interested in building a house not to hire that contractor—
he overpromises and underdelivers.

Now imagine the situation from the contractor's point of view. The
original plan was to buy lumber from a particular supplier that is typically
trustworthy, but one of their trucks broke down, delaying the shipment. The
situation required finding another supplier on short notice, which was difficult, since supplies of the materials were scarce. The contractor moved
heaven and earth to get the job done as quickly as possible—without the
contractor's intervention, the project would have been delayed six months
instead of three.

The **Attribution Error** means that when others screw up, we blame their
character; when *we* screw up, we attribute the situation to circumstances.
By assuming the contractor's actions were due to a character flaw, you made
an error in judgment—the contractor actually went above and beyond the
call of duty, given the circumstances. Because you weren't completely aware
of the circumstances, however, you blamed his character.

Avoiding the Attribution Error makes it easier to stay on good terms
with the people you work with. If you're working with someone who consistently fails to perform to expectations or deliver what they're supposed
to, then you have a legitimate issue that needs to be resolved. Otherwise,
it's beneficial to give people the benefit of the doubt unless a particular
behavior clearly becomes a **Pattern**. When you understand the reason behind a person's actions, it usually makes you see their behavior in a different
light.

When something isn't going as expected, try to find out as much as you can about the circumstances surrounding the behavior you're noticing. More often than not, you'll find that it's a matter of circumstance, not a fundamental character flaw.

SHARE THIS CONCEPT: http://book.personalmba.com/attribution-error/

Option Orientation

The important work of moving the world forward does not wait to be done by perfect men.

—GEORGE ELIOT, NINETEENTH-CENTURY NOVELIST

When something goes wrong, *how* you handle the crisis matters. Mistakes and issues happen all the time, so planning your response in advance goes a long way toward minimizing the impact of the unexpected.

Fixating on the issue is the least productive thing you can do when something goes wrong. By the time you're aware of an issue, preventing it is beyond your **Locus of Control**. The issue has already occurred—the only question is how you plan to respond to it.

Imagine that you report to the CEO of a company that makes microwaves, and you've just received a report that a few of your microwaves have exploded, burning several homes to the ground. That's a major issue. How do you think the CEO will respond if your approach is, "Boss, we have an issue. What do we do? Tell us what to do!"

Unless your CEO is a very patient soul, the response will probably be, "I know we have a $&#@&% issue—help me figure out our options!" Fixate on the hand-wringing, and you'll soon be out of a job.

Instead of dwelling on the problem, focus on your **Options**. Ruminating on the issue doesn't solve anything; what are you going to *do* about it? By focusing your energy on evaluating potential responses, you're far more likely to find a way to make things better.

Here's an alternate approach your hypothetical CEO is probably going to find more useful:

We've received several reports of fires caused by our microwaves. Here are our options—we can have our engineers run a full diagnostic before we *issue a statement and risk further issues, or we can issue an immediate recall. Based on the information we have available right now, it appears our microwaves are at fault, and present a major risk to the safety of our customers. Based on our options, I recommend an immediate recall, which we estimate will cost $4 million.*

Focusing on the potential Options is far more constructive—you're presenting several courses of action and the costs and benefits associated with each, then recommending a solution based on the available information. The CEO (or client) can then review your recommendation and the Options you present, ask follow-up questions, then make the best *Decision* possible. Do this often and well, and you'll develop a *Reputation* for clearheadedness in the midst of crisis.

Focus on Options, not issues, and you'll be able to handle any situation life throws at you.

SHARE THIS CONCEPT: http://book.personalmba.com/option-orientation/

Management

Management is doing things right; leadership is doing the right things.

—PETER DRUCKER, FATHER OF MODERN MANAGEMENT THEORY

Much has been made in business schools of "scientific management" and the need for highly educated, professionally trained managers. In reality, you can't learn to be a competent manager in a classroom—beyond a few simple principles, it's a skill best learned through experience.

Management is simple, but not simplistic. In essence, Management is the act of coordinating a group of people to achieve a specific *Goal* while accounting for ever-present *Change* and *Uncertainty* (both discussed later). It's like taking the helm of a ship during a storm: all you can do is move the wheel back and forth, which is simple, but it takes experience and skill to do it well.

Based on what we've learned thus far, here are six simple principles of effective real-world Management:

1. Recruit the smallest group of people who can accomplish what must be done quickly and with high quality. *Comparative Advantage* means that some people will be better than others at accomplishing certain tasks, so it pays to invest time and resources in recruiting the best team for the job. Don't make that team too large, however—*Communication Overhead* makes each additional team member beyond a core of three to eight people a drag on performance. Small, elite teams are best.

2. Clearly communicate the desired *End Result*, who is responsible for what, and the current status. Everyone on the team must know the *Commander's Intent* of the project, the *Reason Why* it's important, and must clearly know the specific parts of the project they're individually responsible for completing—otherwise, you're risking *Bystander Apathy*.

3. Treat people with respect. Consistently using the *Golden Trifecta*—appreciation, courtesy, and respect—is the best way to make the individuals on your team feel *Important* and is also the best way to ensure that they respect you as a leader and manager. The more your team works together under mutually supportive conditions, the more *Clanning* will naturally occur, and the more cohesive the team will become.

4. Create an *Environment* where everyone can be as productive as possible, then let people do their work. The best working Environment takes full advantage of *Guiding Structure*—provide the best equipment and tools possible and ensure that the Environment reinforces the work the team is doing. To avoid having energy sapped by the *Cognitive Switching Penalty*, shield your team from as many distractions as possible, which includes nonessential bureaucracy and meetings.

5. Refrain from having unrealistic expectations regarding certainty and prediction. Create an aggressive plan to complete the project, but be aware in advance that *Uncertainty* and the *Planning Fallacy* mean your initial plan will almost certainly be incomplete or inaccurate in a few important respects. Update your plan as you go along, using

what you learn along the way, and continually reapply **Parkinson's Law** to find the shortest feasible path to completion that works, given the necessary **Trade-offs** required by the work.

6. **Measure** to see if what you're doing is working—if not, try another approach. One of the primary fallacies of effective Management is that it makes learning unnecessary. This mind-set assumes your initial plan should be 100 percent perfect and followed to the letter. The exact opposite is true: effective Management means *planning* for learning, which requires constant adjustments along the way. Constantly Measure your performance across a small set of **Key Performance Indicators** (discussed later)—if what you're doing doesn't appear to be working, **Experiment** with another approach.

Do these well, and your team will be highly productive. Do them poorly, and you'll be fortunate to get anything useful done at all.

This style of management practice is *not* the command-and-control style of management most people think of when they hear the term. On TV and in most management literature, managers are high-status executives who spend most of their time telling other people what to do and making important decisions. In practice, those behaviors are telltale signs of poor management.

The best managers don't act like big-shot executives: they're more like very skilled assistants, whose primary purpose is to keep the people with **Economically Valuable Skills** focused on improving the **Five Parts of Every Business**: that is, doing things that directly contribute to the company's results. Important decisions are made by the individuals who have the most direct knowledge and experience about the area in question.

In a recent essay, software entrepreneur Joel Spolsky explains why managers should stop calling the shots and start letting people do their jobs:

> *Stop thinking of the management team at the top of the organization.*
> *Start thinking of the software developers, the designers, the product managers, and the front line sales people as the top of the organization.*
> *The "management team" isn't the "decision making" team. It's a support*

function. You may want to call them administration *instead of* management, *which will keep them from getting too big for their britches.*

Administrators aren't supposed to make the hard decisions. They don't know enough. . . . Administrators exist to move the furniture around so that the people at the top of the tree can make the hard decisions. . . .

That's the way it has to work in a knowledge organization. You don't build a startup with one big gigantic brain on the top, and a bunch of lesser brains obeying orders down below. You try to get everyone to have a gigantic brain in their area, and you provide a minimum amount of administrative support to keep them humming along.[4]

Management is a unique skill that requires discipline, patience, clear communication, and a commitment to keeping everyone working together without unnecessary distractions. By recruiting a good team and eliminating as much **Friction** (discussed later) as possible, you'll achieve the results you're seeking.

SHARE THIS CONCEPT: http://book.personalmba.com/management/

Performance-Based Hiring

When all is said and done, a lot more is said than done.
—LOU HOLTZ, PROFESSIONAL AMERICAN FOOTBALL COACH AND
SPORTSCASTER

What if you need to build a team? What if you're responsible for recruiting new employees as your company grows? How do you attract and retain the best employees you can find?

Hiring is a tricky business, and there's no foolproof method to find, attract, and retain star employees and contractors. Mistakes in hiring are almost always expensive, and a bad hire can cost you precious time and money and your team's limited energy and patience.

Good employees and contractors are not necessarily the people who have the fanciest résumé or perform the best in a phone screen or interview: the best hires are people who get things done and work well with other members of your team. Ideally, you're looking for an individual who will contribute valuable work, who's excited about the opportunity, and who you'll enjoy working with every day.

Here's the golden rule of hiring: *the best predictor of future behavior is past performance*. If you want to hire people who will perform well for you in the months and years to come, you need to look for people who have performed well in the past. That means digging deep into what the applicant has accomplished, as well as giving each serious candidate a short-term opportunity to work with you before committing to a longer-term engagement.

The first step in hiring is to publicize that you're looking for help. For most companies, announcing the job typically involves writing a job description, which is either published in a public format or used by a recruiter to search private networks. Either way, don't write the job description like an advertisement: you want to describe what the applicant will actually do on a day-to-day basis if they work for you, with as much unembellished detail as you can share. You're looking for people who are attracted to the work, and it's difficult for applicants to determine whether or not they'll be a good fit unless you describe exactly what the job involves.

Next, identify a basic "acid test" to screen applicants. In weak employment markets, new job postings tend to be overwhelmed with applicants, many of whom are poor candidates. You'll need a way to identify the most promising candidates as quickly as possible. Screening by degree or GPA is common but ineffective, since these don't tell you anything about the candidate's current level of skill. In the application, ask a few basic questions that require a certain amount of specialized knowledge in the field to answer. The most promising candidates will be easy to identify.

Once you've identified a few promising candidates, ask each one to show you examples of two or three of their best projects to date. These projects don't have to be directly related to the job in question, but they should be work that the applicant is proud of and that they believe highlights their skills. The idea is to see examples of what the candidate has accomplished to date, which makes it easier to gauge their relative level of experience and work ethic. If a candidate claims that they have "five years of experience" in product development, but can't show you something they've created, that's a red flag.

Checking references at this point is a good use of time. Along with the examples, request the names and contact information of people they worked with in the process. When you contact a candidate's references, your questions should be simple: e.g., Would they work with the candidate again? If they hesitate or talk around the question, it's a no. If you can't reach a reference when you call, leave a message and ask them to contact you if the candidate is extraordinary. If they are, you'll receive a return call. If they aren't, you won't.

Finally, give promising candidates a short-turnaround project or scenario to see how they think, work, and communicate firsthand. Small projects tend to work best for skilled technical employees, while scenarios work best for candidates who will be responsible for product creation, marketing, sales, business development, finance, and management roles. The outcome of the assignment should be a deliverable of some kind: a report, a pitch, an asset, or a process.

Don't put the candidate in an artificial environment: they should be free to use whatever tools or resources they're comfortable using. They should be free to contact you if they have questions. On completion of the project, bring the candidate in to meet you and present their results. This presentation replaces the interview.

The purpose of the project or scenario is to evaluate the candidate's actual work in a realistic environment. What does the candidate focus on first? What do they notice, and what do they miss? How do they explain their choices and recommendations? How do they respond when you ask questions or disagree with a conclusion?

Assignments like these should be short, requiring no more than a few hours of work. Respect your applicants: your hiring process should not be a cover to obtain free consulting. If you'd prefer to use longer projects to evaluate a candidate, you can always hire them as a part-time consultant, then bring them on full-time if you're pleased with their work.

This general hiring process is a straightforward, effective way to discover and evaluate promising employees and contractors. It's important to note that this process doesn't rely on résumés or traditional interviews, which only really test for how well the candidate writes a résumé and performs in an interview. If you look for past performance and evaluate a candidate's work firsthand, you'll make much better hires.

SHARE THIS CONCEPT: http://book.personalmba.com/performance-based-hiring/

9

UNDERSTANDING SYSTEMS

You do ill if you praise, but worse if you censure, what you do not understand.

—LEONARDO DA VINCI, INVENTOR, ARTIST, AND POLYMATH

Businesses are complex **Systems** that exist within even more complex systems—markets, industries, and societies. A complex system is a self-perpetuating arrangement of interconnected parts that form a unified whole.

In this chapter, you'll learn common elements of all systems, how **Environmental** factors influence the function of systems, and the ever-present nature of **Uncertainty** and **Change.**

SHARE THIS CONCEPT: http://book.personalmba.com/understanding-systems/

Gall's Law

A complex system that works is invariably found to have evolved from a simple system that worked. The inverse proposition also appears to be true: a complex system designed from scratch never works and cannot be made to work. You have to start over, beginning with a simple system.

—JOHN GALL, SYSTEMS THEORIST

Here's a weekend project for you: build a car from scratch. No premanufactured parts or plans allowed. Just a block of metal, a few simple tools, your knowledge, and your imagination. How do you think your project will turn out?

Even if the project takes a year, chances are it will be a complete disaster—if your car works at all (which is very, very unlikely), it'll be far less efficient and reliable than even the worst car from a commercial manufacturer.

Now imagine building a modern computer, creating a cure for cancer, or cloning a human being from scratch without relying on anything someone else has already discovered. Inevitably, you'll suffer through a series of expensive and demoralizing failures. If you succeed, it'll take decades.

Why is it so hard to build working complex *Systems* from scratch? John Gall, one of the first major complex systems theorists, provided the answer.

Here's *Gall's Law*: all complex systems that work evolved from simpler systems that worked. Complex systems are full of variables and *Interdependencies* (discussed later) that must be arranged just right in order to function. Complex systems designed from scratch will never work in the real world, since they haven't been subject to environmental selection forces while being designed.

Uncertainty (discussed later) ensures that you will never be able to anticipate all of these Interdependencies and variables in advance, so a complex system built from scratch will continually fail in all sorts of unexpected ways.

Gall's Law is where environmental *Selection Tests* (discussed later) meet systems design. If you want to build a system that works, the best approach is to build a simple system that meets the *Environment*'s current selection tests first, then improve it over time. Over time, you'll build a complex system that works.

Gall's Law is why *Prototyping* and *Iteration* work so well as a *Value Creation* methodology. Instead of building a complex system from scratch, building a Prototype is much easier—it's the simplest possible creation that will help you verify that your system meets critical Selection Tests.

Expanding that Prototype into a *Minimum Viable Offer* allows you to validate your *Critically Important Assumptions*, resulting in the simplest possible system that can succeed with actual purchasers. Iteration and *Incremental Augmentation*, over time, will produce extremely complex systems that actually work, even as the Environment changes.

If you want to build a system that works from scratch, violate Gall's Law at your peril.

SHARE THIS CONCEPT: http://book.personalmba.com/galls-law/

Flow

A process cannot be understood by stopping it. Understanding must move with the flow of the process, must join it and flow with it.

—FRANK HERBERT, SCIENCE FICTION NOVELIST AND AUTHOR OF *DUNE*

No matter what a **System** actually does, it will have **Flows**—movements of resources into and out of the system. Imagine an automotive assembly line—raw materials like steel, plastic, silicon, rubber, and glass flow in, and a finished car flows out.

Inflows are resources moving into a system. Water into a sink. Money into a bank account. Raw materials into an assembly line. New hires into a company.

Outflows are resources flowing out of a system. Water draining from a sink. Money flowing out of a bank account. Finished goods exiting an assembly line. Employees leaving the company due to retirement, termination, or changing jobs.

Follow the Flows, and you're on your way to understanding how the system works.

SHARE THIS CONCEPT: http://book.personalmba.com/flow/

Stock

Goods in any storehouse are useless until somebody takes them out and puts them to the use they were meant for. That applies to what man stores away in his brain, too.

—THOMAS J. WATSON, FORMER PRESIDENT OF IBM

Follow a system's **Flows**, and you'll inevitably find places where resources tend to pool together.

In this case, a **Stock** isn't a certificate of business ownership—it's a pool or holding tank of resources. A bank account is a good example of a Stock: it's a pool of money waiting to be used. Inventories, queues of customers, and waiting lists are also examples of Stocks.

To increase a Stock, increase **Inflows** and/or decrease **Outflows**. If you want to increase the size of your bank account, put more money in and take less money out. If you're building cars and you're consistently running out of engines, either slow down the line or add more engines to your inventory.

To decrease a Stock, decrease Inflows and/or increase Outflows. If you have too much inventory, stop producing units or increase sales. If waiting lists are too long, increase **Throughput** or reduce the number of people entering the line.

Find the system's Stocks, and you'll discover pools of resources waiting to be used.

SHARE THIS CONCEPT: http://book.personalmba.com/stock/

Slack

> A man with a surplus can control circumstances, but a man without a surplus is controlled by them, and often has no opportunity to exercise judgment.
>
> —HARVEY S. FIRESTONE, FOUNDER OF THE FIRESTONE TIRE AND
> RUBBER COMPANY

Since **Stocks** are pools of resources, it pays to understand *how many* resources you have to work with. **Slack** is the amount of resources present in a Stock. The more resources you have in a Stock, the more Slack you have.

For a **System** to operate efficiently, Stocks should be just the right size—not too big, and not too small. Think of our hypothetical automotive manufacturing system: it's a combination of many smaller systems, each of which is designed to create a Stock of parts.

If there's no Stock of engines waiting to be installed when a car reaches that part of the assembly line, that's an issue—the car will have to wait until an engine is ready, which holds up everything in line behind it. To avoid this issue, it's best to ensure that the Stock is big enough to handle the level of **Outflows** that are required to keep the system running. **Inflows** replenish the Stock as it's depleted.

Large Stocks have the most Slack, but that flexibility comes at a cost. If you have five hundred engines waiting around to be installed, you'll have a lot of funds tied up in inventory, which reduces your cash flow. You'll also have to pay for space to store the engines so they aren't lost or damaged, which increases your costs and decreases your **Profit Margin**.

Small Stocks are more efficient but have less Slack. If you only have a Stock of two or three engines, you won't have a huge amount of resources tied up in inventory, but the probability of running out of engines is much higher if the assembly line speeds up or there's a problem with the engine manufacturing system.

Slack is tricky to manage: too much, and you're wasting time and money. Too little, and your system faces the risk of running out of the resources necessary to continue operating.

SHARE THIS CONCEPT: http://book.personalmba.com/slack/

Constraint

> Once you eliminate your number one problem, number two gets a promotion.
>
> —GERALD WEINBERG, CONSULTANT AND AUTHOR OF
> *THE SECRETS OF CONSULTING*

The performance of a **System** is always limited by the availability of a critical input. Alleviate the **Constraint**, and the system's performance will improve.

In *The Goal: A Process of Ongoing Improvement*, Eliyahu Goldratt explains what he calls the "Theory of Constraints": any manageable system is always limited in achieving more of its **Goal** by at least one Constraint. If you can identify and alleviate the Constraint, you'll increase the **Throughput** of the system.

Creating or increasing the size of a **Stock** in front of a Constraint can help alleviate the issue. If you're constantly running out of engines, increasing the Slack in your engine Stock is the best way to alleviate the Constraint.

By ensuring that the Constraint isn't "starved," you can increase the performance of the entire system.

In order to find and eliminate a Constraint, Goldratt proposes the "Five Focusing Steps," a method you can use to improve the Throughput of any System:

1. *Identification*: examining the system to find the limiting factor. If your automotive assembly line is constantly waiting on engines in order to proceed, engines are your Constraint.

2. *Exploitation*: ensuring that the resources related to the Constraint aren't wasted. If the employees responsible for making engines are also building windshields, or stop building engines during lunchtime, exploiting the Constraint would be having the engine employees spend 100 percent of their available time and energy producing engines, and having them work in shifts so breaks can be taken without slowing down production.

3. *Subordination*: redesigning the entire system to support the Constraint. Let's assume you've done everything you can to get the most out of the engine production system, but you're still behind. Subordination would be rearranging the factory so everything needed to build the engine is close at hand, instead of requiring certain materials to come from the other end of the factory. Other subsystems may have to move or lose resources, but that's not a huge deal, since they're not the Constraint.

4. *Elevation*: permanently increasing the capacity of the Constraint. In the case of the factory, elevation would be buying another engine-making machine and hiring more workers to operate it. Elevation is very effective, but it's expensive—you don't want to spend millions on more equipment if you don't have to. That's why Exploitation and Subordination come first: you can often alleviate a Constraint quickly, without resorting to spending more money.

5. *Reevaluation*: after making a change, reevaluating the system to see where the Constraint is located. Inertia is your enemy: don't assume engines will always be the Constraint: once you make a

few Changes, the limiting factor might become windshields. In that case, it doesn't make sense to continue focusing on increasing engine production—the system won't improve until windshields become the focus of improvement.

The "Five Focusing Steps" are very similar to *Iteration Velocity*—the more quickly you move through this process and the more cycles you complete, the more your system's Throughput will improve.

SHARE THIS CONCEPT: http://book.personalmba.com/constraint/

Feedback Loop

> Systems of information-feedback control are fundamental to all life and human endeavor . . . Everything we do as individuals, as an industry, or as a society is done in the context of an information-feedback system.
>
> —JAY W. FORRESTER, SYSTEMS THEORIST AND PROFESSOR AT MIT

Cause and effect are easy enough to consider, but what happens when the effects become causes themselves?

Feedback Loops exist whenever the output of a *System* becomes one of the inputs in the next cycle. Feedback is how systems learn—if the system is capable of perceiving its *Environment,* that feedback helps the system understand whether it's under control and satisfying the required *Selection Tests.*

Balancing Loops dampen each system cycle's output, leading to system equilibrium and resistance to change. Think of dropping a tennis ball from shoulder height: it'll bounce up and down, each bounce smaller than the last. *Friction* and air resistance dampen each cycle until the energy in the system reaches equilibrium and the ball sits at rest upon the ground.

Balancing Loops stabilize the system, dampening oscillations and keeping the system in a certain state. *Perceptual Control* systems are usually made up of Balancing Loops. Going back to the thermostat example: If the temperature of a room is higher than the *Reference Level,* the cooling system will kick in to move the temperature lower. If the temperature is lower than the Reference Level, the heater will turn on to bring the temperature up. As a result, the system tends to maintain a stable temperature, which is the purpose of the system.

Reinforcing Loops Amplify the system's output with each system cycle. Reinforcing Loops tend to lead to runaway growth or decay over time. Think of a price war between two companies, each of which is competing to have the lowest price. Company A lowers its price, then Company B retaliates by moving its price even lower. As long as each company's Reference Level stays at "our price must be lower than our competitor's," prices will continue to drop until both companies eliminate their **Profit Margins** on that offering.

Compounding is an example of a positive Reinforcing Loop. Each cycle of interest payments makes the principal of the next cycle bigger, resulting in even more interest, continuing the cycle. Over time, accumulated interest can build to enormous sums, which is the purpose of the system.

More often than not, the size of every **Stock** is influenced by several loops, all pulling it in different directions. Consider your bank account balance: there are Feedback Loops controlling your income, rent/mortgage, food expenditures, and other expenses. You're constantly evaluating whether each cycle is too much or not enough, which represents a Balancing feedback Loop. Too much or not enough **Inflow** or **Outflow** causes you to jump into action, which affects the next cycle.

Look around you—there are Feedback Loops *everywhere*. Once you start noticing them, you'll fully appreciate the ever-changing complexity of the systems we live in.

SHARE THIS CONCEPT: http://book.personalmba.com/feedback-loops/

Autocatalysis

> The system that will evolve most rapidly must fall between, and more precisely on, the edge of chaos—possessing order, but with the parts connected loosely enough to be easily altered.
>
> —E. O. WILSON, SYSTEMS THEORIST

Autocatalysis is a concept that comes from chemistry: it's a reaction whose output produces the raw materials necessary for an identical reaction.

An Autocatalyzing *System* produces the inputs necessary for the next cycle as a by-product of the previous cycle, *Amplifying* the cycle. Autocatalysis is a *Compounding*, positive, self-reinforcing *Feedback Loop*—the system will continue to grow until the system changes in a way that produces less output.

Television advertising from the 1950s to the 1990s is an excellent example of Autocatalysis. Companies could spend $1 in advertising and, via increased demand and distribution, get $2 or more in return. That $2, reinvested in advertising, became $4, which became $8, which became $16, etc. Companies like Procter & Gamble, GE, Kraft, and Nestlé used this cycle to become the behemoths they are today.

Now, $1 invested in television advertising is lucky to return $1.20—there are more channels, advertising is more expensive, and people have the technology to filter out unwanted distractions. The loop still works in some circumstances, but it doesn't work as well as it used to.

Autocatalysis doesn't always have to be money: "network effects" and "viral loops" are also examples of Autocatalysis. Every time someone signs up for Facebook, they'll naturally invite even more users to the network. Every time someone sees a funny video on YouTube, they'll pass it along to several friends. That's Autocatalysis.

If your business includes some Autocatalyzing element, it'll grow more quickly than you expect.

SHARE THIS CONCEPT: http://book.personalmba.com/autocatalysis/

Environment

> Reality is that which, when you stop believing in it, doesn't go away.
>
> —PHILIP K. DICK, SCIENCE FICTION NOVELIST AND SHORT STORY WRITER

No *System* stands alone: every system is inevitably affected by all of the other systems around it.

An *Environment* is the structure in which a system operates. The Environment primarily influences or impacts the system's *Flows* or processes, changing the output of the system.

Think of how your body responds when it's either too hot or too cold. Too much or too little heat can be deadly: your body must respond to the change in its Environment to keep operating, either by sweating to shed excess heat or by sheltering to preserve it.

When the Environment changes, the system must change with it to continue operating. According to most leading theories, the dinosaurs became extinct because of changes in the Environment, due to either an ice age or a meteorite impact that kicked up enough dust to blot out the sun. Colder temperatures and less sunlight resulted in major food shortages, resulting in mass extinction.

The conditions present in the Environment affect the operation of the system in that Environment. In 2005, oil prices skyrocketed, and many businesses that relied on oil to manufacture plastics or transport goods suddenly ran into trouble. The increase in variable costs made many businesses less profitable than they were before, and many businesses that couldn't absorb the increase in costs closed.

If you don't want to go the way of the dinosaur, you must always consider how conditions in the Environment affect your system.

SHARE THIS CONCEPT: http://book.personalmba.com/environment/

Selection Test

> Any one response to the universe, however powerful, becomes inappropriate with time and change. Those who become utterly dependent on one means of mastery will find themselves unable to cope with the future.
>
> —FRANK HERBERT, SCIENCE FICTION NOVELIST AND AUTHOR OF *DUNE*

Self-perpetuating **Systems** (like businesses or organisms) can only self-perpetuate as long as they meet the **Environmental** conditions necessary to exist.

A **Selection Test** is an Environmental constraint that determines which Systems continue to self-perpetuate and which ones "die." Mammals like humans have several Selection Tests: breathing enough air, eating enough food, drinking enough water, and retaining enough heat. Businesses also have Selection Tests: enough value provided to customers, enough revenue to cover expenses, enough **Profit** to stay financially **Sufficient**.

Many people think of Selection Tests as "survival of the fittest," but "death of the unfit" is a more accurate description. If a self-perpetuating system fails to satisfy a Selection Test, it will cease to exist. If you can't get enough air, you'll die. If your business can't bring in enough revenue to maintain Sufficiency, it'll die.

As the Environment changes, the Selection Tests change as well. Selection Tests are particularly interesting to watch in the technology market, where the Environment of "what's possible" changes constantly. Businesses that fail to take advantage of major changes in technology quickly find that they're unable to keep up with the new demands customers make for their products.

Changing Environments and Selection Tests are an entrepreneur's best friend—they're what allow small companies to outperform large, entrenched competitors. If you can identify what the Selection Tests in a market really are, you'll be able to compete in that market much more effectively.

Selection Tests are ruthless: satisfy them, and you'll thrive. Fail to adapt to changing conditions, and you'll die.

SHARE THIS CONCEPT: http://book.personalmba.com/selection-test/

Uncertainty

He who lives by the crystal ball soon learns to eat ground glass.

—EDGAR R. FIEDLER, ECONOMIST

What will interest rates look like ten years from now? Where do you think the price of oil will be next year? How about that company stock—is it cheap or overpriced? Is it better to stockpile raw materials now or wait a few months? Businesspeople deal with questions like these daily.

Here's the answer to all of these questions: *nobody knows.* This world of ours is a tremendously uncertain place, which is both a blessing and a curse. Anything can happen, for good or ill—we simply can't know what's around the bend.

There's an enormous difference between risk and *Uncertainty*. In the immortal words of former U.S. secretary of defense Donald Rumsfeld:

There are known knowns. These are things we know that we know. There are known unknowns. That is to say, there are things that we know we don't know. But there are also unknown unknowns. These are things we don't know we don't know.

Risks are known unknowns. If you're planning to pick up a friend from the airport, the probability that their flight will arrive several hours late is a Risk—you know in advance that the arrival time can change, so you can plan accordingly.

Uncertainties are unknown unknowns. You may be late picking up your friend from the airport because a meteorite demolishes your car an hour before you planned to leave for the airport. Who could predict that?

You can't reliably predict the future based on past events in the face of Uncertainty. Unexpected or random events can occur suddenly, which can have major impacts on your goals and plans.

In *The Black Swan*, Nassim Nicholas Taleb, a former hedge fund manager, describes the perils of Uncertainty. No matter how stable or predictable things seem, unpredictable "black swan events" can change everything in an instant.

The term "black swan" was a common expression in sixteenth-century London for something that was impossible or didn't exist—everyone knew that all swans were white. The problem with the term is what eighteenth-century philosopher David Hume called the "problem of induction": until you see every swan that exists, you can never assume the statement "all swans are white" is true. All it takes is *one* black swan to completely invalidate the hypothesis, which happened when black swans were documented in Australia in 1697 by Dutch sea captain Willem de Vlamingh.

The moment before they happen, the probability of "black swan" events occurring is essentially zero. In the wake of a black swan event, the probability of its occurring is a moot point: the event changes the **Environment** in which the system operates, sometimes drastically changing **Selection Tests** without warning. You can't know in advance if (or which) black swan events will occur: all you can do is be flexible, prepared, and **Resilient** (discussed later) enough to react appropriately if and when they do.

Even the most detailed analysis with reams of historical data can't save you from Uncertainty. The primary drawback of the financial models taught in most MBA programs is Uncertainty: your pro forma, Net Present Value (NPV), or Capital Asset Pricing Model (CAPM) model is only as good as the quality of your predictions. Many a business has been ruined by financial predictions that turned out to be wrong. How likely is it that your ten-year financial projection predicts absolutely everything that will happen with 100 percent accuracy? Who says tomorrow is going to be anything like today?

Many people make a business of selling certainty, which *doesn't exist*. Prediction, forecasting, and other forms of business soothsaying are popular because they provide the illusion that the future is knowable and controllable. Exercises in prediction aren't worth the cost—if there were a foolproof way to predict gas prices, interest rates, or stock prices, the people with that magic knowledge would be enormously wealthy and would have no need to sell anything to you.

Absorbing the ever-present nature of Uncertainty is an exercise in seeing the world as it really is, not as we want it to be. Instinctually, we all *want* to feel like we know what will happen in the future, particularly given how prone we are to **Loss Aversion** and **Threat Lockdown**. Contemplating Uncertainty feels bad, because not knowing what's going to happen feels like a threat. Instead of fixating on predicting invisible and unknowable threats, it's better to channel your energy into enhancing your ability to handle the unexpected.

Don't rely on making accurate predictions—things can change at any time. Planning for flexibility in response to Uncertainty via **Scenario Planning** is far more useful than pretending to be a seer.

SHARE THIS CONCEPT: http://book.personalmba.com/uncertainty/

Change

> It is not the strongest of the species that survives, nor the most intelligent, but the one most responsive to change.
>
> —CHARLES DARWIN, NATURALIST AND PIONEER OF EVOLUTIONARY THEORY

All systems **Change**—there is no such thing as a **System** in stasis.

Complex systems are in a constant state of flux. There is a great deal of

Uncertainty in *how* a system will Change over time, but it is certain that the System *will* Change. Plans that do not take Change into account are of limited value.

Change is a fact of life. Psychologically, it's very difficult to internalize that some things are random: there's no rhyme or reason to many of the things that happen in the world. Because of our natural **Pattern Matching** abilities, we tend to see patterns where none exist and tend to attribute random Changes to skill if the Changes are good or misfortune if they're bad. As a result, we're *Fooled by Randomness*—the title of Nassim Nicholas Taleb's first book.

You will never develop your business to the point that everything is perfect and unchanging. Many business owners and managers share an unexamined belief that by moving a business from "good to great," it'll be "built to last," continuing to outperform competitors for decades to come. It's a pleasant dream, but measuring yourself against that yardstick is unrealistic—it requires an unchanging world.

The only thing you can do about Change is increase your flexibility to handle a wide variety of different circumstances. The more flexible you are, the more **Resilient** (discussed later) you'll be when things inevitably Change.

SHARE THIS CONCEPT: http://book.personalmba.com/change/

Interdependence

> When we try to pick out anything by itself, we find it hitched to everything else in the universe.
>
> —JOHN MUIR, NATURALIST

Nothing in the world exists in isolation.

Complex **Systems** almost always rely on other systems in order to operate. Your refrigerator requires electricity to operate. When your local power plant fails, your refrigerator fails as well. That's **Interdependence**.

Highly Interdependent systems are sometimes referred to as "tightly coupled" systems. The more tightly coupled the processes in a system are, the more likely failures or delays will affect other parts of the system.

Tightly coupled systems are typically time dependent, rigidly ordered, and have very little *Slack*. There's often only one path to a successful outcome, and a failure in any part of the system can "cascade" to the rest of the system.

If you've ever seen a Rube Goldberg machine or played the children's board game Mousetrap, you've seen a tightly coupled system. In a cascade of dominoes, when one domino fails to knock over the next, the entire System grinds to a halt.

If you've ever heard the project management term "critical path," you know the importance of Interdependencies. The critical path contains only the tasks that must be completed *in order* for the project to be finished on schedule. If something on the critical path changes, that *Change* cascades to everything else on the path. Any delay in a task on the critical path will delay the entire project.

"Loosely coupled" systems have low degrees of Interdependence. Loosely coupled systems are more relaxed: they're typically not time dependent. You may able to use "parallel processing," completing multiple steps at a time. There's plenty of slack, and you may be able to accomplish your goal using many different strategies.

Think of an orchestra, which consists of a conductor and many instrumentalists. If the first violin hits the wrong note, the quality of the performance will be affected, but the mistake won't necessarily cascade to the rest of the orchestra.

You can make a system less Interdependent by removing *dependencies*. A dependency is an input that's required before the next stage of a process can take place. The more dependencies there are in a system, the higher the likelihood of delay or system failure.

Eliminating dependencies makes a system less tightly coupled. Think back to the automotive assembly line example: if you must put in the engine before the windshield is installed, an engine problem will delay the entire system. If it doesn't matter in which order the parts are installed, it's possible to assemble a finished vehicle in more than one way.

In *The 4-Hour Workweek*, Timothy Ferriss shares a method that made his business work far more efficiently. Initially, when a customer service representative had a problem with a customer, they were required to obtain approval from Tim before resolving it. By instituting a policy that allowed representatives to do anything necessary to solve the problems that cost less than $400 without approval, Tim made his business system less dependent upon him for operation.

Eliminate unnecessary dependencies, and you'll reduce the risk of a cascading failure.

SHARE THIS CONCEPT: http://book.personalmba.com/interdependence/

Counterparty Risk

> The man who makes everything that leads to happiness depend upon himself, and not upon other men, has adopted the very best plan for living happily.
>
> —PLATO, ANCIENT GREEK PHILOSOPHER

If your **System** relies on other people in order to function, that poses a major risk to the operation of your system.

Counterparty Risk is the possibility that other people won't deliver what they have promised. If your house burns down, you can only make a claim on your homeowner's insurance if the company you purchased the insurance policy from is still in business. If it's not, you're in trouble.

If your manufacturing system relies on a third-party vendor to supply certain parts and they're not able to honor their commitments, your manufacturing line stops.

If you outsource work to a contractor and that contractor doesn't perform as promised, your project will be delayed.

Too much Counterparty Risk increases the risk of catastrophic system failure. In the 2008 Wall Street crash, the world's largest investment banks stood on the brink of insolvency because they all relied on one another in the event something went wrong.

Investment banks and financial firms like Goldman Sachs, JPMorgan Chase, and Lehman Brothers made a practice of buying "credit default swaps," a form of financial **Insurance**, from other large firms. If a highly **Leveraged** deal went south, these investment banks thought the Insurance they had purchased would protect them from multimillion-dollar losses, so they took on more and more Leverage, increasing their risk exposure.

When the housing market collapsed and the banks started losing money on the mortgage securities they held, they tried calling in their credit default swaps. Lo and behold, the other banks they had purchased the swaps from had also lost a huge amount of money on mortgage-backed securities and couldn't honor the obligations. Every large investment bank was a counterparty to the risk of the other banks in the system. Because they all relied on one another, when one bank fell, they all fell.

Counterparty Risk is *Amplified* by the *Planning Fallacy*. Your partners can't predict the future any more than you can, and everyone has a tendency to be optimistic regarding plans and deadlines. Make plans and commitments, but always have a plan for when the project doesn't go as expected.

When your system relies on the performance of someone outside of your control, do all that you can to prepare for the possibility that they won't perform as expected.

SHARE THIS CONCEPT: http://book.personalmba.com/counterparty-risk/

Second-Order Effects

> While we are free to choose our actions, we are not free to choose the consequences of our actions.
>
> —STEPHEN COVEY, AUTHOR OF *THE SEVEN HABITS OF HIGHLY EFFECTIVE PEOPLE*

A few years ago, Kelsey and I had the opportunity to visit the kingdom of Bahrain, a small island country a few miles off the east coast of Saudi Arabia. Now known for its international banking prowess, pearl diving, and international F1 racing track, it wasn't too long ago that Bahrain was known for its unique ecosystem.

A few short decades ago, the interior of Bahrain was lush with natural greenery—an island oasis said to be the original site of the Garden of Eden. Now the interior of the island is a stark desert, and local plant life is maintained via irrigation. What changed?

Bahrain is surrounded by a network of underground freshwater springs, which were responsible for both the island's plant life and spurring the local oysters to cultivate pearls of remarkable quality. As the country's single large city, Manama, developed, land in the city center became scarce, so developers adopted a process called "land reclamation," which involved excavating dirt from the interior of the island and depositing it on the coast, "reclaiming" land from the sea.

This approach was successful in creating new land, but at a much steeper cost than anticipated—the island's network of springs dried up, turning the country into a desert.

Every action has a consequence, and those consequences have consequences, which are called **Second-Order Effects**. Think of a line of dominoes—a single push causes a chain of events to occur. Once the chain starts, it's difficult (if not impossible) to stop or reverse the cascade of cause and effect.

Rent control in New York City after World War II is another sobering example of unintended consequences. Originally intended to provide returning veterans with affordable housing, the policy capped rent prices (and the ability of landlords to raise them) in certain areas of the city. Affordable housing for veterans is a noble idea, right?

Here's what the city planners didn't expect: every year, the cost to maintain properties in New York City continued to rise, but landlords couldn't raise rent prices to compensate for their increased costs. By law, rent control couldn't be removed unless the original leaseholder moved or the building was condemned, so landlords refused to maintain their property—it was a waste of money. Financially, it was better to let the building deteriorate around the remaining tenants.

The effect of this policy over time was a steep decline in the quality of property, and eventually supply, as buildings were condemned, making housing even more expensive. A policy intended to make housing more affordable actually destroyed housing supply and made it *more* expensive—the opposite of the original intent.

Changing some aspect of a complex system *always* introduces Second-Order Effects, some of which may be antithetical to the original intent of the change. Elements in a complex system can be interrelated or dependent upon one another in millions of different ways, and **Uncertainty** guarantees that you probably don't know exactly how. Every action has a consequence, and those consequences *always* have consequences—even if you don't know what they are or don't want them to happen.

Approach making changes to a complex system with extreme caution: what you get may be the opposite of what you expect.

SHARE THIS CONCEPT: http://book.personalmba.com/second-order-effects/

Normal Accidents

> The problem is not that there are problems. The problem is expecting otherwise and thinking that having problems is a problem.
>
> —THEODORE RUBIN, PSYCHIATRIST AND COLUMNIST

The space shuttle—a vehicle capable of exiting the bounds of Earth's gravity with human travelers aboard—is clearly an extremely complex *System*. A highly engineered airplane strapped to three rockets holding millions of cubic feet of explosive hydrogen gas is the epitome of a highly *Interdependent* system. *Any* error has the chance of cascading catastrophically, and every time the shuttle is launched, millions of things could potentially go wrong.

In 1986, the space shuttle *Challenger* suffered a catastrophe—a seal in one of the rockets froze, becoming extremely brittle. When the seal was superheated during takeoff, it failed. The *Challenger* exploded seventy-three seconds after liftoff, killing everyone aboard.

It's tempting to believe that it's possible to create a system in which nothing ever goes wrong. Real-life systems always prove otherwise—count on it.

The theory of *Normal Accidents* is a more formal way of expressing a universal proverb: shit happens. In a tightly coupled system, small risks accumulate to the point where errors and accidents are inevitable. The larger and more complex the system, the higher the likelihood that *something* will eventually go very, very wrong.

Overreacting to Normal Accidents is actually counterproductive. When something goes wrong, our instinctive response is to become hypersensitive, locking things down and adding more controls to prevent the unfortunate event from happening again. This response actually makes things worse: locking things down and adding more systems only makes the system *more tightly coupled*, increasing the risk of future accidents.

NASA's response to the *Challenger* tragedy is extremely instructive: instead of completely shutting down or adding more systems that could compound the issue, NASA engineers recognized the inherent risk and focused on finding other solutions to the problem that would minimize the risk of the issue reoccurring without adding more systems that could potentially fail.

The best way to avoid Normal Accidents is to analyze breakdowns or "close calls" when they happen. Instead of going into the systems equivalent of *Threat Lockdown*, which can create even bigger issues in the long term, looking at near misses can provide crucial insight into hidden Interdependencies. By analyzing the issue, it's possible to construct contingency plans in the event a similar situation happens in the future.

In 2003, the space shuttle *Columbia* suffered a catastrophe of a different sort: the carbon fiber heat shields designed to protect the shuttle as it re-entered Earth's atmosphere failed, and the shuttle disintegrated. Again, NASA focused on how to prevent the issue from happening again without making the system even more tightly coupled. When the space shuttle *Discovery* suffered damage to its heat shields on takeoff a few years later, NASA engineers were prepared, and the crew landed safely.

Normal Accidents are a compelling reason to keep the systems you rely on as loose as you possibly can. There are many positive things to be said for systems, but expecting zero failures is unrealistic in the extreme. Loose systems may not be as efficient, but they last longer and fail less catastrophically.

The more complex a system is and the longer it operates, the more likely it is to suffer a major failure. It's not a matter of *if*—it's a matter of *when*. Be watchful for system failure, and be prepared to respond to it quickly.

SHARE THIS CONCEPT: http://book.personalmba.com/normal-accidents/

10

ANALYZING SYSTEMS

If you can't understand it, you can't change it.

—ERIC EVANS, TECHNOLOGIST

Before you can improve a *System,* you must understand how well it's currently operating. Unfortunately for us, that's tricky business—it's simply not possible to stop the world however long you want while you take careful measurements.

Systems must be analyzed as they're working. Analyzing a system in operation is difficult, but definitely possible—if you know what to look for.

In this chapter, you'll learn how to *Deconstruct* systems into smaller parts you can understand, measure what's important, and discover how parts of the system interact with and depend on one another to function.

SHARE THIS CONCEPT: http://book.personalmba.com/analyzing-systems/

Deconstruction

Out of perfection nothing can be made. Every process involves breaking something up.

—JOSEPH CAMPBELL, MYTHOLOGIST AND AUTHOR OF *THE HERO WITH A THOUSAND FACES*

Complex *Systems,* as we've already discussed, are made up of many *Interdependent Flows, Stocks,* processes, and parts. As a whole, the system may be too complex to take in all at once—if there are more than seven or eight variables or dependencies, the **Cognitive Scope Limitation** kicks in and confusion takes over.

If that's true, how can anyone analyze extremely complex systems?

Deconstruction is the process of separating complex systems into the smallest possible subsystems in order to understand how things work. Instead of trying to understand the system all at once, you break up the system into parts, then work on understanding the subsystems and how they interact with one another.

Deconstruction is the reverse-engineering aspect of **Gall's Law**. Remember: complex systems that work inevitably evolved from simpler systems that also worked. If you can identify simpler subsystems and focus on understanding how they work and how they fit together, you can eventually understand how the entire system works.

If you know nothing about how cars work, popping the hood of your vehicle and examining the contents is an exercise in confusion—there are so many parts that it's hard to know where to begin. Understanding the system is not impossible, however—identifying important subsystems like the engine, transmission, and radiator can give you valuable insight on how the entire system functions.

Once you've identified important subsystems, temporarily isolating them in your mind can help you understand how they work. Instead of focusing on how the entire car works, you simply concern yourself with the engine for a while. Where does the subsystem begin? What **Flows** are involved? What processes take place inside the system? Are there **Feedback Loops** involved? What happens if **Inflows** *don't* come in? Where does the system end? What are the **Outflows**?

It's important not to lose sight of **Interdependence** when using isolation to Deconstruct a system, since each subsystem is part of a larger system. Identifying *triggers* and *endpoints*—the parts of the system that interact with other subsystems—is just as important. Triggers teach you what makes a subsystem start operating, and endpoints show you what makes the system stop.

In addition, it's important to understand the conditionals present in a system—if-then or when-then relationships that influence the operation of the system. For example, an engine requires an Inflow of gasoline vapor to operate. If that Inflow is present, a spark from the spark plug ignites it, providing energy that pushes a piston that powers the rest of the system. If that Inflow is absent or a spark doesn't come from the spark plug, the energy is absent and the system stops, making both the Inflow of gasoline vapor and the spark from the spark plug conditions of the system's operation.

Creating diagrams and flowcharts can help you understand how each Inflow, process, trigger, conditional, endpoint, and Outflow comes together. Explaining complex systems in words alone can be limiting—for best results, draw diagrams of the Flows, Stocks, conditionals, and processes involved. Well-constructed flowcharts can help you understand the Flow of a system as it operates, which can go a long way toward helping you fix the system when things break down.[1]

To analyze a system, Deconstruct complex systems into subsystems that are easier to understand, then build your understanding of the system from the ground up.

SHARE THIS CONCEPT: http://book.personalmba.com/deconstruction/

Measurement

In God we trust . . . all others bring data.

—W. EDWARDS DEMING, PRODUCTION MANAGEMENT EXPERT AND
PIONEER OF STATISTICAL PROCESS CONTROL

Once you've understood the parts of the **System** and how they interact with one another, it pays to ask another question: *how well* is the system operating? To do that, we rely on measuring the system as it's operating.

Measurement is the process of collecting data as the system is operating. By collecting information related to the core functions of the system, it's much easier to understand exactly how well the system itself is performing.

Measurement also allows systems to be compared with one another. For example, it's possible to use several different types of microprocessors to build a computer—which one should you use? By measuring various characteristics of each processor—cycle time, power consumption, heat generation, etc.—it's possible to choose the best processor for your computer, resulting in better performance.

Measurement helps us avoid **Absence Blindness** when analyzing a system. Remember: we have a hard time seeing things that aren't present. Measuring different parts of a system in operation helps to identify potential issues before they arise.

For example, diabetes is a condition that represents a fault in the **Feedback Loop** that controls the body's blood glucose levels. Too much or too little blood glucose is life threatening, so if the body produces too much or too little insulin to keep blood glucose levels stable, that's a major issue.

Even though insulin levels are extremely important to a person with diabetes, you can't figure out a person's insulin or blood glucose level just by looking at them. Without measurement, Absence Blindness is the rule until the condition becomes bad enough to become visible, which typically takes the form of the person passing out or going into shock.

To avoid this situation, people with diabetes make a habit of measuring their blood glucose and insulin levels throughout the day.

Measuring something is the first step to improving it. Peter Drucker famously opined, "What gets measured gets managed." It's true. If you don't know how much money your business is collecting or spending, it's difficult to know whether or not any change you make to your business system is actually an improvement. If you want to lose weight, you first must know how much you weigh right now, then track how any changes you make affect your weight.

Without data, you're blind. If you want to improve anything, you must measure it first.

SHARE THIS CONCEPT: http://book.personalmba.com/measurement/

Key Performance Indicator

It is better to have an approximate answer to the right question than an exact answer to the wrong question.

—JOHN TUKEY, STATISTICIAN

Here's the primary problem with **Measurement**: you can measure a million different things. Measure too much, and you'll inevitably suffer from the **Cognitive Scope Limitation**, drowning in a sea of meaningless data.

Some Measurements are more important than others: **Key Performance Indicators (KPIs)** are Measurements of the critical parts of a **System**. Measurements that don't help you make improvements to your System are worse than worthless: they're a waste of your limited **Attention** and energy. If your intent is to improve the system you're examining, you don't have to pay Attention to everything—just a few key Measurements that actually matter.

Unfortunately, it's easy to fixate on things that are easy to measure instead of things that are actually important. Take, for example, a business's revenue—seems pretty important, right? It is, but only to a point: revenue is important only because it's a key component of profit. It doesn't matter if you collected $1,000,000 in revenue if you spent $2,000,000 to collect it. As Theo Paphitis, a serial entrepreneur and host of the hit BBC series *Dragons' Den*, memorably put it: "Profit is sanity. Turnover is vanity." Alone, revenue is not a KPI.

The same thing goes for other in-process Measurements. For example, if you're managing a team of programmers, it's tempting to measure their output in "lines of code"—a visible, easy-to-collect measure. Here's the problem: more code is not necessarily better. A talented programmer can make a program better by rewriting it using *fewer* lines of code. If you fixate on quantity, removing ten thousand lines looks like a setback, even if it's actually a huge improvement.

The situation gets even worse if you *reward* programmers based on lines of code: **Incentive-Caused Bias** will ensure that your code looks like the programming equivalent of *War and Peace*.

Typically, business-related KPIs are directly related to either the **Five Parts of Every Business** or **Throughput**. Here are a few questions I use to identify a business's KPIs:

Value Creation: How quickly is the system creating value? What is the current level of **Inflows?**

Marketing: How many people are paying Attention to your offer? How many prospects are giving you **Permission** to provide more information?

Sales: How many prospects are becoming paying customers? What is the average customer's **Lifetime Value?**

Value Delivery: How quickly can you serve each customer? What is
   your current returns or complaints rate?

Finance: What is your **Profit Margin**? How much **Purchasing Power** do you
   have? Are you financially **Sufficient**?

Any Measurements directly related to these questions are probably
KPIs. Anything that's not directly related to a core business process or a
system's Throughput is probably not.

Try to limit yourself to only three to five KPIs per system. When collecting Measurements, it's tempting to build yourself a "dashboard" that
contains every piece of information you'd ever want to see. Resist the temptation: if you overload yourself with too much data, you'll be far less likely
to see **Changes** that are critically important. You can always dig deeper
into the data at your disposal if necessary.

Find your system's KPIs, and you'll be able to manage your system without drowning in data.

SHARE THIS CONCEPT: http://book.personalmba.com/key-performance-indicator/

Garbage In, Garbage Out

> Let us watch well our beginnings, and results will manage them-
> selves.
>
> —ALEXANDER CLARK, NINETEENTH-CENTURY U.S. AMBASSADOR AND
> CIVIL RIGHTS ACTIVIST

If you analyze poor-quality data, the resulting analysis will be worthless at
best, and misleading or damaging at worst.

The quality of the input you use always has an impact on the quality of
the output. If you build an object from poor-quality materials, that object
will be unattractive and unreliable. If you eat a lot of junk food, don't move
around much, and pay attention to too much news and reality TV, you'll
feel apathetic instead of energetic. If the people working on a project aren't
skilled or excited, the end result will inevitably suffer.

Garbage In, Garbage Out is a straightforward principle: put useless input
into a **System,** and you'll get useless output. Your ability to understand a
system is directly related to your ability to observe what's going on in that

system. The quality and quantity of the data you collect about the system represents an upper limit to how well you'll be able to understand what's happening in the system as it's operating.

If you don't want garbage when you're done, don't use garbage when you begin. Being mindful of what you're starting with can help you ensure that the end result of the process meets your expectations.

To improve your results, improve the quality of what you start with.

SHARE THIS CONCEPT: http://book.personalmba.com/garbage-in-garbage-out/

Tolerance

> The road to wisdom? Well, it's plain / And simple to express: / Err / and err / and err again, / but less / and less / and less.
>
> —PIET HEIN, MATHEMATICIAN AND POET

Many inexperienced businesspeople expect perfection: any sort of mistake or variance, however small, is a cause for concern.

Take, for example, a business's Web site. Most businesspeople are aghast when their Web site goes down, an event that prompts concerned calls to the system administrator or responsible party. Often the words "Make sure our Web site never goes down" are spoken.

That's not realistic: perfection is impossible. One hundred percent reliability is a pipe dream. *Normal Accidents* are a fact of life, so it pays to account for them in planning. The more reliability you need, the more your system is going to cost.

A *Tolerance* is an acceptable level of "normal" error in a system. Within a given range of measurements, the system is performing as intended. As long as the errors don't exceed a certain threshold, urgent intervention is not required.

Tolerances are often referred to as being "tight" or "loose." A tight Tolerance is one in which there's little room for error or variability, which is common if the component or system is critical to the performance of the system. A loose Tolerance allows significant room for error or variability and is common when small mistakes produce no major repercussions.

The reliability of a system is often measured in terms of a percentage. When a system is 95 percent reliable in a given area, it will produce a result within the intended Tolerances nineteen out of twenty times. The higher the reliability, the higher the percentage.

When you hear someone talk about "five nines" reliability, that means the system produces the intended result 99.99999 percent of the time. This level of reliability is extremely impressive, and just as expensive to achieve. Often, systems companies use this reliability measurement as a Tolerance, and they write a contract called a "Service Level Agreement" (SLA) that promises to compensate customers if errors exceed a certain threshold.

Tight tolerances are very useful and a positive indicator of quality: after all, you don't want mistakes or variations. Work to achieve tighter Tolerances for the critical parts of your system over time.

SHARE THIS CONCEPT: http://book.personalmba.com/tolerance/

Analytical Honesty

That which can be destroyed by the truth should be.

—P. C. HODGELL, PROFESSOR AND AUTHOR OF *THE GOD STALKER CHRONICLES*

My last position at Procter & Gamble involved creating an online Marketing **Measurement** strategy: figuring out a way to measure the effectiveness of P&G's advertising on the Web. P&G spent millions of dollars every year on banner ads, search engine advertising, and online video placements. My job was to figure out if the investment was worth it.

One of the things my team discovered while putting together our recommendations was disturbing: the **System** we were using on most of our Web sites to measure unique visitors was wrong. Instead of simply counting human visitors, the system was treating visits from search engine programs as "visitors" as well, even though they weren't people. Computer programs don't care about laundry detergent and shampoo, but the system was counting them as potential customers.

It's not uncommon for search engine spider programs to visit a Web site many times a day looking for new information, so the system was overstating how many people were visiting each Web site by a significant margin. Put simply, it was a *Garbage In, Garbage Out* situation, and it made our measurements much less useful.

Naturally, we recommended upgrading the tracking system to collect visitor data more accurately. Almost universally, the teams declined. They knew they were getting crappy data, but they didn't seem to care. Weird, right?

Here's the rub: installing the new tracking system would make each Web site's unique visitors measurement—considered a *Key Performance Indicator* by most teams—go down dramatically. Even though the new system was clearly more accurate, installing it would make the team look bad. Instead of correcting the issue, they chose to continue living a lie. As a result, they seriously compromised their ability to improve their Web site's actual performance.

Analytical Honesty means measuring and analyzing the data you have dispassionately. Since humans are social creatures, we tend to care deeply about how others perceive us, which gives us a natural incentive to make things look better than they actually are. If your purpose is to actually make things better, this tendency can get in the way of collecting accurate data and conducting useful analysis.

The best way to maintain Analytical Honesty is to have your measurements evaluated by someone who isn't personally invested in your system. *Incentive-Caused Bias* and *Confirmation Bias* are all too easy to succumb to if your social status is on the line. Having an experienced but dispassionate third party audit your measurement and analysis practices is a neat workaround for these tendencies: you might not like what you hear, but at least you'll be fully aware of potential issues.

Don't look at your data through rose-colored glasses: always strive to be honest with yourself about what the data indicates you can improve.

SHARE THIS CONCEPT: http://book.personalmba.com/analytical-honesty/

Context

If you don't understand something, it's because you aren't aware of its context.

—RICHARD RABKIN, PSYCHIATRIST

You brought in $200,000 of revenue this month. Is that good or bad?

It depends. If you brought in $100,000 last month, it's good. If your expenses are $400,000 this month, it's bad.

Context is the use of related **Measurements** to provide additional information about the data you're examining. In the example above, knowing your revenue isn't very useful without additional information. Knowing last month's revenue and this month's expenses provides necessary Context, giving you a clearer picture of the situation.

Aggregate Measurements almost never tell you anything useful. Aggregate measures are worthless when it comes to making tangible improvements because they lack Context. Knowing 2 million people visited your Web site this month tells you absolutely nothing useful. Without context, you can't determine **Change** or effectiveness, which limits your ability to improve the **System**.

Try to avoid the temptation to focus on a single "magic number" when tracking your results. Relying on a single number sounds like a useful simplification, but it's not—removing Context blinds you to important Changes in the data. Knowing your "total quality score" or that revenue went up or down a few points won't tell you why it happened, whether or not it's important, or if it's due to random fluctuations or a significant Change in the system or its **Environment**.

As a general rule: examine no measures in isolation—always look at them in Context with other Measurements.

SHARE THIS CONCEPT: http://book.personalmba.com/context/

Sampling

If you don't believe in sampling theory, next time you go to the doctor
and he wants to take a little blood, tell him to take it all.

—GIAN FULGONI, FOUNDER AND CHAIRMAN OF COMSCORE, INC.

What do you do if your **System** is too large or complex to collect data on every process?

Sometimes it's not practical to measure the **Flows** of an entire system. If you're managing a **Scalable** system, it's often not possible to test every unit or find every error. How can you identify potential problems quickly when your system is cranking out millions of units or completing millions of transactions?

Sampling is the process of taking at random a small percentage of the total output, then using it as a proxy for the entire system. If you've ever had your blood taken at the doctor's office, you'll have a good idea of what Sampling entails. The doctor or nurse draws a small amount of blood, which is then sent to a laboratory for analysis. If testing reveals anomalies in the sample, it's likely that the same issue is present in the bloodstream in general.

Sampling can help you identify systemic errors quickly without testing all of the output of the system, which can be time-consuming and expensive. If you're manufacturing mobile phones, you don't have to test every single phone that comes off the line. If you test one in twenty phones, you can still identify errors quickly enough to fix the system if something goes wrong. Depending on how quickly and accurately you need to spot errors, you can increase or decrease the Sampling rate.

Random "spot checks" are also a form of Sampling. Many retail stores employ "secret shoppers" to periodically test customer service or the skills of their sales staff. These shoppers are hired to express interest in specific items, ask certain questions, make a return, or generally be annoying. Since the staff doesn't know which customers are real and which ones are not, it's an effective way for the management of a store to test their staff without scrutinizing them every second of every day.

Sampling is prone to bias if the sample is not truly random or uniform. For example, measuring the average household income in the United States by surveying property owners in Manhattan will skew the data considerably higher than if you survey property owners in West Virginia. For best results, use the largest random sample you possibly can.

If you need to test for quality, Sampling can help you collect good data without incurring enormous costs, provided you stay on the lookout for potential bias that can skew the data.

SHARE THIS CONCEPT: http://book.personalmba.com/sampling/

Margin of Error

Everyone generalizes from one example. At least, I do.
—STEVEN BRUST, SCIENCE FICTION AUTHOR

Suppose you purchase a trick coin from a magician's shop, and you want to be sure the coin is actually biased to land on heads most of the time.

How can you be sure you didn't buy a dud? You start flipping the coin, of course.

Let's assume that in the first five flips, you get two heads and three tails. Should you ask for a refund?

It's probably worthwhile to make sure your results are accurate before jeopardizing the magician's good name. **Margin of Error** is an estimate of how much you can trust your conclusions from a given set of observed **Samples**.

Since you only flipped the coin five times, you can't be absolutely sure it's a dud: your sample size is very small. Each coin flip makes your sample size larger.

If you go on to flip the coin one thousand times and it comes up tails two-thirds of the time, you can be relatively sure that the coin is biased, but not in the way you expected. Since a nonloaded coin should come up heads half the time, your large sample size makes it likely the magician gave you a tails-loaded coin by mistake.

Each additional sample you make increases your available data and helps ensure your set of observed samples is representative of the general population you're studying. The more Samples you take, the lower your Margin of Error becomes, and the more faith you can have in the conclusions you make from examining the samples as a whole. (Unavoidable biases in sampling can be accounted for by increasing your Margin of Error.)

The math behind how to estimate Margin of Error is beyond the scope of this book. It's relatively easy once you get the hang of it, particularly if you use a spreadsheet or database for your analysis. If you need to calculate Margin of Error or other, related estimates, like "confidence intervals" or "credibility intervals," I recommend picking up *Principles of Statistics* by M. G. Bulmer for an in-depth primer.

In general, beware of misleading conclusions based on small and/or nonrepresentative sample sizes. Whenever you're presented with an average or a probability based on data you're not familiar with, it always pays to investigate the size of the sample and how it was collected. Sample sets that are too small or biased can significantly influence the final analysis.

When it comes to analytical confidence, more data is always better—collect the largest set of samples you can.

SHARE THIS CONCEPT: http://book.personalmba.com/margin-of-error/

Ratio

He who refuses to do arithmetic is doomed to talk nonsense.

—JOHN MCCARTHY, COMPUTER AND COGNITIVE SCIENTIST WHO COINED THE
TERM "ARTIFICIAL INTELLIGENCE"

A *Ratio* is a method of comparing two *Measurements* against each other. By dividing your results by your input, you can measure all sorts of useful relationships between different parts of your *System.*

For example, assume that for every 30 customers who enter your store, 10 of them make a purchase. Your "closing Ratio" would be 10 divided by 30: 1/3.

Let's say you train your sales staff in techniques that result in 15 paying customers out of 30 who enter the store. Your new closing Ratio is 15 divided by 30: 1/2.

Percentages are simply Ratios with a base of 100. Your first closing Ratio, converted into a percentage, is 33 percent. Your second would be 50 percent.

HERE ARE SOME USEFUL RATIOS TO TRACK:

—Return on Promotion: *For every $1 you spend in advertising, how much revenue do you collect?*

—Profit per Employee: *For every person you employ, how much profit does your business generate?*

—Closing Ratio: *For every prospect you serve, how many purchase?*

—Returns/Complaints Ratio: *For every sale you make, how many choose to return or complain?*

Financial Ratios are very helpful when examining financial statements. Ratios like **Return on Investment**, *Return on Assets, Return on Capital, Inventory Turns,* and *Day Sales Outstanding* are very useful in determining the health of a business. For a full introduction to common Financial Ratios, I recommend *Financial Intelligence for Entrepreneurs* by Karen Berman and Joe Knight with John Case.

Tracking Ratios over time can provide a directional indication of how a system is changing. If your closing Ratio or Return on Investment keeps going up, that's a very good thing. If it's going down over time, it would pay to investigate to find out why.

Be creative: study your business, then construct Ratios that highlight the most important parts of your system.

SHARE THIS CONCEPT: **http://book.personalmba.com/ratio/**

Typicality

> It ain't what you don't know that hurts you. It's what you know that ain't so.
>
> —WILL ROGERS, AMERICAN COWBOY AND COMEDIAN

The average household net worth of a person who reads the *Wall Street Journal* is $1.7 million. Seems that *WSJ* readers are extremely well off, right?

Yes, but less than you might think. Bill Gates and Warren Buffett read the *Wall Street Journal,* and their wealth is measured in the billions—significantly more than even the top 0.01 percent of business professionals.

Simply by existing, high-net-worth executives like Gates and Buffett skew the average much higher than it would be otherwise. If you're relying on the average to tell you how much the typical *Wall Street Journal* reader is worth, you're making a mistake.

Many forms of analysis rely on defining *Typicality*: identifying a normal or typical value for some important measurement. There are four common methods of calculating a typical value: *mean, median, mode,* and *midrange*.

A *Mean* (or average) is calculated by adding the quantities of all data points, then dividing by the total number of data points available. Averages are simple to calculate but are prone to Gates and Buffett Syndrome: the presence of outliers that skew the average too high or low to be representative. (Exclude the outliers, however, and the average becomes more accurate.)

A *Median* is calculated by sorting the values in order of high to low, then finding the quantity of the data point in the middle of the range. Medians are actually a specific form of analysis called a percentile: the median is the value that expresses the fiftieth percentile. By definition, 50 percent of the values in the set will be below the Median. Calculating the Median and comparing it to the Mean can tell you if the average is being influenced by a few heavy hitters.

A *Mode* is the value that occurs most frequently in a set of data. Modes are useful for finding clusters of data—a set can have multiple modes, which can alert you to potentially interesting *Interdependencies* in the *System* that produced that data.

A *Midrange* is the value halfway between the highest and lowest data points in a set of values. To calculate the Midrange, add the highest and lowest values, then divide by two. Midranges are best used for quick estimates—they're fast, and you only need to know two data points, but they can be easily skewed by outliers that are abnormally high or low, like Bill Gates's bank balance.

Means, Medians, Modes, and Midranges are useful analytical tools that can indicate typical results—provided you're careful enough to use the right tool for the job.

SHARE THIS CONCEPT: http://book.personalmba.com/typicality/

Correlation and Causation

Correlation isn't causation, but it sure is a hint.

—EDWARD TUFTE, STATISTICIAN, INFORMATION DESIGN EXPERT,
AND PROFESSOR AT YALE UNIVERSITY

Imagine a billiards table: if you know the exact position of every ball on the table and the details of the forces applied to the cue ball (impact vector, impact force, location of impact, table friction, and air resistance), you can calculate exactly how the cue ball will travel and how it will affect other balls it hits along the way. Professional billiards players are skilled at *Mentally Simulating* these relationships so well that they can rapidly clear entire tables.

That's *Causation*: a complete chain of cause and effect. Since it's possible to calculate a complete chain of causality, you can say that striking the cue ball *caused* a ball to fall into the corner pocket. If you hit the cue again in exactly the same way in exactly the same situation, you'll get the same result every single time.

Here's another thought experiment, using hypothetical data: people who suffer heart attacks eat, on average, 57 bacon double cheeseburgers every year. Does eating bacon double cheeseburgers cause heart attacks? Not necessarily. People who suffer heart attacks typically take 365 showers a year and blink their eyes 5.6 million times a year. Do taking showers and blinking your eyes cause heart attacks as well?

Correlation is not Causation. Even if you notice that one measurement is highly associated with another, that does not prove that one thing *caused* the other.

Imagine you own a pizza parlor, and you create a thirty-second advertisement to air on local television. Shortly after the commercial goes live, you notice a 30 percent increase in sales. Did the advertisement cause the increase?

Not necessarily—the increase could be due to any number of factors. Maybe a convention was held in town that day, so there were more visitors in town than usual and they needed a quick place to eat. Maybe school let out and families went out to eat to celebrate. Maybe you offered a special two-pizzas-for-the-price-of-one promotion at the same time, and that's what actually brought more people in the door. So many things happened at the same time, it's hard to be certain.

In fact, the commercial may have actually caused a *decline* in sales—maybe people found it unappealing or offensive, but another factor caused such a huge increase in sales that it overshadowed the decline.

Causation is always more difficult to prove than Correlation. When analyzing complex **Systems** with many variables and **Interdependencies**, it's often extremely difficult to find true causality. The more changes that happen in a system over a period of time, the higher the likelihood that more than one change had an impact on the result you're trying to analyze.

Adjusting for known variables can help you isolate the potential causes of a change in your system. For example, if you know that families go out to celebrate the end of school or that an annual convention is coming up, you can adjust for that seasonality by using historical data.

The more you can isolate the change you made in the system from other factors, the more confidence you can have that the change you made intentionally actually caused the results you see.

SHARE THIS CONCEPT: http://book.personalmba.com/correlation-causation/

Norms

Those who cannot remember the past are condemned to repeat it.
—GEORGE SANTAYANA, PHILOSOPHER, ESSAYIST, AND APHORIST

If you want to compare the effectiveness of something in the present, it's often useful to learn from the past.

Norms are measures that use historical data as a tool to provide **Context** for current **Measurements**. For example, by looking at past data you may discover trends in your sales data directly related to the date the sale was made, which is called *seasonality*. Seasonality is a good example of why Norms are often useful. If you're in the business of selling Christmas ornaments, comparing sales during Q4 (the last quarter of the year—October through December) to Q3 sales (August through September) probably isn't useful—no one purchases Christmas ornaments in August. Far better to compare this year's Q4 sales with last year's Q4 sales to see if you performed better than last year's comparable period.

When Measurement practices **Change**, Norms based on the previous Measurements are no longer valid. At P&G, we had a method of evaluating the effectiveness of certain types of advertising. Drawing on several years' worth of data, it was possible to compare new advertisements with old advertisements that had been successful. If the new advertising didn't beat the Norm in testing, it wasn't used.

If the company suddenly decided to use a different testing methodology, the Norms would no longer be valid—it would be comparing apples and oranges. Change the Measurement methods, and you immediately invalidate any Norms based on them. If you still want to use Norms, you must build your database of historical information once again.

Past performance is no guarantee of future performance. Remember, we're dealing with complex **Systems**—things always Change over time. Just because something was useful in the past does not mean it will continue to perform as well in perpetuity. For best results, reexamine your Norms periodically to make sure they're valid.

SHARE THIS CONCEPT: **http://book.personalmba.com/norms/**

Proxy

> How many legs does a dog have if you call the tail a leg? Four. Calling a tail a leg doesn't make it a leg.
>
> —ABRAHAM LINCOLN

What do you do if it's not possible to measure something directly?

A **Proxy** measures one quantity by measuring something else. For example, in democratic political **Systems**, votes are used as a Proxy to measure the "will of the people." It's not possible to subject every citizen in the country to a brain scan that reveals detailed preferences, so votes are used as the **Next Best Alternative**.

Proxies are used all the time in scientific measurement. Ever wonder how scientists know how hot the sun is, or how old certain rocks are? They measure Proxies like the wavelength of electromagnetic rays or the decay of known radioactive isotopes, then apply well-proven relationships and formulas to determine the answer.

Useful Proxies are closely related to the primary subject—the closer, the better. Take Web site analytics—you may want to know exactly where and how long people pay **Attention** to different parts of the Web page, but again, you can't brain scan each visitor to your Web site. Tracking the position of the mouse cursor, however, can be a useful Proxy for Attention. According to a study done by researchers at Carnegie Mellon University:

> . . . *84% of the times that a region was visited by a mouse cursor, it was also visited by (users') eye gaze. In addition, 88% of regions that were not gazed by the eye were also not visited by a mouse cursor.*[2]

Because mouse movements and eye fixation (i.e., Attention) are highly Correlated, mouse movements are a good Proxy for visitor Attention. The better the **Correlation**, the better the Proxy.

For best results, ensure that the Proxy is actually related to the intended subject. Proxies can be tricky or misleading if they seem to measure one thing but actually measure another. Think back to the example of trying to measure programmer productivity by counting lines of code as a **Key Performance Indicator**. As we discussed earlier, "lines of code" is certainly a Proxy for programming effectiveness, but more code is sometimes an *inverse* signal of productivity, making it a useless Measurement for the stated objective.

Used with care, Proxies can help you measure the immeasurable—just be sure your Proxy is directly and highly Correlated with the subject of interest.

SHARE THIS CONCEPT: http://book.personalmba.com/proxy/

Segmentation

Analytics nirvana rule: never report a metric (even God's favorite KPI) without segmenting it . . . There is no KPI so insightful all by itself, even in a trend or against a forecast, that can't be made more impactful by applying segmentation.

—AVINASH KAUSHIK, AUTHOR OF *WEB ANALYTICS: AN HOUR A DAY*

Very often, aggregate data sets contain hidden nuggets of gold—if you can find them. **Segmentation** is a technique that involves splitting a data set into well-defined subgroups to add additional **Context**. Splitting the data into predefined groups can uncover previously unknown relationships. For example, knowing that orders increased by 87 percent this month is good, but knowing that 90 percent of those new orders came from women in Seattle is even better. Find out what made those women order, and you'll be able to use that information to further capitalize on your success.

There are three common ways to Segment customer data: Past Performance, Demographics, and Psychographics.

Past Performance Segments customers by past known actions. For example, you can Segment customer sales data using previous sales data, comparing sales to new customers with sales to customers who have previously purchased from you. **Lifetime Value** calculations are a form of Segmentation by Past Performance.

Demographics Segment customers by external personal characteristics. Personal information like age, gender, income, nationality, and location can help you determine which customers are your **Probable Purchasers**. Knowing that your best customers are males between the ages of twenty-three and thirty-two who live in major metropolitan areas and have over $2,000 per month in disposable income can be quite useful—you can focus your **Marketing** efforts on reaching more prospects who have those characteristics.

Psychographics Segment customers by internal psychological characteristics. Typically discovered via surveys, assessments, or focus groups, Psychographics are attitudes or worldviews that influence how people see themselves and the world at large.

Psychographics can be very useful in creating or adjusting your **Value Creation, Marketing,** and **Sales** strategies. For example, if you're selling home security systems, it's likely that your Probable Purchasers will believe statements like "the world is a dangerous place" and feel somewhat in danger even when in their homes. Experimenting with promoting your product in survivalist and self-defense magazines and Web sites—markets whose customers might have similar beliefs—might not be a bad idea.

Segment your data, and you'll find many useful hidden connections worth investigating.

SHARE THIS CONCEPT: http://book.personalmba.com/segmentation/

Humanization

People are the center of the universe. Not stuff.
—STOWE BOYD, SOCIAL TECHNOLOGIST

Analyzing data is comforting to the quantitative-minded, but to really use data properly, you must go beyond juggling numbers to understand what they're telling you.

When analyzing data from a *System,* it's easy to forget that it often pertains to the actions of real human beings. For example, imagine a customer service department that answers customer complaints by telephone. Numerically, reducing hold times from ten minutes to eight minutes sounds great—that's a 20 percent improvement!

Put the champagne away: what the data-centric viewpoint misses is the fact that you still have a dissatisfied customer waiting on the phone for eight minutes, which still *feels* like an eternity. Every minute on hold makes that customer angrier, which affects their perception of the company. That 20 percent improvement pales in comparison to the *Reputation* hit your business takes every time that customer tells their friends and associates how horrible your company is to deal with.

Humanization is the process of using data to tell a story (*Narrative*) about a real person's experience or behavior. Quantifiable measures are helpful in the aggregate, but it's often necessary to reframe the measure into actual behavior to really understand what's actually happening.

Many businesses Humanize by developing a series of personas: fictional profiles of people developed from data. When I developed home cleaning products for P&G, market research data told us that two broad *Segments* existed: people who valued regular deep cleaning ("Unless I'm on my hands and knees cleaning with bleach and elbow grease, I'm not satisfied") and people who wanted cleaning to be quick and convenient ("I'm too busy to clean—as long as it looks good enough, I'm happy").

Using this information, we combined these characteristics with other data like household income, family statistics, and hobbies to create a profile of a fictional person. Once the profile was developed, it became easier to use the data we had to make decisions—instead of relying on statistics to evaluate an idea, we could rely on our intuition by asking ourselves if "Wendy" would like it.

Don't just present data—tell a story that helps people understand what's happening, and you'll find your analysis efforts more useful.

SHARE THIS CONCEPT: **http://book.personalmba.com/humanization/**

11

IMPROVING SYSTEMS

In theory there's no difference between theory and practice.
But, in practice, there is.

—JAN L. A. VAN DE SNEPSCHEUT, COMPUTER SCIENTIST

Creating and improving **Systems** is the heart of successful business practice. The purpose of understanding and analyzing systems is to improve them, which is often tricky—changing systems can often create unintended consequences.

In this chapter, you'll learn the secrets of **Optimization**, how to remove unnecessary **Friction** from critical processes, and how to build Systems that can handle **Uncertainty** and **Change**.

SHARE THIS CONCEPT: http://book.personalmba.com/improving-systems/

Intervention Bias

For every complex problem there is an answer that is clear, simple, and wrong.

—H. L. MENCKEN, ESSAYIST

Before making a change to a system, it's important to understand that human beings are predisposed to do something rather than nothing. As we discussed, **Absence Blindness** leads us to value things we can see over things we can't. This predisposition affects how we work on systems: **Intervention**

Bias makes us likely to introduce changes that aren't necessary in order to feel in control of a situation.

Many corporate policies have their roots in Intervention Bias. When something bad happens, it's tempting to "fix" the situation by installing additional layers of limitations, reporting, and auditing. The result isn't an improvement in **Throughput** or efficiency: it's an increase in **Communication Overhead**, waste, and unproductive bureaucracy.

The best way to correct for Intervention Bias is to examine what scientists call a "null hypothesis": examining what would happen if you did nothing or assumed the situation was an accident or error.

Imagine a company that allows its employees to purchase any book they want or need, no questions asked. Books are inexpensive sources of high-quality information, so making it easy for employees to obtain them makes sense.

All is well until one employee abuses the privilege and orders hundreds of novels for personal enjoyment. What should be done?

Many companies would respond by eliminating the policy and requiring a manager's approval for all book purchases. But this change wouldn't fix the situation, because it isn't a widespread issue. Instead, it would annoy or anger employees who use the privilege responsibly, waste time for everyone by increasing paperwork and bureaucracy, and reduce employee productivity by increasing the amount of time it takes to find information they can use to improve the business.

The correct response in this case is to do *nothing*. One employee has abused the privilege, so the situation can be handled with a single discussion, without a major change in policy. The damage is limited, and there's no sense in penalizing everyone for a single person's poor judgment. It is a **Normal Accident**, so overreaction is counterproductive.

Examining the null hypothesis before intervening will help you avoid Intervention Bias and ensure you make the best possible decisions.

SHARE THIS CONCEPT: http://book.personalmba.com/intervention-bias/

Optimization

Premature optimization is the root of all evil.

—DONALD KNUTH, COMPUTER SCIENTIST AND FORMER PROFESSOR
AT STANFORD UNIVERSITY

Optimization is the process of maximizing the output of a **System** or minimizing a specific input the system requires to operate. Optimization typically revolves around the systems and processes behind your **Key Performance Indicators**, which measure the critical elements of the system as a whole. Improve your KPIs, and your system will perform better.

Maximization typically focuses on the system's **Throughput**. If you want to earn more money, create more units to sell, or serve more customers, you're Optimizing for Throughput. Making **Changes** to the system that increase Throughput means your system is performing better in a specific, measurable way.

Minimization typically focuses on in-process inputs required for the System to operate. If you're trying to increase your **Profit Margin**, costs are one of the key inputs. Minimize your costs, and your margins will increase.

By definition, if you're trying to Maximize or Minimize more than one thing, you're not Optimizing—you're making **Trade-offs**. Many people use the term Optimization to mean "making everything better," but that definition doesn't help you actually *do* anything.

In practical terms, trying to Optimize for many variables at once doesn't work—you need to be able to concentrate on a single variable for a while, so you can understand how the Changes you make affect the system as a whole. You're trying to find **Causation** (not **Correlation**) in your Changes, and hidden **Interdependencies** can make it difficult to understand which Changes produced which results.

Remember: you can't reliably Optimize a system's performance across multiple variables at once. Pick the most important one and focus your efforts accordingly.

SHARE THIS CONCEPT: http://book.personalmba.com/optimization/

Refactoring

> Elegance is necessarily unnatural, only achievable at great expense.
> If you just do something, it won't be elegant, but if you do it and then
> see what might be more elegant, and do it again, you might, after an
> unknown number of iterations, get something that is very elegant.

—ERIK NAGGUM, COMPUTER PROGRAMMER

Not all changes to a **System** are designed to affect the System's output. Sometimes it's more effective to reengineer a process without changing the end result at all.

Refactoring is the process of changing a system to improve efficiency without changing the output of the system. The term comes from computer programming—programmers will spend hours rewriting a program that, if all goes well, does *exactly the same thing* when they're finished. What's the point?

The primary benefit of Refactoring isn't improving the output—it's making the system itself faster or more efficient. By rearranging the processes the system uses to produce the result, it's possible to make the program run faster or require fewer resources while operating.

Refactoring starts by **Deconstructing** a process or system, then looking for **Patterns**. What are the critical processes that absolutely must be done right in order to achieve the desired objective? Do those processes have to be completed in a certain order? What are the current **Constraints**? What appears to be particularly important? Collect as much information about how the system works as you can, then sit with it for a while.

More often than not, you'll start to notice things about the system that don't make sense—things that you've done a certain way because it seemed like a good idea at the time but that aren't the best way to approach the task now.

Once Patterns begin to emerge, you can rearrange the system to group similar processes or inputs together. Think of rearranging an assembly line: if you constantly have to stop what you're doing and travel all the way across the factory to obtain a necessary component, rearranging things so the component is always close at hand is probably a good idea. The system will still produce the same thing when you're done, but you'll have removed a little inefficiency from the system that adds up to significant losses in productivity.

If your *Goal* is to make the system faster or more efficient, Refactoring is critically important.

SHARE THIS CONCEPT: http://book.personalmba.com/refactoring/

The Critical Few

> Typically, causes, inputs, or effort divide into two categories: (1) the majority, that have little impact, and (2) a small minority, that have a major, dominant impact.
>
> —RICHARD KOCH, AUTHOR OF *THE 80/20 PRINCIPLE*

Vilfredo Pareto was a nineteenth-century economist and sociologist who was very interested in the topic of land ownership and the social distribution of wealth. After collecting and analyzing a great deal of data, Pareto found a curious *Pattern:* over 80 percent of the land in Italy was owned by less than 20 percent of the population. The Italian economy wasn't distributed evenly, or in the bell-curve-shaped distribution many people assumed: wealth was highly concentrated among a relatively small group of individuals.

As Pareto studied other areas of life, he consistently found the same Pattern: in Pareto's garden, for example, 20 percent of the pea pods produced 80 percent of the peas. What was going on?

In any complex *System,* a minority of the inputs produce the majority of the output. This Pattern of persistent nonlinearity is now called the Pareto principle, or the 80-20 rule. Personally, I prefer to refer to it as the *Critical Few*.

Once you understand this common Pattern, you'll find it in many areas of life:

- In many businesses, less than 20 percent of the customers account for more than 80 percent of annual revenue.

- Less than 20 percent of a business's employees typically do 80 percent or more of the highly valuable work.

▶ You wear less than 20 percent of the clothing in your closet over 80 percent of the time.

▶ You spend over 80 percent of your time communicating with less than 20 percent of your personal contacts.

The nonlinearity of the Critical Few can often be extreme. For example, less than 3 percent of the world's population is in possession of over 97 percent of the world's total wealth. Over time, political power (in both countries and companies) also tends to concentrate in the hands of a few people, which results in a very small group of individuals making decisions that directly affect the lives of hundreds of millions of people. Far less than 1 percent of movies ever produced become blockbusters, and less than 0.1 percent of books ever written become best sellers.

For best results, focus on the critical inputs that produce most of the results you want. In *The 4-Hour Workweek*, Timothy Ferriss used the Critical Few to identify his best performing customers. Out of the 120 customers Ferriss was serving, 5 accounted for 95 percent of the revenue. By focusing on those top-performing wholesalers and putting the rest on "autopilot," Ferriss doubled his monthly revenue and cut his work time from eighty hours to fifteen hours a week.

The same approach is often useful to weed out results you *don't* want. While conducting his business analysis, Ferriss realized that two particular customers accounted for most of his frustration and fire fighting. "Firing" these energy-sucking customers, even though they represented significant sources of volume, liberated his time and energy. As a result, he was able to secure distribution with three additional high-volume customers that boosted the bottom line without the constant headaches.

Noncritical inputs are significant **Opportunity Costs**. If you're spending most of your time in unproductive meetings, for example, you're wasting time that could be used to actually get important things done. The same goes for noncritical expenses: they represent money that you could be using to far greater effect.

Find the inputs that produce the outputs you want, then make them the focus of most of your time and energy. Ruthlessly weed out the rest.

SHARE THIS CONCEPT: http://book.personalmba.com/critical-few/

Diminishing Returns

The last 10 percent of performance generates one-third of the cost
and two-thirds of the problems.

—NORMAN R. AUGUSTINE, AEROSPACE EXECUTIVE AND FORMER U.S. UNDER
SECRETARY OF THE ARMY

If you have $10 in your bank account, finding $5 in the pocket of your
freshly laundered pants is a cause for celebration. If you have $10,000,000
in your bank account, the same situation is a pleasant afterthought.

In a similar vein, eating one cookie is great. Eating two cookies is even
better. Eating a hundred is actually worse. More is not always better. (The
same relationship applies to drinking beer and taking vitamins.)

All good things are subject to **Diminishing Returns**—after a certain point,
having more of something can actually be detrimental. When I was in
marketing at P&G, we spent a lot of time and effort analyzing the results
of our advertising. In the first few weeks of running a television commercial, it was easy to see if it was performing as expected. If the commercial
was performing well, we'd allocate more money to it, but that would only
work for so long.

No matter how much people liked the commercial, at a certain point it
would "wear out," and the company would no longer produce $1 of revenue
for every dollar the company spent showing that ad. That was the "Point of
Diminishing Returns"—if we spent more dollars showing the same commercial, the company would start losing money. Far better to spend those
funds promoting the product in a different way.

It's always better to spend a little time and energy to get the big wins
than to do nothing. In *I Will Teach You to Be Rich*, Ramit Sethi recommends
applying what he calls the "85% Solution." So many people get wrapped up
in making the perfect decision that they wind up overwhelming themselves
and doing nothing. Focus on doing a few simple things that will produce
most of the results you're looking for, then call it a day.

Don't feel like you have to Optimize absolutely everything to perfec-
tion. **Optimization** and **Refactoring** are affected by the **Critical Few** as well—a few
small changes can produce enormous results. After you've picked the "low-
hanging fruit," further Optimization can cost more in effort than you'll

reap in returns. That's a good point to stop. Perfectionism is a trap for the unwary.

Optimize and Refactor up to the point you start experiencing Diminishing Returns, then focus on doing something else.

SHARE THIS CONCEPT: **http://book.personalmba.com/diminishing-returns/**

Friction

> The world is wide, and I will not waste my life in friction when it could be turned into momentum.
>
> —FRANCES E. WILLARD, EDUCATOR AND SUFFRAGIST WHO SPEARHEADED
> THE CAMPAIGN TO ADOPT THE EIGHTEENTH AND NINETEENTH AMENDMENTS
> TO THE U.S. CONSTITUTION

Imagine a hockey puck on the ground in front of you. You're suitably armed with a hockey stick, and the objective is to move the puck from its present location to the goal, which is located one mile away.

First, assume the puck is sitting in a field of tall grass, which is waving in the wind. Each whack of the hockey stick will move the puck only a few feet, since the tall grass robs the puck of energy. At this rate, you'll have to hit the puck thousands of times before you get to the goal, and you'll exhaust your energy quickly. It'll take you many frustrating hours to reach the goal.

Now let's assume you mow the field until the grass in front of you is very short. Each time you hit the puck, it goes twenty feet or more—a huge improvement. The puck comes in contact with less grass, which means that it travels a longer distance with every strike. You'll still have to work to get the puck to the goal, but you'll achieve your objective more quickly and with less effort.

Finally, let's assume you flood the field with water and freeze it, until the landscape is a smooth plane of ice. Now the puck will travel hundreds of feet every time you hit it, because the ice doesn't rob the puck of energy—the puck glides along the surface effortlessly. At this rate, you'll only need to hit the puck a few times before you've achieved the objective, and you won't be tired when you're done.

Friction is any force or process that removes energy from a *System* over time. In the presence of Friction, it's necessary to continue to add energy to a system to keep it moving at the same rate over time. Unless additional energy is added, Friction will slow the system down until it comes to a stop. Remove the Friction, and you'll increase the system's efficiency.

Every business process has some amount of Friction. The key is to identify areas where Friction currently exists, then experiment with small improvements that will reduce the amount of Friction in the system. Removing small amounts of Friction consistently over time *Accumulates* large improvements in both quality and efficiency.

Removing even small amounts of Friction from your *Marketing*, *Sales*, and *Value-Delivery* processes can generate major improvements in *Profit*. For example, retailers like Amazon.com go to enormous lengths to minimize the amount of effort it takes for a customer to place an order. From allowing customers to purchase items with a single click (which automatically charges and ships the order to the customer's default credit card and address on file) to automatically recommending related items for purchase, Amazon aims to make it as easy as possible for its customers to buy online.

Amazon Prime, a service that automatically upgrades every order a customer places to two-day shipping, is a textbook example of the benefits of reducing Friction. In exchange for a small annual fee, the Prime customers receive their purchases by mail in two days or less, without spending time in a retail store.

When a customer signs up for Amazon Prime, the customer's annual order volume increases by 150 percent on average, and 82 percent of Prime members choose to purchase items on Amazon even when the item is less expensive at a competing retailer. As a result, orders from Amazon Prime customers total an estimated 20 percent of the company's overall U.S. sales . . . all from finding new ways to reduce Friction in the buying process.[1]

Introducing Friction intentionally can sometimes encourage people to behave in a certain way or make a particular decision. For example, adding a small amount of Friction to your returns process, like requiring the customer to provide a receipt or explain the reason for the return, can decrease the number of people who return your product. You don't want to add too much, since that can negatively impact your *Reputation* (customers get angry if you make them work too hard for a refund), but a little Friction in the right place can help prevent frivolous returns.

Work on removing Friction from your business system where appropriate, and you'll generate better results for less effort.

SHARE THIS CONCEPT: http://book.personalmba.com/friction/

Automation

The first rule of any technology used in a business is that automation applied to an efficient operation will magnify the efficiency. The second is that automation applied to an inefficient operation will magnify the inefficiency.

—BILL GATES, FOUNDER AND CHAIRMAN OF MICROSOFT

Remove enough *Friction*, and people may not have to be involved in a process at all.

Automation refers to a *System* or process that can operate without human intervention. Factory production lines, utility networks, and computer programs use Automation to minimize the amount of human involvement necessary to complete a task. The less human effort required to operate the system, the more efficient the Automation.

Automation is best for well-defined, repetitive tasks. For example, if I had to manually reply to a letter or e-mail every time someone wanted to read my list of recommended business books, I'd quickly go insane. Fortunately, I can just put the list up on my Web site—every time someone requests the list, it's delivered to them automatically, without any effort on my part. My reading list has been viewed by hundreds of thousands of readers from around the world, and Automation is what makes it possible.

Find a way to Automate your system, and you open the doors to *Scale* via *Duplication* and *Multiplication*, improving your ability to create and deliver value to more paying customers.

SHARE THIS CONCEPT: http://book.personalmba.com/automation/

The Paradox of Automation

> One machine can do the work of fifty ordinary men. No machine can
> do the work of one extraordinary man.
>
> —ELBERT HUBBARD, AUTHOR OF *A MESSAGE TO GARCIA*

Automation can be great, but it has very important drawbacks worth understanding.

Imagine a fully Automated production line that makes computer processors that sell for $200 per unit. All the human operators have to do is push a button, and the production **System** starts cranking out 2,400 finished products per minute. Life is good, right?

Yes, with a *very* important caveat. Imagine that a drill used to bore holes in the silicon wafer becomes misaligned and starts drilling microscopic holes through the middle of the processor core. Every second the system keeps working, forty chips are ruined.

Assume each processor costs $20 in raw materials—that means the factory starts losing $800 every second the error isn't found. Every minute the system keeps running, the company loses $48,000. And that's just the direct cost—if you take into account that each processor would sell for $200, the company is losing $528,000 a minute: $48,000 in direct costs and $480,000 in opportunity costs.

Sound far-fetched? Consider this: In late 2009, Toyota identified a major issue with the accelerator pedal in several popular vehicle models, which were top sellers for many years. The error was **Multiplied** across every vehicle Toyota made, and the recall cost over *five billion dollars*.

Before the recall, Toyota was considered the best automotive manufacturer in the world. They still are in many respects, but their **Reputation** and financial situation suffered a major blow. Even the best can fall if costly mistakes are allowed to Multiply.

Here's the **Paradox of Automation**: the more efficient the Automated system, the more crucial the contribution of the human operators of that system. When an error happens, operators need to identify and fix the situation quickly or shut the system down—otherwise, the Automated system will continue to Multiply the error.

Dr. Lisanne Bainbridge, a psychologist at University College London, was one of the first to rigorously study the ramifications of efficient and reliable systems.[2] She was the first to identify and express the "paradox" of Automated systems: efficient Automated systems reduce the need for human effort, but make human involvement even more critical.

Efficient Automation makes humans *more* important, not less.

SHARE THIS CONCEPT: http://book.personalmba.com/paradox-of-automation/

The Irony of Automation

> There will always be a set of circumstances that was not expected, that the automation either was not designed to handle or other things that just cannot be predicted. As system reliability increases, the more difficult it is to detect the error and recover from it.
>
> —DR. RAJA PARASURAMAN, PROFESSOR OF PSYCHOLOGY AT GEORGE MASON UNIVERSITY

Efficient **Automated Systems** make skilled human intervention critically important to prevent the **Amplification** of errors, so it's best to keep skilled operators on hand at all times, right?

That's easier said than done: businesses typically don't pay highly skilled employees to sit around in a room all day doing nothing, which is what they'll be doing as long as the system appears to be reliable. Even if they do, the operators will spend most of their time being bored out of their skulls.

Here's the **Irony of Automation**: the more reliable the system, the less human operators have to do, so the less they pay **Attention** to the system while it's in operation. Remember the Mackworth Clock and the vigilance studies conducted on British radar operators in World War II from our discussion of **Novelty**? Humans get bored extremely quickly if things stay the same, and the more reliable the system, the *more things stay the same*.

Ironically, reliable systems tend to dull the operator's senses, making it very difficult for them to notice when things go wrong—the moment when their attention is most sorely needed. As a result, the more reliable the system, the lower the likelihood that human operators will notice when something goes wrong—particularly if the error is small.

Left long enough, small errors can become the "new normal," which is how a company like Toyota ends up with a five-billion-dollar recall. (By the way, don't make the *Attribution Error* and think that Toyota's engineers were stupid or careless—if you rely on Automated systems, it could easily happen to you.)

The best approach to avoid major Automation errors is rigorous, ongoing *Sampling* and *Testing*. Remember, *Normal Accidents* can and will occur. If you assume that errors will be made and plan a battery of tests to find the most critical errors, you can keep your system operators engaged and increase the probability of finding important errors quickly.

Keep your Automated system's operators mentally engaged, and they'll be far more likely to notice when errors inevitably occur.

SHARE THIS CONCEPT: http://book.personalmba.com/irony-of-automation/

Standard Operating Procedure

> The measure of success is not whether you have a tough problem to
> deal with, but whether it's the same problem you had last year.
>
> —JOHN FOSTER DULLES, FORMER U.S. SECRETARY OF STATE

What do you do when a customer has a complaint or asks for a refund? What happens when you run out of toner for the laser printer? Who takes the helm if the manager is out of town and there's an emergency?

A *Standard Operating Procedure (SOP)* is a predefined process used to complete a task or resolve a common issue. Business *Systems* often include repetitive tasks, and having a standard process in place can help you spend less time reinventing the wheel and more time doing productive work.

Well-defined Standard Operating Procedures are useful because they reduce *Friction* and minimize *Willpower Depletion*. Instead of wasting valuable time and energy solving a problem that has already been solved many times before, a predefined SOP ensures that you spend less time thrashing and more time adding value.

Standard Operating Procedures are also effective ways to bring new employees or partners up to speed quickly. Having a central source of SOPs can help new employees or partners learn how you work far more effectively than informal training. Storing your SOPs in some sort of central electronic database is best—it ensures that everyone can instantly reference the most up-to-date procedures available.

Don't let your Standard Operating Procedures lapse into bureaucracy. Remember, the purpose of an SOP is to minimize the amount of time and effort it takes to complete a task or solve a problem effectively. If the SOP requires effort without providing value, it's Friction.

For best results, review your SOPs on a periodic basis—once every two to three months is ideal. If you find outdated, wasteful, or unnecessary work in your SOPs, change them. Neither you nor your customers are served by unnecessary red tape.

Create Standard Operating Procedures for important recurring tasks, and you'll see your productivity skyrocket.

SHARE THIS CONCEPT: http://book.personalmba.com/standard-operating-procedures/

Checklist

> No matter how expert you may be, well-designed checklists can improve outcomes.
>
> —STEVEN LEVITT, COAUTHOR OF *FREAKONOMICS*

Want to make sure an important task is done correctly every single time? Create a checklist.

A *Checklist* is an *Externalized*, predefined *Standard Operating Procedure* for completing a specific task. Creating a Checklist is enormously valuable for two reasons. First, Checklisting will help you define a *System* for a process that hasn't yet been formalized—once the Checklist has been created, it's easier to see how to improve or *Automate* the system. Second, using Checklists as a normal part of working can help ensure that you don't forget to handle important steps that are easily overlooked when things get busy.

Pilots have extremely detailed Checklists for takeoff and landing for a reason: skipping a step is easy, but can have major consequences for everyone on board. Even pilots with decades of flying experience always use Checklists to make sure everything is done right and in the proper sequence. As a result, plane crashes are extremely rare—statistically, it's safer to fly commercially than to drive.

Even simple processes can benefit from **Systemization** and the use of Checklists. In 2001, a study on the effects of Checklisting was conducted by Dr. Peter Pronovost, which was described in detail in Atul Gawande's *The Checklist Manifesto* and in an article Gawande published in the *New Yorker*. [3] The study was conducted in a hospital in Detroit that had the highest rate of ten-day IV line infections (a costly and life-threatening condition) in the country. Pronovost's objective was to determine whether or not using Checklists would reduce the rate of infections.

Here's the entirety of the intervention: whenever a doctor inserted an IV line, they were instructed to use the following Checklist.

Step 1: Wash hands with soap.

Step 2: Clean the patient's skin with chlorhexidine antiseptic.

Step 3: Put sterile drapes over the entire patient.

Step 4: Wear a sterile hat, mask, gloves, and gown.

Step 5: Put a sterile dressing over the catheter site once the IV line is in.

None of these steps is particularly complicated. In fact, many doctors resisted the study, since they felt that being forced to use a Checklist for such a simple procedure was insulting, given their status as highly trained specialists. Even more insulting, the head nurse was empowered to stop the doctor if they weren't using the Checklist—an unusual role reversal that had many doctors fuming.

Nevertheless, the results of this study over two years were astounding: the ten-day IV line infection rate dropped from 11 percent to 0 percent and saved the hospital over $2 million in related costs. As it turns out, forgetting even basic, commonsense procedures is easy in a busy, stressful environment.

Checklisting can produce major improvements in your ability to do quality work, as well as your ability to delegate work effectively. By taking the time to explicitly describe and track your progress, you reduce the likelihood of major errors and oversights, as well as prevent **Willpower Depletion** associated with figuring out how to complete the same task over and over again. In addition, once your Checklist is complete you can use it as the basis for full or partial Automation of the system, which will allow you to spend time doing more important things.

For best results, create explicit Checklists for the **Five Parts of Your Business**, then make sure they're followed every single time.

SHARE THIS CONCEPT: http://book.personalmba.com/checklisting/

Cessation

There is nothing so useless as doing efficiently that which should not be done at all.

—PETER DRUCKER, FATHER OF MODERN MANAGEMENT THEORY

Sometimes the best way to improve a **System** is to stop doing so much.

Cessation is the choice to intentionally stop doing something that's counterproductive. Due to **Absence Blindness**, we're predisposed to attempt to improve a system by doing something—it "feels wrong" to do nothing. That doesn't mean that doing nothing is a bad strategy: it's often more effective.

In *The One-Straw Revolution*, Masanobu Fukuoka wrote about his experiments with natural farming, which mostly involved letting nature take its course and intervening as little as possible. While most farms were introducing chemicals and machinery into agriculture, Fukuoka was consciously doing *nothing*—and reaping the rewards of high yields and ever-increasing soil richness. Here's what he had to say about the virtues of cessation:

> Human beings with their tampering do something wrong, leave the damage unrepaired, and when the adverse results accumulate, work with all their might to correct them. When the corrective actions appear to be successful, they come to view these measures as splendid accomplishments. People do this over and over again. It is as if a fool were to stomp on and break the tiles of his roof. Then when it starts to rain and the ceiling begins to rot away, he hastily climbs up to mend the damage, rejoicing in the end that he has accomplished a miraculous solution.

Instead of trying to do too much, Fukuoka only did what was absolutely necessary. As a result, his fields were consistently among the most productive in the area.

Cessation takes guts. It's often unpopular or unpalatable to do nothing, even if doing nothing is actually the right solution. As an example, "pricing bubbles" are often caused by government intervention in certain markets, which has the *Second-Order Effect* of artificially decreasing the costs of certain actions, leading to rampant speculation. When reality sets in and the bubble "pops," as it did with dot-com companies in 2000 and the housing market in 2008, it's politically unpopular for the government to do nothing, even though *doing something is what caused the situation in the first place*. More often than not, the government acts, which causes another, bigger bubble a few years later.

Firing customers, quitting your job, discontinuing a product, or pulling out of a market you can't succeed in are all tough decisions, but these decisions may put you in a better position in the long run.

Doing something is not always the best course of action. Consider doing nothing instead.

SHARE THIS CONCEPT: http://book.personalmba.com/cessation/

Resilience

> Placing a system in a straightjacket of constancy can cause fragility to evolve.
>
> —C. S. HOLLING, ECOLOGIST

Turtles aren't the sexiest creatures in the animal kingdom. They can't run fast. They can't fly. They don't have big sharp teeth or claws. They can't puff themselves up to look menacing or poison their enemies with deadly venom. Compared to the raw power of a tiger or a falcon, turtles are rather lame.

What turtles *do* have is a variety of protective strategies—they can swim quickly, use camouflage, snap with their jaws, and if all else fails, retract into their shell and wait for the threat to pass.

Creatures elsewhere in the animal kingdom are in big trouble if they're cornered by a predator. Turtles have a fighting chance—they win because they're the armored tanks of nature. They can also eat many different things and go into hibernation when times get tough. That's why they live so long.

Tigers, on the other hand, rely on their strength, power, and speed to chase down their prey. When times are good, tigers are the kings of the jungle. If prey becomes scarce or they lose their hunting prowess due to age or injury, death takes them quickly and mercilessly—no second chances.

What the business world needs is more turtles and fewer tigers.

The world is a fundamentally *Uncertain* place. Unexpected things happen—some good, some bad. You never know when Mother Nature, Lady Luck, or a hungry predator will decide that today is not your day.

Resilience is a massively underrated quality in business. Having the toughness and flexibility to handle anything life throws at you is a major asset that can save your skin—literally and metaphorically. Your ability to adjust your strategy and tactics as conditions *Change* can be the difference between survival and disaster.

Resilience is never "optimal" if you evaluate a *System* solely on *Throughput*. Flexibility always comes at a price. A turtle's shell is heavy—it could certainly move faster without it. Giving it up, however, would leave the turtle vulnerable in the moments when moving a little faster just isn't fast enough. In an effort to chase a few more short-term dollars, many businesses trade Resilience for short-term results—and pay a hefty price.

The big investment banks are a classic example. Keeping cash reserves on hand to handle the unexpected has become "ultraconservative" and "inefficient"—it's become a "best practice" to *Leverage* the entire company many times over times to squeeze out a few more cents in earnings per share each quarter, leaving the business explosively vulnerable to a very small decline in revenues.

Operating a business with no cash reserves, no insurance, and high levels of debt may improve your returns for a few months or quarters, but the moment your revenues decline even by a little or someone decides to sue the business, you're sunk.

Leverage works just like rocket fuel—depending on how it's used, it can propel your business to dizzying heights or make the entire operation explode. Unfortunately, many of the advanced financial manipulation tactics taught in business schools implicitly trade Resilience for paper returns—and once-successful businesses pay the price by going out of business when times get tough.

Preparing for the unexpected makes you more Resilient. On a personal level, investing in a home emergency/first aid kit, car kit, and extra resources like food and water isn't paranoid—supplies like these are cheap insurance for the intelligent. The same goes for purchasing insurance and building up reserves for unexpected events. You may never need them, but you'll be glad they're there if you do.

HERE'S WHAT MAKES A BUSINESS RESILIENT:

—*Low (preferably zero) outstanding debt*

—*Low overhead, fixed costs, and operating expenses*

—*Substantial cash reserves for unexpected contingencies*

—*Multiple independent products/industries/lines of business*

—*Flexible workers/employees who can handle many responsibilities well*

—*No single points of failure*

—*Fail-safes/backup systems for all core processes*

Planning for Resilience as well as performance is the hallmark of good management. Resilience is certainly not sexy, mostly because the benefits suffer from ***Absence Blindness***. It can, however, save your hide when times get tough.

Think less like a tiger and more like a turtle, and your business will be able to withstand pretty much anything.

SHARE THIS CONCEPT: http://book.personalmba.com/resilience/

Fail-safe

> "Always" and "never" are two words that you should always re-
> member never to use.
>
> —WENDELL JOHNSON, PSYCHOLOGIST AND PIONEER OF SPEECH PATHOLOGY

Every Wednesday at noon, a generator kicks on outside of the house I grew up in. If all goes well, it'll run for ten minutes, then turn off automatically until the next testing cycle, silently waiting to spring into action again when the power goes out.

My father once worked as a firefighter and emergency medical technician and has refined "being prepared" into a high art. The generator is designed to turn on automatically the moment the primary electricity to the house fails, taking over the house's electrical demands seamlessly. The generator is fed via a propane tank behind the garage, which has enough fuel to keep the generator running for a week. If a storm knocks out power to the area, Dad is prepared to handle it.

Dad's preparedness rubbed off on me. Now that we live in the mountains of Colorado, we have to be prepared for the possibility of our car breaking down somewhere remote or cold and we can't rely on AAA (or cell phone coverage) to save us.

Kelsey often makes fun of me for stocking our vehicles with extra clothing, sleeping bags, snowshoes, and satellite-driven personal locator beacons, but I don't mind. If something happens, we'll be glad we were prepared—I consider the investment in equipment a cheap, durable *Insurance* policy.

A *Fail-safe* is a backup *System* designed to prevent or allow recovery from a primary system failure. If the primary system fails in some way, well-designed Fail-safes can keep the system from collapsing unexpectedly. You can find backup systems anywhere consistent performance is critical.

Actors in high-profile Broadway shows have understudies. If "the show must go on," it pays to know you'll always have a replacement for any actor who can't perform. Most shows even have a few "swing" actors—performers who are ready to stand in for *any* role at a moment's notice.

External hard drives back up critical computer data. If the hard drive in your computer crashes, you can still access the data via the backup drive, so you won't lose everything. Some businesses even take the precaution of storing backup drives off-site in case of fire or natural disaster.

Airplanes have systems that sense a failure in cabin pressure, automatically deploying face masks attached to an oxygen tank. If the airplane's pressurized cabin fails for some reason, the passengers won't lose consciousness—a very good thing indeed.

Fail-safes are not efficient in the sense that you're investing time and resources in a system you hope you'll never use. Backup systems and Insurance, from one perspective, can be seen as a waste of money—why spend valuable resources on something you hope you'll never need?

Here's why: by the time you need a Fail-safe, it's too late to develop one. In order to be effective, Fail-safes must be developed *before* you need them. If you wait to develop backup systems until you need them, it's too late to make a difference. Paying for homeowners' Insurance can feel like a waste of money until your house burns down. If you wait to buy Insurance until something bad happens, it's already too late.

Try to separate your Fail-safe and primary system as much as possible. One of the reasons people rent safe deposit boxes in banks is to protect certain items from loss in the event of fire or theft—if something happens to the house, the items in the safe deposit box will still be okay. The practice of backing up data to an off-site data center serves the same purpose: if something happens to the business's primary computers, the data is still safe in another location.

Fail-safes that are highly **Interdependent** with the primary system can actually introduce additional risks. One of the worst things you can do is make your backup system a part of the system you're trying to protect. For example, it wouldn't do my father much good if a failure in the generator cascaded to the house's primary electrical system and knocked out the power unexpectedly. An **Automated** computer backup system doesn't do you any good if it could potentially delete all of your original files.

As much as possible, *never have a single critical point of failure*. If your system relies on critical inputs or processes in order to function, it's a good idea to plan for situations where those inputs aren't available or those processes are disrupted. What would you do if the primary system fails?

Plan in advance to develop Fail-safes for all critical systems, and you'll make your system as **Resilient** as you possibly can.

SHARE THIS CONCEPT: http://book.personalmba.com/fail-safe/

Stress Testing

> To make no mistakes is not in the power of man; but from their errors and mistakes the wise and good learn wisdom for the future.
>
> —PLUTARCH, ANCIENT GREEK HISTORIAN AND ESSAYIST

Let's say you've developed what you believe is a robust, **Resilient System,** but you want to ensure that your preparations actually work. How would you go about **Testing** it?

Stress Testing is the process of identifying the boundaries of a system by simulating specific *Environmental* conditions. Instead of staying in systems engineer mode, Stress Testing inverts your mind-set into "demon mode." What would it take to break what you've built?

In the early days of the Personal MBA, every time I launched a new version of the reading list, my Web server would go down in a blaze of glory—the system couldn't keep up with all of the people trying to visit the Web site. I upgraded to several different systems, but each time, it wasn't enough.

I continued having server issues until I got serious about Stress Testing. Instead of waiting for an influx of traffic that would cause my site to go down, I set about "breaking" my system intentionally, then trying different approaches to make the system more Resilient under stress.

Using an *Automated* tool,[4] I simulated a huge number of visitors hitting my Web site at the same time. The tool continuously increased the number of visitors requesting my Web site, then tracked how long my Web site took to respond. As the requests went up, my site's performance decreased until the server failed.

Using the data I collected from the Stress Test, I made several major improvements to my Web site's infrastructure and systems. Now, thousands of people can visit my site at precisely the same moment without noticeably affecting performance—a huge improvement.

Stress Tests can help you learn more about how your system works. If you're in the manufacturing business, you could simulate a sudden order of thousands of units—can you keep up? If you're doing customer support, you could simulate a massive influx of questions or complaints—could you handle it? Your ability to test is only limited by your available time and imagination—let your inner demon run wild, then fix any major problems you find before they affect real customers.

SHARE THIS CONCEPT: http://book.personalmba.com/stress-testing/

Scenario Planning

A prudent person foresees danger and takes precautions. The simpleton goes blindly on and suffers the consequences.

—PROVERBS 27:12

As we've discussed many times in this book, no one can predict what will happen tomorrow, let alone ten years from now. That's a problem when your plans and *Goals* depend on things completely outside of your *Locus of Control*. What can you do to prepare for an *Uncertain* future?

Scenario Planning is the process of systematically constructing a series of hypothetical situations, then *Mentally Simulating* what you would do if they occured. You may not be a seer, but *Counterfactual Simulation* gives you a powerful capability: imagining things that *might* occur, then figuring out what you'd do if they did. Scenario Planning is essentially detailed, thorough, and systematic Counterfactual Simulation applied to major decisions.

Scenario Planning always starts with a simple question: "What would I do if. . . ?" The "what if" part is the Counterfactual, and it's what kicks your planning brain into gear, helping you imagine possible responses. By writing down all of your potential courses of action in that circumstance, it's possible to develop several responses to any situation you can imagine.

Scenario Planning is the essence of effective strategy. Trying to base your actions on predictions of interest rates, oil prices, or stock values is a fool's game. Instead of trying to predict the future with 100 percent accuracy, Scenario Planning can help you prepare for many different possible futures. Instead of rigidly focusing on only one option, your business will become more flexible and *Resilient*, improving your ability to *Change* and adapt to a changing world.

Most large businesses use Scenario Planning as the basis of a practice called "hedging": purchasing various forms of *Insurance* to reduce the *Risk* of unfavorable future events. For example, manufacturers care about oil prices because they increase the cost of importing raw materials and shipping finished products to their customers, both of which can suddenly and dramatically decrease their *Profit Margins*. By purchasing financial instruments called "futures," the businesses can make money if the price of oil goes up, which helps to offset the losses they would incur if oil prices increase.

Scenario Planning is easy to skip, particularly if you already have a lot of work to do. The time you spend in Scenario Planning can be some of the most valuable time you spend building your business, but it's easy to overlook if you're constantly struggling to simply keep your head above water. Regularly setting nonnegotiable time to step back and plan for the future is always time well spent—don't skip it.

Don't waste time trying to predict an unknowable future—construct the most likely scenarios and plan what you'll do if they occur, and you'll be prepared for whatever actually happens.

SHARE THIS CONCEPT: http://book.personalmba.com/scenario-planning/

Sustainable Growth Cycle

After victory, tighten the straps on your helmet.

—TOKUGAWA IEYASU, EARLY-SEVENTEENTH-CENTURY SHOGUN

It's a mistake to assume any system can grow indefinitely, without limit. Systems tend to have a natural size, and exceeding this size can cause many problems. Elements of a system that are out of control need to be eliminated.

Take cell growth, for example. The cells in your body tend to grow to a certain size and to multiply at a rate that ensures new cells replace cells that die. When these proportions are in balance, your body works quite well. When cells grow or multiply out of control, the situation can threaten the existence of the system. Cancerous cells need to be removed to ensure the health of the entire body.

Businesses and biological organisms have many things in common: they're made up of many interrelated parts and systems that change and grow over time. If the *Five Parts of Every Business* grow out of control or out of proportion to one another, the situation can threaten the health of the organization.

The *Sustainable Growth Cycle* is a pattern I've noticed in businesses that are able to grow year after year without major difficulties. This cycle has three distinct phases: expansion, maintenance, and consolidation.

In an *Expansion phase*, the company is focused on growing. New offers are created and tested. New markets are explored. New business units are built and staffed, and future plans are created. Early data about what works is collected for later use.

In a *Maintenance phase*, the company is focused on executing the current plan. The **Marketing**, **Sales**, and **Value-Delivery** parts of the business are in full swing, and emphasis is placed on fully exploring the potential of the current business structure. Systems are put in place to ensure the execution.

In a *Consolidation phase*, the company is focused on analysis. Information about the performance of the business is examined in detail in an attempt to figure out what's working and what's not. Things that aren't working are cut back or eliminated, and things that are working are given more resources.

Think of plant cultivation: the best gardeners allow plants to grow, ensure they have enough resources to thrive, then cut back the plants that don't. This cycle repeats, season after season. Every cycle is essential.

Many entrepreneurs become frustrated when their business seems to hit a "plateau" and growth appears to stop. Spending time on maintenance or consolidation seems like a waste, or a flaw in the business idea. That's not the case at all: these phases are necessary to ensure the business succeeds, and they should be respected.

A business that fixates on expansion but shortchanges maintenance and consolidation will experience the commercial equivalent of cancerous growth. Parts of the business will grow out of control, consuming too much time, energy, and resources compared to what they contribute to the health of the business. New opportunities will be explored while proven opportunities are ignored or forgotten.

Maintenance and consolidation are necessary to bring the system into balance. Once the system is humming along, the growth cycle kicks in automatically.

A healthy business cycles between expansion, maintenance, and consolidation often. No matter which part of the cycle you're in, it's important to recognize that it's necessary and essential to the health of the business. By giving each cycle the appropriate time and attention, you'll ensure the long-term success of the business.

SHARE THIS CONCEPT: http://book.personalmba.com/sustainable-growth-cycle/

The Middle Path

A master in any art avoids what is too much and what is too little;
they search for the mean and choose it.

—ARISTOTLE

Business is never easy—it's an art as much as a science.

The **Middle Path** is the ever-changing balance point between too little and too much—just enough. No one can tell you what the Middle Path is—you have to be walking the path to know, and it changes constantly. Getting the balance right in the midst of **Uncertainty** is the difference between a competent business professional and a great one.

The best approach to anything almost always lies somewhere between "too little" and "too much." Just as in cooking, "business recipes" can only teach you so much. You may know the ingredients, the techniques, and the tools, but actually cooking a dish still requires attention, effort, and taste.

No one has it "all figured out." No one is absolutely certain that something will work, or has a complete lack of fear that things won't work out as planned. The people who experience the most success in this world are the people who accept the Uncertainty and fear as best they can, learn from their experiences, and keep trying new things.

Try to find the Middle Path, then stay on it as best you can. Find the right balance, and you can accomplish anything.

SHARE THIS CONCEPT: http://book.personalmba.com/middle-path/

The Experimental Mind-set

The only way you learn to flip things is just to flip them!

—JULIA CHILD, WORLD-RENOWNED CHEF, AFTER FLOPPING A POTATO
PANCAKE ONTO THE FLOOR DURING HER TV SHOW

When improving yourself or your business, it's often not clear what approach will create the intended result. That's where the **Experimental Mind-set** comes in handy.

Constant **Experimentation** is the only way you can identify what will actually produce the result you desire. Often, the best (or only) way to learn things is to jump in and try. At the beginning, you may be in over your head, but there's no faster way to learn what works. Once you're committed to exploring something, you'll learn far more quickly than if you'd cowered on the sidelines.

You learn the most from what doesn't go well. As long as your mistakes don't kill you, paying **Attention** to what doesn't work can give you useful information you can use to discover what does. All failures are temporary—what you learn in the process always helps you move forward.

Experimentation is learning through play. There's no need to build yourself up as a "serious businessperson" who cringes at the thought of the slightest mistake. You'll make thousands of mistakes over the course of your career, and that's perfectly okay. Every Experiment teaches you something new, and every new lesson you learn increases your capability to accomplish great things.

Experimentation is the essence of living a satisfying, productive, fulfilling life. The more you Experiment, the more you learn, and the more you'll achieve.

SHARE THIS CONCEPT: http://book.personalmba.com/experimental-mindset/

Not "The End"

A truly good book teaches me better than to read it. I must soon lay it down, and commence living on its hint. What I began by reading, I must finish by acting.

—HENRY DAVID THOREAU

Many of my readers and clients ask me:

"This business education stuff is great, but when will I be done?"

Wrong question, grasshopper. Self-education, whether it's about business or anything else, is a never-ending process. There's never a point where you'll say, "Okay, I'm done—no more learning for me." Every new concept you come across is a gateway to thousands of other opportunities for exploration.

That's what makes self-education so fun and rewarding: there's always something new to learn.

In Eastern philosophy, *Tao* means "way" or "path"—a journey you're in the process of undertaking. Tao has no beginning and no end—it just is. Educating yourself about anything is a Tao—there's no end to the process. The journey itself is the reward.

Even masters of the art of moneymaking like Warren Buffett are always looking for new things to learn. When asked in an interview with students from the University of Nebraska–Lincoln about what superpowers he'd like to have, Buffett answered: "I'd like to be able to read faster." Most of what Buffett does on a daily basis is read financial reports and learn new concepts, looking for new ways to increase the value of his company.

Even the wealthiest person on earth has things to improve and more to explore. That ongoing curiosity is what made them successful in the first place.

There will certainly be milestones along your path: completing a book, mastering a new skill, launching a business, closing a sale. Eventually, however, you'll find that there's a new path for you to take, and the journey continues.

There's never a limit to how much you can grow.

Now that you've read this book, please visit http://personalmba.com and subscribe to the Personal MBA e-mail update. I revise my recommended reading list every year and publish new material every month. There's no cost to subscribe, and I'd be happy to keep you up-to-date with the most useful business information I discover.

I'd like to leave you with a few words of wisdom from B. C. Forbes, the founder of *Forbes* magazine, who wrote an essay in 1917 called "Keys to Success." I refer to it often, and find that it's a great reminder of what business and life are all about:

> *Your success depends on you.*
> *Your happiness depends on you.*
> *You have to steer your own course.*
> *You have to shape your own fortune.*
> *You have to educate yourself.*

You have to do your own thinking.

You have to live with your own conscience.

Your mind is yours and can be used only by you.

You come into this world alone.

You go to the grave alone.

You are alone with your inner thoughts during the journey between.

You make your own decisions.

You must abide by the consequences of your acts . . .

You alone can regulate your habits and make or unmake your health.

You alone can assimilate things mental and things material . . .

You have to do your own assimilation all through life.

You can be taught by a teacher, but you have to imbibe the knowledge. He cannot transfuse it into your brain.

You alone can control your mind cells and your brain cells.

You may have spread before you the wisdom of the ages, but unless you assimilate it you derive no benefit from it; no one can force it into your cranium.

You alone can move your own legs.

You alone can move your own arms.

You alone can utilize your own hands.

You alone can control your own muscles.

You must stand on your feet, physically and metaphorically.

You must take your own steps.

Your parents cannot enter into your skin, take control of your mental and physical machinery, and make something of you.

You cannot fight your son's battles; that he must do for himself.

You have to be captain of your own destiny.

You have to see through your own eyes.

You have to use your own ears.

You have to master your own faculties.

You have to solve your own problems.

You have to form your own ideals.

You have to create your own ideas.

You must choose your own speech.

You must govern your own tongue.

Your real life is your thoughts.

Your thoughts are your own making.

Your character is your own handiwork.

You alone can select the materials that go into it.

You alone can reject what is not fit to go into it.

You are the creator of your own personality.

You can be disgraced by no man's hand but your own.

You can be elevated and sustained by no man but yourself.

You have to write your own record.

You have to build your own monument—or dig your own pit.

Which are you doing?

I hope you've enjoyed this book and found it useful—if you have, please spread the word. If you have questions or comments, don't hesitate to reach out—you can always contact me directly at josh@personalmba.com.

Thanks for reading, and best wishes on your journey through the fascinating and ever-changing world of business.

Have fun!

ACKNOWLEDGMENTS

To Kelsey: we did it. Thank you for your unwavering love, confidence, and support.

To Mom and Dad: thanks for teaching me to read at such an early age. I owe my curiosity about the world and open heart to your example.

To Seth Godin: thanks for the inspiration, and for changing my life in all sorts of remarkable ways.

To Charlie Munger: thanks for sharing what you know with the world; I'm a better person because of it.

To Todd Sattersten and Jack Covert: thanks for introducing me to the team at Portfolio—without your generosity, this book wouldn't exist.

To Ben Casnocha and Ramit Sethi: thanks for encouraging me to take on this project, for reviewing rough drafts, introducing me to Lisa, and inspiring me with your example.

To Carlos Miceli, who graciously assisted in creating the Web site that accompanies this book.

To Lisa DiMona: your reputation preceded you, and it's not difficult to see why. Your enthusiasm, dedication, and patience are world-class. Thanks for everything you do.

To Adrian Zackheim: thanks for taking a chance on a young man with a crazy idea, and for consistently publishing great work. The books you've published have improved my life, and I'm happy to be able to contribute to the cause. I hope it sells a million.

To David Moldawer: I expected an intelligent, experienced, and tough editor. You're all that and more: a trusted friend. Thanks for your keen eye and sharp wit: you left this book much better than you found it.

To Will Weisser, Maureen Cole, Richard Lennon, Joseph Perez, Oliver Munday, Jaime Putorti, Noirin Lucas, Michael Burke, and everyone behind the scenes at Portfolio: many years ago, I promised myself that if I ever decided to write a book, I'd only work with a publisher if I could work with the best. Your experience and professionalism in taking this book to market is astounding—I couldn't ask for a better team.

To Eric Gonzalez, Enoch Ko, Steven McGuinnity, Peter Millonig, Denver Rix, Marina Murray, Joseph Magliocco, and Tim Shadel: thanks for your help in identifying and correcting errors in the first edition. I appreciate your sharp eyes and suggestions for improvement.

To my clients and readers: without you, this book wouldn't exist. Thanks for your support, feedback, and encouragement—I hope you find this resource useful, and that you accomplish everything you set out to achieve.

APPENDIX A

HOW TO CONTINUE YOUR BUSINESS STUDIES

We write by the light of every book we ever read.
—RICHARD PECK, AUTHOR

The next best thing to knowing something is knowing where to find it.
—SAMUEL JOHNSON, ESSAYIST AND MAN OF LETTERS

This book is a high-level overview of an extremely wide body of useful business literature. If you're interested in continuing your studies, I highly recommend starting with any of these books:

BUSINESS CREATION

- ► *Go It Alone!* by Bruce Judson
- ► *The Lean Startup* by Eric Ries
- ► *The Knack* by Norm Brodsky and Bo Burlingham
- ► *Ready, Fire, Aim* by Michael Masterson
- ► *Escape from Cubicle Nation* by Pamela Slim
- ► *Bankable Business Plans* by Edward G. Rogoff

VALUE CREATION AND TESTING

- ► *Rework* by Jason Fried and David Heinemeier Hansson
- ► *The New Business Road Test* by John W. Mullins
- ► *How to Make Millions with Your Ideas* by Dan S. Kennedy

MARKETING

- *All Marketers Are Liars* by Seth Godin
- *Permission Marketing* by Seth Godin
- *The 22 Immutable Laws of Marketing* by Al Ries and Jack Trout
- *Getting Everything You Can Out of All You've Got* by Jay Abraham

SALES

- *The Psychology of Selling* by Brian Tracy
- *Pitch Anything* by Oren Klaff
- *The Ultimate Sales Machine* by Chet Holmes
- *Value-Based Fees* by Alan Weiss
- *SPIN Selling* by Neil Rackham

VALUE DELIVERY

- *Indispensable* by Joe Calloway
- *The Goal* by Eliyahu M. Goldratt
- *Lean Thinking* by James P. Womack and Daniel T. Jones

FINANCE AND ACCOUNTING

- *Financial Intelligence for Entrepreneurs* by Karen Berman and Joe Knight with John Case
- *Simple Numbers, Straight Talk, Big Profits!* by Greg Crabtree
- *The 1% Windfall* by Rafi Mohammed
- *Accounting Made Simple* by Mike Piper
- *How to Read a Financial Report* by John A. Tracy
- *Venture Deals* by Brad Feld and Jason Mendelson

THE HUMAN MIND

- *Thinking, Fast and Slow* by Daniel Kahneman
- *Brain Rules* by John Medina

- *Making Sense of Behavior* by William T. Powers
- *Driven* by Paul R. Lawrence and Nitin Nohria
- *Deep Survival* by Laurence Gonzales

PRODUCTIVITY AND EFFECTIVENESS

- *Getting Things Done* by David Allen
- *The Power of Full Engagement* by Jim Loehr and Tony Schwartz
- *StrengthsFinder 2.0* by Tom Rath
- *Bit Literacy* by Mark Hurst
- *10 Days to Faster Reading* by Abby Marks-Beale and the Princeton Language Institute

PROBLEM SOLVING

- *The 80/20 Principle* by Richard Koch
- *Accidental Genius* by Mark Levy
- *Learning from the Future* edited by Liam Fahey and Robert M. Randall

BEHAVIORAL CHANGE

- *The Power of Less* by Leo Babauta
- *The Path of Least Resistance* by Robert Fritz
- *Re-Create Your Life* by Morty Lefkoe
- *Self-Directed Behavior* by David L. Watson and Roland G. Tharp

DECISION MAKING

- *Sources of Power* by Gary Klein
- *Smart Choices* by John S. Hammond, Ralph L. Keeney, and Howard Raiffa
- *Ethics for the Real World* by Ronald A. Howard and Clinton D. Korver

COMMUNICATION

- *On Writing Well* by William Zinsser
- *Presentation Zen* by Garr Reynolds
- *Made to Stick* by Chip Heath and Dan Heath
- *The Copywriter's Handbook* by Robert W. Bly
- *Show Me the Numbers* by Stephen Few

POWER AND INFLUENCE

- *Influence* by Robert B. Cialdini
- *How to Win Friends and Influence People* by Dale Carnegie
- *Crucial Conversations* by Kerry Patterson, Joseph Grenny, Ron McMillan, and Al Switzler
- *The 48 Laws of Power* by Robert Greene

NEGOTIATION

- *Bargaining for Advantage* by G. Richard Shell
- *3-D Negotiation* by David A. Lax and James K. Sebenius
- *The Partnership Charter* by David Gage

MANAGEMENT

- *First, Break All the Rules* by Marcus Buckingham and Curt Coffman
- *12: The Elements of Great Managing* by Rodd Wagner and James K. Harter, PhD
- *Growing Great Employees* by Erika Andersen
- *The Essential Drucker* by Peter F. Drucker

LEADERSHIP

- *Tribes* by Seth Godin
- *Total Leadership* by Stewart D. Friedman
- *What Got You Here Won't Get You There* by Marshall Goldsmith

▶ *The New Leader's 100-Day Action Plan* by George B. Bradt, Jayme A. Check, and Jorge E. Pedraza

▶ *The Halo Effect* by Phil Rosenzweig

PROJECT MANAGEMENT

▶ *Making Things Happen* by Scott Berkun

▶ *Results Without Authority* by Tom Kendrick

SYSTEMS

▶ *Thinking in Systems* by Donella H. Meadows

▶ *Work the System* by Sam Carpenter

ANALYSIS

▶ *Turning Numbers into Knowledge* by Jonathan G. Koomey, PhD

▶ *Marketing Metrics* by Paul W. Farris, Neil T. Bendle, Phillip E. Pfeifer, and David J. Reibstein

▶ *The Economist Numbers Guide* by Richard Stutely

STATISTICS

▶ *Thinking Statistically* by Uri Bram

▶ *How to Lie with Statistics* by Darrell Huff

CORPORATE SKILLS

▶ *The Unwritten Laws of Business* by W. J. King

▶ *The Effective Executive* by Peter F. Drucker

▶ *The Simplicity Survival Handbook* by Bill Jensen

▶ *Hire with Your Head* by Lou Adler

CORPORATE STRATEGY

▶ *Purpose* by Nikos Mourkogiannis

▶ *Competitive Strategy* by Michael E. Porter

▶ *Blue Ocean Strategy* by W. Chan Kim and Renée Mauborgne

▶ *Seeing What's Next* by Clayton M. Christensen, Scott D. Anthony, and Erik A. Roth

CREATIVITY AND INNOVATION

▶ *The Creative Habit* by Twyla Tharp

▶ *Myths of Innovation* by Scott Berkun

▶ *Innovation and Entrepreneurship* by Peter F. Drucker

DESIGN

▶ *The Design of Everyday Things* by Donald A. Norman

▶ *Universal Principles of Design* by William Lidwell, Kritina Holden, and Jill Butler

CONSULTING

▶ *Getting Started in Consulting* by Alan Weiss

▶ *Secrets of Consulting* by Gerald M. Weinberg

PERSONAL FINANCE

▶ *Your Money or Your Life* by Vicki Robin and Joe Dominguez with Monique Tilford

▶ *The Millionaire Next Door* by Thomas J. Stanley, PhD and William D. Danko, PhD

▶ *I Will Teach You to Be Rich* by Ramit Sethi

▶ *Fail-Safe Investing* by Harry Browne

PERSONAL GROWTH

▶ *Lead the Field* by Earl Nightingale

▶ *The Art of Exceptional Living* by Jim Rohn

▶ *A Guide to the Good Life* by William B. Irvine

FORTY-NINE QUESTIONS TO IMPROVE YOUR RESULTS

Good questions help your brain look at the world in a different way. By simply holding a question in your mind and pondering potential answers, you can find unexpected paths to get from where you are now to where you want to be.

Below is a list of questions I created for myself a few years ago. The intent of the list was to help me figure out what I wanted to improve about my life, both as a person and as a professional. These questions helped me figure out who I was and what I wanted during a particularly difficult time in my career, and I hope they help you as much as they've helped me.

DO I USE MY BODY OPTIMALLY?

- ▶ What is the quality of my current diet?
- ▶ Do I get enough sleep?
- ▶ Am I managing my energy well each day?
- ▶ How well am I managing daily stress?
- ▶ Do I have good posture and poise?
- ▶ What can I do to improve my ability to observe the world around me?

DO I KNOW WHAT I WANT?

▶ What achievements would make me really excited?

▶ What "states of being" do I want to experience each day?

▶ Are my priorities and values clearly defined?

▶ Am I capable of making decisions quickly and confidently?

▶ Do I consistently focus my attention on what I want versus what I don't want?

WHAT AM I AFRAID OF?

▶ Have I created an honest and complete list of the fears I'm holding on to?

▶ Have I confronted each fear to imagine how I would handle it if it came to pass?

▶ Am I capable of recognizing and correcting self-limitation?

▶ Am I appropriately pushing my own limits?

IS MY MIND CLEAR AND FOCUSED?

▶ Do I systematically externalize (write or record) what I'm thinking about?

▶ Am I making it easy to capture my thoughts quickly, while as I have them?

▶ What has my attention right now?

▶ Am I regularly asking myself appropriate guiding questions?

▶ Do I spend most of my time focusing on a single task, or am I constantly flipping between multiple tasks?

▶ Do I spend enough time actively reflecting on my goals, projects, and progress?

AM I CONFIDENT, RELAXED, AND PRODUCTIVE?

▶ Have I found a planning method that works for me?

▶ Am I "just organized enough"?

▶ Do I have an up-to-date list of my projects and active tasks?

▶ Do I review all of my commitments on a regular basis?

▶ Do I take regular, genuine breaks from my work?

▶ Am I consciously creating positive habits?

▶ Am I working to shed nonproductive habits?

▶ Am I comfortable with telling other people "no"?

HOW DO I PERFORM BEST?

▶ What do I particularly enjoy?

▶ What am I particularly good at doing?

▶ What environment(s) do I find most conducive to doing good work?

▶ How do I tend to learn most effectively?

▶ How do I prefer to work with and communicate with others?

▶ What is currently holding me back?

WHAT DO I REALLY NEED TO BE HAPPY AND FULFILLED?

▶ How am I currently defining "success"?

▶ Is there another way of defining "success" that I may find more fulfilling?

▶ How often do I compare myself with my perceptions of other people?

▶ Am I currently living below my means?

▶ If I could only own one hundred things, what would they be?

▶ Am I capable of separating necessity and luxury?

▶ What do I feel grateful for in my life and work?

Pick up a notebook, set aside an hour, and spend time with yourself answering these questions. Make it fun: treat yourself to a nice lunch or dinner at a restaurant you like, and write as you eat. By the time the check arrives, you'll have more than a few new ideas about how to change your life or business for the better.

NOTES

INTRODUCTION: WHY READ THIS BOOK?

1. http://sethgodin.typepad.com/seths_blog/2005/03/good_news_and_b.html.

2. http://personalmba.com/best-business-books/.

3. Janet Lowe, *Damn Right: Behind the Scenes with Berkshire Hathaway Billionaire Charlie Munger* (Wiley, 2003), p. 75.

4. *Outstanding Investor Digest,* December 29, 1997.

5. Peter D. Kaufman, ed., *Poor Charlie's Almanack*, 3rd ed. (Walsworth, 2008), p. 64.

6. This is not just a problem with business schools: it's a problem with college in general. College tuition has increased 7–14 percent annually since the 1980s, while salaries have stagnated, so the return on investment (ROI) of college education has decreased dramatically. See "College: Big Investment, Paltry Return" by Francesca Di Meglio, *Bloomberg BusinessWeek*, http://www.businessweek.com/bschools/content/jun2010/bs20100618_385280.htm.

7. Fittingly enough, Mr. Gates didn't graduate from college and doesn't have an MBA. Most successful and wealthy individuals didn't go to business school—they started as entrepreneurs and taught themselves.

8. http://grad-schools.usnews.rankingsandreviews.com/best-graduate-schools/top-business-schools/mba-rankings.

9. http://poetsandquants.com/2011/11/14/mba-tuition-rises-5-7-this-year/.

10. http://management.fortune.cnn.com/2011/11/18/mba-costs-soar-salaries-not-so-much/.

11. http://www.businessweek.com/interactive_reports/mba_pay_the_haul_of_lifetime.html.

12. http://mbacaveatemptor.blogspot.com/2005/06/wharton-grads-caveat-emptor-for.html.

13. http://www.aomonline.org/Publications/Articles/BSchools.asp.

14. See Daniel Pink's book *Drive: The Surprising Truth About What Motivates Us* (Riverhead, 2009).

15.   Including Perceptual Control Theory, which we'll discuss in chapter 6.

16.   http://www.tnr.com/article/economy/wagoner-henderson.

17.   Leverage is the use of debt to amplify financial Return on Investment (ROI), which has a side effect of amplifying downside risk if the business doesn't succeed. We'll discuss Leverage and ROI in detail in chapter 5.

18.   For an example of how this works, read http://www.nytimes.com/2009/10/05/business/economy/05simmons.html.

19.   www.sba.gov/advo/stats/sbfaq.pdf.

20.   For detailed tips on how to take good notes while you read, visit http://book.personalmba.com/bonus-training/.

CHAPTER 1: VALUE CREATION

1.   For an example of how I do this, visit http://book.personalmba.com/bonus-training/.

2.   A legally binding contract or promise not to share information about a business or business idea with others.

3.   Louviere called the approach "MaxDiff" testing: http://en.wikipedia.org/wiki/MaxDiff.

4.   For an example of how to conduct Relative Importance Testing for your business idea, visit http://book.personalmba.com/bonus-training/.

5.   http://www.kifaru.net/radio.htm.

6.   http://www.youtube.com/user/miguelcaballerousa.

CHAPTER 3: SALES

1.   http://www.petradiamonds.com/im/press_display.php?Id=2010/26feb10.

2.   You can find the formulas at http://en.wikipedia.org/wiki/Discounted_cash_flow.

CHAPTER 4: VALUE DELIVERY

1.   For an example of how I do this, visit http://book.personalmba.com/bonus-training/.

2.   Before the advent of the printing press, bibles were copied and illuminated (decorated and illustrated) by cloistered monks, who spent years working on a single copy.

3.   http://www.kk.org/thetechnium/archives/2008/01/better_than_fre.php.

4.   We'll discuss Toyota's recall woes later in "The Paradox of Automation."

5.   "Inside the Box," *Wired*, March 2010.

CHAPTER 6: THE HUMAN MIND

1. For detailed workouts using a sledgehammer, visit http://www.shovelglove.com/.

2. I use the Philips goLITE BLU light therapy device and highly recommend it. It's small, bright, easy to travel with, and works wonders.

3. You can also take a vitamin D3 supplement, which is a good idea if you're deficient— most people are. A simple blood test by your doctor can verify the levels of many essential nutrients—always consult with your MD before making any major changes to your diet or supplement intake.

4. For more on the neurophysiology of the brain, check out *Kluge: The Haphazard Construction of the Human Mind* by Gary F. Marcus (Faber & Faber, 2008).

5. http://macfreedom.com.

6. http://www.proginosko.com/leechblock.html.

7. http://www.timessquarenyc.org/facts/PedestrianCounts.html.

8. http://en.wikipedia.org/wiki/Austrian_business_cycle_theory.

9. http://en.wikipedia.org/wiki/Tulip_mania.

10. http://en.wikipedia.org/wiki/Dot-com_bubble.

11. http://en.wikipedia.org/wiki/United_States_housing_bubble.

CHAPTER 7: WORKING WITH YOURSELF

1. http://www.pomodorotechnique.com/.

2. http://www.pnas.org/content/103/31/11778.abstract.

3. http://www.ingentaconnect.com/content/hfes/hf/2006/00000048/00000002/art00014.

4. http://www.paulgraham.com/makersschedule.html.

5. http://personalmba.com/training.

6. Personally, I work with the folks at Timesvr.com—they're skilled, fast, friendly, and cost effective.

7. http://davidseah.com/pceo/etp.

8. http://govleaders.org/powell.htm.

9. For a complete look at my personal productivity system, visit http://book.personalmba.com/bonus-training/.

10. http://www.markforster.net/autofocus-system/.

11. For an example of how I do this, visit http://book.personalmba.com/bonus-training/.

12. http://www.bulletproofexec.com/how-to-make-your-coffee-bulletproof-and-your-morning-too/.

13. http://www.theatlantic.com/magazine/archive/2009/06/what-makes-us-happy/7439/3/.

CHAPTER 8: WORKING WITH OTHERS

1. The first edition of this book attributed the source of this list to Dr. Michael Sutcliffe of the University of Cambridge. Many thanks to Marina Murray for the correction.

2. You can read the whole story at http://www.earlytorise.com/2007/11/30/lessons-from-a-persian-rug-merchant-in-jaipur/.

3. http://www.nytimes.com/interactive/business/buy-rent-calculator.html.

4 http://www.avc.com/a_vc/2012/02/the-management-team-guest-post-from-joel-spolsky.html.

CHAPTER 10: ANALYZING SYSTEMS

1. For an example of how I do this, visit http://book.personalmba.com/bonus-training/.

2. http://portal.acm.org/citation.cfm?id=634067.634234.

CHAPTER 11: IMPROVING SYSTEMS

1. http://www.businessweek.com/magazine/content/10_49/b4206039292096.htm.

2. http://www.bainbrdg.demon.co.uk/Papers/Ironies.html.

3. http://www.newyorker.com/reporting/2007/12/10/071210fa_fact_gawande.

4. LoadImpact.com.

INDEX